Pension Plans and Public Policy

William C. Greenough & Francis P. King

PENSION PLANS
AND
PUBLIC POLICY

Columbia University Press
New York
1976

Library of Congress Cataloging in Publication Data

Greenough, William Croan, 1914–
    Pension plans and public policy.

    Includes index.
    1. Old age pensions—United States. 2. Retirement
income—United States. 3. Old age pensions—United
States—Finance. I. King, Francis Paul, 1922–
joint author. II. Title.
HD7106.U5G825   331.2′52′0973   76-13608
    ISBN 0-231-04070-9

Columbia University Press
New York   Guildford, Surrey
Copyright © 1976 Columbia University Press
Printed in the United States of America

ACKNOWLEDGMENTS

We are greatly indebted to the many friends and colleagues, both within and outside the pension field, with whom over many years we have discussed the idea of writing a book of this kind, and who have encouraged us to do so. They are too many in number to name here.

Financial assistance for the preparation of this study was provided by the Ford Foundation. We acknowledge with gratitude the foundation's grant and its interest in the project.

It was our good fortune to have been able to benefit directly from the criticism and comments on various chapters of the manuscript by Paul Fisher, Curtis R. Henderson, Joseph A. Kershaw, Murray W. Latimer, Dan M. McGill, Robert J. Myers, and James H. Schulz. We are also indebted to Roger R. Conant for assistance in the preparation of the chapter dealing with investments of pension funds, to Thomas J. Cook for assistance with manuscript revision and bibliographical materials, and to Barry M. Black and Thomas G. Walsh for expert actuarial assistance.

Carol Indiviglio carried the major burden of the preparation of successive drafts of the manuscript and supervision of study files and other materials. Her skill and efficiency contributed greatly to the timely completion of the project. Carolyn White, Ruth Landa, and Adele Arndt capably assisted in typing of manuscript drafts.

The views expressed in this study are the authors' and should not be ascribed to TIAA-CREF or to the Ford Foundation.

WILLIAM C. GREENOUGH
FRANCIS P. KING

September 1976
New York, N.Y.

CONTENTS

INTRODUCTION   ix

1   INCOME OF THE AGED   1

2   THE BEGINNING OF AMERICAN PENSION PLANS   27

3   SOCIAL SECURITY   68

4   PRIVATE PENSION PLANS   109

5   PUBLIC EMPLOYEE RETIREMENT PLANS   121

6   INVESTMENTS OF PENSION FUNDS   135

7   PUBLIC POLICY—THE VESTING OF PENSION BENEFITS   153

8   PUBLIC POLICY—FINANCING PENSION BENEFITS   176

9   PUBLIC POLICY—INCOME OBJECTIVES AND RETIREMENT AGES   210

10   FOREIGN SYSTEMS OF SOCIAL AND PRIVATE PENSIONS   242

NOTES   283

INDEX   303

INTRODUCTION

A society's income support system for people in their old age is one of its most important institutions. In the United States the system for the support of the elderly, like so many of our other institutions, is pluralistic, comprising Social Security, welfare, private pensions, public employee pensions, and individual savings and investment. Paid employment also supports some older people.

This volume examines in depth the three major components of our old-age income support structure: Social Security, private pensions, and public employee pensions. In one way or another each of the major components relates benefit payments in old age to the worker's employment history. Under these systems today's employment is the touchstone of tomorrow's benefits. Each of the components involves many billions of dollars as payments or reserves and influences enormously the economic life of the nation. Social Security old-age and survivor benefit transfers have reached over $56 billion each year and private and public employee pension plans now pay out over $22 billion a year.

Unfortunately, public discussion and understanding of pension plans—including both structure and economic and social impact—have not matched the magnitude and importance of the institutions involved. Most of the literature is technical and limited in objective, of primary interest to actuarial, legal, or investment specialists. Our aim is to provide a discussion responsive to the interests not only of the experts, but also of others who seek a broader perspective on pension plans: legislators; people on a decision-making level in business, government, and labor; staff advisers; interested college professors and students; individuals who as taxpayers support public employee retirement systems and Social Security; and those who are themselves members of specific retirement plans. The effort is to provide a broad overview of income support for the aged and to present analysis and public policy conclusions related to the overview.

A very rapid growth in private pension plans occurred during and after World War II; by the early 1970s nearly half of the private work force was employed by firms with private pension plans. But in recent years the gaps and weaknesses of a basically positive and constructive system have attracted more attention than its strengths. Implicit in almost all of the commentary, however, beginning with the report of a presidential commission in 1965, was a recognition of the great value of private pension plans, especially if certain recommended improvements were introduced. Significant changes have now been made. The passage in 1974 of the Employee Retirement Income Security Act (ERISA) brought to a conclusion almost ten years of active discussion about private pensions, instituting numerous reforms and setting important new standards; its greatest significance was its affirmation that, as a matter of public policy, private pensions are expected to play a stronger role in providing income support for the nation's workers in their old age. In a real sense, the 1974 Pension Reform Act marks the end of a period of youth of our private pension system and the beginning of a period of maturity.

The 1974 Pension Reform Act specifically exempted public employee retirement plans from its various standards and requirements, although it did provide for a special study of these plans. In this study we have classified public employee retirement systems (federal, state, and local) as part of the "private" pension system because public and private plans exhibit common basic features: an underlying principle of reserve funding, comparable approaches to benefit structure, and common purposes. They are, or should be, distinctly different from the transfer system represented by the Social Security program. As later chapters note, many if not most of the government employee plans are at present underfunded and many government plans do not meet the standards that have been prescribed by government for the pension plans of private employers. This is one of the major issues with which future legislation must deal.

Information about present sources and levels of income being received by the elderly is important background to a discussion of public policy issues regarding pension plans and the Social Security program. Chapter 1, "Income of the Aged," offers an overview of the income available to people 65 and over.

The pension plans of private and governmental employers should be examined in the light of their origins and history. To provide such perspective, chapter 2, "The Beginning of American Pension Plans," offers a summary of developments from the establishment of the first such plan a hundred years ago to the landmark Pension Reform Act of 1974.

Although distinct from private pensions in both financing and philosophy, the federal Social Security system is an integral part of our total income support system for the aged. Chapter 3 describes the principal features of Social Security and discusses important issues related to future benefits and costs of this gigantic intergenerational transfer system. It raises questions as to the directions such a system should take in a slow-growth economy with an aging population.

Chapters 4 and 5 describe the private and public employee retirement systems currently in operation—types of plans, size, and coverage. Chapter 6,

"Investments of Pension Funds," describes the changes that have occurred over the years in investment policies and practices in the private and public employee plans.

The heart of this study comprises the three chapters with the words "public policy" in their titles: chapter 7, "Public Policy—Vesting," chapter 8, "Public Policy—Financing Pension Benefits," and chapter 9, "Public Policy—Income Objectives and Retirement Ages." These chapters cover what we believe to be fundamental aspects of pension policy and management for the post-1974 era.

In chapter 10 we describe the interrelationship of social insurance programs and private pension plans in foreign countries whose populations live in urban and industrial environments comparable to our own. This look at the way other nations have handled issues relating to income support in old age offers interesting insights into the variety of policy decisions possible and the variations in systems that result.

The Older Americans Act of 1965 expressed a national policy objective for income in old age: "The older people of our Nation are entitled to . . . an adequate income in retirement in accordance with the American standard of living." The same objective was repeated as a recommendation of the 1971 White House Conference on Aging. Can our people achieve this goal when they are older? Is the goal appropriate? Is it stated with sufficient clarity? Whatever goals are affirmed, we believe that they can be reached only through better understanding of social insurance and private pensions as a total system. We hope that this study will contribute to the discussion and debate that is a necessary part of setting realistic goals and establishing effective mechanisms for reaching them.

Pension Plans and Public Policy

— 1 —

Income of the Aged

Man's actions are the picture book of his creeds.
Ralph Waldo Emerson

A look at what is known of the income situation of elderly people in the United States is an indispensable starting point for a discussion of public policy regarding social insurance and private pensions. Although the stress in this chapter is on income, there is no intention to downgrade the importance in old age of health, housing, services, or of all the other aspects of life that determine its quality. It is evident that the overall economic picture of the aged is not altogether encouraging, though it is quite true that many people now leaving the work force for reasons of age are better off than their predecessors of just a few years ago.

If income levels of the aged are to be examined, we first must determine who is aged and who is not. Because chronological age often corresponds poorly to functional age, identification of the "aged" is bound to be arbitrary, yet some demarcation must be made. The commonly used dividing line is 65, the age at which unreduced benefits are first payable under the Social Security program and also the mandatory retirement age of many retirement plans.

"Old age" is a label that deserves less usage. Its subjective overtones, its ambiguity, and the lengthy span of years the term tries to cover all suggest that other terminology might be better. Can we say, for example, that 65 is as old in 1975 as it was in 1900, when life expectancy from birth was about 20 years less than it is now? In some situations it seems better to talk about "pre- and postretirement" ages. These too may differ in different circumstances. Sixty-five may be too late a retirement age for a chorus girl, a policeman, or a fireman if each is to discharge normal duties, but not too late for the effective functioning of a business leader, judge, or congressman. The term "pensionable age" deserves some attention. Some people may consider themselves retired at age 40, but that does not mean there is an obligation to provide a pension starting at that age. A problem in dealing with old age and retirement is that most of our data are collected in terms of age regardless of circumstances of work or health.

Another way of approaching age designations is to attempt to determine the ages at which a society can afford to allow people to step away from the productive activities of the worker to the nonproductive activities of the nonworking consumer. Perhaps "old age" in this context should incorporate society's judgment of the age at which the community can afford the departure of the worker from the work force.

CHART 1.1

Population Age 65 and Over, 1900–2000

Millions of people

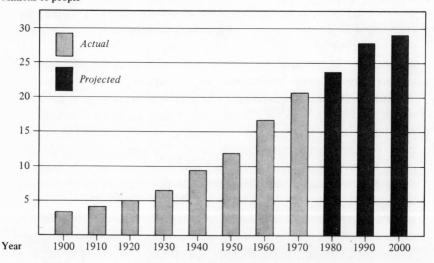

Source: U.S. Bureau of the Census, Current Population Reports, Series P-23, No. 43 (1973), p.2.

The first step toward answering any of the above questions is to look at our aged population, focusing on both historical and current information.

An Increasing Aged Population. The number of elderly people in the United States has been steadily increasing, decade by decade. In 1900 there were 3.1 million Americans age 65 and over; by 1940 that number had tripled to 9 million, and today the figure stands at 21.1 million, about the same as the total population of the 22 smallest states. The aged population is not expected to remain at today's level—more people will enter the 65-and-over category than will leave it by dying. Chart 1.1 shows the number of persons age 65 and over at the end of each decade since 1900, with projections through 2000. The Census Bureau figures project a rise in the aged population from the present 21 million to 28.8 million by the year 2000; in about the year 2010 there will be a further surge in the aged population. Such increases can be predicted with considerable accuracy 65 to 84 years before the year in which the number of aged is counted. The high birth rates in the "baby boom" years from 1945 to 1957 will increase the aged population in the decade between the year 2010 and 2020 by 9.3 million, a 30 percent increase in that decade alone.

The sheer numbers of aged persons and the steep rate of growth in the aged population pose a challenge to our systems of income support for people outside the productive work force because of age. Not only are the aged increasing in numbers; they are also an increasing proportion of the total population.

**Table 1.1 Proportion of Total U.S. Population Age 65 and
Over, 1900–1972**

Year	65 and Over	Year	65 and Over
1900	4.1%	1940	6.8%
1910	4.3	1950	8.1
1920	4.6	1960	9.2
1930	5.4	1970	9.8
		1972	10.1

Sources: U.S. Bureau of the Census, *Current Population Reports,*
Series P-23, No. 43 (1973), p. 5; U.S. Department of HEW, *New Facts
About Older Americans,* June 1973.

Increasing Proportion of the Aged. In 1900 only 4 out of every 100 Americans were over age 65 (an aged population of 3.1 million out of a total population of 76.2 million). Since 1900 there has been a steady rise in the proportion of the aged to the population as a whole. By 1972 10 out of every 100 Americans were age 65 or over; in 72 years the proportion of the U.S. population over 65 more than doubled, from 4.1 percent to 10.1 percent. Table 1.1 shows the growth by ten-year periods.

One might expect the numbers of aged persons to increase as our national population increases, but why an increase in the proportion of aged? Several factors have been at work. One is immigration. Immigrants are generally in the younger age categories. If immigration rates decline, as they have in this country since the end of the great waves of European immigration in the 19th century, the initial swelling of the younger population due to immigration will be repeated, in another sense, when these groups reach old age.

Mortality rate changes have a double effect. Improvements in medical care and health facilities are first reflected in lower mortality rates among the young and middle-aged population. Later on, these people swell the ranks of the aged, where lower mortality rates among the elderly help maintain the size of the 65-and-over population. This is illustrated by the fact that in 1900 the life expectancy of a man age 65 was 11.5 years and of a woman of the same age 12.2 years. In 1970 the life expectancy at 65 had risen to 13 years for men and 16.6 years for women.[1]

With immigration at a low level and mortality below age 50 also at a low level relative to the past, fertility levels become the main determinant of age composition of the U.S. population. An increase in the fertility rates, such as occurred during the "baby boom" years, will swell the younger population. Later on, this population surge will begin to enlarge the ratio of the aged population to the whole. Over the long term, the effect of a declining birth rate is to reduce the growth of the population under 65, thereby increasing the ratio of the aged population to the younger categories.

Predicting future birth rates, while difficult, is important if we are to develop sound policies based on the proportion of the future population that will require income support systems for old age. The U.S. Bureau of the Census Series E projection, using current rates of mortality and immigration, assumes a moderately low "replacement level" fertility rate of 2.1 children as the average number of births per woman before completion of childbearing. This latest census projection forecasts an increase in the proportion of persons age 65 or older in the population, rising from the 10 percent we now have in 1970 to 11 percent in 2000, to 13 percent in the year 2020. Estimates of the proportion of persons age 60 and over in the year 2020 give a figure of about 19 percent.[2]

CHARACTERISTICS OF THE AGED POPULATION

The 20 million aged people, 10 percent of our population, are distributed over a range of ages that extends from the entry age of the group as we have defined it, 65, to over 100. (The Census Bureau currently reports 7,000 persons age 100 and over, 70 percent of them women.) As age advances, aged persons' needs change, and these changes may take place at a fairly rapid rate, particularly in the areas of health care, housing, transportation, services, and personal assistance. People in the higher age brackets among the elderly are not in the same situations as most people between 65 and 75.

The proportion of persons in the higher age group (75 and over) has been rising. Of the over-65 population in 1900, 29 percent were 75 and over. By 1970 this proportion had risen to 39 percent, and the trend is expected to continue. By the year 2000, 43 percent of the aged population, or 12.6 million persons, will be 75 years of age or older.[3]

The certainty that within 30 years we will have more than 12 million people over age 75 in this country must influence our public policy stance not only on the question of the provision of income for the aged, but also on housing, health care, services, and transportation. Another important policy question is how far under age 75 we are to go in the determination of the age groups to be supported as pensionable persons. It should be recognized that if retirement ages as low as 60, 62, or even 55 are to be incorporated into one segment of the economy or another, with resulting pressures for extension into other segments, increased costs may well have the effect of diminishing the chances of adequate support levels for the growing numbers of those of truly advanced age.

Sex Composition. Among the aged 65 and over in 1970, women outnumbered men by more than 3 million: there were 11.7 million women and 8.4 million men. By 1985 it is projected that women age 65 and over will outnumber men in that age group by almost 5 million.[4] The preponderance of women is due to their greater longevity. A recent report by the World Health Organization of mortality rates in 34 countries indicates that the margin in favor of women is increasing. Innate biological or genetic factors apparently produce the differential, not environmental or economic differences.[5]

In 1900 the ratio of men to women in the 65-and-over group was just about even. The explanation for the equal ratio in 1900 is attributable in part to the greater number of men than women coming into the United States in the last half of the 19th century, and to the rate of female mortality, including the high level of childbirth deaths, leaving fewer women than men, proportionately, to arrive at the age of 65. Now there are about 138 women in the 65-and-over category for every 100 men; by the year 2000 it is expected that there will be about 150 women for every 100 men. The difference increases with age. Among persons 75 years and older there are at present about 145 women for every 100 men, and by 2000 this difference is expected to rise to about 170 women for every 100 men.

Public policy decisions regarding the aged must thus take into account the fact that a majority of people over 65 are women. Their greater longevity means that many will be the survivors of men, upon whom they may have been dependent for varying periods of time for the major part of their income. This raises questions regarding the extent and adequacy of benefits for survivors provided under social insurance and under private pension plans. Increasingly, as more women enter the work force with career objectives, there may also be greater numbers of men who are dependent on the woman's earnings for shorter or longer time periods. It may soon be necessary, as life styles and marriage patterns continue to change, to redefine eligibility for survivorship benefits under our social insurance and private pension plans.

Marital Status—Living Arrangements. With so many women among the aged, one would expect to find many widows and many women living alone. This is the case. Only about one out of three women aged 65 or over was married and living with her husband in 1972 (38 percent). All the rest of the over-65 women were either widowed (52.8 percent), divorced (2.5 percent), or never had married (6.6 percent). Table 1.2 shows the percentage distribution of people 65 and over by marital status in 1900 and in 1972.

Collection of data on the living arrangements of older persons is based on three living modes: (1) in a family setting, either with a spouse or with relatives, (2) alone or with nonrelatives, and (3) in institutions. In 1972 about 5 percent, or approximately one million older people, lived in institutions of all kinds. In the noninstitutional population more than one third of all older persons in 1972 (6.1 million: 1.4 million men and 4.7 million women) lived alone or with nonrelatives. The difference between men and women here is startling; 41 percent of all older women lived alone, but only 17 percent of all older men did. A little less than two thirds of the people over 65 in 1972 lived with a spouse or other relative. Since there are many more older women than older men, the proportion of older men in family settings (83 percent) was higher than that of women (59 percent). The proportion of all older people living in family settings decreases rapidly with advancing age.

There is obviously much truth to the saying, ''How you live tells who you are.'' Data on marital status and living arrangements offer a fairly clear picture of the situation of older persons in these respects. Generally, the figures show that men and women of older ages are found in increasingly isolated situations as couples are split by the death of a spouse, with far more widows than widowers. Other recent studies show that among married couples fewer are living with relatives than did so 20 years ago.[6]

Where the Aged Live. In 1972 more than one third of all persons aged 65 and over lived in the five most populous states—California, Illinois, New York, Pennsylvania, and Texas. Each of these states had more than one million persons in this category, and the aged populations of New York and California will soon reach two million. But seven other states had an unusually high proportion of older persons. With the national average at 10 percent, Florida in 1972 reported 15.5 percent of its population as aged 65 and over, Arkansas 12.7 percent, Iowa and Nebraska 12.3 percent, South Dakota 12.2 percent, and Kansas and Missouri 12.1 percent. The 1970 census

Table 1.2 Marital Status of People 65 and Over, 1900 and 1972

Status	1900		1972	
	Men	*Women*	*Men*	*Women*
Married	67.1%	34.2%	77.0%	38.1%
Widowed	26.4	59.3	15.7	52.8
Other				
Divorced	0.5	0.3	1.8	2.5
Never married	5.7	6.0	5.5	6.6

Source: U.S. Department of HEW, *New Facts About Older Americans,* June 1973.

Note: Totals may not equal 100% because of rounding.

reported that about one third of all aged persons lived in central cities. Over half (55 percent) lived in urbanized areas, the balance in rural or semirural areas.[7]

The aged are not a very mobile part of our population, despite the reputed mobility of American citizens. During 1971, 8.7 percent of those aged 65 and over moved from one residence to another, with only 1.4 percent moving to a different state. In contrast, in the same 1971 period 41.2 percent of pesons aged 20 to 24 moved to another residence and 8.6 percent moved to another state.[8]

Older People in the Labor Force. For the year 1972, government data indicate that 3.1 million people age 65 and over were "in the labor force," that is, were working or said they were actively seeking work. Department of Labor statistics reveal that the proportion of the aged population finding employment is declining. In 1950 about a quarter of the people 65 and over were in the labor force, compared with the present 16 percent; Labor Department projections predict a participation rate of about 13 percent by 1985.[9] These percentages combine men and women. Among women, labor force participation for those aged 65 and over has remained the same over the past 20 years, about 10 percent. Among men the rate is higher—26 percent in 1972—but that proportion is expected to drop to 22 percent by 1980.

Several things should be kept in mind regarding these labor force figures. Large proportions of those aged 65 and over are in low-paid work. The proportion of people who report themselves as self-employed after 65 and therefore in the work force is much higher than the proportion of self-employed in the under-65 work force. Part-time work is included in the figures, and those who are "actively seeking work" may range from the perservering to the nominal. Until more sophisticated and sensitive data-collection methods are introduced, labor force data regarding older persons should be viewed cautiously. It is easier to collect accurate data on sex and age than on whether a person is in or out of the work force.

Surveys of New Social Security Beneficiaries. In the late 1960s the Social Security Administration began a survey to attempt to clarify the circumstances under which beneficiaries were beginning their old-age income. The law had been amended in 1956 for women and 1961 for men to provide old-age benefits at age 62, with actuarial reduction. Questions soon arose as to whether the increasing numbers of workers who were beginning benefits before age 65 (and thus accepting the actuarial reduction) were doing so because they desired early retirement and could afford it, because they couldn't find work, because they could find only intermittent or part-time work and needed an income supplement, or because they were disabled, although not seriously enough in ill health to qualify for disability benefits. Basically, the question was whether the early retirees were truly retiring, with an adequate level of income, or were instead using the Social Security benefits as a form of unemployment compensation in the absence of other alternatives.

The Survey of Newly Entitled Beneficiaries (SNEB in the short-hand of the Social Security Administration) takes a sample each month of people who are awarded benefits, and from time to time prepares reports on the survey results. The first SNEB report covered the last half of 1968 and revealed that 50 percent of the men initially awarded retired-worker benefits began their benefits before age 65, with actuarial reduction, and that two thirds of the women did so.[10]

The distribution of ages at award of Social Security benefits for the period surveyed is shown in Table 1.3. As indicated in the table, 60 percent of the

Table 1.3 Social Security Awards, Last Half 1968: Age at Entitlement and Payment Status

Payment Status at Award and Age at Entitlement	*Men*	*Women*
Number of Awards (thousands)	325	216
Benefits Payable	60%	81%
Reduced benefits	50	68
Age 62	31	52
Age 63	10	8
Age 64	9	8
Full benefits	10	13
Age 65	7	8
Age 66 or over	4	5
Benefits Postponed	40	19
Age 62 to 64	5	3
Age 65 or over	34	16

Source: Lauriat and Rabin, ''Men Who Claim Benefits before Age 65: Findings from the Survey of New Beneficiaries, 1968,'' *Social Security Bulletin* 33 (November 1970):4.

men being awarded Social Security benefits began receiving payments, either reduced or unreduced. The remainder, 40 percent of the total, postponed benefits at award; these individuals are, in general, persons aged 65 who file a claim only to be eligible for benefits under Medicare. If they are insured, they become entitled to retired-worker benefits, but because they are still employed, they do not draw the benefits at award. (Nothing is lost by filing for entitlement at age 65 because the annual recomputation may increase benefit rates to reflect additional earnings.) A report covering the first half of 1969 found that among men initially entitled to retired-worker benefits, 60 percent were under 65.[11] Among all currently payable regular Social Security retirement benefit awards, there has been a steady trend (since reduced benefits were first made available to men in 1962) toward an increase in the ratio of people awarded reduced benefits to those awarded unreduced benefits.

What is the situation of the people who are under 65 when they choose to begin their Social Security retirement benefits? About 50 percent of current awards to men were to those aged 62 at entitlement. About one in five of these men had not worked for at least 12 months before his entitlement, a situation described as "almost as if they were in a queue waiting for the minimum age for retired-worker benefits to arrive." [12] About 40 percent of men entitled before age 65 continued to work, but earnings were low so that they also qualified for some Social Security benefits.[13]

Those who supplemented their benefits with earnings include a disproportionate share of self-employed men (at least those who described themselves as self-employed) and of wage earners in the service industries and in unskilled blue-collar jobs. These partly retired men generally had lower benefits than the nonworking men in the beneficiary group. They rarely were entitled to pensions from a public employee or private pension plan. Many reported health problems. In contrast, the men who stopped working when they started to receive their Social Security benefits included a high concentration of skilled blue-collar workers and men with second-pension rights.[14] The large majority of this group had full-time, year-round earnings above the retirement test in their former jobs. Retirement for these men was often abrupt rather than gradual.[15]

Declining health was the reason most men gave for leaving their jobs and claiming Social Security benefits before age 65. Other reasons included elimination of their job, poor results from their own business, or reaching a compulsory retirement age. Most of those who claimed full benefits at 65 cited compulsory retirement as the reason. Only two out of five of this group said they wanted to retire.[16] In terms of benefits, the men entitled at age 62 had less favorable earnings records than those beginning benefits at later ages.[17]

The data of the Survey of Newly Entitled Beneficiaries suggest that early retirements tend to represent situations in which individuals are less likely to have a second pension, often have to work to supplement benefits, and have a lower average monthly wage history underlying their Social Security benefits. The individual is less likely to be a skilled worker, and very often has worked in the services rather than in highly unionized production enterprises. Early retirees who must supplement their benefits—the partly retired—tend to have lower incomes than those who have quit work entirely.

By age 65 most men and women have withdrawn permanently from the work force due to compulsory retirement, poor health, unemployment, job dissatisfaction, or desire to retire. It is clear that under present employment policies the time has come by age 65 to provide a satisfactory level of retirement income for the rest of life. However, about half of the men and two thirds of the women now begin Social Security benefits before age 65 and as a result accept actuarially reduced benefits, with declining health or unemployment cited as important reasons for doing so. These factors affect the public policy decisions to be made in Social Security and are discussed in Chapter 3.

INCOMES OF AGED PERSONS

For the collection of statistics on income, some fairly precise definitions of income are required. If incomes are to be evaluated as high or low, or as below, near, or above a poverty line, some generally acceptable criteria are necessary. Three main government agencies have undertaken these tasks: the Census Bureau, the Department of Labor, and the Department of Health, Education, and Welfare.

Components of Income. The government agencies which collect income data generally define income as including earnings, Social Security benefits, veterans' pensions, benefits from federal and state retirement systems, benefits from pension plans of employers or unions, income from assets (interest, dividends, net rents from property), public assistance and welfare payments, and cash contributions from relatives or friends not living in the household. All of these items are measurable directly in dollars, and the information is relatively simple to collect. Certain other types of money or money-equivalent receipts, however, are not included, mainly because the items are more difficult to collect and to evaluate than simple dollar amounts; these include the value of wages in kind and of subsidized housing, "rental value" of owner-occupied homes, the value of food produced and consumed on farms, the value of food stamps, and government contributions to health benefits.

The addition of a money income value due to home ownership would affect, if measurable, approximately three fourths of all aged couples, i.e., those who own their own homes, usually unmortgaged. What difference this would make in incomes reported is hard to say. Home ownership entails costs of maintenance, repair, heating, property taxes, and the like, all of which figure in rents, so that some net values would have to be calculated before a usable figure could be obtained. Research experts note that if imputed income values are to be added to the incomes of the aged, the same values would have to be used in income studies of the under-65 population, including the addition of employer contributions to pension and other benefit plans, stock option plans, expense accounts, and capital gains operations. To count these "nonincome flows" would require major changes in the definitions applicable to all income levels. Thus, practical and conceptual considerations stand in the way of taking into account the nonmoney income factors that enable people to live better than seems possible on their money incomes.[18]

Incomes. In looking at the elderly for the purpose of examining income, we look mainly at two groups, couples (two-person, husband-wife combinations) and persons living alone or with nonrelatives. The latter are sometimes called "unrelated individuals" for want of a better term.

In 1974, 67 percent of the 8 million families (two or more individuals) headed by a person aged 65 and over received an annual income under $10,000, 28 percent received an income under $5,000, and 8 percent received an income under $3,000 per year. Among the 6.5 million persons 65 and over living alone in 1974, 77 percent had incomes under $5,000, 51 percent had incomes under $3,000, and 8 percent had incomes under $2,000.[19] These figures include situations in which older people (couples *or* individuals) are living with their children, or their children are living with them.

The data for older families allow comparison of the incomes of older people with those of families and individuals under 65. The comparison is necessary if we are to view incomes of the elderly in perspective. In 1974 the median income of families with heads 65 and over, as reported by the Bureau of the Census, was $7,298. For families with heads under 65, the figure was $13,418, nearly twice as much as the older group. For individuals the median income of persons 65 and over was $2,956 compared with $6,328 for individuals under 65; here the under-65 median income is more than twice that of the older group. The differences may be understated because the figures for the under-65 individuals include persons as young as age 14.[20] The ratios of the median incomes of the elderly to incomes of younger people have remained about the same since 1960.

Measuring Poverty. The first official estimates of the numerical extent of poverty were offered in the January 1964 "Economic Report of the President" by the Council of Economic Advisors. The council arbitrarily chose a family income of $3,000 per year as the dividing line between poor and nonpoor and analyzed 1959 data. Since then, work by the Social Security Administration's Office of Research and Statistics has refined the methods, and it is this Social Security method which has been accepted by the Office of Management and Budget for official figures on poverty and which is followed by the Bureau of the Census.[21]

On the average, incomes of older people are about half those of people under 65 and are concentrated toward the low-income categories. What proportion are at or below the poverty threshold? For 1974 the Bureau of the Census set its poverty threshold at $2,958 for a family of two whose head is 65 or older, and at $2,352 for an unrelated individual 65 or over, either living alone or with someone other than a relative. For the under-65 families and individuals, the Census Bureau set somewhat higher figures, $3,294 for a family of two and $2,557 for an individual.[22] The difference is due to the bureau's adjustments of the figures for age differences in expenditure patterns. It is commonly accepted that in the calculation of measurements of income adequacy, older people have lesser needs for the same items than do younger persons and families.

With this 1974 poverty threshold, we find that about 8 percent of elderly families and 36 percent of elderly individuals were at or below the poverty line of the Census Bureau in 1974. Overall, of the 21.1 million aged Americans, about 13 percent, 2.7 million people, were living in poverty in 1974.[23]

The "Near Poor" Threshold. In essence, the official poverty threshold establishes the minimum amount of money that is sufficient to meet living expenses. People with a little more money than that, but not much more, are still poor. Perhaps in tacit acknowledgment that all is not well once the poverty threshold is crossed, a "near poor" threshold has appeared in some government publications. The threshold for the "near poor," according to the Department of Health, Education, and Welfare, "is established at 25 percent above the specific poverty levels." [24]

"Near poor" has an official synonym—"low income." "Poor" in 1974 meant for an older individual an income of $2,352; "near poor," or "low income," that year meant an income threshold of $2,940. For older couples in 1974, "poor" was $2,958, and "near poor-low income" was $3,698. What happens to the statistics when the poor threshold is elevated to the "near poor-low income" threshold, a 25 percent lift? The percentage of elderly families at or below the (new) threshold rises from 8.3 percent to about 15 percent, and the percentage of elderly individuals in this larger poor category rises from 36 percent to 51 percent. Among families 538,000 are added to the poor roles and among individuals 975,000 join the ranks.[25]

A poverty index alone, although useful, is hardly the best instrument with which to measure adequate living standards for elderly individuals and couples. The people at and below the poverty thresholds, whether "poor" or "near poor," are people who do not have enough money to live on. That situation is not changed by a step upward across the threshold unless the step is a giant one. Better measurements are necessary if we are to assess the responsiveness of social insurance plans and private pensions to the needs of elderly people.

The Retired Couples' Budgets. Since 1960, the Bureau of Labor Statistics has issued a Retired Couple Budget, and more recently has designed two additional retired couple budgets, one at a somewhat lower standard than the original one, which is now called intermediate, and one somewhat higher. In essence, the budget represents a detailed listing of items and their quantities to meet the normal needs of a retired couple, as judged adequate by experts, for a hypothetical standard of living. An existing inventory of clothing, furniture, and appliances is assumed. The three budgets differ in quality and quantity of content and vary considerably in some categories, such as taxes and gifts. Updating is based on changes in the Consumer Price Index and in consumer expenditure patterns. Equivalency factors permit the conversion of the budget for a family to a budget for an individual or for different types of families.[26]

The step from the poverty threshold to the "lower" Bureau of Labor Statistics retired couple budget for 1974 is a giant 43 percent, from $2,958 to $4,228. To step up to the BLS "intermediate" budget requires a 104 percent increase, and to the "higher" budget a 203 percent increase. Here are the BLS estimated budget levels for 1974 for an urban retired couple at the lower, intermediate, and higher levels of living:

1974 BLS Budget Level	Total	Consumption	Other
Lower	$4,228	$4,046	$182
Intermediate	6,041	5,678	363
Higher	8,969	8,277	692

Information from U.S. Bureau of Labor Statistics, *News* (August 1, 1975), p. 2.

The BLS budget figures are urban averages, and they can vary widely among different urban situations. The lower budget, shown as $4,228,

Table 1.4 Intermediate Budget Costs for an Urban Retired Couple, Autumn 1974

Component	Budget Costs	Distribution	Change from Autumn 1973
Total Budget	$6,041	100.0%	11.0%
Consumption	5,678	93.9	11.0
Food	1,766	29.2	10.4
Housing	2,043	33.8	11.1
Transportation	527	8.7	14.1
Clothing	328	5.4	9.0
Personal care	176	2.9	12.8
Medical care	537	8.8	11.2
Other consumption	301	4.9	8.7
Other Items	363	6.0	11.0

Source: U.S. Department of Labor, Bureau of Labor Statistics, *News* (August 1, 1975), pp. 2, 3.

ranged from a low of $3,765 in Baton Rouge, Louisiana, to a high of $5,872 in Anchorage, Alaska. In the same cities, the intermediate budget ranged from $5,403 to $7,784, and the higher budget from $8,094 to $11,001. New York City levels were near the Anchorage levels.

How does the BLS assume older people on an intermediate budget spend their money? The distribution of expenditures may be of some interest to those who might wish to judge for themselves the standard of living the budget affords. Table 1.4 breaks the budget down into eight major components. Expenditures for housing took 34 percent of the budget, food over 29 percent.

Eight percent of elderly families in 1974 were at or under the poverty threshold. How many elderly families do not achieve the lower, intermediate or higher budget levels developed by the BLS? Table 1.5 shows that when the BLS standards are established as an income standard about 18 percent of older families fail to meet the lower standard test, 39 percent the intermediate standard, and 62 percent the higher standard. The figures refer to the 8 million elderly families in 1974.

Poorer Than the Rest. The aged are poorer than the population as a whole. For people living alone or with nonrelatives, the proportion 65 or over who are below the "near poor" level is 51 percent, and for the population as a whole 29.1 percent. The figures support the results of other studies which reveal that many persons who are poor in old age have not previously

Table 1.5 Older Families Below the Bureau of Labor Statistics Budget Levels, 1974

BLS 1974 Budget Level	Dollar Cost	Older Couples	
		Number [a]	Percent
Lower	$4,228	1.4	17.4
Intermediate	6,041	3.1	38.8
Higher	8,969	5.0	61.9

Sources: U.S. Department of Labor, Bureau of Labor Statistics, *News* (August 1, 1975), p. 2; U.S. Bureau of the Census, *Current Population Reports,* Series P-60, No. 99 (July 1975), p. 9.

[a] Millions of families; total families in 1974 was 8.0 million.

occupied such a low-income status—the "newly poor." In both the family and unrelated individual categories, the proportion of blacks in the poor and near poor groups is higher than for whites in all age groups.

The budgets of the Bureau of Labor Statistics add a new dimension to the conventional measurements of marginal or submarginal income status, which concentrate on poverty. The BLS intermediate level budget is useful in the development of standards for the function of social insurance and pension programs. It was designated by the 1971 White House Conference on Aging as the *minimum* standard to be adopted for all aged couples in the United States. While it may be too high as a level for welfare support of aged persons, the intermediate level does suggest a minimum goal suitable to a combination of Social Security and private pension benefits, given a fairly constant employment history and the selection of a survivor income option under private pension coverage.

About 40 percent of retired couples have incomes that do not come up to the intermediate level. Table 1.6 gives the proportion of couples below that level for the years 1967 through 1974.

Table 1.6 Aged Families With Incomes Below the BLS Intermediate Budget Level, 1967–1974

		Families Below Intermediate Level	
Year	Intermediate Budget	Number [a]	Percent
1967	$3,857	2.5	56.2
1969	4,233	2.3	50.0
1970	4,489	2.5	53.4
1971	4,776	2.4	47.9
1972	4,967	2.2	44.5
1973	5,414	2.6	39.3
1974	6,041	3.1	38.8

Sources: U.S. Department of HEW, Administration on Aging, "BLS Retired Couple Budget," Statistical Memo No. 2 (October 4, 1972), No. 10 (January 19, 1972), and No. 28, Supplement No. 46 (April 18, 1974); U.S. Bureau of the Census, *Current Population Reports,* Series P-60, No. 97 (January 1975), p. 51 and No. 99 (July 1975), p. 9.

[a] Millions of families.

SOURCES OF THE INCOME OF THE AGED

The sources of income are derived from special sample surveys, the most comprehensive of which are undertaken from time to time by the Social Security Administration. Unfortunately, these surveys are not made often and publication is frequently delayed. The most recent survey provides information for the year 1967. Earlier data offer an opportunity to assess changes in the proportion of aggregate income (by source) of the aged since 1950, as shown in Table 1.7.

It is not surprising that the proportion of the aggregate income of persons 65 and over coming from Social Security has increased manyfold, from 3 percent in 1950 to 34 percent in 1967. The Social Security program was barely ten years old in 1950. Proportionate income from private pension plans rose over the 17-year period from 3 to 5 percent. The proportion of income from government employees' pensions also increased, from 4 to 7 percent, and the total from these two pension sources rose from 7 to 12 percent. Because the totals equal 100 percent for each period shown, an increase in any sector automatically affects the percentages in other sectors.

The decline from 50 to 29 percent of the proportion of employment repre-

Table 1.7 Sources of Aggregate Income of the Aged, 1950, 1960, and 1967

Source	1950	1960	1967
Employment	50%	33%	29%
Assets	29	20	15
Social Security	3	26	34
Government [a] and private pensions	7	11	12
Veterans' benefits	2	4	3
Public assistance	9	6	4
Other	—	—	3 [b]

Sources: *1967 data:* Lenore E. Bixby, "Income of People Aged 65 and Older: Overview from 1968 Survey of the Aged," *Social Security Bulletin* 33 (April 1970):11. *1950 and 1960 data:* Juanita M. Kreps, ed., *Employment, Income, and Retirement Problems of the Aged* (Durham: Duke University Press, 1963), p. 148, using data developed from Lenore E. Epstein, "Money Income of Aged Persons, mid-1960," *Social Security Bulletin* 24 (1961): 12–17; "Background Paper on Income Maintenance," White House Conference on Aging (1960), p. 7.

[a] Includes Railroad Retirement System.   [b] New category.

sents a major shift. With the growth of the role of Social Security and other pension plans, there has also been a decline in the proportion of income from invested assets in the form of interest, dividends, rents, and the like from 29 percent in 1950 to 15 percent in 1967.

Income from Work. The median income of aged couples who work (one or both in the labor force) tends to be substantially higher than for couples not working. In 1967 the median income for aged couples where both worked was $5,450, where only the man worked, $4,390, and where only the woman worked, $4,362. Where neither worked the median was $2,621. Of aged couples not working in 1967, 60 percent had less than $3,000 in income; on the other hand, 60 percent of the aged couples with at least one member working received more than $4,000.

Couples are more likely to benefit from employment than single persons. Forty-six percent of the 6.0 million aged married couples in 1967 had one or both members in the labor force sometime during the year. At the same time, only 15 percent of the 9.8 million nonmarried aged individuals received income from earnings. The median income of unmarried aged individuals in 1967 who did not work was $1,241, while the median income of those who worked was $2,293, more than double.[27] Nonmarried men were more likely to have income from earnings than nonmarried women, 19 percent versus 14 percent.[28]

Income from Social Security. As noted, in 1967 34 percent of the aggregate money income received by persons 65 and over came from Social Security, and benefit increases since 1968 have raised the percentage considerably. Most aged persons now receive some benefits from Social Security; the 1968 Social Security survey found that eight out of ten "aged units" (a unit is either a couple or an individual) were receiving either the regular benefit or a "special age 72" benefit.

Because aged married couples are more likely to have income from earnings, Social Security benefits represent a somewhat smaller proportion of their total income than they do for nonmarried persons, who are less likely to have income from earnings. Overall, 30 percent of the total income of married couples came from Social Security, compared with 40 percent of the total income of nonmarried persons.[29]

The aged units who were not receiving Social Security benefits in 1967 were in poor financial condition. They included some 1.1 million women without husbands. Nearly half (46 percent) of these women had incomes of

less than $1,000 per year; two fifths of them relied on public assistance for
their main support. Among the women aged 73 and over, 60 percent were
on welfare.[30]

A significant portion of people receiving Social Security benefits have no
other income. About a fourth of the couples who were beneficiaries in 1967
and two fifths of the nonmarried beneficiaries had no income beyond their
Social Security benefits.[31]

Without Social Security benefits, many more aged persons would be officially poor than are now so classified. It was estimated for 1967 that
without Social Security, one half of all beneficiary couples would have been
"poor" (instead of one fifth) and four fifths of all nonmarried beneficiaries
(instead of one half). The Social Security survey staff also provided some
other estimates of the income situation of older people, had Social Security
not been operative in 1967. They estimated that without Social Security the
proportion of aged couples with enough income to meet the Bureau of Labor
Statistics "moderate" budget would drop from one third to one fifth, and
that for unmarried people, nine out of ten would be in the "poor" or "near
poor" categories.[32]

Pension Income. Twelve percent of the money income received by persons 65 and over in 1967 came from the pension plans of private or public
employers. For that year it was estimated that 1.9 million of the 15.8 million
aged units received income from a private pension and that 1.5 million units
received income from the pension programs for federal civilian and military
personnel, state and local government employees, and railroad workers.[33]
Nearly all private pensioners and about two thirds of those receiving public
employee pension income in 1967 also received Social Security benefits.[34]
The private and public employee pensioners were the economically elite.
The Social Security survey shows that for 1967 they had median incomes
about $1,000 higher than those without "second pension" benefits. Studies
also indicate that recipients of private pension benefits received higher Social Security benefits than the aged whose only retirement income source
was the Social Security payment, were more likely to have personal savings,
and held higher-paid jobs before retirement.[35]

Aged single women were the least likely persons to receive private retirement plan benefits and the most likely to have as retirement income only the
benefits of Social Security. Their underprotection under private plans was
due largely to the relative lack of vesting and survivor protection in private

plans, their concentration in industries with low private-plan coverage, and irregular patterns of labor-force attachment.[36] Table 1.8 shows that while about 13 percent of aged single men received Social Security plus private plan benefits, only 5 percent of aged single women did.

Newer generations of retirees tend to have higher incomes than the aged population as a whole, and a larger proportion of them are eligible for second pensions. In the 24-month period between July 1968 and June 1970, 2.3 million workers became newly entitled to Social Security benefits. Of these, about one in four was entitled to a second pension benefit (public or private) from his most recent job.[37] The median annual private pension payment was estimated to be $2,080.[38]

Table 1.9 shows the distribution of new Social Security beneficiaries in the 1968–1970 period according to receipt of a second pension. The figures show that as recently as the 1968 to 1970 period, 69 percent of men beginning their Social Security retirement income had no second pension benefit, public or private, and 81 percent of the retiring women workers had no second pension.

If aged persons with a second pension in addition to Social Security are much better off than those with just Social Security alone, retired public employees with second pensions are in turn much better off than retired privately employed persons with such pensions. The 1968 survey disclosed that

Table 1.8 Source of Retirement Benefits of Persons Aged 65 and Over, 1967

Benefits	Percent Distribution		
	Married Couples	Nonmarried Persons	
		Men	Women
Social Security only	62	69	76
Social Security plus private plan	19	13	5
Social Security plus other public plan	7	6	5
Other public plan only	3	5	3
No retirement benefit	9	8	12

Source: Walter Kolodrubetz, "Employee Benefit Plans in 1968," Social Security Bulletin 33 (April 1970), p. 45.

the median annual public employee pension of persons also receiving Social Security benefits was $1,800 for couples (compared with a median of $972 for couples under private pensions), $1,394 for nonmarried men (compared with $864 under private pensions), and $1,005 for nonmarried women (compared with $664 under private plans).[39] On the average, employees of federal, state, and local governments are better off in retirement than employees whose working lifetimes were spent in the private sector.

Home Ownership. Couples aged 65 and over are very likely to own their own homes. The 1968 survey found that 77 percent of aged married couples owned their homes, while aged individuals—widows, widowers, the non-married—are less likely to live in premises they own; 37 percent of the non-married reported home ownership.[40]

By the time homeowners reach age 65, it has been assumed that most of them have completely paid off their mortgages. The 1968 survey confirmed this; more than four fifths of the elderly homeowners owned their homes free of mortgage. Homes of the elderly at the higher income levels were less likely to be free of mortgage than homes of persons at lower income levels, reflecting perhaps a greater propensity of those with higher incomes to move into new homes on retirement. While 70 percent of homeowners with incomes of $10,000 per year or more owned their homes mortgage-free, 80 percent or more of those with annual incomes of $2,500 or less owned their homes mortgage-free.[41]

There is a direct relationship between the income of the elderly and home

Table 1.9 Second Pensions Among Persons Receiving Social Security Benefits, 1968–1970

	Total	Men	Women
Number of Persons (thousands)	2,317	1,388	929
Receiving Second Pension	24%	29%	17%
Private pension, total	17	21	10
Public pension, total	8	9	7
Both private and public	1	1	—
Not Receiving Second Pension	74	69	81
Not Reported	2	1	2

Source: Lenore E. Bixby and Virginia Reno, "Second Pensions Among Newly Entitled Workers: Survey of New Beneficiaries," *Social Security Bulletin* 34 (November 1971), p. 5.

ownership. Overall, the median income of homeowners, as revealed by the 1968 survey, was 38 percent higher than that of nonowners. Among married couples, median income of homeowners was 14 percent higher than non-owners. [42]

Financial Assets. The majority of the elderly cannot count on much income from savings. Overall, 71 percent of the aged surveyed in 1968 reported liquid assets. Asked the amount of their holdings of various financial assets (money in banks, left with insurance companies, U.S. savings bonds, stocks and bonds), half of the married couples reporting in the 1968 Social Security survey reported assets of less than $2,000. Two thirds of the non-married persons had less than $1,500.

The proportion of the elderly reporting any assets varies with their incomes. Ninety-five percent of the elderly persons, including couples and nonmarried persons, with incomes of $7,500 per year or more reported assets, compared with 58 percent of those with incomes of less than $1,500 per year. [43]

The most frequently reported type of asset was money in the bank: 74 percent of the married couples and 58 percent of the nonmarried men and women reported assets in the form of bank deposits. United States savings bonds were reported by 18 percent of married couples and 10 percent of nonmarried persons. These relatively high figures possibly reflect the popularity of such savings bonds during World War II.

Ownership of stocks and corporate bonds was limited to about one in ten aged units. Married couples were a bit more likely to report assets in stocks and bonds (13 percent) than nonmarried elderly persons (8 percent). Not surprisingly, stock and bond ownership increases with income reported. Among aged married couples, 35 percent of those with an annual income of $7,500 or more reported such assets, compared with 3 percent of those whose incomes were under $2,000 per year. [44]

Table 1.10 shows the percentages of elderly persons reporting each type of asset in the 1968 Social Security survey of the aged. Reported income from financial assets was consistent with assets reported. Thus, 67 percent of all aged units reported financial assets of less than $3,000, and 70 percent reported income from assets of less than $150. The income figures are generally consistent with an income yield of 4 to 5 percent. Half the married couples who reported any income from assets had income amounts less than $3,000 per year, and half of the nonmarried had incomes from their assets of less than $210 per year. On the higher income side, 15 percent of married couples reporting income from assets received $1,000 or more per year as income from their assets. Among nonmarried persons with assets, 7 percent received income from assets of at least $1,000 per year.[45]

Public Assistance. Public assistance payments represented about 4 percent of the aggregate income of persons 65 and older in 1967. About 12 percent of all aged units (couples and individuals) reported receiving some income from public assistance sources. Among the 12.4 million aged units receiving Social Security benefits in 1967, 8 percent also received public assistance. Of the 2.2 million aged units who did not receive Social Security benefits, 31 percent reported income from public assistance.[46] The aged who receive public assistance are relatively advanced in old age, often infirm, and frequently require help from others in their daily living. More than two thirds of the recipients of public assistance are women.[47]

ADEQUACY OF INCOME

Since 1950, when President Truman directed the Federal Security Agency to convene the first White House Conference on Aging, two later conferences in 1961 and 1971 have also been held and many conference recommen-

Table 1.10 Financial Assets of Aged Units, 1967

Type of Asset	All Units	Married Couples	Nonmarried Persons
Any liquid assets	71%	80%	65%
Money in:			
Banks	64	74	58
Credit unions	4	6	2
Savings and loan	22	26	19
Insurance companies	10	13	8
Other	3	3	3
U.S. savings bonds	13	18	10
Stocks and corporate bonds	10	13	8
Loans or mortgages	4	6	3

Source: Janet Murray, "Homeownership and Financial Assets: Findings from the 1968 Survey of the Aged," *Social Security Bulletin* 35 (August 1972):12.

dations have been implemented. Among them were Medicare and Medicaid, increased Social Security benefits, establishment of the Administration on Aging, and the training of manpower to serve older people. Yet adequate incomes for aged people remain a problem. Income was the first of nine areas of specific concern listed by the 1971 White House Conference on Aging.

An adequate and assured income is not the only need of aged couples and nonmarried aged individuals, but it is most assuredly the first. A booklet published by the Department of Health, Education, and Welfare just prior to the 1971 White House Conference on Aging attempted to describe the life and circumstances of older citizens in an "ideal world."

Every older person would have enough income to pay for nutritious food, a comfortable home, the clothes he needed, transportation when he needed it, medical care and medicines, and participation in the total life of his community.[48]

Many of the problems of the aged today would almost solve themselves if aged persons had higher incomes. Beyond income, how many in the eight other areas of specific concern of the recent White House Conference would be areas of lesser concern if elderly people had enough income at their disposal to meet their fundamental needs? Health, housing, employment and retirement, retirement roles and activities, education, nutrition and transportation, and spiritual needs? With all of these, adequate income helps.

This is not to say that the elderly do not need special services that personal income alone cannot buy. Health care facilities, convalescent care, household assistance, assistance in the preparation of meals, aid in transportation, facilities for recreation and social activities, an adequate national supply of living units—all these require national and community efforts. If facilities and services are not available when and where they are needed by the elderly, elderly needs will remain unmet regardless of income. But income is the starting point if individuals and couples are to enjoy a dignified and satisfying "third age." We have not met the challenge. There are too many "poor" and "near poor." Even our official definitions of poverty suggest an interest on the part of public officials in sweeping the problem under the rug. Too few of the elderly have a decent, reasonable, moderate level of income.

The figures in this chapter detail the low income status of most of the elderly. They also point the way toward orderly and soundly conceived responses to the problem.

Our Social Security program has already become a substantial source of income for elderly persons. Each generation of newly retired people, on the average, derives a greater percentage of income from this national program. In contrast, the statistics on the presence of a second pension are discouraging. Aside from reform of the welfare system, the main challenge we face lies in arranging for a better system of second pensions.

We must also take into more careful account the fact that, ultimately, there are far more elderly women than men. Provision for assured lifetime pensions of women workers and of workers' dependents (spouses) should be as important an element in private pensions as it is under the Social Security program.

Above all, as will be brought out in the public policy chapters, we should establish as a principle of private pensions that a worker earns an increment in his future pension for each year he works. The fact that only 12 percent of the aggregate money income going to aged persons as recently as 1967 comes from the second pensions of public and private employers reflects in part the failure of pension plans throughout this century to vest their benefits early, thus assuring pension portability in our highly mobile and dynamic society, and in part the absence of pension plans in many sectors of private employment.

Our national success in achieving reasonable income levels for people when they leave the work force due to age and enter the retirement years depends ultimately on our willingness to develop a comprehensive public policy for a better combination of first and second pensions—of basic Social Security plus employer- or union-sponsored pensions. That will be the winning combination in the battle for dignified survival in old age.

The weak link in our system of income support for the elderly has been on the side of private pension plans. The effect of private plans in the aggregate is still limited, though the first plans began over a century ago. How pension plans got started, and how they have developed is the subject of the next chapter.

—2—

The Beginning of American Pension Plans

And time that gave now doth his gift confound.
Time doth transfix the flourish set on youth
And delves the parallels in beauty's brow,
Feeds on the rareties of nature's truth,
And nothing stands but for his scythe to mow:
  And yet to times in hope my verse shall stand,
  Praising thy worth, despite his cruel hand.

William Shakespeare

Concern for the well-being of aged persons in American society dates from colonial times, but private pension plans as an aspect of concern are much more recent in their origin. The first formal private pension plans generally emerged along with the conditions created by the industrial revolution: the large employing organization, the corporate structure of business and industrial firms, impersonal employer-employee relationships, efficiency-seeking methods of management, growing urbanization of the working population, and increased health and safety hazards of large-scale industrial and transportation enterprises. Some of the same factors stimulated early beginnings in pension plans for government employees.

Pension historians generally cite 1875 as the year in which the first formal pension plan was established, that of the American Express Company, then closely associated with the business of railroad transportation. Murray Latimer, in his monumental two-volume study of American pension plans pub-

lished in 1932, describes the American Express plan as the first noncontributory private plan in North America, following by one year the start of the
contributory plan of the Grand Trunk Railway of Canada.[1]

Unlike the retirement benefits provided by present-day plans, the benefits
of the early American Express plan applied only to "permanently incapaci-
tated" workers, i.e., disabled elderly employees. To be eligible for the
benefits the disabled worker had to have served the company for at least 20
years and to have reached age 60. Also, there had to be a recommendation
for retirement by the general manager and approval by the executive committee of the board of directors. The annual allowance was one half of the
worker's annual average pay during the ten years preceding retirement, with
a maximum of $500 a year. Forty years later the company was still operat-
ing with the same plan, except that the retirement of a permanently disabled
worker could take place at any age provided he had had at least 20 years of
service.[2] The plan was discontinued when the express business was transferred to the American Railway Express Company in 1918, and a new plan
was adopted in 1921.[3]

CARE OF THE AGED—
AMERICA'S FIRST HUNDRED YEARS

Perhaps the principal significance of the year 1875 in U.S. pension history is
that it marks the end of an era in American thought that held that the social
and economic needs of aged people could be satisfied solely by individual,
family, or community resources. During the new American nation's first
century, economic and social conditions made it natural for the family to
serve as the principal institution of old-age support. The economic life of the
nation, largely rural and based mainly on agriculture, emphasized the family
and indeed depended on it. A relatively independent producing unit in an agricultural economy, the family tended to retain most or all of its members,
of whatever generation, as a part of that functioning unit. One generation
would provide its children with livelihood on the land, gradually decreasing
activity as age advanced and as the children grew old enough to assume
ownership responsibilities. The cycle continued and at any one time two or
three generations might exist in a relationship of mutual support. Although
the physical labor of older family members decreased, the aged still played

an important supervisory role in the family structure, participating in the productive enterprise of the farm or artisanship, and sharing in the working and supportive processes.

In the more populated trade or business centers the pattern was much the same. An individual would continue in business as long as health permitted. Members of the younger generation would follow the occupational footsteps of their parents, providing economic security for the parents who had earlier provided children with their opportunities for training and work.

For workers not self-employed in agriculture or trade—the people in the employ of others for wages or salary—old-age support was perhaps less certain, depending on continuation of employment in old age (there were no mandatory retirement ages), on the fruits of frugality and savings, or on support of family members. The very poor aged were the objects of public or private charity or, if infirm and without other means of support, the poorhouse.

The system of "self-support" for the elderly during the first three quarters of the 19th century was reinforced by certain factors underlying the family structure in an agricultural society. For one thing, the era was marked by strong traditions of individualism and personal independence. The opening of the West to settlers and the enactment of the Homestead Act provided new opportunities for many who in similar circumstances today would have no hope of starting a new life on a frontier. A spirit of self-reliance, stimulated by seemingly endless opportunities to exercise that spirit, beckoned almost every man toward his and his nation's "manifest destiny," with little apparent concern for individual security. Furthermore, the society itself was a youthful one and remained so. The successive waves of 19th-century immigration from abroad brought mainly young people, and the average life expectancy for those born at mid-century was only 45 years (compared with 70 at present). There were proportionately fewer old people to consider and to care for. Altogether, the number, the proportion, and the situation of old people was greatly different from today.

However, in the late 19th century far-reaching changes began to take place in virtually every aspect of American life, including the economic and social situation of the elderly. Industrialization, the dramatic impact of the railways, and the accelerating movement of America to urban centers created vast changes and posed new and unfamiliar problems.

THE TWENTIETH CENTURY

The first organized pension plans were a tiny aspect of various attempts to respond to conditions in a society that was changing from rural to urban, from agricultural to industrial, from multigenerational family self-sufficiency to a cash-exchange base. Compared with such issues as hours of work, working conditions, pay scales, and the right of employees to organize, pensions occupied a low priority. The recognition due pension plans as a means of meeting needs of employees in their old age was slow in coming; by 1900 only about a dozen plans had been started.

The lead was taken by the railroads, which employed large numbers of workers in hazardous jobs. The pioneering American Express plan was followed in 1880 by a plan established by the Baltimore & Ohio Railroad Company. By 1905 a total of 12 formal pension plans had been set up by U.S. railroads, covering 488,000 people, or about 35 percent of all railroad employees. At the same time, many other railroads were reported by the Interstate Commerce Commission as paying pensions or gratuities to retired employees without benefit of formal plan.[4]

Other industry groups pioneering in the establishment of formal pension arrangements before 1900 included municipal utility companies, street railways, banking institutions, and a handful of manufacturing companies whose plans did not last long. The first enduring pension plan in a manufacturing firm was established in 1901 as part of the relief fund for employees of the Carnegie Steel Company. The normal age for retirement was set at 60 years after 15 years of service, and the pension allowance was 1 percent of the average salary throughout the whole period of service, multiplied by the number of years of service. The plan, with modifications, was taken over by the successor U.S. Steel Corporation in 1911.[5]

The period of greatest early growth in pension plans was between 1900 and 1920. By 1920, most of the major railroads, utility companies, banks, mining companies, and petroleum companies had set up formal pension plans, and parallel pension plan growth was recorded for manufacturers of machinery, agricultural implements, chemicals, paints and varnishes, food products, rubber, paper and printing products, and electrical apparatus. After 1920 the pension plan growth rate declined, both in the numbers of plans newly adopted and in the numbers of employees newly covered, since the largest companies had already established plans. By the end of 1929,

Latimer concluded that a total of 421 industrial pension plans had been established since 1875, that 397 were still in operation, and that employees of corporations with pension plans numbered 3,745,000, about 10 percent of the nonagricultural labor force, although not all were eligible for plan membership.[6] Because of the eligibility rules, perhaps less than 10 percent of plan members would ever qualify for benefits.[7]

NATURE OF THE EARLY PLANS

Over three fourths (77 percent) of the 397 pension plans established between 1875 and 1929 and still operating in 1929 were noncontributory, that is, paid for wholly by the employer. These noncontributory plans covered 96 percent of all employees of firms reporting a pension plan in effect. The remaining 23 percent of plans, covering 4 percent of employees, required an employee contribution or, in a few plans, offered contributing employees a benefit on top of an employer-pay-all base.[8] Latimer notes that under the plan of the Pennsylvania Railroad, started in 1900, the employer paid the whole cost, and that this plan became "the model for large numbers of American formal plans. . . ." Latimer observed that the noncontributory approach was popular because it appeared to further important employer objectives:

If the dominating influence were the desire for a humane method of retirement, there would seem to be no reason against the employees contributing to a fund and having a voice in administration. That they do not do so leads to the conclusion that the railroads have preferred to bear the entire cost in order to retain full control of the schemes. This policy has the advantages, at least in the opinion of the managements, of not complicating relations with trade unions, retaining full control of retirements and final judgment on the fulfillment of qualifications, discouraging strikes, and permitting retirement for the good of the service and the public safety.[9]

Retirement Age. Among the plans operating in 1929, the retirement age at which members became eligible for benefits was sometimes set at 65, sometimes 70. Among the railroad plans, age 70 was usually the maximum age for continuation of employment, as reasons of safety governed the mandatory retirement of operating personnel. In addition, a continuous service of at least 20 years was required, and for disability benefits, 20 or 25 years. Some plans contained a provision for voluntary retirement, usually applied to employees 65 years of age with 20 years of service. A typical pension plan in manufacturing called for voluntary retirement at either 60 or 65 years of age, after 20 or 25 years of service, while a pension for incapacity might typically have required 15 to 20 years of service. The uniformity of provisions among various plans is ascribed by Latimer's 1932 study to a tendency for new plans to copy older plans.[10]

Latimer also notes that employers with retirement plans, particularly the railroads, tried to avoid hiring workers at the higher ages, partly in order to assure that all employees who worked to the retirement age could fulfill the service requirements for retirement benefits. However, hiring age limits were initially established for reasons not primarily related to pension plans, since the limits may have predated plan installation, but rather to the character of the work. Where retirement plans had come into existence, workers hired above a certain age were sometimes specifically excluded from the pension plans.[11]

Except for a small number of contributory plans, none of the plans in effect in 1929 provided for the vesting of benefits for employees who terminated employment before reaching the prescribed retirement age, nor did the pension literature of the time find the absence of such vesting worthy of comment.

Benefits. Benefit amounts were typically based on service and salary or wage history. A 1931 report by the National Industrial Conference Board found that the earliest plans had made the final year's income or the average of the last three to ten years the basis for computing the pension, but that the procedure had later fallen into disfavor, after more attention was paid to actuarial techniques in the calculation of pension costs, because it was "impossible to forecast" what an individual's earning capacity would be during his final years of service.[12] Latimer observed that "most pension plans operating in 1929 seem to have been framed with the idea of relating the benefit to the employee's standard of living at the time of retirement," but that rising prices in the 1916–1920 period had caused some concern about the rapidly rising costs of the "final average" plans and had cut down the proportion of such plans during the mid-1920s.[13]

The percentage factors applied to the calculation of benefits varied between 1 and 2 percent. Among the noncontributory plans, accounting for more than three fourths of total plans, three fourths were in the 1 percent formula group.[14]

None of the plans attempted to provide for adjustments of the retirement payments to accord with price changes. The one exception to the provision of fixed benefits once the pension started was the plan of the Perfection Stove Company, adopted in 1913, which provided for the adjustment of pensions according to the percentage change each six months in the average hourly earnings of all employees.[15]

Financing. Benefits of the majority of plans operating in the late 1920s were financed from the current income of the employing companies. Latimer reported that 60 percent of noncontributory plans in 1929 were paying their pensions from the employer's current income, 25 percent had set up an in-company balance sheet reserve, and the remaining 15 percent had set up trust funds or were using insured arrangements.[16] Among contributory plans, the use of trust fund reserves was more common than among noncontributory plans.

Trust fund operations did not necessarily indicate a much greater degree of financial solvency than other methods, however. A 1925 Conference Board study concluded that the majority of all pension plans were using "methods of hand-to-mouth disbursements by the company to meet pension charges as they arise," and that even among plans in which some degree of prefunding was evident, the accumulating reserves were insufficient to meet faster-growing long-term liabilities.[17]

In addition to noting inadequacies of funding of the early plans, the 1925 Conference Board study expressed concern about the methods of assessing plan costs. Judging most of the plans unrealistic in terms of their assessment of future wage levels, labor turnover, rates of disability, and changes in the numbers and age composition of the work force, the report observed that "the great majority of pension plans in American industry have been established with no accurate calculation of their future costs and with no adequate provision for financing them." [18]

A few years later, in 1931, in a pamphlet offering information to industrial executives on pension plans, the Conference Board urged that pension reserves be set up at the time benefits accrue and noted that the principle of funding with adequate reserves "is so obviously sound that it is difficult to explain the absence of this provision in the set-up of many pension plans." [19]

Employee Rights. Employers were presumably aware that the pay-as-you-go financing methods generally in use and the level of reserves in funded plans could not be depended upon to assure or guarantee benefits under all possible future circumstances. Consequently, they were hesitant to commit themselves or their successors to the unalterable maintenance of an obligation the full burden of which was not foreseeable. In no case, therefore, did any of the 400 or so industrial pension plans in operation in the late 1920s contain any contractual obligation for the future maintenance of benefit promises or payments.[20]

While there was clear advantage to the expression of good and sincere intentions in formal plan language in the recognition of long and faithful service, careful precautions were taken to make sure that payments of pensions would be at the employer's option and that the employer undertook no legal obligation if business conditions made it difficult to pay pensions or if, for any other reason, it was decided that pensions not be paid either to particular individuals or to all. Most of the plans contained a clause similar to the following:

> The right to change from time to time any of the foregoing provisions and substitute others in their stead and the right to revise or alter from time to time the plan under which this pension system has been established or to abandon said system is hereby reserved.

In addition to prudent guardianship of the employer's rights of plan discontinuance or alteration, employers pursued clarification of the position of the employee in language which became virtual boilerplate in every industrial plan. The following were typical:

> Neither the establishment of this annuity plan nor any of its provisions nor the granting of an annuity or any other action now or hereafter taken by the annuity board or by the officers of the ***corporation shall be held or construed as creating a contract or giving to any employee the right to be retained in the service or any right to an annuity. All employees remain subject to discharge as always in the same manner and to the same extent as if the annuity plan had never been created.[21]

> The allowances are voluntary gifts from the company and constitute no contract and confer no legal rights upon any employee. The continuance of the retirement allowance depends upon the earnings of the company and the allowances may at any time be reduced, suspended, or discontinued on that, or any other account, at the option of the Board of Directors.[22]

> Neither the creation of the Fund nor any provision or action in reference or relating thereto or the distribution or application thereof or anything done under or because of or in relation to such Fund, shall be construed as constituting or effecting a contract, expressed or implied, or giving any employees, beneficiary, or other person, any legal rights, or right of action at law or in equity, either before or after pension

granted, nor giving any employee the right to be retained in the service, and all employees remain subject to discharge to the same extent as if this Fund had not been created, the creation of such Fund and all provisions made in reference or relating thereto, being purely voluntary on the part of the Company for the benefit of employees who shall have rendered it long and faithful service.[23]

As a result of studies of these provisions, Conant described industrial pension systems as "if and maybe" propositions. In effect, he stated, such a system says to the worker:

If you remain with this company throughout your productive lifetime,
If you do not die before the retirement age,
If you are not discharged or laid off for an extended period,
If you are not refused a benefit as a matter of discipline [i.e., because of joining a union, asking for a raise, or, in some cases, for "immoral" conduct],
If the company continues in business, and
If the company does not decide to abandon this plan, you will receive a pension at the age of __, subject to the contingency of its discontinuance or reduction, after it has been entered upon.[24]

ADJUDICATION OF EMPLOYEE RIGHTS

It was inevitable that employees would be adversely affected by administrative implementation of the standard pension plan disclaimer clauses, and would press their claims in the courts. *McNevin v. Solvay Process Company* (1898), was apparently the first court case to interpret an industrial pension plan. *Solvay* arose from a dispute regarding eligibility for pension benefits under a noncontributory plan. McNevin, who had joined the company in 1890, was discharged by a foreman in 1895 with no reason given to him. A reason was later entered on the company records.

Under its pension plans, the Solvay Company issued to each employee a passbook that contained a copy of the pension rules and was regularly posted with pension amounts credited to the employee. One of the plan provisions was that in case of discharge "without cause of dissatisfaction" the amount credited to the employee should be paid "according to the rules." One rule stated that if an employee left the company for any cause, including dismissal, the trustees could hold back all or part of his account for a period not exceeding five years, on condition of paying him interest upon the sum. This rule and the entering of credits on the passbook might have led an employee to think there was something dependable about his pension credits—Mc-

Nevin apparently thought so. But other rules placed the administration in the hands of the company directors, authorized them to decide questions without appeal, and stated that the sums credited to employees were to remain the property of the company until actually paid. Some of the rules seemed to take away what others assured.

A lower New York court decided in favor of the plaintiff employee, but a higher court reversed the decision.[25] The reversal, affirmed by the highest New York State court, was based on the plan rule authorizing the company's directors to decide all questions without appeal. The opinion of the Appellate Division stated that "in this case the defendant's trustees [directors] decided after a hearing of the plaintiff that he was not, when the action was begun, entitled to payment of any portion of the fund credited to him, and it seems to me that, under the terms of a gift, this decision is final, unless within the discretion of the defendant's trustees it shall be modified in the future."

The court's opinion rested squarely on the authority of the trustees to make decisions without appeal. But an important underlying part of the discussion in this case was the court's interpretation of the pension as a gift involving no employee right, as illustrated in an earlier part of the opinion:

> It is conceded that this pension fund has been created voluntarily and is a gift by the defendant, and the question upon which this case turns is whether, when a sum is credited to the employee on the passbook furnished by the defendant, the employee has a vested right in the sum so credited, or whether, under the terms by which the fund is established, the employee acquires no vested right until the gift is completed by actual payment to the employee. It must be conceded . . . that a person or corporation . . . has the right to fix the terms of his bounty and provide under what circumstances the gift shall become vested and absolute. Under the regulations established . . . none of the employees has a vested right in any part of this fund, even though credited upon their passbooks, until the gift is completed by actual payment.[26]

A few years later, in *Dolge v. Dolge* (1902), there came to the same court another case involving the rights of an employee who had not qualified for retirement but to whom certain sums had been credited from year to year in connection with a pension, insurance, and endowment plan, also by the passbook method. The House of Dolge, manufacturers of felts, failed in 1898, and in an action to dissolve the Dolge partnership certain employees presented claims as preferred creditors. The passbook contained printed rules classified under the headings "Pension Law," "Insurance Law," and

"Law of Endowment." Among the rules was one disavowing responsibility in the following words:

It is distinctly understood that all and every of the provisions of this law are voluntary on behalf of said House of Dolge, and that this law does not, nor do any of the provisions herein contained, confer any legal right or create any legal right in favor of any employee. . . .

The court held that, far from being preferred creditors, the employees were not creditors at all. Its opinion was that there was no binding agreement and that the plan, as adopted by Alfred Dolge, was "simply a benevolent plan" solely within his discretion to carry out or not.

Merely giving credit upon their passbooks for certain amounts did not constitute a valid gift. To sustain a gift of this character, there must have been on the part of Dolge an intent to give, and an actual payment and complete delivery of the money to or for the employee, wholly divesting Dolge of the control of it.[27]

The *Solvay* and *Dolge* cases sustained the gift principle of pension benefits and effectively ended the use of the passbook mechanism for operating noncontributory plans. A retrospective comment made in 1930 summed up the two cases:

It is notable in present practice that the accruing of credits to the employee's pension account, as well as the passbooks in which these were recorded (features of the plans described in *McNevin v. Solvay Process Company* and in *Dolge v. Dolge*) have been abandoned. They were too close to an admission of liability to survive as features of the wider use of pension plans. . . .[28]

The fate of the Dolge pension plan and its members was an early indicator of the fact that a pension offer remains an illusion unless it is contractual in nature and is backed by adequate financial reserves. Dolge's intentions were of the best. Alfred Dolge was a pioneer in a variety of steps to improve the lot of the factory worker. A sympathetic review of his work published in the American Journal of Sociology in 1897 gives no suggestion of the financial weakness of his firm.[29] The review described the Dolge pension provisions and told of the periodic credits in employee passbooks as if there were no questions of their inviolability. Male employees past age 21 with five years' service were credited each year "with the amount which the manufacturing record has shown to be earned over and above the wages paid him." These credits were payable with interest at age 60 or upon the death of the employee if he had not reached that age; if the employee should "quit the ser-

vice of the House, interest ceases and the principal is paid as specified." An
employee could borrow against his endowment account but had to give col-
lateral. The review raised no questions regarding possible financial misfor-
tune and the decisions that would necessarily face a receiver if such misfor-
tune should come. But the lesson was soon drawn; afterward, in a
publication of 1899, an observer of the labor scene noted that "[Dolge's]
failure of business in 1898 showed the desirability of making such schemes
independent of the financial fortunes of the House, if possible." [30]

DECLINE OF THE RAILROAD PLANS

As noted earlier, the railroads were among the first of the industrial employers to establish pension plans, starting with the B&O and the Pennsylvania. This was consistent with the fact that the early pension plans tended
to appear in the more prosperous industries and the larger concerns, among
which were the railroads—new, growing, and able to attract massive
amounts of capital. By 1934 about 90 percent of all employees of Class I
railroads were covered by noncontributory private pension plans. The last
Class I railroad retirement plan was established in 1929.

The later decline of the railroads illustrates the problems pension plans encounter if they have not made sound financial arrangements to back up their
pension promises. Until the late 1920s the railroads continued to flourish and
to represent attractive employment opportunities. Beginning with the Great
Depression, railroad revenues declined sharply and at the same time the
number of railroad workers expecting to be retired because of age or years
of service was increasing. Had the railroads been able to continue as profitable business enterprises, they would probably have had less difficulty in
meeting their heavy pension promises. But the plans had not accumulated
sufficient reserves to meet their obligations, and current revenues were insufficient to support these underfunded plans. Of the 82 pension plans
operated by the Class I roads in 1929, only one had followed the policy of
fully funding the accumulating service credits.

With virtually no pension reserves established to meet pension liabilities,
and with many of the roads operating in the red in the late 1920s and early
'30s, companies resorted to various expediencies to ease the financial pressures. Railroad wage rates were cut by 10 percent in 1932. Virtually all
companies reduced pensions by 10 percent and a few cut them by from 15 to

40 percent. Some railroads slowed the rate of retirements and a few abandoned the compulsory retirement age of 70.

These emergency measures were not enough. Without sufficient pension reserves, with a declining capacity to sustain a pay-as-you-go retirement system amidst the economic shambles of the Great Depression, and with growing competition from the trucking industry, the railroads' benevolent and optimistic pension promises were turning into a financial monster. As the Depression deepened, layoffs increased. From 1929 through 1933 roughly 800,000 railroad employees were laid off. But the oldest in service were retained and the potential pension burden did not materially decrease; in 1934 approximately 25 percent (250,000) of the employed rail workers were 65 or would reach that age within four years, or had completed 30 years of service.[31]

There was little prospect that the troubled railroads could make good on their pension promises for the quarter-million older employees due to retire within three or four years. Strong pressure developed for some kind of legislative action to bail the railroads out. Failures and employment cutbacks among smaller industrial enterprises had also deprived employees of their pension expectations, but the railroads were large enterprises and hundreds of thousands of people were involved. Their predicament could not be ignored, and the political implications were great.

The federal government responded with a plan to take over and administer the pension promises of the railroads. The government approach was to inject substantial federal appropriations to cover immediate obligations, and for the future to develop a plan incorporating employee and employer contributions under a federally run plan. An initial attempt at legislation was declared unconstitutional. Subsequent legislation resulted in the Railroad Retirement Act of 1935, amended in 1937, and the Carriers' Taxing Act of 1937. These acts covered all employees of the railroads, employees of related transportation companies and associations, and railroad labor union employees. The system now operates something along the lines of Social Security and functions as a substitute Social Security system for railroad employees.[32]

The present-day Railroad Retirement System thus grew out of a set of pension plans that failed, were rescued with public funds, and were transformed into a quasi-public system for the employees of the industry. This hybrid arrangement, under which general public revenues are added to employee and employer contributions, is unique among American pension plans. It embodies an acknowledgment that private pension plan failures are, at times at least, matters of public policy requiring corrective public action. Had railroads at their outset been mandated by public policy to set aside adequate pension fund reserves, benefits for qualifying employees could have been paid independently of the fortunes of the railroads themselves. Employee protection would have been afforded regardless of the vicissitudes of the particular industry.

Pension plan failures in other industrial areas have not been as massive nor in such a homogeneous industry. As a result, they have not led to federal bailouts. Unfortunately, the catastrophic failure of the railroads' pension plans did not at the time lead to any movement for pension reform.

PENSION PLANS AND LABOR

While the larger industrial employers were establishing their pension plans in the early years of the 20th century, the trade unions, independently of employers, were attempting their own programs of member benefits. Labor leaders understood the value of union-sponsored welfare programs in attracting union members. In the 1890s Sidney and Beatrice Webb noted that union welfare programs reflected "the belief of trade union officials in the advantage of developing the friendly society side of trade unionism [and] rests frankly on the adventitious aid it brings to working-class organizations." [33] James Lynch, a president of the International Typographical Union, observed in 1914 that "the officials of the great trade unions . . . recognize the value of benefit features as builders of unions, as conservators of the membership of these unions, entirely aside from their assistance to members as safeguards against financial loss during adversity." [34]

The earliest mutual aid activities of the trade unions concentrated not on old-age pensions, but on the much more immediate needs of both the workers and their unions: death benefits, sickness benefits, disability benefits, and whatever arrangements the union might be able to make for some kind of wage replacement during strikes or unemployment. Pensions, to the extent that unions were able to manage some kind of pension program, were initially related to the need for a continuing benefit during permanent disability, and somewhat later, to the movement for the establishment of homes for aged union members who could no longer work. The lack of emphasis on provisions for the aged is perhaps explained by the fact that in the early years of the trade union movement the intensity of the struggle to gain members, raise wages, and shorten hours left little energy for items of longer-term priority. Also, the militancy of the movement made it attractive primarily to young men, so that concern for old-age dependency was rarely voiced.[35]

Old-Age Plans. The first union plan to provide for periodic old-age payments, as distinct from lump-sum or periodic benefits for permanent disability, was established by the Patternmakers in 1900. The plan was not funded and depended on the union treasury. The first plan with a degree of funding for old-age payments was established in 1905 by the Granitecutters. Also, by 1905 the Cigarmakers Union had developed what was regarded as a model union-run plan for sickness, unemployment, and death benefits and permanent and total disability payments.[36] These were small unions. The first large union to adopt its own pension program was the Typographical Union in 1906–7; this plan was the consequence of the unemployment of many of the union's older workers following acrimonious strikes over the eight-hour day. None of these plans provided benefits as a matter of right, and the payments depended largely upon the state of the union treasury.[37]

The first union plan offering old-age benefits as a matter of right rather than as gratuities was established by the Brotherhood of Locomotive Engineers in 1912. Two other railroad unions followed, the Locomotive Firemen and Enginemen (BLFE) and the Trainmen (BRT); these two plans included homes for the aged and disabled, pensions for old age and total disability, and pensions to widows of aged or disabled members.

Weakness of Union Plans. By 1928, it was estimated that about 40 percent of trade union membership belonged to national unions offering one form or another of old age and permanent and total disability benefits. But the funds for the benefits necessarily had to be derived from assessments on union members. As the numbers of older union members increased, the assessments on all members had to be increased, often when other claims on the union treasury were being made for the fight for better wages, shorter hours, and better working conditions. To increase union dues became more difficult, and within a few years after the Great Depression began almost all of the union welfare plans had collapsed. In 1930 the New York State Commission on Old-Age Security judged trade union pension funds to be "in all cases technically bankrupt. . . . The attaining of solvency will necessitate huge increases in contributions and . . . members of the unions are not prepared to stand such increased contributions.'' [38] The unions' efforts to develop their own arrangements for old age and disability benefits had foundered on the weaknesses of the assessment system, the coming of the Depression, and on other union priorities.

After the adoption of Social Security in 1935 only a handful of national unions continued to offer old-age homes or old-age pensions, notably the carpenters, electrical workers, pressmen, railroad conductors, and the locomotive engineers.[39]

Attitude Toward Employer Plans. Labor had largely failed in its attempts to maintain its own welfare plans. While the large employers had made considerable strides in the development of their own pension plans, labor did not view these plans with much warmth. In the mid 1930s it appeared that there had been little change in the labor attitude phrased in 1914 by James Lynch of the International Typographical Union that "wage earners look askance at these company-instituted and company-controlled funds, as they give the impression that they are instituted in order that the worker may be more firmly bound to the industry and less liable to form industrial organizations for the regulation of hours, wages, and working conditions.'' [40] In establishing their plans, management had frankly emphasized these advantages: (1) improvement of general morale, (2) improvements in safety resulting from the retirement of superannuated employees, noted especially by railroad management, (3) stability of the work force through reduction of turnover in anticipation of pensions, (4) enhancement of the enterprise's attractiveness to superior workers, and (5) reduction in strikes and in the weakening of union appeals.

Looking back on the early company pension plans, a 1949 American Federation of Labor publication characterized the typical company plan as "strictly an instrument of, by, and for management," and as a cheap means of getting rid of superannuated employees, an invisible chain by which workers were attached to a particular company through the promise of a pension and the threat of its loss if they quit or were fired.[41]

A Transition Period. The Great Depression seriously shook American confidence in the virtues of individual thrift and in personal savings as a way to prepare for old age. With 13 million people out of work, savings erased, and long-standing traditions of self-reliance undermined, the 1930s were becalmed years for both union welfare plans and employer-sponsored pension plans. In this atmosphere the passage of the Social Security Act of 1935, America's first national social insurance legislation, was virtually inevitable. This was to be the main pension development until after World War II.

As the 1940s began, the demands of military and economic mobilization for World War II turned aside, for the time being, much of the attention that might have otherwise been directed toward improvements in provisions for old-age income. During the war, however, there was some resurgence of employer interest in pensions, partly as a result of the provisions of the 1942 Internal Revenue Code, the operation of excess-profits taxes, and the wage stabilization program.

By 1945 some doubt was expressed as to whether there had been a net gain in pension coverage over the pre-Depression years.[42] Furthermore, Social Security, less than a decade after it went into effect, was a disappointment to labor.[43] Despite its "late start" provisions, Social Security had by no means produced instant results, nor were the unions comfortable with the Old Age Assistance Program, the part of Social Security designed as a stopgap measure until the system matured. Also, there were no provisions for disabled workers in the law, and the assistance portion incorporated a means test, unacceptable to labor. The Advisory Council on Social Security in 1948 found three major deficiencies in the old-age insurance program: (1) inadequate coverage, (2) unduly restrictive eligibility requirements, and (3) inadequate benefits.[44]

A New Start. At the close of the 1940s the stage was set for a renewal of union interest in pension plans, not in mutual assistance or fraternal benefits, but in the negotiation of pension plans with employers through collective bargaining. Conditions were ready for the next phase of union welfare activity. The Internal Revenue Act of 1942 had placed the tax treatment of pension plans in a clearer light and had delineated criteria regarding nondiscrimination of employee classes within plans. Combined with the sharp increases in corporate and excess-profits tax rates of the 1940s, the special tax treatment that was accorded pension plans under the 1942 act enhanced employer receptiveness to union pension demands.[45] The wage stabilization policy of the National War Labor Board during World War II maintained wage stability at the price of "greater flexibility on secondary lines," specifically on fringe benefits. This wartime focus on fringe benefits popularized the idea and helped create in the minds of labor leaders and workers the notion that they were entitled to such benefits as a matter of right.[46]

The Mine Workers' Plan. The first struggle of a large union for a negotiated pension plan was that of John L. Lewis and the United Mine Workers of America. Although the plan that came out of this struggle had spectacular weaknesses, it focused attention on the question of pensions for union members and dramatized an interest in welfare funds that had not arisen from earlier negotiated plans; some of these had also used pooled funds and royalty contributions, but none had borne such public notice. Professor Jack Barbash observes that "psychologically it is likely that the miners' welfare fund was the single most influential force in the negotiated pension movement." [47]

John L. Lewis had first advanced demands for a welfare fund in the 1945 bituminous coal negotiations. But, as Lewis reported, "the plan was rejected by the operators and not pressed by mine workers." [48] Demands for a welfare fund were resumed the next year; the mine owners again refused, and a strike ensued that lasted from April 1 to May 22, 1946. Secretary of the Interior J. A. Krug, acting for the U.S. government, seized the mines. Krug and Lewis entered into an agreement on May 29, 1946, which established a welfare and retirement fund, to be financed by a contribution of five cents a ton from employers. Although Lewis demanded that the fund be managed by the union alone, Krug refused, stating that he could not "take the responsibility of arranging for a health and welfare fund to be administered solely by the union." Later in the year another strike broke out as the result of Lewis' charge that a government interpretation relating to the fund was breaching the contract. Although the miners returned to work, the fund was still not operative because the parties could not agree on the neutral trustee. The mines were returned to the private operators on June 30, 1947, with the expiration of the statute authorizing government operation of the mines. Shortly thereafter, under new negotiations, the employer contributions to the fund were set at ten cents a ton. The plan was again delayed because the trustees of the fund could not agree on specific items, including the fundamental question of whether the program should be funded on a reserve basis or set up on a pay-as-you-go basis. The latter was decided upon. After another strike, an injunction, a contempt order against Lewis, a stalemate on the seating of the neutral trustee, suits to prevent the fund from making pension payments, the negotiation of a new contract in 1948, and a federal court's approval of the pension plan, the first pension check was sent out in September 1948.

The strife and publicity that characteristically surrounded the mine workers' union and the personality of John L. Lewis, the numerous mine worker strikes in the late 1940s, and the colorful later history of the mine workers' retirement plan did little directly to further the development of sound pension plans, but these events did draw attention to welfare and benefit concepts. While other union leaders recognized that a new dimension had been added to the negotiation process, or soon would be, they also recognized that pension negotiations could not take priority over wage questions and other more immediate needs, and that where pensions were being considered, the interests of older workers might not take precedence over those of younger workers, at least for a time.[49]

The Steel Plans. In 1949 pensions became an issue in the steel industry negotiations. The union presented pension demands under a 1949 wage reopening provision in a contract due to expire in 1950. With the exception of Inland Steel, the companies took the position that pensions were not bargainable under the reopening clause because pensions were not wage rates within the meaning of the applicable contract provision. In support of its pension demands, the union asserted the inadequacy of the old-age benefits under Social Security and the companies' obligations to pay all of the costs of the pension "as a cost of doing business comparable to the cost of maintaining and replacing machinery."[50] The companies favored joint contributions, and a strike was threatened.

President Truman, in the face of a threatened national steel strike, appointed a fact-finding board to make recommendations. The board found that although the existing contract expiring in 1950 did not mention pensions, under the law a contractual exclusion of a matter that is bargainable occurs only when the exclusion is made explicit, so that there was an immediate obligation for such negotiations under the Taft-Hartley Act (enacted in 1947). The board accepted the union's "human depreciation" theory and also found that the cost of the pensions could be met without "unduly narrowing the profit margin of the industry or its ability to hold or even lower its prices." The steel industry objected to the cost conclusions and to the noncontributory principle. After three postponements, a nationwide steel strike went into effect, lasting for 42 days.

Bethlehem Steel settled first for a noncontributory plan, partly because the firm had had a noncontributory pension plan in effect since 1923. Others followed. The minimum pension benefit was set at $100 a month after 25 years of service and attainment of age 65, or where higher 1 percent of average monthly earnings over the last 10 years of service times years of service.[51]

The Automobile Industry. At about the same time, pension negotiations were going on in the automobile industry. In 1947, Ford workers had rejected pensions in favor of a direct wage increase, but by 1949 Walter Reuther of the United Automobile Workers was ready to say: "Slackening of the rise in the cost of living enables us to turn our attention to other matters, . . . pension plans and social security." [52] Negotiations started June 2, 1949. The union asked for joint union-management pension plan administration, fixed employer contributions stated in cents per hour, a noncontributory program, standards of benefits that together with Social Security would constitute a modest but adequate budget, integration with Social Security so that the private plan would become a supplement to that benefit, and actuarial soundness.[53] The resulting settlement provided for a joint board to oversee the pension benefits structure, within the single-employer plan. The company was to appoint the bank trustees for the pension fund and to be solely responsible for determining the funding of past service. The plan was noncontributory, providing $100 monthly normal pension at 65 or older after 30 years of credited service, automatic retirement at age 68, prorated benefits for employees age 65 years or older with less than 30 years of service, and a total and permanent disability benefit for employees between 55 and 65 with 30 years of service.[54]

The concluding phase of the inauguration of pension negotiations in the automobile industry was marked by a United Automobile Workers strike against Chrysler in 1950 that lasted 104 days. As Reuther said some years later:

> It was not about the size of the pension. It was about whether the pension would be based on pay-as-you-go or whether it would be a funded plan. And the Chrysler workers, about 90,000 of them, walked the bricks for 104 days on that principle alone, because we felt that we should not start down the road of a pension program except as we funded the pension and backed up the benefits with an actuarially sound fund.[55]

The Negotiated Plans. Some observers questioned the longer-term soundness of the separate negotiation of pension provisions by individual bargaining units. Clark Kerr, Director of the University of California Industrial Relations Center, noted a potential for interunion rivalry and a need for a more comprehensive approach in dealing with the unusually complicated subject matter.[56] A 1949 report of the House Ways and Means Committee saw "the demands for security by segments of the population threaten[ing] to result in unbalanced, overlapping, and competing programs." [57]

It is difficult to say what alternatives to the negotiation of pension plans, employer by employer, union by union, would have been available, unless single-employer plans were to be abolished. Certainly the single-employer plans established without negotiation differed substantially from one another and were just as likely to provide benefits that would be unbalanced, overlapping, or competing. Yet the plans met important employer and union objectives. Ultimately, the problems noted by Clark Kerr and by the Ways and Means Committee Report could only be dealt with by a national policy on private pensions that went far beyond the Internal Revenue Act, the one existing expression of national policy on the subject.

Another view of the future of negotiated pension benefits was that they might go beyond a stopgap role. Robert M. Ball, an official of the Social Security Administration, suggested that a major peril that might ensue from the further development of negotiated pension plans was the prospect that they might be "considered as long-range plans designed to do the major part of providing retirement protection." [58] However, fears that negotiated pension plans would tend to supplant Social Security have turned out to be unfounded.

While unions began to pay more attention to the negotiation of pension benefits, they also continued to urge the improvement of Social Security. The view of labor was that "protection must be more stable, continuous, and broader in scope than can be achieved in private and isolated plans." [59] The UAW claimed "that employer support for improvements in the public program [Social Security] is a direct result of the collective bargaining pressure for workers' security programs." [60]

That union negotiators would emphasize financial soundness of pension plans, however defined, and the avoidance of pay-as-you-go plans, suggests that labor organizations had learned a good deal from their own earlier experiences with benefit plans, most of which had failed because of funding inadequacies. At the same time, labor found it necessary, for the moment at least, to forego other important features of pension plans, such as early vesting, and permanent and total disability benefits. Initial negotiations opted for "maximum retirement security for the greatest number of older workers who will be eligible for retirement within the period for which the plan was originally negotiated," and this meant foregoing for the moment many desirable features of pension plans.[61]

MULTIEMPLOYER PLANS

The strongest early advances in pension negotiations were in the single-employer plans of the steel and automobile industries, both characterized by a few relatively large employers. However, the initiation of collectively bargained multiemployer pension plans took place as a result of the United Mine Workers' negotiations. Other industries were also taking the multiemployer pooled-pension approach. Among these were construction, food, apparel, and transportation, characterized by seasonal and irregular employment, small establishments, and such frequent job changes that few workers remained with a single employer long enough to qualify for pensions.[62] The single-employer pattern was not well suited to the typically high job turnover rates in the construction, service, and apparel industries. In these, the necessary pension mechanism was found in the form of a pooled fund that would receive contributions from more than one employer and disburse benefits to members regardless of which particular employer (or employers) in the group the eligible employee had worked for.

Some precedents for pooled employer funds for employee benefits had been worked out in the "needle trades." In 1938 the New York Children's Dressmakers' Union proposed that "employers contribute a percentage of their payroll into a pooled fund" for vacation pay. This proposal served to meet two critical problems in the industry: loss of vacation money because of job loss and failure to pay when an employer went out of business.[63] Various pooled welfare funds were later established in the needle trades; the first explicitly earmarked retirement fund was negotiated in 1944 by the International Ladies Garment Workers' Cloak Joint Board.[64]

The mid-1950s marked the beginning of real collective bargaining advancements in multiemployer pension plans. By 1954 the growth of multiemployer plans in the building trades warranted collections of statistics on such plans by the Bureau of Labor Statistics. James Hoffa negotiated his first pension plan for the Teamsters union in 1955.

While pooled multiemployer pension funds are governed through equal board representation of employers and unions (a requirement of Section 302 of the Taft-Hartley Act), the unions have tended to become the dominant partners. One reason has been that the employers are many and the union is one. The union is a continuing focal point of interest and continuity in the operation of the fund, and has of course been instrumental in establishing it. On the other hand, employer members of the boards of trustees do not necessarily represent all participating employers and may not identify themselves with pension affairs beyond making the contributions required of them.[65] The 14 employer trustees of the Western Teamsters' Fund, for example, do not possess any formal mandate beyond their selection for the representation of the 19,000 employers in the plan.[66]

PENSION PLANS FOR PUBLIC EMPLOYEES

In the beginning, pension plans for public employees provided benefits only in the case of death—a death benefit for survivors—or a pension for disability. Furthermore, the earliest plans did not provide their coverage very broadly, but were only for special groups of public employees—policemen first, followed by firemen and teachers. Nor were the early public employee systems statewide, as is now so common. Rather, they were established by municipalities. The financing at first was either wholly by the governmental employer or wholly by the employees themselves. The pioneering public plans began to appear in the decades preceding the establishment of the earliest industrial plans.

What was apparently the first municipal benefit plan was started for members of the New York City police force in 1857. The plan provided a pension in the event of disability or a lump-sum payment in the event of death and was financed by miscellaneous sources, such as donations and the proceeds of confiscated and unclaimed property. Twenty years later nondisability retirement benefits were made a part of the plan (1878) and employee contributions were introduced.[67]

The predecessor plans for the public teacher retirement systems were voluntary employee associations. In 1869 New York City teachers founded the Mutual Life Assurance Association to make lump-sum payments to survivors of deceased teachers from assessments levied on members as needs arose. This forerunner of a later pension plan had no legislative sanction and

no support from the employing municipality or school board. In the 1860s
there was apparently no thought that the employer or the public should interest itself in the efforts of teachers to help themselves.[68]

The public school teachers of New York City and Brooklyn began to seek
pension legislation as early as 1879, but while these efforts were repeated
from time to time, it was not until 1894 that they were successful. Paul
Studenski, a professor of economics and student of public pensions writing
in 1920, describes the establishment of the first teachers' retirement system
in the United States:

> The Board of Education in New York City was opposed to retirement legislation
> and the task of winning over the legislators and the governor was a difficult one. In
> 1894, after several failures, the teachers prepared a very mild measure. It provided
> for the establishment of a fund the resources of which were to come from deductions
> made from the pay of the teachers because of absence. No contributions were
> required of the teachers. Despite the opposition of the Board of Education, the sup-
> port of the governor was secured and thus in 1894 the first legislation creating a
> teachers' pension fund in this country was enacted.[69]

In 1895 and 1896, voluntary associations were formed by public school
teachers in seven other large cities, but none of these received support from
the employing governments until 1907.[70] In 1895 compulsory teacher retirement funds were established in Brooklyn, Detroit, and Chicago, and voluntary funds in St. Louis and San Francisco. In 1896 compulsory plans were
established in Buffalo and Cincinnati, and a voluntary plan was started on a
statewide basis in New Jersey. Studenski described the provisions of the
early teacher plans:

> The provisions of most of these funds were patterned after the provisions of the
> New York fund. In most of them annuities were fixed at $600, the exceptions being
> the associations of Cincinnati and Omaha, with annuities of $500 and $400 respec-
> tively, and the association of Brooklyn which provided annuities of one half the fixed
> salary of the retiring teacher. Annuities were to be paid to those members who retire
> from the teaching service under either of the following conditions: (1) completion of
> a certain length of service, which varied from 30 to 40 years in different systems,
> frequently with a lower requirement by five years for women than for men; (2) a
> proof of disability, irrespective of the length of service. The money necessary for the
> payment of these benefits was to be provided by means of annual dues from the
> members of the association at the rate of 1 percent of their salary and was to be sup-
> plemented by donations and voluntary contributions from the public.[71]

The early public retirement plans initially focused on benefits and paid
only modest attention to the question of revenue and to the long-term nature

of the obligations being undertaken. Many began with no regular source of support other than contributions from members, usually about 1 percent of salary. Since benefit calculations usually indicated that the contributions would not go all the way toward meeting obligations, the plans usually provided that the benefits could be decreased if funds were not sufficient. While it was contended that these saving clauses made the plans financially sound, they also made them unstable and the benefits unpredictable.

The question of upgrading the early pension plans, both in terms of benefits and funding methods, soon became pressing. Especially concerned with the problem was the Carnegie Foundation for the Advancement of Teaching. The studies and reports of this foundation, issued over a number of years, did much to advance public understanding of the importance of sound financial methods in pension planning.

In making suggestions in 1912 for a feasible pension system for public schools, the Carnegie Foundation had recommended compulsory participation and contributions from both employer and employee. It also stressed the importance of actuarial soundness, a concept that was generally neglected in the early plans.

The amount of the contribution should be determined by thorough actuarial investigation, but each teacher shall form a unit, and the annuity which he is to receive shall be based upon his own payment plus that granted by the state. Such an arrangement is just and fair, and is capable of actuarial computation. Every individual, whether he survives, resigns, or dies, thus furnishes the basis for the action taken.[72]

In 1911 Massachusetts became the first state to establish a statewide retirement plan for nonteaching employees. The plan followed the completion of the first systematic study by a state government of the problems of pensions for public employees. The Massachusetts pension study commission was created by the state legislature in 1907 and made its report in 1910. It reviewed the pension situation in the state, discussed the purposes of pension plans, noted the shortcomings in the noncontributory plans then operating, and recommended a general contributory retirement plan for all classes of public employees in the state.[73] The recommendation was for separate but similar general pension laws for state employees, county employees, and employees of cities and towns. Enactment for state employees followed in 1911 and became effective promptly. The system for city and town employees was enacted in 1910 but, by 1921, had not been accepted by any city or town. The system for county employees was established in 1911 and was accepted by four counties within the next 10 years. A system for teachers was enacted in 1913.[74]

The work of the legislative commission on public employee pensions in Massachusetts and the studies in New York by the Carnegie Foundation and by municipal study groups signified a growing realization of the value of retirement systems in public employment, of the importance of the search of sounder funding methods than were initially employed, and of proper assessment of the cost of retirement systems. The pension studies of the time regularly exposed both the temptations and the dangers of establishing liberal pension benefits without paying attention to adequate levels of employer and employee contributions. A five-year study of New York City pension plans by the New York Bureau of Research (1913–1918), for example, is described by Professor Studenski as having "brought to light the essential unsoundness of the pension arrangements maintained by the city and the actual bankrupt condition of most of the city's various departmental pension funds." [75]

During the 1920s, retirement plans for groups of public employees grew in numbers and coverage. The search for a sound financial base continued. Generally, the plans tended to follow the early pattern of separate coverage for special employee groups such as policemen, firemen, and teachers, on the one hand, and for general state employees on the other. In some states consolidations of plans brought teachers and other employees into the same plan; in others, teacher plans have remained separate. The evolution of plans included the addition of provisions for retirement without disability under stated requirements for age or service, and compulsory membership. The principle of joint contributions by both employees and employers gained wide acceptance. By the early 1940s, about one half of all state and local employees had some type of coverage under a retirement system. By the time of the 1962 Census of Governments, it was estimated that three out of four public employees had such protection.[76]

PENSION PLANS FOR THE NONPROFIT SECTOR

Early Single-Employer College Plans. Near the end of the 19th century, three of the most prominent of American universities, Columbia, Yale, and Harvard, established formal plans for the retirement of faculty members. In 1892 Columbia provided that a professor aged 65 with 15 years of service might be retired at half pay at his request or that of the trustees. In 1897 Yale provided retirement on half pay at age 65 to those who had served as long as 25 years in a rank higher than that of assistant professor. In 1899 Harvard established a plan under which a person age 60 with 20 years of service as assistant professor or higher might retire at a pension of one sixtieth of his last year's salary for each year of credited service, the pension not to exceed two thirds of his last year's salary; the university could require retirement at 66. None of the plans required a contribution from faculty members and none made disability a requisite for retirement. By 1905, two other institutions had established similar plans, Cornell University and the University of California.[77]

The present pension system for most institutions of higher education—colleges, universities, research institutions—occupies a unique place in American pension history. While a few business and industrial employers were establishing single-employer pension plans, one at a time, and while public employee plans were tentatively starting on a city-by-city basis, a remarkable philanthropic gift in 1905 brought colleges and universities a prototype multiemployer system, providing for job mobility without loss of pension benefits for covered employees among nearly 100 employers. This system was the Carnegie free pension plan for college faculties. It included both private and public institutions. Although it was later phased out, the experiment eventually led to the establishment of the nonprofit Teachers Insurance and Annuity Association, a national multiemployer pension system for higher education.

The Carnegie Free Pension System. A pattern of seriatim establishment of single-employer, nonportable pension plans would probably have continued in U.S. colleges and universities had it not been for Andrew Carnegie's interest in higher education. In 1890, when Carnegie became a trustee of Cornell University, he was shocked, he later wrote in his autobiography, "to find how small were the salaries of the professors. . . ." He concluded that it was next to impossible for a professor to save for his old age. Little attention had been paid to the idea of retirement security for college teachers, and the problem made a deep impression upon him.

Some 10 or 12 years later Henry S. Pritchett, president of the Massachusetts Institute of Technology, visited Carnegie at his summer home in Scotland. Carnegie asked Pritchett what his mission in Europe was and the latter replied, "I am searching for a $25,000 professor at a $7,500 salary."

The two men talked about ways to improve the economic standing of college teachers and the importance to teachers and to higher education of provisions for old age. Carnegie had sold his steel business in 1900, retired, and was now engaged in distributing his fortune. Earlier, in two articles in the *North American Review* (1899), he had given careful formulation to what he called "the gospel of wealth," by which he meant that surplus personal wealth should be used for service to humanity.[78] Carnegie, whose own formal schooling ended at age 12 when his family emigrated from Scotland to America, had perceived a vital link between education and democracy, and it seemed to him that in the distribution of his fortune for the public good he should give most of it for educational purposes.[79] Carnegie knew that all his millions could not greatly raise teachers' salaries, but he believed he might help education by providing from his own funds free pensions for teachers in leading colleges and universities.

The result of Carnegie's thought and action was the establishment of the Carnegie Foundation for the Advancement of Teaching to provide retirement pensions for the teachers of universities, colleges, and technical schools in the United States, Canada, and Newfoundland. Henry S. Pritchett left the presidency of MIT to become the first president of the foundation. The Carnegie Foundation was incorporated in 1905 by an Act of the Congress of the United States. The officers of the foundation proceeded at once to establish a list of private, nondenominational colleges and universities of "requisite stature and qualifications." In order that professors in state universities might be included in the pension fund, Carnegie later supplemented his original $10 million gift with an additional $5 million. The principal requirements for association were that the college have no denominational connection, offer a full four-year course in arts and sciences, require completion of high school for entrance, employ at least six professors whose time was fully devoted to college or university work, and have an endowment of at least $200,000.[80]

The benefits of the free pension system were liberal. The plan provided for an annual payment to the retired faculty member of $400 more than half of his average salary for the last five years of service for those who attained age 65 after having held the rank of professor for 15 years. Provision was made for the continuation of benefits to a surviving spouse. With this inducement, colleges moved quickly to meet the foundation's qualifying requirements. The average pay of professors in American colleges in 1906 was $1,550 a year.[81]

The eligibility list for the free pensions remained open for just 10 years. By 1912 there were 72 accepted institutions; ultimately there were 95. In November 1915, after a decade of experience with the plan, the free pension lists were closed to newly hired faculty. In addition to persons already pensioned, only teachers already serving the participating institutions would receive foundation allowances. A broader approach to pension coverage would be sought for employees of all educational institutions.

It had become apparent that even Andrew Carnegie's vast personal fortune could not fund benefits for the increasing numbers of faculty in the 95 participating colleges and universities, let alone in the rapidly expanding ranks of new institutions. Higher education was growing much more rapidly than had been estimated in 1905. Salaries were increasing, perhaps pushed a bit for persons over 60 by the inducement of free pensions related to final-five average salary. The initial calculations of potential cost had used existing mortality tables on the advice of actuaries, but the foundation soon observed that the pensioners on their roles were living longer than the actuarial tables suggested they would. Thus, expanding higher education, increasing salaries, and mortality miscalculations forced the closing of the lists. Financial deficiencies continued to mount, and supplementary gifts to the foundation from the Carnegie Corporation became necessary to support the long-term commitments that had been made. The last eligible professor retired in 1965.[82] By 1972 the foundation had paid out more than $82.5 million in free pensions to approximately 6,200 retired faculty members and their widows. In June 1972, 57 years after the pension roles were closed to new appointees, benefits were still being paid to 625 persons, 220 to retired professors and 445 to widows of professors.[83]

The experience of the free pension system helped form its successor. To qualify for a retiring allowance under the foundation rules it was not necessary that a teacher spend any particular length of time in any one of the associated institutions, although he or she did have to stay within the system. This permitted free movement of professional talent among the 95 employers. The foundation's aims for the successor system gave high priority to this concept of portability of retirement benefits. The search also emphasized assurance of benefits as a matter of contractual right and the need for sound methods of pension funding, including contributions from the colleges and their staff members.

The efforts of the Carnegie Foundation to design a more practicable and durable pension system for the colleges led in 1916 to the organization of a study group, the Commission on Insurance and Annuities. Represented on the commission were the American Association of University Professors, the Association of American Universities, the National Association of State Universities, and the Association of American Colleges. Technical advice was secured from the Actuarial Society of America and the American Institute of Actuaries. The recommendations of the commission led to the establishment in 1918 of the Teachers Insurance and Annuity Association (TIAA) to provide fully vested, portable annuities under a contractual contributory system. TIAA operates as a central service organization for retirement and insurance plans, with eligibility limited to colleges, universities, independent schools, and certain other nonprofit institutions engaged primarily in education or research. The TIAA retirement plan in each institution is funded through individual TIAA annuity contracts for each participating faculty and staff member. The contract provides for immediate vesting in the individual of the retirement and survivor benefits, including those purchased by employer contributions. Under the contract, if a person leaves the institution before retirement—to change jobs, for example—all accrued benefits remain intact in the contract regardless of age, rank, or years of service. The annuities cannot be surrendered for cash. The investment of employer and employee contributions, all actuarial and accounting services, and the payment of benefits is carried out by TIAA. The annuity contract provisions are uniform throughout the system. The participating institutions, however, determine the level of employer and employee contributions; and these are normally expressed as a percentage of salary credited monthly to individual annuity contracts. The institutions also determine who is eligible for their plan, when participation begins, and when retirement occurs.

Ten years after TIAA was established, 139 institutions were participating in the system. In 1975, 2,799 eligible organizations were participating, with contributions being received for 317,000 plan members and benefits being paid to 51,000.

During 1950 and 1951, TIAA developed the variable annuity and in 1952 established the College Retirement Equities Fund (CREF), the first variable annuity fund. CREF was designed to enable participants to obtain a broader diversification of investments and to help maintain the purchasing power of annuity income over the long run through lifetime common-stock investments. CREF serves as a companion organization to TIAA and the two together form the nationwide college pension system.

Other Nonprofit Retirement Plans. Religious denominations were also among the nonprofit organizations pioneering pension programs. The church plans are generally administered by organizations created by authority of a parent church and operated in close association with it. In 1973, the Church Pension Conference reported 29 church pension plans presently in operation.[84] The Presbyterian Ministers' Fund in Philadelphia, Pennsylvania, with antecedents going back to 1759, was the first chartered life insurance company in America. Today the fund offers life insurance and annuities to members of the clergy of all faiths.

The early church arrangements for pensions were directed toward the needs of surviving widows and children of ministers. Needs tests were applied and the funds were obtained from voluntary contributions from church members. By the early 20th century, however, when the uncertainty of relief funds and the use of needs tests brought the charitable approach under question, more systematic approaches were sought. Numerous studies of the programs were carried out in the early part of this century, such as that commissioned by the general Convention of the Protestant Episcopal Church in 1910. "The cry of the 1910 Convention," a church publication noted many years later, "became an adequate, comprehensive Church-wide system of pensions to be granted not on a humiliating confession of penury, but by right of service and thus insure our clergy an old age of at least ordinary comfort, security and peace." [85]

By 1920 eight church pension plans were in operation. In the 1920s more church organizations developed pension plans; many of these later plans incorporated fixed contributions, in contrast to the fixed formula benefits typical of the earlier plans. The first pension system of the fixed contribution type was the Annuity Fund for Congregational Ministers, started in 1921. Today about half the church plans use the defined contribution approach.[86]

The National Health and Welfare Retirement Association, which provides centralized pension and insurance benefit administration for community chest, united fund, and health organizations throughout the United States, was established in 1945 and serves approximately 4,000 organizations and 80,000 participants.

THE FEDERAL CIVIL SERVICE RETIREMENT SYSTEM

The Federal Civil Service Retirement System came into being in 1920. The first references to the need for a retirement plan for federal employees seem to have been related to the question of efficiency in government raised by the continuation in office of aged civil servants. It is reported that President Jackson "found many grown old in the service and removed them on charges of inefficiency." [87] There is no indication as to how they were removed or what happened to them. A House committee of 1845 reported that "the list of [federal] officers becomes a pension role" and described detrimental effects on efficiency. Later surveys of superannuation in the federal service were made in 1893, 1900, 1902, and 1903. Beginning in 1899 the Civil Service Commission in its annual reports recommended the adoption of a retirement system financed in whole or in part from employees' salaries. As early as 1900, Washington clerks in federal service formed an association to urge a retirement act. There were wide differences of opinion as to the desirable provisions of a plan and only in 1917 did there appear to be united support for a contributory plan.[88]

When the Civil Service Retirement Fund was created by Congress in 1920, 330,000 civil servants became participants. The number rose gradually with the growth of federal government to nearly 600,000 in 1939 and then much more rapidly to a high of about 3 million in 1944 as war expansion got underway. As of June 30, 1972, the Civil Service Commission estimated membership at 2,588,000.[89]

The scope of the system's coverage has increased substantially over the years, as have the classes of employees eligible. Amendments of 1942 and 1946 extended coverage to all officers and employees of the executive, judicial, and legislative branches of the federal government and of the municipal government of the District of Columbia, with the exception of those covered by other retirement plans. The Legislative Reorganization Act of 1946 extended coverage to members of Congress.

Other Federal Government Retirement Systems. Separate retirement systems cover military personnel of the United States and the employees of the

Federal Reserve System and the Tennessee Valley Authority, quasi-public corporations. The two Federal Reserve plans were started in 1934; one covers the Federal Reserve Board employees and the other the employees of the Federal Reserve Bank. The TVA plan was begun in 1939. Unlike members of the Federal Civil Service Retirement System, members of the TVA, Federal Reserve, and military plans participate in the federal Social Security program.[90] The earliest military pensions were paid to soldiers of the American Revolutionary War; subsequent legislation gradually developed the retirement system presently operated for military personnel by the Department of Defense.

FEDERAL REGULATION OF PENSION PLANS

Federal regulation of private pension plans dates from the early 1920s in an amalgam of taxation principles and social principles. The Internal Revenue Code and Treasury regulations have had a considerable influence on private pension plans in the United States, and the evolution of the code as applied to pensions and profit-sharing plans is a significant part of the history of American pension plans.

The 1920s. The first industrial pension plans were usually paid out of current company earnings as a current business expense—a pay-as-you-go basis—but it was not too long before it became evident that there were advantages in establishing at least some reserves and separate trust or insurance arrangements. By the early 1920s many of the pay-as-you-go plans had been transformed into trusts, although by no means fully funded, and new plans were being initially established as trusts.

Almost immediately a question arose as to the taxability of the income of such trusts and of the status of employer contributions under the relatively new U.S. income tax laws. In 1926, pension trusts created by employers for the exclusive benefit of some or all employees were made exempt from federal income tax. It was also provided that employer contributions to such trusts, and the income therefrom, would not be taxable to the beneficiaries until actually distributed. These provisions had been applied earlier (in 1921) to trusts created by employers as part of a stock bonus or profit-sharing plan.[91]

In 1928, to clear up an ambiguity in the 1926 legislation, employer contributions to an exempt trust on account of past service were specifically authorized as a deductible business expense. The provision was drawn so that contributions to a pension trust on account of past service could be allocated over a period no shorter than 10 years, regardless of whether a reserve had previously been established. However, the provision did not apply to insurance companies, so that an entire past service liability paid to an insurance company could be deducted in the year paid. (This difference was removed in the 1942 amendments to the Internal Revenue Code.)

In 1938, a "no diversion" requirement was added to the tests for an exempt trust. The law provided that under the trust instrument it must be impossible at any time prior to the satisfaction of all liabilities with respect to employees and their beneficiaries under the trust for any part of a corpus or income to be used for, or diverted to, purposes other than the exclusive benefit of employees or their beneficiaries.

In 1942 the tax laws regarding pension plans were substantially amended. During the interim years—the early 1920s to 1942—the tax treatment of pension trusts and contributions was rather uncomplicated and can be briefly summarized: the net income of trusts established for the benefit of employees was not subject to tax; employer contributions to pension trusts were deductible from the gross income of the employer in determining taxable net income. Such amounts became subject to income tax only when distributed in the form of pensions. A pension was personal income that could be taxed only to the extent that it exceeded the pensioner's own contribution toward it. Since employees' contributions under contributory pension plans were not deductible when computing taxable net income, the lines of income to be taxed were thus kept clear and double taxation avoided.

The 1942 Revisions. By 1942 it had become apparent that the existing laws and regulations were too simple and needed refinement. Under the earlier legislation, pension trusts on behalf of "some or all employees," as referred to in the Revenue Acts of 1921, 1926, and 1928, had been utilized to develop trusts that included as participants only small groups of officers and favored key employees in the higher income brackets, apparently as a means of tax avoidance (or deferment) for persons in a position to create a trust in the first place. The challenge was to develop statutes that would be more effective in achieving a desired goal of broader employee welfare while preventing the use of employee trusts primarily as tax avoidance devices.

Remedial proposals were developed by the Department of the Treasury and submitted to the House Committee on Ways and Means on March 3,

1942. The Treasury proposed that pension trusts, in order to retain their tax exempt status, should be required to meet certain standards with respect to vesting, covered employees, and maximum employee benefits. The statement of Mr. Randolph Paul, Tax Adviser to the Secretary of the Treasury, was that pension trusts be required to meet three basic standards in order to be tax exempt:

First, the right of the employee to his portion of the employer's contribution to the trust, and to its earnings, as well as to his own contribution, should be fully vested.

Second, the trust should cover either 70 percent or more of all employees, excluding employees who have been employed for less than a minimum period not exceeding five years, and casual, part-time and seasonal employees, or such employees as qualify under a classification set up by the employer and found by the Commissioner not to be based upon any favoritism for employees who are officers, shareholders, supervising employees, or highly compensated employees.

Third, the system of contributions and benefits under the trust should not discriminate in favor of officers, shareholders, supervising employees, or highly compensated employees.[92]

Although immediate vesting had been suggested by the Treasury spokesman, the proposal was substantially modified in a memorandum submitted on March 23, 1942. A gradual vesting proposal was substituted. It was proposed that when an employee had reached a certain age and had participated in a plan for a certain number of years (the Treasury statement suggested age 40 and 15 years of plan membership), the employee's rights under the plan would be vested to the extent of one third of accrued benefits, and that at the end of five-year intervals thereafter he should obtain a further vested interest of one third at each point so that at the end of 10 more years his benefits would have vested in full. Under plans with a contributory element, the rights of the employee with respect to his own contributions to the trust and the earnings thereon would be fully vested immediately upon making the contribution.[93]

The Treasury's proposal for gradual vesting represented a sharp change from the full vesting originally recommended. It was later confirmed that a number of representatives of various groups had told the Treasury that a vesting requirement, however stated, would substantially increase the expense or reduce the benefits under existing plans. Although employers took the initiative in bringing about the elimination of the vesting requirement, they were not solely responsible for its abandonment. In the 1942 revenue revision hearings, a vice-president of the American Telephone and Telegraph Company and the president of the National Federation of Telephone Workers both testified in opposition to a vesting provision.[94] The AT&T representative maintained that "to vest rights in individual employees in these funds before retirement as Mr. Paul proposes . . . would mean the termination of the [AT&T] plan." The union representative expressed a fear of plan termination due to increased costs if vesting were required and said that the union preferred collective bargaining as a basis for pension changes.[95] The president of a prominent actuarial consulting firm also testified against the setting of a vesting standard. In addition to offering technical and cost arguments, his testimony before the Ways and Means Committee maintained that compulsory vesting would "defeat basic purposes" in establishing pension plans, plans which "are designed to provide a pension for the employee after he has retired and not to establish additional compensation for the employee who leaves service before retirement. . . . If an employee leaves without a right to the employer reserve," he added, "the reserve is transferred to protect other employees." [96]

In the subsequent bill reported to the House by the Committee on Ways and Means and in the accompanying report there were no references to vesting as a condition for the tax exemption of employers' contributions to a pension trust. Vesting ceased to be a live issue at the committee stage and it was not revived during the later hearings before the Senate Finance Committee.[97]

Although a vesting standard was lacking, the Internal Revenue Code of 1942 constituted a complete revision and rewriting of the sections of the code dealing with pension plans (and deferred compensation and profit-sharing plans). In the light of the Treasury's abortive recommendations for a vesting standard in 1942, it is interesting to speculate what the level of pension protection for aged persons today might have been had the full vesting provisions originally recommended been adopted in 1942, or even the gradual vesting proposal. It seems inevitable that more than 30 years of operation of a vesting requirement for private pension plans would have helped make private pension benefits far more significant in the income of aged persons than they are today.

The new tax code of 1942 brought further into view and placed in statutory form the public policy principle that federal tax laws could and should be used as a means of requiring employers to meet certain expressed standards in voluntarily established private pension plans. Prior to 1942, the code dealt narrowly with pension contributions and trust earnings. The new code, without going very far, entered as a matter of public policy the area of plan provisions. To qualify for the statutory tax treatment of employer contributions to pension trust funds and profit-sharing trusts under the new code, a plan was required to be: (1) for the exclusive benefit of the employer's employees or their beneficiaries; (2) for the purpose of distributing the corpus and income to the employees; (3) impossible for the employer to use or divert the fund before satisfying the plan's liabilities to the employees and their beneficiaries; and (4) nondiscriminatory as to extent of coverage— a large percentage of regular employees must be eligible to participate, and neither contributions nor benefits were to discriminate in favor of officers, stockholders, or highly compensated employees or supervisory employees.

Amendments to the pension sections of the code between 1942 and 1974 were not fundamental in nature. A 1962 amendment to Section 401(a) added a "termination-vesting" provision. Although the 1942 revisions had attempted to prevent discrimination in favor of officers or highly compensated employees, there was nothing to prevent a pension plan from being established, continued in operation for a fairly short time on behalf of long-service employees entitled to benefits under the plan, very often managers and highly compensated employees, and then terminated once these employees had retired. The termination-vesting provision of 1962, in Section 401(a) (7), sought to correct the abuse by providing that "a trust shall not constitute a qualified trust under this section unless the plan of which such trust is a part provides that, upon its termination or upon complete discontinuance of contributions under the plan, the rights of all employees to benefits accrued to the date of such termination or discontinuance, to the extent then funded, or the amounts credited to the employees' accounts are non-forfeitable."

The Labor Management Relations Act of 1947. This law, the Taft-Hartley Act, extensively amended and supplemented the original basic labor relations law of 1935, the Wagner Act. The amendments were particularly far-reaching with respect to employees' legal rights, and administrative machinery and procedures. The general declaration of policy of the Taft-Hartley Act included this statement of purpose:

It is the purpose and policy of this Act, in order to prescribe the legitimate rights of both employees and employers in their relations affecting commerce, to provide orderly and peaceful procedures for preventing the interference by either with the le-

gitimate rights of the other, to protect the rights of individual employees in their relations with labor organizations whose activities affect commerce, to define and pro-
scribe practices on the part of labor and management which affect commerce and are
inimical to the general welfare, and to protect the rights of the public in connection
with labor disputes affecting commerce.[98]

Among the areas of collective bargaining covered by the act were "rates
of pay, wages, hours of employment, or other conditions of employment.
. . ."[99] Within a year after the passage of the act a question arose between
the Inland Steel Company and the steelworkers' union as to whether the
Taft-Hartley Act imposed a duty on employers to bargain with representatives of their employees on the subject of pensions. The National Labor
Relations Board considered the question and decided in a ruling of April,
1948, that companies were required to bargain on pension plans. The ruling
was based on the dual grounds that the term "wages" as defined in the statute includes any emoluments of value such as pension or insurance benefits,
and that the provisions of pension plans come within the definition of "conditions of employment."[100]

When the company took the ruling to the federal courts, the Federal Court
of Appeals (Seventh Circuit) affirmed the view of the NLRB that retirement
plans were included under the act as a proper subject for collective bargaining; it skirted the wages issue and concluded that a pension plan was a condition of employment. The court's opinion in the Inland Steel case read in
part as follows:

> While, as the Company has demonstrated, a reasonable argument can be made that
> the benefits flowing from such a plan are not "wages," we think the better and more
> logical argument is on the other side, and certainly there is, in our opinion, no sound
> basis for an argument that such a plan is not clearly included in the phrase, "other
> conditions of employment.". . . . It surely cannot be seriously disputed but that
> such a pledge [to provide pensions under a plan] on the part of the Company forms a
> part of the consideration for work performed. . . . In this view, the pension thus
> promised would appear to be as much a part of his "wages" as the money paid him
> at the time of the rendition of his services. But again we say that in any event such a
> plan is one of the "conditions of employment."[101]

The Inland Steel case immediately joined the ranks of important land-
marks in U.S. law regarding employee pension plan protection. In September, 1949, a presidential fact-finding board recommended that the companies
in basic steel incorporate social insurance and pension systems in their collective bargaining agreements.[102] As we have noted, unions in the early de-

cades of the century were skeptical of employer-sponsored pension plans, viewing them as paternalistic devices, as means of holding down wages, and as a means of making the labor force immobile. The rarity of contributory plans, furthermore, deprived the unions of the weight of the argument that the employees themselves were also involved in the administration and function of the plans. The Inland Steel case, however, by making pensions a negotiable issue, marked a turning point in the unions' attitude toward pension plans. Thereafter, many private plans ceased to be a matter of voluntary, unilateral action by an employer.

Section 302 of the Taft-Hartley Act affects pension plan administration directly by prohibiting sole union administration of a welfare fund to which an employer contributes and by requiring the establishment of a trust for welfare fund contributions. The roots of the provision were in John L. Lewis' demand in the 1945–46 negotiations that the pension fund for the United Mine Workers be administered unilaterally by the union. Secretary of the Interior Krug had resisted the demand and insisted on a joint employer-union administration of the fund. Largely as a result of the Lewis-Krug encounter, Section 302 was incorporated into the Taft-Hartley Act as a means of preventing indiscriminate use or diversion of welfare funds by union officers. Senator Claude Pepper of Florida characterized the section on the floor of the Senate as proceeding "on the theory that union leaders should not be permitted, without reference to the employees, to divert funds paid by the company, in consideration of the services of employees, to the union treasury or the union officers, except under the process of strict accountability. . . ." Without such restraints employees would have no more rights in the funds supposedly established for their benefit than their union leaders choose to allow them.[103]

That the provisions of the section had not wholly prevented such diversions in the jointly administered Mine Workers' plan was suggested later in testimony presented to the Senate Subcommittee on Welfare and Pension Funds of the Committee on Labor and Public Welfare as it began its investigations in 1955 on "the degree to which this provision [Section 302] has been observed. . . ." The extent of the United Mine Workers' pension fund mismanagement came out only many years later, in the federal court case of *Blankenship v. Boyle* (1971).[104]

The Welfare and Pension Plans Disclosure Act of 1958. The Welfare and Pension Plans Disclosure Act sought to strengthen the Taft-Hartley protection of pension plan participants from financial mismanagement by requiring plans qualified under the Internal Revenue Code to file with the Secretary of Labor each year a report disclosing the financial operations of welfare and pension plans.[105] The intent of the law was to utilize disclosure of financial practices as a means of controlling situations of embezzlement, kickbacks, and conflicts of interest. However, the information required was not sufficient to reveal questionable financial practices or plan operations, and audits were not provided for. Staffing by the Labor Department for examination of the required reports was never adequate. The act was replaced in 1974 by the more comprehensive Employee Retirement Income Security Act.

The Employee Retirement Income Security Act of 1974. Little significant change took place in U.S. legislation regarding private pension plans in the three decades following the 1942 changes in the Internal Revenue Code. But by the mid-1960s a change in atmosphere could be detected. In 1964, heavy losses in pension expectations were occasioned by a widely publicized shutdown of the South Bend, Indiana, Studebaker Corporation plant. In the same year, Professor Merton C. Bernstein published a comprehensive and influential analysis of private pension plans and their possible future directions, *The Future of Private Pensions*. In 1965 a pension policy study group appointed by President Kennedy issued a report, "Public Policy and Private Programs—A Report to the President on Private Employee Retirement Plans by the President's Committee on Corporate Pension Funds and Other Private Retirement and Welfare Programs." This document offered numerous recommendations for legislation regarding standards of pension vesting, funding, plan termination provisions, fiduciary protection, and recommended further studies of the problem areas it had identified. Shortly after this report was released, Congressional hearings on needs for improved pension legislation were initiated, and these led to the introduction of a number of proposals for pension reform. In the Senate, Senator Jacob K. Javits (New York) introduced a bill in 1967 generally aiming at implementation of the recommendations of the President's Committee of two years before.[106] In the House, Representative John H. Dent (Pennsylvania) introduced bills in 1969 proposing pension reform.[107] Subsequently, other pension bills were introduced in both chambers, further hearings were held, fact-finding studies were carried out by the Treasury and Labor departments, and on September

2, 1974, a comprehensive new pension act was signed into law, the Employee Retirement Income Security Act of 1974.

The 1974 Pension Reform Act established basic new requirements in virtually every area of pension administration and funding, including rules of participation and eligibility, minimum vesting standards, reporting and disclosure to government and to plan participants, funding standards, actuarial standards, fiduciary conduct, and past service liability amortization rules. It established a Pension Benefit Guaranty Corporation within the Labor Department to protect plan participants through insurance in the event of plan termination. The act's standards are applied to private plans, except for church or church-related plans, but not to public employee plans.

The passage of the 1974 pension act denoted a shift in public policy regarding private pensions from a tax-based orientation to one more fundamentally related to employee security. It effectively strengthened the nation's potential over the longer term for better levels of combined Social Security and second-pension income in old-age. Many questions must still be resolved, however, and these questions are examined in the following chapters.

−3−

Social Security

Je veux qu'il n'y ait si pauvre paysan en mon royaume
qu'il n'ait tous les dimanches sa poule au pot.

Henri IV

The federal Social Security system has been one of the most successful "social engineering" experiments ever tried in this country. Over its lifetime—now more than four decades—Social Security has helped alleviate want and worry from millions of elderly and disabled people and from survivors of covered workers. The original program passed by Congress in 1935 was designed to help prevent economic insecurity caused by loss of earnings in retirement. Survivor, disability, and medical benefits were added later. Coverage, also far narrower than it is now, was limited until 1951 to workers in commerce and industry.

At present, Social Security is compulsory for more than nine out of ten people in paid employment. The only large categories of workers not covered are public employee groups—federal civil service and employees of certain state and local governments. Approximately 101 million men and women worked in covered employment in 1974.[1] In that year, about 93 percent of the elderly (aged 65 or over) either were already recipients of benefits or would be when they or their spouses stopped working, and 96 percent of those reaching age 65 were eligible for benefits.[2] About 30.3 million men, women, and children—one out of every seven Americans—received monthly cash benefits in mid-1974. Social Security benefit payments amounted to about $4.9 billion per month.[3] It was estimated in 1970 that without Social Security one half of beneficiary couples instead of one fifth, and four fifths of nonmarried beneficiaries instead of one half, would have incomes below the poverty level. [4]

THE BEGINNING OF U.S. SOCIAL SECURITY

In 1889, nearly 50 years before the U.S. Social Security Act, Otto von Bismarck, the Iron Chancellor of Germany, established the first social security system providing old-age pensions. This bold step called for compulsory participation of workers in a plan for old-age insurance supported by contributions from workers and employers, with benefits related to earnings levels. Austria followed Germany in 1906 with a contributory social insurance plan, and Romania in 1912. In England the development of social security had its roots in voluntary associations and friendly societies begun in the early 1860s. A noncontributory, income-tested government pension system was established in 1908, followed in 1925 by a contributory plan of flat benefits that contrasted with the German and other systems of wage-related benefits. By 1928 all of the European states had established contributory old-age insurance plans; in 1933 one writer observed that "China, India, and the United States are the only large countries still remaining without any national system of old age security." [5]

Theodore Roosevelt had warned in his "Confession of Faith" before the 1917 national convention of the Progressive party that "we must protect the crushable elements at the base of our present industrial structure. . . . It is abnormal for any industry to throw back upon the community the human wreckage due to its wear and tear." He urged that "the hazards of sickness, accident, invalidism, involuntary unemployment, and old age should be provided for through insurance." [6] Notwithstanding these sensitive remarks by one of America's great individualists, many Americans tended to look upon adversities such as unemployment and poverty in old age as weaknesses of individuals and not of the economy or of the society. The contrary voices of Eugene V. Debs and Norman Thomas attracted few followers. Not until the cataclysm of the Great Depression did Americans generally conclude that forces stronger than the individual were at work and that other nations had advanced beyond the United States in social programs.

It was an unbelievably deep depression. By late 1932 a creeping bank paralysis had spread across the nation, and by 1933 unemployment had risen to an unprecedented 13 million persons, nearly one out of every five in the civilian work force.[7] It was estimated that during September and October of 1934, 18.5 million persons were receiving emergency relief.[8] Concurrently, drought had turned the cereal bowl into the dust bowl. In his second inaugural address, President Franklin D. Roosevelt said: "I see one third of a nation ill-housed, ill-clothed, ill-fed." [9]

By late 1934, some 36 organizations were agitating for old-age pensions. The most spectacular of the reformers was Francis E. Townsend, who proposed a pension of $200 a month to anyone over age 60, to be paid only if spent immediately. The money would be raised by a sales tax. The general idea was that the tax would support the pensions, which, being spent at once, would increase the sales tax revenue and improve business, which in turn would support the pensions. The Townsend movement made considerable headway, although it was in competition with another idea, the "share the wealth" plan of Senator Huey Long of Louisiana. But there was much opposition. The $200 monthly payment ($400 for a couple) was in significant contrast with the average wage of the time, which was between $75 and $100 a month. Professor Edwin E. Witte, an economist at the University of Wisconsin, concluded that the Townsend plan would divert half the national income to the 10 million elderly people, and that it would be "a cruel fraud perpetrated upon the aged poor." [10]

Many of the federal government's measures to meet the crisis of the depression were necessarily temporary, but President Roosevelt came to realize that many aspects of the crisis were symptoms of a need for greater attention to underlying social and economic forces. In his message to Congress of June 8, 1934, he stressed the need for more than temporary measures, emphasizing decent housing, productive work, and "some safeguards against the misfortunes which cannot be wholly eliminated in this man-made world of ours." [11]

To develop proposals and make recommendations for the implementation of long-range measures of economic security, the President established by executive order (June 29, 1934) a Committee on Economic Security composed of Frances Perkins, Henry Morgenthau, Henry A. Wallace, Homer Cummings, and Harry Hopkins (respectively, Secretaries of Labor, Treasury, and Agriculture, Attorney General, and Federal Emergency Relief Administrator). The committee was assisted by an advisory council of distinguished private citizens and a technical board, headed by Arthur J. Altmeyer, Assistant Secretary of Labor. Professor Witte became Executive

Director, coordinating all of the activities of the Committee on Economic Security and its staff.[12]

As discussion of the proposed program developed, Roosevelt took special pains to assure the country that the new plan was a sound program started on a reasonable scale: "It is overwhelmingly important to avoid any danger of permanently discrediting the sound and the necessary policy of federal legislation for economic security by attempting to apply it on too ambitious a scale before actual experience has provided guidance for the permanently safe direction of such benefits." [13] The work of the planning and technical committees led to a final report to the President, dated January 15, 1935. This report contained the recommendations leading to landmark legislation later in the year, the Social Security Act, passed and signed August 14, 1935.[14]

It was thus from a weedy, depression-ridden garden that the remarkably sturdy American Social Security system sprang. When President Roosevelt signed the Social Security Act he described it as "a cornerstone in a structure which is being built, but is by no means complete—a structure intended to lessen the force of possible future depressions, to act as a protection to future administrations of the government against the necessity of going deeply into debt to furnish relief to the needy—a law to flatten out the peaks and valleys of deflation and of inflation—in other words, a law that will take care of human needs and at the same time provide for the United States an economic structure of vastly greater soundness." [15] The Great Depression had highlighted the problem of economic insecurity and given impetus to the development of the federal program. Witte, in an article written 20 years later, doubted "very much whether [the Social Security Act] or any similar measure could have passed, at least for many years, had it come before the Congress later than 1935." [16]

The 1935 act was put together quickly by the brain trust and college professors. It soon appeared that the benefits would have to be improved and the methods of determining benefit amounts and insured status changed. There was time for alterations to be made, since the original act had provided for taxes to begin in 1937 and benefits in 1942. The changes were incorporated in the Social Security Amendments of 1939, which substantially recast the whole program, added survivors' benefits, and advanced the starting date for monthly benefits from 1942 to 1940.

SOCIAL SECURITY FROM 1939 TO 1949

During World War II and its aftermath, practically no change was made in the infant social program other than to postpone payroll tax rate increases. Understandable during the war, this neglect continued for five years thereafter while the nation was preoccupied with the problems of readjustment to a peace-time economy, the employment of 11 million returning servicemen, and transitions in employment for millions of defense industry workers. There were some scholarly discussions about the incidence of the Social Security payroll taxes, vigorous discussion by experts regarding the size and importance of the reserve fund, and growing concern about the absence of health insurance and disability programs. The low benefit levels of the program came increasingly under criticism.

SOCIAL SECURITY FROM 1950 TO 1971

The year 1950 began a period of new growth for the Social Security system, gradual at first, then accelerating. Amendments in 1950 brought under coverage the nonagricultural self-employed and Americans employed outside the United States by American employers. Workers in Puerto Rico and the Virgin Islands were added. Coverage of state and local government employees not under a retirement system was made elective by the employer, and coverage of employees of nonprofit organizations was made elective by employer and employee. Changes in 1954 made it possible for state and local government employees belonging to a state retirement system to be covered by election of employer and employees, and brought in self-employed farm workers and professional people. The armed forces, along with additional professional people, were covered by changes made in 1956. Total disability benefits were added for workers aged 50 and over by 1954 law; four years later the disability coverage was extended to all covered workers regardless of age. Medicare for persons 65 and older was added in 1965 and long-term (two years or more) disabled beneficiaries in 1972. Benefit levels were raised 10 different times between 1950 and 1972.

The addition of disability and Medicare benefits, the periodic increases in benefit amounts (including increases for persons already retired), and increases in minimum benefits required increased taxes. The amount of income on which taxes are levied, the "earnings base," rose in stages from

$3,000 in 1937 to $9,000 in 1972. The tax amount paid by each employee, expressed as a percentage of the wage base, rose from 1.5 percent (of $3,000) in 1950 to 5.2 percent (of $9,000) in 1972, with a tax of an equal amount paid by the employer.

THE 1972 CHANGES

By far the largest benefit changes made in the Social Security program were voted by the Congress in 1972 to become effective in 1973 and later.

The Earnings Base. The Social Security earnings base was increased from $9,000 to $10,800 on January 1, 1973, and was scheduled to increase to $12,000 on January 1, 1974. A 1973 amendment subsequently increased the 1974 earnings base to $13,200. On January 1, 1975, it became $14,100 under new automatic change provisions.

Tax Rates. Effective January 1, 1973, the total tax rate applicable to covered incomes within the earnings base was increased from 5.2 percent to 5.85 percent each for the employer and the employee. The new rate applied to the increased earnings base raised maximum employer plus employee Social Security taxes from $936 in 1972 to $1,650 in 1975, an increase of 76 percent in three years.

The Old Age, Survivors, Disability, and Health Insurance (OASDHI) tax for 1976 is composed of three parts, as follows:

Percent of taxable earnings base

	Employee Pays	Employer Pays	Total Tax	
Old-Age and Survivors Insurance (OASI)	4.375%	4.375%	8.75%	⎫
Disability Insurance (DI)	.575	.575	1.15	⎬ 9.9%
Medicare Part A (HI)	.9	.9	1.8	⎭
Total	5.85	5.85	11.7	

The combined employer-employee OASDHI tax rate is scheduled to rise to 12.1 percent in 1978, 12.6 percent in 1981, 12.9 percent in 1986, and 14.9 percent in 2011, with the increases due primarily to higher projected health insurance costs. The OASDI tax is scheduled to remain at its 9.9 percent combined total until 2010, and to increase to 11.9 percent for 2011 and after.

Benefits. Beginning with payments made in October 1972, Social Security benefits were increased 20 percent across the board. Further increases scheduled for 1974 amounted to 11 percent, and the first of the "escalator" benefits, a rise of 8 percent, occurred July 1, 1975.

Average Benefits. One evidence of Social Security's new maturity is that average benefits have more than doubled in less than a decade. Just before the 1968 benefit increase, the *average* Social Security benefit to newly awarded retired workers was $88. By mid-1975, that amount had increased to about $210, a 138 percent gain in just seven years. The cost of living in the same period went up 58 percent.

Average monthly benefit award figures in selected years from 1967 to 1975 were reported by the Social Security Administration as follows:

	May 1967	May 1971	July 1975
Retired workers	$ 88	$134	$210
Disabled workers	102	155	239
Aged widows and widowers	77	116	195

Special Minimum Benefits. The 1972 amendments established an alternative to the regular minimum stated Social Security benefits by setting up a "special minimum" affecting persons having 20 or more years of coverage. Ranging in 1975 from $99 per month for workers with 21 years of coverage to $180 for those with 30 or more years, the special minimum serves to provide a basic level of benefits to persons who have worked under Social Security coverage for a long time, but at low wages. Benefits under the special minimum are not increased under the Consumer Price Index escalator provisions.

The Automatic Escalator Clause. The most far-reaching change of the 1972 Social Security amendments was a provision for the automatic increase of benefits according to future increases in the cost of living, first effective in 1975. Cost-of-living escalators have been features of numerous European social insurance systems for some years but had not been given serious consideration in the United States until the annual rate of inflation began to exceed 4 percent (in 1968).

The automatic Social Security benefit increase takes place in June of any year when the Consumer Price Index of the Department of Labor shows an increase of 3 percent or more as measured from the first quarter of the preceding year (or since any other quarter of the previous year for which

Congress legislated a benefit increase) to the first quarter of the year in question. The escalator increase is in proportion to the change in the CPI since the previous escalator increase or since the most recent legislated increase, whichever is later.

The 1972 amendments provided that whenever benefits are automatically increased, the Social Security earnings base will increase. The new earnings base is set by comparing the average of taxable wages in the first quarter of the year of the benefit increase with such average at the time of the previous increase, and then raising the earnings base by the proportionate change. Increasing the earnings base increases the dollar amount of the Social Security tax payable by employer and employee for wage earners between the old and new base levels. These extra tax dollars are designed to help finance the automatic benefit increase. Decreases in the CPI do not decrease benefits or the taxable earnings base, however.

Benefit Increase for Delayed Retirement. The 1972 amendments introduced for the first time a small increase in benefits for persons who do not begin their benefits until after age 65. An actuarial reduction for the beginning of benefits between ages 62 and 65 has been in effect since 1956 for women and since 1961 for men (five ninths of 1 percent reduction for each month the worker is under age 65). Under the increase provision, benefits payable to persons who continue in employment after age 65 and postpone the start of Social Security benefits are increased by one twelfth of 1 percent for each month of covered employment after age 65 and before age 72.

Wives' Benefits. The wife age 65 or over of a worker receiving retirement benefits is entitled to a benefit equal to one half of her husband's benefit. This is the wife's full benefit. She may also receive a full benefit regardless of age if an eligible child is present; at age 62 or over she may receive an amount reduced from the full benefit.

Widows' and Widowers' Benefits. Until the 1972 amendments, a widow's benefit was 82.5 percent of her husband's former benefit if she was age 62 at claim, with actuarially reduced amounts at 60 or 61 (or from 50 to 59 if disabled). This was raised to 100 percent for age 65 at claim by the 1972 amendments, with actuarially reduced amounts at ages 60 to 64.

A widower is entitled to the same benefit based on his wife's Social Security account as a widow on her husband's account, except that in order to receive the benefit a widower must prove that he was a dependent, i.e., that he received at least one half of his support from his wife.

Supplemental Security Income for the Aged, Blind, and Disabled. As it
stands today, the Social Security Act covers three main service categories:
(1) social insurance, which includes the Old-Age, Survivors, and Disability
Insurance program, Unemployment Insurance, and Health Insurance for the
Aged and Disabled (Medicare), (2) public assistance and welfare services,
and (3) children's services.

The 1972 amendments not only made important changes in the social insurance programs, but in the public assistance and welfare service categories
as well. Effective January 1, 1974, the programs of Old-Age Assistance,
Aid to the Blind, and Aid to the Totally Disabled, all of which provided for
aid to state programs, were combined into a new federally administered program entitled Supplemental Security Income for the Aged, Blind, and Disabled. The new program (SSI) is administered by the Social Security Administration, not as part of OASDHI but as a federal welfare program.

The new SSI program makes from general revenues basic needs-tested
payments to aged, blind, or totally disabled persons. Like OASDHI, the SSI
benefits are automatically adjusted for cost-of-living increases. National welfare eligibility standards are established. Aged persons over 65 are granted
full assistance payments if they have no additional income over $20 per
month and have no assets beyond a house, a car, personal effects, and savings of $1,500 for an individual or $2,250 for a couple. The federal program
does not require the liens on homes that are imposed by some state welfare
plans or the qualifications in some states that adult children must meet a
means test before assistance will be provided to parents.[17] The SSI program
fully or partially supplants state administered welfare programs for the aged.
States may augment the federal program by providing additional monthly
payments; approximately 27 states do so under their own eligibility standards.

Effects of the 1972 Changes. Overall, the 1972 Social Security amendments brought the program to a new level of maturity. It may now be expected that, at least for the time being, changes (other than in financing) will
be made to adjust imbalances among various classes of people within the
program rather than to alter the substance or magnitude of the program as a
whole.[18] The new one-way link with the CPI means that benefits will keep
up with living-cost changes. The tax base will rise automatically to help
meet the costs of higher benefit levels. In commenting on the 1972 changes,
Robert M. Ball, a former Commissioner of Social Security, said: "The

changes in Social Security enacted this year . . . so significantly modern-
ized our Social Security program that we can say in truth we have a new
Social Security program—a program that provides a new level of security to
working people of all ages and to their families." [19]

SOCIAL SECURITY PRINCIPLES

As one of the principal designers of the Social Security system recently observed, "Social Security" has become a "common and comforting expression" in the American language, identifying a "meaningful factor" in meeting the contingencies of life for 9 out of 10 Americans.[20] Yet 40 years ago
this great social enterprise, now taken for granted, was just an idea in the
minds of advisers to the President, and the term "Social Security" was unknown to the American people.

Many of the "alphabet soup" agencies created under the New Deal were
by their nature temporary measures designed to help meet extreme conditions of emergency. The AAA, NRA, WPA, CCC, and others have long
since disappeared (Agricultural Adjustment Administration, National Recov-
ery Act, Works Progress Administration, Civilian Conservation Corps). But
the Social Security program was constructed of more solid stuff. The first
Social Security Act marked the genesis of a new and enduring social institution, designed to meet important and continuing needs. In its present-day
form that institution now touches the lives of practically every living American, either through benefits being received or anticipated, or through the
payment of taxes or contributions toward Social Security. There is every indication that most workers willingly contribute to the Social Security program in the expectation of a reliable measure of future financial independence for their families and for themselves. In human terms, the program
has been strikingly successful.

If this vast program has shown strength and capacity for growth, it is appropriate to explore the reasons. Congress and successive administrations
have recognized that to be effective Social Security would have to meet
changing conditions. Changes have taken place and flexibility has been a
feature of the program. As we have noted, the original limited coverage was
gradually expanded to almost all workers except federal civilian and some
other governmental employees. The original limited scope and low levels of
benefits have been increased dramatically. From a narrow, experimental

beginning, Social Security has become a mature social insurance program.

Throughout its growth, however, Social Security has remained close to a basic set of principles. The system continues to be national, compulsory, and contributory, with benefits paid as a matter of right and coverage almost universal. Associated with these basic principles are others that also express the purposes and limits of the program and distinguish this wage-related social equity system from the individual equity of public employee retirement plans and private pension plans. The following basic principles can be discerned as underlying the American social insurance system and as primarily responsible for its acceptance and success. Each is discussed separately below.

1. Nationwide plan.
2. Very broad coverage.
3. Compulsory participation.
4. Protection against major financial hazards.
5. Replacement of earnings.
6. Contributory—supported financially by employers and employees.
7. Benefits a matter of right.
8. Benefits related to concepts of social adequacy.
9. Payroll-tax financing.
10. Pay-as-you-go (current) financing.

1. Nationwide plan. The uniform provisions of Social Security are effective in all 50 states and in the District of Columbia, Puerto Rico, the Virgin Islands, Guam, and American Samoa. Few people would now dispute the importance of the Social Security program and its nationwide uniformity for the basic earnings-related old-age benefit program. Social insurance can be effective only to the extent that all workers and dependents are covered; exceptions dilute the program. America's work force is far too mobile in both the public and private sectors, far too much in need of assured basic income protection, to have it otherwise.[21] In 1935 there were discussions as to whether such a plan would be constitutional, but that problem and any economic, social, and political obstacles to a national plan have been laid to rest. No modern democratic nation has been able to assure its citizens a basic level of income protection in old age without a wage-related social insurance system operating midway between welfare programs and private pension plans.

2. *Very broad coverage.* The original Social Security acts in 1935 and 1939 left large gaps in coverage. About 6 out of 10 jobs in paid employment were then covered; now, 9 out of 10 paid jobs are covered. No worker is excluded because his wages are too high; the program applies its uniform earnings base to every covered individual.

A fundamental decision on coverage was made in 1935 when Congress defeated the Clark Amendment. Senator Champ Clark of Missouri led a successful fight in the Senate for an amendment to exempt from the compulsory old-age insurance all employees of companies with private pension plans. Because many large employers, such as American Telephone and Telegraph, General Electric, and U.S. Steel, had pension plans, there was pressure to avoid duplicate coverage by exempting from coverage participants of existing plans. The company plans, however, incorporated lengthy vesting delays and offered benefits only for those employees who remained with one employer virtually for life. Many if not most workers would have ended up with neither private nor social protection when in fact both were needed. The Clark Amendment was eliminated in conference and there were no further discussions of exclusions of this type in private employment.[22]

Of the approximately 9 million workers not now covered under Social Security, about 7 million are under the exempt employments of federal, state, or local government.[23] This gap in Social Security coverage and in the shared pooling of the contributions to pay for the program raises the question of whether any paid employee should be exempt from participation in a national social insurance plan. The existence of sizable areas of employment not covered gives rise to serious inequities in benefit protection, particularly for the many workers who move between covered and noncovered jobs. Some of these workers get windfall Social Security benefits based on relatively short coverage while others just miss getting enough coverage to qualify for benefits. In addition, there are opportunities for windfall benefits for entire groups of state and local employees because of the group-voluntary basis of such coverage and provisions for termination of coverage after it has been in effect for seven years. Many exempt federal and state workers arrange to hold covered jobs just long enough to permit them to qualify for weighted minimum Social Security benefit levels that were intended for low-income people. A more equitable distribution of both costs and benefits would be effected through the inclusion of all paid employment under the program. Universal coverage would assure all workers of benefits that could be supplemented by private and public employee pension plans designed with the knowledge that Social Security benefits will also be payable.

3. Compulsory participation. Except for the excluded groups noted previously, participation of employed persons in Social Security is required by law. Almost everyone is thus protected and taxed. To be effective, contributory social insurance programs must be made compulsory. Social Security would not work if participation were voluntary. Too many people would exclude themselves only to face later the risks of old age and disability without the economic protection they otherwise could have had.

Employers of covered groups and self-employed persons are required by the Federal Insurance Contributions Act (FICA), part of the Internal Revenue Code, to withhold Social Security taxes from employees and to transmit these taxes along with the employer's taxes to the Internal Revenue Service for the accounts of the Social Security trust funds. Civil and criminal penalties are prescribed for failure to make the payments.

If the compulsory feature is sometimes thought to be a limitation of the freedom of the individual to make his own decisions regarding economic security, it may also be regarded as a means of gaining economic freedom. The program provides a financial underpinning for nearly all workers in the society so that they or their dependents will have a basic assured money income in old age or in case of early death or disability. This assurance is a necessary part of modern living in a complex society.

Professor Richard A. Musgrave has pointed out that "increasingly, social insurance has become a budgeting aid for the middle class. . . ." [24] In fact, this feature applies to all income levels, but social insurance is far more than a compulsory budgeting aid. It assures all workers that all others are insured against the financial risks covered by the program. The burden of the cost of the support program as a whole thus falls fairly evenly. Otherwise, it would be likely that those who had voluntarily foregone current expenditures in favor of future security ultimately would also have to shoulder the cost of the security of persons who had failed, for whatever reason, to make old-age income provisions in advance. The compulsory feature also results in confining welfare or assistance payments to smaller groups and reducing the welfare payment burden.

4. Protection against life's major financial hazards. The major financial hazards facing workers and their families are the consequences of death or disability during the income-earning years, unemployment, or the risk of outliving income sources in old age. OASDHI covers all of these but unemployment, which is covered under a separate program. It provides benefits for the families of workers who die, monthly income for workers who become totally disabled, and retirement income for the worker and dependents. In addition, the health insurance portion, Part A, provides hospital insurance benefits for covered persons over age 65.

5. *Replacement of earnings.* When Congress passed the Social Security Act, it made clear that a primary objective was to help prevent economic insecurity due to loss of earnings in retirement by providing cash income for those who had substantially withdrawn from the labor force. There was no intention of constructing a plan to tax all workers during their working years in order to increase personal income sharply at age 65 for those who continued to work full time. In other words, as a matter of principle under social insurance, there was no intent under the provisions of the program to tax younger *working* people to pay benefits to older *working* people.

Consequently, the Social Security law provides for deductions from benefits payable to a working beneficiary under age 72 (including working dependents entitled to Social Security benefits) if earnings exceed certain levels. This earnings test, or work test, is based on the philosophy that in a social insurance system there should not be a diversion of a part of social transfer funds from one segment of the working population to another segment of the working population. Loss of earned income or very low earnings, as well as the attainment of age 62 or 65, is thus made a condition for eligibility for Social Security old-age retirement benefits. The partial replacement of earnings lost because of age has remained a fundamental part of the system.

The work test or retirement test is the method of determining whether a person has essentially withdrawn from the work force. Some earnings are permitted without loss of Social Security benefits, but substantial earnings are not. If a beneficiary under age 72 earns more than the annual exempt amount ($2,520 in 1975 and adjusted with rising average earnings each year), benefits are withheld at the rate of $1 in benefits for each $2 in earnings above that amount. Regardless of annual earnings, a beneficiary may receive full benefits for any month in which he or she neither earns more than the monthly measure ($210 in 1975) nor performs substantial services in self-employment.

A recent survey of social insurance in over 100 countries found that over

80 percent of the systems have retirement test provisions and that the number has been increasing.[25] The test is controversial in the United States, however, and each year Congress receives additional demands for weakening it. It has been critized because it takes into account earned income but does not consider a beneficiary's income from such nonwork sources as interest on savings, dividends, rents, or pension payments. However, if the test took account of income other than earnings from work, it would penalize private savings and it would no longer be a retirement test but an income test. If it became an income test, the fundamental idea that Social Security benefits are intended as a partial replacement of earnings from work would be diluted or lost. Successive Advisory Council reports have concluded that the test is consistent with the basic purpose and principles of Social Security—to replace, in part, earnings lost because of retirement, disability, or death. The exempt amount is designed largely to accommodate low-income individuals who do not have access to private savings or private pension payments to supplement Social Security benefits and are most likely to depend on earned income to supplement benefits.

The retirement test of Social Security has been controversial partly because of failure to distinguish between social insurance and individual insurance, and partly because of failure to acknowledge precisely what is being insured by the social program. A person can ask to have an individually owned annuity start payments at age 65 regardless of whether he or she continues to work; if it is requested that the start of payments be delayed, the resulting monthly benefits will then be higher. The premiums he or she has paid cover the cost either way. Whether the individual works or not while receiving the benefits is not relevant. On the other hand, Social Security aims to replace earnings when earnings are no longer being received, and in setting the cost, the "risk" of starting payments even though an individual continues full-time work is not insured in the Social Security system. It has been estimated that to cover it would increase the Social Security tax by about 0.5 percent of taxable payroll, or by about $4 billion a year. Or the extra cost could be accounted for by reducing all Social Security benefits by about 4 percent. Thus, in considering the work test, important questions of social adequacy, the risk insured against, and the purpose of a social insurance program are involved, and it is appropriate to ask whether it is a proper priority to increase taxes or lower benefits in order to pay benefits to persons who are working, many at wages as high as they ever had.

Recently, about 1.4 million (or 6.4 percent) out of 22 million Social Security old-age beneficiaries 65 and over reported earnings over $2,400 per year. Of these, 0.9 million had some benefits withheld (4.1 percent) and 0.5 million (2.3 percent) had all benefits withheld during the year 1973.[26]

As a political compromise, the Social Security law in 1950 was changed to provide benefits at age 75 regardless of whether the worker continued in employment. Then, in the 1954 legislation, the age was lowered to the present 72. This was a patchwork provision resulting in sharply increased income for the few people, mainly self-employed, who continued to work in remunerative jobs after age 71. It is inconsistent with a philosophy of social insurance benefits as *replacements* for earnings rather than *additions* to earnings. Pressures to increase allowable earnings beyond the present scale with escalator or to lower the age should be resisted.

6. Contributory. From the outset the OASDI system has been supported through equal contributions from employers and their employees. The contributory feature has been accepted almost without controversy. Labor, management, and workers have all favored contributory taxes as the prudent way of financing Social Security. Labor has been especially strong in its support over the years. In addition, there are important psychological advantages in levying OASDI taxes on the same amount of salary that is used in the computation of benefits. This relationship between benefits and taxes has generally strengthened the program and is in no way inconsistent with the social transfer aspects of the program. Although it is recognized that those who have retired so far have paid far less in the way of taxes than their benefits cost, nonetheless there is a sense of fair and appropriate participation in the contributory financing of benefit expectations.

An important advantage to the financing of Social Security through employer and employee contributions is that this direct financing helps illuminate the cost of additional benefit liberalizations, since the current costs, at least, are reflected in the taxes. Financing the program entirely from payroll contributions helps dampen unreasonable demands for increases in benefits. The link between contributions and benefits also fosters a sense of responsibility regarding the program, since workers and employers know that higher benefits mean higher taxes. Especially at present, when the program must deal with a substantial long-range deficit, it is particularly important that any further liberalizations be financed in a manner that will not obscure the relationship between benefits and contributions.

Some writers and speakers claim that Social Security taxes are regressive because the employee tax when related to *total* earnings—covered plus non-covered—is a lower percentage of total earnings for workers whose earnings exceed the taxable wage base. This view, however, does not take into account that Social Security is a package of benefits and contributions and that both taxes and benefits are related to and limited to the taxable earnings base. The Social Security taxes are in fact mildly progressive, since benefits are weighted in favor of workers with lower earnings histories (about 120 percent of the first $110 of average monthly earnings and 44 percent of the next $290), while workers whose taxable earnings are higher receive benefits that are relatively attenuated (only 20 percent of the last $100 of average monthly earnings).

7. Benefits as a matter of right. Among the ways that Social Security differs from income-tested or needs-tested welfare and assistance programs is that insured status and other statutory provisions determining entitlement to benefits do not include needs criteria. The covered worker who meets the requirements as to the number of three-month periods (quarters) in covered employment and who has substantially retired from work in accordance with the work test receives his retirement benefits as a matter of right. Whether one is well-off or poor or has other sources of income does not affect the right to Social Security benefits. This aspect of the program provides incentive for individual investment and savings and for private plan coverage so that a higher standard of living can be maintained beyond what Social Security provides. Insured status and average monthly earnings under the program determine whether benefits are payable and what amounts should be paid.

8. Benefits related to concepts of social adequacy. A social insurance system sets benefit levels according to some concept of what is adequate for the purpose, balancing benefits achieved with the burden of the cost, and with the interrelationships of the program with needs-test assistance programs at lower income levels and private pension programs and individual savings at higher income levels. Achieving a consensus of what is adequate is not easy; many different interests and viewpoints are involved. Over a period of time, changes in concepts of adequacy may be expected to occur as changes in economic and social circumstances take place.

The discussions as to benefit levels at present encompass two main groups—the so-called expansionists, who generally favor higher taxes and benefit levels than those currently provided, and the so-called moderates, those who believe that the system as it has now evolved generally plays an appropriate role for a tax-supported transfer system. Both moderates and expansionists recognize the importance of assistance or welfare programs for those who have had only intermittent association with the work force and for their dependents.

Under present law, Social Security benefits when supplemented by private pensions can result in retirement incomes of more than 100 percent of earned income for many retirees. As a result, many expansionists envision a future in which Social Security would do virtually the whole job; that is, social insurance would supplant reserve-fund private and public employee plans.

The moderates regard a tripartite old-age income support system as the most realistic and economically viable approach: Social Security at approximately its present level of maturity with the built-in CPI escalator, plus private and public employee pensions supplementing as at present the basic level of social protection, plus underlying needs-test welfare assistance. Their viewpoint is that a social insurance system works best in conjunction with private pensions as supplements at all earnings levels. They believe private pensions should be strongly encouraged as a matter of public policy to further strengthen independent retirement protection directly related to the worker's earnings.

Part of the test of adequacy of a social insurance program is in the type of benefits provided. OASDI provides not only for retirement benefits, but for survivor and disability benefits of considerable value. In addition, adequacy is expressed through a degree of social equity transfer designed to achieve broad social purposes. While the OASDI program's benefits are wage-related to an extent, the relationship is diminished at earnings levels nearer the top of the covered earnings base with benefits weighted in favor of low-paid workers. In contrast, under the individual equity of private pensions, the contributor to the system receives benefit protection directly related to the amount of his or her contributions. Under a social insurance system, full individual equity should not and cannot be achieved because of the need to accomplish various social objectives, including relatively larger benefits for workers with low earnings. The same social equity objectives and weighting also pertain to families, with benefit schedules under the social insurance system providing higher benefits but the same tax rate for married compared with single workers, workers with children compared with childless workers, and more liberal benefits for wives and widows than for husbands and widowers. These and other social equity elements of the federal program have coalesced into the existing broad basic floor of social support, largely a social equity system, but with aspects of individual equity through its system of partly wage-related benefits, paid as a matter of right.

In practice, the adequacy objectives of the program take into account the parallel structure of the private pension system (including public employee retirement plans), although it is acknowledged that the private pension sector has yet to fulfill its potential. What constitutes adequacy for one might seem affluence to another and penury for a third. Thus it is difficult to formulate a precise and specific definition of the adequacy objective. Successive Social Security Advisory Council reports have emphasized that it should not be expected that OASDI perform the entire job of assuring economic security for the aged and disabled and their families or for survivors. Yet, as the primary means of partially replacing earnings, OASDI is the core of the nation's total system of income protection. Private efforts are deemed essential to fulfill needs and desires for protection above and beyond the floor level of Social Security.

In terms of dollars, the maximum monthly primary Social Security benefit payable to a person retiring at age 65 in 1975 is $341.70 for a man and $360.40 for a woman. (The male-female benefit difference will be phased out by 1978). The dollar amounts of the benefits have increased substantially since the beginning of the program, although there were no increases during the first 10 years of benefit payments, 1940 through 1949. The 1950 and 1952 increases restored the purchasing power of the benefits, and the 1954 increase raised the adequacy level of the benefits, to a degree, in real terms. Then the increases up to 1969 generally restored benefit levels from time to time to match increases in living costs. During the period from 1969 through 1972 the adequacy floor was substantially raised as a result of three benefit increases totaling 52 percent over a period when the cost of living rose by 23 percent. Chart 3.1 uses constant (1975) dollars to show the changes and real values of the old-age benefits beginning with the first benefit payment year, 1940. The increases of 1973 and 1974 (totaling 11 percent) helped restore the real value of the benefits that had been lost by inflation since the 1972 change. The 1975 increase marks the first benefit increase resulting from the automatic escalator provision.

The minimum Social Security benefit is another element of the program's purpose of providing for social equity. The present law provides that the primary insurance amount shall not be less than a stated amount ($101.40 in 1975), no matter how small the average monthly earnings. The minimum monthly benefit is designed to provide a better level of benefits for workers with a substantial history of covered earnings but at very low wages. Now that the Supplemental Security Income program (SSI) has been introduced, however, it has been proposed that the minimum be frozen and gradually eliminated and that benefits related to need be handled through SSI and financed from general revenues. This would alleviate the problem in which the minimum is often paid to people who are well-off compared with the people for whom it was intended. For example, U.S. civil service employees and public employees in some states, whose regular jobs are not

CHART 3.1

Social Security Retirement Benefits in Constant 1975 Dollars, 1940–1975
(primary insurance amount)

Monthly benefit

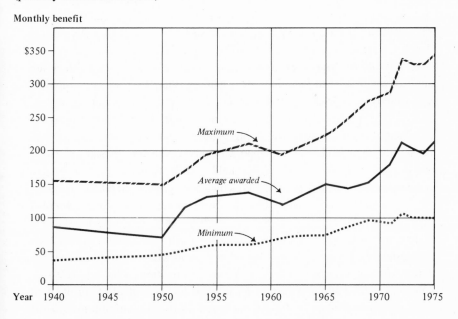

Source: Social Security Administration, Bureau of Labor Statistics Consumer Price Index.

covered by Social Security, frequently hold another job concurrently or at some time in their career just long enough to qualify for minimum Social Security benefits. A 1968 study of retired federal civil servants found that 40 percent were also receiving Social Security benefits and that about a third of these were receiving the windfall minimum, which amounts to over 100 percent of the average monthly wage that entitled the worker to the minimum.[27]

In keeping with its social role as an income-transfer system meeting basic needs while leaving room for and encouraging group private pension coverage and individual efforts, Social Security provides for taxes on earnings only up to the amount of the taxable wage base. If there is to be retirement income related to earnings above the Social Security base, individual efforts and private pension coverage are the methods of providing it, and are necessary if total retirement income is to bear a reasonable relationship to total preretirement earnings.

In order to provide about the same overall replacement ratio for earnings both above and below the earnings base, most private pension plans and many public employee plans integrate benefits by setting the pension formula or contributions related to earnings within the Social Security base so that the total of the combined OASDI benefit and the plan benefit based on salary below the base is approximately the same percentage of earnings as is the plan benefit alone above the base.[28]

9. Payroll-tax financing. As already noted, Social Security taxes are applied within a stated earnings base and are shared equally by employer and employee. OASDI is financed exclusively from this earmarked tax and no general revenues are applied, either for benefits or administration. When the Social Security system was being planned, and at times since then, the possibility of general revenue support for the system was considered. However, over the years Congress has held that with minor exceptions (the special age-72 benefits, pre-1957 noncontributory wage credit for members of the armed services, credits for Americans of Japanese ancestry interned during World War II), Social Security cash benefits should be financed out of payroll taxes. Such financing helps distinguish OASDI from purely welfare programs, permits greater understanding and identification of Social Security costs, and reinforces the government's obligation under implied social contract to maintain the program in the future for the benefit of current contributors. In addition, the fact that covered workers contribute toward the cost of the program supports the principle of benefits paid as a matter of right without a needs test and encourages a responsible attitude toward the program.

In considering the cost of the program, it is necessary to take into account that Social Security is more than a program of retirement insurance. Even if a worker does not become disabled prior to reaching retirement age, and even if he no longer has a dependent spouse or young children when he dies, he nevertheless enjoyed dependents' and survivors' insurance protection for many years. Like any other insurance protection, this protection has both a cost and a value. Part A of the hospital insurance program is also financed by the OASDHI tax.

The next big effort in Social Security financing is already developing—partial financing of the benefits through general revenues. A number of bills have been introduced in Congress to provide a subsidy for Social Security benefits from general taxation. In this connection it is well to remember that the only way needs-related welfare benefits can be financed is through general revenues. There is no other way to finance benefits for people who have never been solidly in the labor force, or whose needs far outrun their resources. Thus the federal government is already using general revenues on a large scale for social welfare programs.

In order to keep the contrast between needs-tested benefits (welfare) and benefit expectations as a matter of right (Social Security), it is important to use wage taxes to finance benefits related to earnings. The wage tax with related benefits has provided a strong Social Security system. This relationship and structure are far too important to weaken by breaking the link between benefits and taxes.

As a final point, Social Security and its beneficiaries already receive a large "subsidy" from general revenues in the form of foregone taxes. Social Security benefits are free from all federal taxes. Benefits now being paid amount to almost $60 billion a year. If those benefits were included in taxable income on the same basis as private pension plans (everything includable in taxable income except benefits purchased by already-taxed employee contributions), the tax revenue would be several billions of dollars. Foregone taxes by state and local taxing units would add to the total. The foregone revenue represents a social policy decision with respect to federal taxation of Social Security benefits, and therefore can be considered a large contribution from governmental general revenue sources to the system and its beneficiaries.

Table 3.1 reviews the Social Security tax rate history and indicates the frequent changes that have been made in the rate to accommodate extension of benefits covered or increases in benefit amounts. It also projects currently scheduled rates for the future. Tax collections will of course rise as a result of increases in average covered wages and increases in the earnings base because of the operation of the CPI-escalator provisions. Cost projections show that the presently scheduled future taxes are too low.

Along with tax rate increases, increases in the taxable earnings base, now automatic, have also taken place over the years to help finance the program. The base grew from $3,000 in 1937, when taxes were first collected from a much more limited group of covered workers, to the 1975 base of $14,100. Table 3.2 reviews the earnings bases that have been in effect. The accelerated growth of the program, particularly in benefit levels, is suggested by

Table 3.1 OASDHI Employee and Employer Tax Rates, Each, 1937–1975, and Scheduled for 1976–1998 (percent of taxable earnings)

Calendar Year	OASDI Rate	Hospital Insurance Rate	Total Rate
1937–1949	1.00% [a]		1.00%
1950–1953	1.50 [a]		1.50
1954–1956	2.00 [a]		2.00
1957–1958	2.25		2.25
1959	2.50		2.50
1960–1961	3.00		3.00
1962	3.12		3.12
1963–1965	3.62		3.62
1966	3.85	.35%	4.25
1967	3.90	.50	4.40
1968	3.80	.60	4.40
1969–1970	4.20	.60	4.80
1971–1972	4.60	.60	5.20
1973	4.85	1.00	5.85
1974–1977	4.95	.90	5.85
1978–1980	4.95	1.10	6.05
1981–1985	4.95	1.35	6.30
1986–1998	4.95	1.50	6.45

Source: "Annual Statistical Supplement," Social Security Bulletin (1973), p. 29.

[a] OASI only.

the fact that the first 100-percent increase in the earnings base spanned a period of just under 30 years (1937–1966), while the next 100-percent increase took place within 7 years (1968–1975). The table also suggests why a worker's average monthly earnings calculation at retirement may be so much below the earnings on which taxes are paid in the year just preceding retirement.

Tax rate and earnings base changes have not taken place at the same time; one earnings base may have had more than one tax rate applied to it during the period it was effective. Table 3.3 shows the exact dollar amount of the employee maximum tax each year through 1975, the product of the prevailing tax rate and the applicable maximum earnings base.

10. Pay-as-you-go (current) financing. The financing method of the Social Security program would be unacceptable in a private pension plan and would violate the provisions of the 1974 Pension Reform Act. While Social Security maintains reserves or trust funds (separate accounts in the Treasury for OASI and DI), they are not comparable to the private pension reserves built up during an employee's working years to be paid out on an actuarial basis during retirement. Instead, the Social Security taxes are immediately paid out by the government to persons who are already beneficiaries. Such funds as are held in the trust accounts are built up by relatively modest ex-

Table 3.2 Changes in the Social Security Earnings Base

Period	Earnings Base
1937–1950	$ 3,000
1951–1954	3,600
1955–1958	4,200
1959–1965	4,800
1966–1967	6,600
1968–1971	7,800
1972	9,000
1973	10,800
1974	13,200
1975	14,100
1976 and after	Automatic adjustments

Source: 1975 Annual Report of the Board of Trustees, OASI and DI Trust Funds, Table 1.

cesses of receipts over disbursements, functioning largely, and importantly, as contingency funds to absorb the initial cost of increased benefits as legislated by Congress, the decreases in the payroll tax due to declines in employment, and the program's administrative expenses. For many years the trust fund equaled about one year's program expenditure, but this ratio has been declining since 1972.

The pay-as-you-go method reflects the social transfer process in operation. Money is paid from one generation to another, with the amount taken from the one generation being measured by the other generation's entitlements under the provisions of the Social Security Act and its amendments. This current cost method is theoretically sound for OASDI because government has the continuing power to tax future workers to pay benefits in the future to those who are now working.

Taxpayers and Congress want to know what their decisions will cost

Table 3.3 Maximum Employee Social Security Tax,
1937–1975

Calendar Year	Maximum Tax
1937–1949	$ 30.00
1950	45.00
1951–1953	54.00
1954	72.00
1955–1956	84.00
1957–1958	94.50
1959	120.00
1960–1961	144.00
1962	150.00
1963–1965	174.00
1966	277.20
1967	290.40
1968	343.20
1969–1970	374.40
1971	405.60
1972	468.00
1973	631.80
1974	772.20
1975	824.85

them. Consequently, current and expected future costs of the Social Security program receive careful scrutiny. Although never a simple matter, projecting future costs of Social Security was much easier before the introduction of the 1972 escalator provisions. The adoption of the automatic features has made future costs dependent on future prices and wages. Costs can no longer be determined on the basis of today's benefit schedule plus demographic assumptions because the benefit schedules will move up automatically with the CPI. Nor can the payroll tax receipts any longer be projected on the basis of scheduled earnings bases because they are now linked to changes in average earnings levels and because CPI changes will determine their application. Economic conditions have always affected levels of employment and taxable earnings under the program, but now under the automatic provisions economic conditions will also directly affect benefits, the contributions, the earnings base, and the exempt amount under the work test. Under these circumstances, it is evident that projections of the expected financial operations of the program are subject to substantially greater risks, that the actual levels of benefits and taxes are subject to substantially greater degrees of change, and that costs will be higher than anticipated.

Already this new sensitivity of the program to economic conditions has shown itself. In 1974 the regular actuarial review and cost projections for OASDI included two major assumptions: wages increasing at an average rate of 5 percent per year and the CPI increasing at an average rate of 3 percent per year. Under these and other assumptions it was concluded by the trustees of the program that over the long term there would be an excess of benefit payments over tax receipts of 2.98 percent of covered payroll, gradual at first, then increasing. Between 1974 and 2045, the cost of OASDI was projected at an average 13.89 percent of taxable payroll. This was the amount required to meet benefits. The combined employer and employee tax was expected to provide only an average 10.91 percent of covered payroll as system income, a difference of 2.98 percent, which signifies a cost deficit of 27 percent.[29] In the light of changing economic conditions it appears that even this long-term estimate of a one-fourth deficit in financing is much too low.

A nearer term and startling cost development grew out of the calculation of the first automatic increase (June 1975). It had originally been estimated that the 1975 benefit increase would be 4.4 percent. It was actually 8 percent. This led to a considerable change in the forecasting assumptions used

for the 1975 trustees' report compared with that of 1974. As a consequence
it is now forecast that over the short term from 1976 to 1980, Social Security disbursements will exceed income in each of those years because of the
operation of the escalator feature. Furthermore, it appears that by as soon as
1980 some means of strengthening the financial support of the new escalator
system will have to be found if the trust funds are to remain solvent.

It is revealing to examine the trustees' 1975 assumptions regarding the
next five years. Table 3.4 shows these assumptions for wages, the CPI, and
the unemployment rate. Table 3.5 shows a forecast of annual benefit increases averaging 8.2 percent per year, and an expected rise in the earnings
base to $19,800 in 1979. Since 1951, the taxable earnings base has ranged
from 79 to 85 percent of total wages in employment covered by the program. The present automatic increases in the earnings base would retain the
current ratio of about 85 percent. Table 3.6 shows the annual expected
changes in the OASI trust fund, which is expected to decline from $35.614
billion in 1975 to $18.173 billion in 1980, or to about 20 percent of 1980 in-
come. As the table indicates, OASI excess expenditures are expected to
rise to over 4 billion dollars in 1979. Adding to this the annual expected deficits of the DI program, total OASDI expenditures will exceed income by 6
billion in 1979. While the trust funds themselves are operating as intended
under the circumstances—as contingency reserves to meet unanticipated
costs and unexpected economic conditions—it seems clear that more than
just temporary or short-term forces are at work.

This is in fact the case. The 1975–1979 estimates are clear signals that the

Table 3.4 Assumed Future Increase in Average Wages, CPI, and Unemployment, 1975–1980

Year	Wages	CPI	Unemployment
1975	6.2%	9.0%	8.8%
1976	9.0	6.6	8.0
1977	11.0	6.5	7.0
1978	8.8	5.7	6.2
1979	7.7	4.6	5.4
1980	7.0	4.0	4.8

Source: 1975 Annual Report of the Board of Trustees of the OASI and DI
Trust Funds, p. 36.

new benefit increases and escalator provisions have introduced wholly new cost levels into the pay-as-you-go system. Until recently, the pay-as-you-go system raised few alarms because it operated under a relatively stable set of circumstances; taxpayers and expert planners alike were spared visions of alarming cost escalations. In this atmosphere it was not surprising that an expansionist philosophy developed and that expansionists urged even higher levels of benefits and taxes, higher by far than those actually legislated by the 1972 changes.

Now that the new cost levels have become visible and substantial deficits are foreseeable for both the near term and over the longer range, it becomes apparent in the final analysis that pay-as-you-go, like any other funding method, has its own imperatives—the support capacity of the economy and the willingness of the taxpayers to pay. Between now and 1983, when the OASI trust funds would be exhausted as a source for replenishing annual deficits (the DI fund is expected to be exhausted in 1980), Congress must face the task of putting Social Security back on a pay-as-you-go basis and of keeping taxes and benefit payments in balance; it seems inevitable that public awareness of the cost of the program will rise.

Current cost methods of financing cannot be administered responsibly without careful and realistic future projections that take into account all relevant variables, including benefits promised and payable and available sources of funds. The new escalator features of the program not only may be expected to escalate benefits and costs but to escalate the difficulty of making reasonably accurate cost predictions. Henceforth, it seems likely that

Table 3.5 Assumed Changes in Benefits and Earnings Base, 1975–1979

Year	Benefit Increase	Earnings Base
1975	8.0%	$14,100
1976	6.6	15,000[a]
1977	6.4	16,500
1978	6.3	18,300
1979	4.8	19,800

Source: 1975 Annual Report of the Board of Trustees of the OASI and DI Trust Funds, p. 37.

[a] The actual earnings base for 1976 is $15,300.

Social Security actuarial forecasts will prove at times to be even wider of the mark than they have in the past, and to require greater adjustments. This represents a new challenge to the stability of the system as it enters its fifth decade.

THE FUTURE OF SOCIAL SECURITY

The continued health of Social Security as an institution depends not only on meeting its near-term financial crisis but on making sure that in the longer run financing methods are sound and costs are under control. The automatic escalator provisions have introduced higher costs and make them harder to predict, but on the positive side the new provisions have helped focus attention on the financial impact of the method of current funding and on how benefits are to be paid for in the future.

Long-range Financing Problems. In measuring the long-range financial requirements of OASDI, long-range cost predictions for the program are normally expressed as a percentage of total covered earnings, meaning earnings subject to the OASDI tax (presently 9.9 percent of taxable earnings, shared equally by employer and employee). Absolute dollars are not normally used because of the constant change in the number of workers, beneficiaries, earnings and benefit levels, and other factors. To meet the short-term deficit,

Table 3.6 Estimated Future Income, Disbursements, and Status of the Trust Fund, OASI, 1975–1979 (in millions by calendar years)

| | | | OASI Trust Fund | | |
| | | | Net Decrease | Fund at End of Period | Fund As Percent of Income |
Year	Income	Disbursements			
1975	$58,610	$60,773	$−2,163	$35,614	60%
1976	63,788	68,072	−4,284	31,330	49
1977	72,169	76,198	−4,029	27,301	37
1978	80,095	84,404	−4,309	22,992	28
1979	88,178	92,997	−4,189	18,173	20

Source: 1975 Annual Report of the Board of Trustees of the OASI and DI Trust Funds, Table 11, p. 41.

the 1975 Advisory Council on Social Security has urged a prompt increase in the tax of 1 percent, shared equally by employer and employee.[30]

The present 9.9 percent cost covers benefits now being paid only because the trust funds are absorbing the difference between income and expenditure. An immediate tax increase will only be a stopgap remedy, however, if it is limited to 1 percent. The 1975 OASDI trustees' report foresees the cost of the program rising under present provisions to 11.2 percent of the increasing taxable earnings, on the average, between 1975 and 1999, to 14.3 to 16.5 percent during the period between 2000 and 2024, and to 19 to 25 percent during the period from 2025 to 2049. The range of costs within each period depends on assumptions used in projecting average wages and the cost of living index.[31]

Demographic factors are also accounted for in these projections; the sharp rise in costs between 2020 and 2030 is due to a rapid increase in the ratio of workers to beneficiaries. Today there are 30 beneficiaries for every 100 workers; in the year 2030 it is estimated that there will be 45 beneficiaries for each 100 workers.[32] In the future there will be more retired people to support and relatively fewer people to support them.

How can the high future costs be met? There are three possible approaches: increase the taxes, decrease the benefits, or combine these two.

Taxes. Increasing taxes could involve (1) using general revenues, (2) increasing the taxable earnings base, (3) increasing the employer tax only, or (4) increasing both employer and employee taxes.

(1) Using general revenue has been advocated many times before to meet previous increases in Social Security costs. It has always been rejected, largely because it would involve a significant change in the nature of the program itself. The 1975 Advisory Council stated that ''the deficit can and should be dealt with through the conventional system of earmarked payroll contributions.'' [33] The council concluded that general revenue financing would obscure the cost-benefit relationship and the tie between contributions and benefits, would increase unreasonable benefit demands, and could lead to reduced public acceptance of the program.

(2) Increasing the taxable earnings base has been advocated by Social Security expansionists for many years, in earlier times to cover the cost of recommended benefit increases, at present to cover the future deficit. An immediate increase—$24,000 has been proposed—would raise more money. But

it also raises questions about the influence of the change on the purpose of the program itself. Social Security was designed from the beginning as only one of three elements in the income maintenance program, public assistance on the lower side and pension plans and private savings operating alongside Social Security and covering earnings above the Social Security limit. It was concluded by the 1975 Advisory Council that raising the limit to $24,000 would cause Social Security to interfere with the private savings element and would extend coverage to a level of income where "enforced" savings would seem inappropriate. Furthermore, increasing the earnings base to $24,000 would not bring in the necessary increases in funds. There is an important place for Social Security, and the earnings base helps determine it, but that place is now well established and changes ought not to be at the expense of private pension protection and the tripartite income support system.

Another important consideration is the effect on capital formation of raising the earnings base. Private pension plans are one of our major sources of investment capital. The effects of a diversion of funds from private pension savings and investment into the Social Security transfer system could be harmful to an already threatened economy in terms of higher interest rates, inflation, lack of adequate capital for modernization and new capacity, the proper management of environmental considerations, improvements in transportation, coming needs in the energy sector, and housing. Ironically, diverting a part of private pension savings flow to Social Security could make it more difficult, not less, to finance the Social Security program, which to a great degree depends on the overall health of the U.S. economy. Ultimately, unmet capital needs have a double-barreled impact on government, reducing tax revenues and increasing the cost of unemployment insurance and welfare, thus expanding the gap between Social Security tax collections and benefit payments. Actual and prospective capital shortfalls documented by studies carried out by the New York Stock Exchange and other organizations point to the urgent need for developing national policies that will stimulate, not restrict, savings and investment. One study estimates a staggering $650-billion gap between the domestic supply of investment capital expected to be available between 1974 and 1985 and the amount of capital that will be needed to meet our national economic requirements.[34]

OASDI trust funds do not function as investment capital, since they are invested in government securities. If the accumulated OASDI trust funds were to approach the levels that would normally be required for full funding of a private pension system, the result would be a tremendous reduction in sources of private capital. When Social Security was first established it was thought that employee and employer contributions could be put into a fund which would be built up over the years as reserves comparable to those in private pensions. It soon became apparent that a full reserve was unnecessary and that it was in fact undesirable to accumulate such large reserves. Were OASDI to be funded fully, it has been estimated that the fund needed would be in excess of $2 trillion, an amount over six times the present federal debt and ten times the present level of state and municipal debt. It would be nearly three times the assets of all domestic commercial banks. If full funding of the Social Security program were to be attempted, it would take all personal savings for the next 28 years, even without funding new obligations incurred during the 28 years.[35]

(3) Increasing the employer tax only would require an increase of perhaps as much as 20 percent in taxes paid just to meet near-term deficits. Over the longer term, the increase would have to be greater. There has been considerable discussion among economists of just how the employer tax falls, whether it is shifted to employees or is shifted unevenly among industries. Employers in labor-intensive and service industries are thought to bear a heavier OASDI tax burden than employers in more automated areas. Increases in the employer tax only could lead to increased costs of doing business, higher prices, lower wages, and perhaps decreases in employment. In view of these complex considerations and the success of the program under the present method of equally shared employer and employee taxes, it would appear unwise to alter fundamentally the role of employer and employee in paying for the program.

(4) A joint increase in both the employer and employee tax appears as the reasonable and consistent way of continuing to raise income for this wage related program. During the next 25 years, a 1.1- to 1.3-percent increase in the total employer and employee tax has been suggested by the 1975 Advisory Council as sufficient to meet the financial gap of this period. Later, as demographic changes heavily influence plan costs, further increases will be required, but they alone may not have to be the sole means of meeting the financial requirements. Considerable savings can be realized by redesigning the benefit formula. This would not mean a reduction in current benefits, but would effect a desirable elimination of higher costs and unintended instabilities resulting from the recent escalator changes.

DECOUPLING THE FORMULA

At present the OASDI system contains a flaw that was probably included inadvertently. Under it the ratio of the OASDI old age benefit to a worker's taxable wages just before retirement can vary radically according to changes in wages and price levels that have occurred during his covered service, factors over which the system has no control. Depending on the relationship of the CPI and wage levels during the worker's career, replacement ratios can move capriciously either up or down. A "replacement ratio" is the relationship between a worker's monthly benefit and the monthly wage he earns just before he retired, died, or was disabled. Thus, if a worker earns $600 a month just before retirement and received a monthly benefit of $300, he would have a replacement ratio of 50 percent. Replacement ratios should be stable over long periods of time, even though absolute benefit levels will naturally continue to rise with wages and prices.

Under the 1972 amendments, if the CPI were to rise nearly as fast or faster than wages, the future scheduled Social Security benefits would go up faster than necessary to stay abreast and the benefits as a percentage of final salary (replacement ratio) would rise substantiallly. If the increase in CPI lags much behind increases in wages, the reverse is true and the replacement ratio would be dramatically lower. Table 3.7 demonstrates this situation under a constant assumption of a wage increase of 5 percent a year and CPI increases of 4, 3, and 2 percent. Under the present "coupled" operation of the plan, two people retiring in 1975 each start out with the benefit equal to

**Table 3.7 Replacement Rates for Annual Wage Increases of 5
Percent (percent of final salary)**

| | Annual Increase in CPI: | | |
Year of Retirement	4%	3%	2%
1975	61%	61%	61%
1985	67	61	55
2000	84	66	51
2025	130	80	49
2050	165	85	44

Source: 1975 Report of the Advisory Council on Social Security, p. 51.

about 60 percent of final salary as shown in Table 3.7. However, persons retiring in 2025 would receive a benefit of 130 percent of final salary if inflation had averaged 4 percent a year but only 49 percent if inflation had averaged 2 percent a year. This peculiarity was not anticipated and should be corrected.

The core of the problem is that under the present benefit increase mechanism not only are the benefits of retired people raised when the CPI rises, the desirable goal legislated in 1972, but so are the future benefits of present workers. The standard table from which OASDI benefits are calculated must now be revised each year. Thus, if the CPI rises 8 percent, then each of the percentages applied to the average monthly wage in the benefit table moves up by 8 percent. The escalator has the desirable effect of increasing the benefits for all persons who are already retired, but it also increases the future benefits for those who are still working because they will eventually obtain the advantages of the higher benefit schedule when they retire. And the increase is compounded, because at the same time those who are still working will also receive an increase in wages and in the taxable wage base, and this too will increase their average monthly earnings and thereby further increase their future benefits. Then, when benefits begin, the CPI escalators will trigger further benefit increases. In other words, the benefit increases for those still working are "coupled" with the benefit increases for retired persons in a manner that produces the instability in replacement ratios illustrated in Table 3.7.

To stabilize the replacement ratios, the Advisory Council and the trustees of the OASDI trust funds have recommended that the system be decoupled. With decoupling, the system would be corrected so that a person's benefits would rise solely in accordance with wages during his working years and with the CPI in the years after retirement. The 1975 Advisory Council investigated a number of methods by which the change could be made and emphasized that the change can be accomplished by more than one formula. The council has stated that a decoupled system can be designed so as to prevent any material change in current benefit levels or replacement ratios. The design and installation of such a system would of course take some time because a careful testing would be required, and the specific formula adopted would depend upon the year it actually went into operation.

The savings in cost for future years that would be achieved by the use of a decoupling arrangement have been studied by the trustees of the system and

are summarized in Table 3.8. This table compares expected expenditures for
the support of the program for 1985 to 2050 and shows three different assumptions regarding rates of wage increase and of CPI increase: average
earnings increase of 5 percent and CPI increase of 3 percent, average earnings increase of 6 percent and CPI increase of 4 percent, and average earnings increase of 7 percent and CPI 5 percent. For the period from 1975 to
1980, higher wage and CPI assumptions have been made. The table shows
that there are significant differences in the cost of the program as a percentage of taxable payroll between the system as it is presently constituted and
the system as it would operate under a decoupling modification.

The current OASDI tax totals 9.9 percent of taxable earnings. In the absence of a decoupling amendment, future taxes can be expected to rise as
high as 25 percent of taxable earnings. With decoupling, future costs are estimated, under the stated assumptions, as somewhere between 16 and 17
percent. Estimates of future costs of the OASDI program have traditionally
turned out to be optimistically low. If this is the case with the estimates of-

**Table 3.8 Estimated Average Cost of OASDI Under Coupled and Decoupled
Approaches, 1975–2049**

	Average Cost as a Percent of Taxable Payroll Under Assumed Earnings and CPI Increase Rates [a]		
	5% Earnings; 3% CPI	6% Earnings; 4% CPI	7% Earnings; 5% CPI
Present coupled approach			
1975–1999	11.12%	11.16%	11.19%
2000–2024	14.31	15.12	16.42
2025–2049	19.05	22.09	24.91
Proposed decoupled approach			
1975–1999	11.17%	11.06%	10.95%
2000–2024	13.63	13.43	13.28
2025–2049	16.95	16.78	16.56

Source: 1975 Annual Report of the Board of Trustees of the Federal OASI and DI Trust Funds,
Tables 23, 24.

[a] Earnings and CPI rate assumptions shown are for 1980 and after. Higher assumptions are used for
the 1975–1980 period.

fered in Table 3.8, as it probably is, it seems likely that an amount as large as 15 percent of taxable payroll will have to be collected to finance the least expensive decoupled program in the 2000–2024 period, and perhaps 20 percent in the 2025–2049 period. This vast financial burden has been assumed by *present* legislation for workers many of whom have not yet been born. And it forces this financial burden on generations of workers who will face great and as yet not fully known problems of fuel and energy shortages, agriculture production problems, resource conservation, social changes, and the necessary supportive productivity levels.

After 40 years of growth and development of the Social Security system, a growth that has brought its benefits and future obligations to a far higher level than was envisioned at the outset, it now becomes urgent to consider the question of balance between the benefit promises and the capacity of the economy and the willingness of workers to meet those commitments. With an awesome future financial burden already in prospect, it seems essential that as a matter of public policy the greatest restraint be exercised henceforth in enlarging commitments even further.

BENEFIT PROPOSALS

Each year proposals have been made in Congress to add one or two more benefits to Social Security. Each item has its price tag for all workers paying Social Security taxes—many billions of dollars each for lowering the retirement age, eliminating the actuarial reduction for early retirement, eliminating the work test, or adding medical care under age 65. The cost would be hundreds of millions or billions for disability benefits for homemakers or for adding spouses' benefits on top of workers'. Congress will have to decide whether to add various new benefits and increases in taxes to finance them, or whether to leave to individuals and employers the right to choose priorities and whether to prepay certain kinds of services for themselves. Each of these items represents a transfer *from* someone as well as *to* someone. Therefore social policy on each side of the equation, "taxes from someone" as well as "benefits to someone," must be considered. Some of the items represent real needs, whereas others represent only a presumed injustice when comparing social insurance with private, or individual, insurance.

In Social Security the individual has no choice; there is only one model. Each idea for a new or expanded benefit sounds good and is expressed in social terms. But multibillion dollar benefits have been added almost casually. This is a compliment to the current popularity of the program, but it leaves much to be desired in terms of public choices and priorities and fiscal responsibility. There is real danger that ad hoc additions will leave this excellent basic program a complex patchwork and a heavy financial burden on workers. Public policy will in coming years have to make some difficult choices. Resources are not infinite, and, more important than that, at some level of Social Security taxes the burden on workers may become unacceptable to them, with dire consequences for the system.

It may even be necessary to cut back when reasonable and socially sound opportunities are available. For instance, in the period in which the ratio of retired to active workers will be rising to approximately 45 retirees to 100 workers, it would be desirable to give consideration to extending gradually the retirement age. The present age 65 was fixed over 40 years ago and was an admittedly arbitrary selection at the time. During those 40 years many advances have been made in health care and life expectancy rates have increased. Changing the age upward would help maintain a reasonable ratio of workers to beneficiaries. The Advisory Council has suggested that an increase from 65 to 68 might be accomplished gradually starting in 2005 by increasing the retirement age by one month every six months, ending in 2023 with a new age 68 retirement age, with the early retirement age advanced to 65. Serious attention should be given to this possibility.

A BASIC INCOME TRANSFER SYSTEM

There are three types of transfer under the OASDHI program. One is the insurance-type transfer to survivors or to those who suffer disability. These transfers are accomplished through payments from the taxes paid by workers who live to the families and survivors of those who die prematurely, or from the taxes paid by workers who stay healthy to those who become disabled. In 1974 benefits were being paid to nearly 7 million survivors and dependents under age 65, and to 2 million disabled workers. The second type, and by far the largest, is the intergenerational transfer, from the working generation to the retired generation. More than 20 million people are receiving retirement benefits as workers or dependents. The third type of transfer is the social-adequacy transfer to meet presumed needs—from higher-paid persons to lower-paid persons, from single persons to married, from men to women, and from smaller families to larger. The insurance-type survivor and disability benefits have worked well and raise no serious equity problems at their present levels. The old-age benefits and the social-adequacy transfers have raised the major questions and controversy. In general, the Social Security system can be considered a compact between generations. In the expectation that its turn will come, the current generation of workers supports the current generation of elderly. The major public policy questions that arise have to do with the amounts of intergenerational transfer that should occur and that can reasonably, or acceptably, be financed in the future.

Social Adequacy. At any given point in its history Social Security has been attacked as being unfair to some group—the young, the single, the married with a large family, the working elderly, nonworking men with working wives, or women compared with men, or men compared with women. The question generally hinges on the objective of social adequacy compared with individual equity. Under Social Security, social adequacy of benefits is a most useful and important consideration, but it is impossible for any system to provide social adequacy and full individual equity at the same time. The primary job of Social Security is to provide socially adequate benefits. It cannot do this and concurrently accept the idea that the single person has paid for and should therefore receive the same size benefits as a married person, or that the person who has paid twice the taxes of another should have twice the benefits, or that the person over age 62 who keeps on working full-time at high salary has a right to receive Social Security benefits on top of his wages, or that a younger worker of today should when he retires receive as generous an actuarial bargain as those who have already retired. These are the responsibilities of private pension plans.

Yet continually proposals are made for patching up benefits for this or that "unfairly treated" group, often using inaccurate analogies with private pension plans. There is an alternative to this patching process, wherein Social Security would concentrate its benefits in the areas of the greatest social needs and not attempt to pay relatively high benefits related to the upper part of salary. (The wage base now covers about 85 percent of total earnings in covered employment.) For instance, the cost of added Social Security benefits for persons now entering the work force may well be greater than equivalent benefits under privately invested pension plans. Present Social Security benefit replacement ratios can meet social objectives and still allow plenty of room for funded, vested private pension plan benefits. The manner of accomplishing this would be to assure strong Social Security benefits up to the middle income levels. The demand for, and reasonable aspiration to, benefits above that level can be provided through private plans that fully reflect the individual's own employment and savings history.

Terminology. Much of the complaint about unfair treatment for a particular classification of people covered by Social Security, either workers or beneficiaries, is caused by the terminology used in Social Security. The framers of Social Security adopted the well-regarded word "insurance" for the new social program. A tour de force in public relations, it also had a superficial relevance. But it has caused confusion over the years. It has led directly to the demand for a larger amount of individual equity in what is fundamentally a social insurance plan, such as payment of benefits to people who continue to work (elimination of the work test), payment of increased benefits for later retirement, payment of benefits for early retirement (instead of disability or unemployment benefits), and equal payments to single and married beneficiaries.

Although the debate goes on, the name "insurance" is so strongly fixed now that there is little chance of eradicating it. But it is important to distinguish the difference in meaning when "insurance" is used with the social program and when it is used with individual equity private programs.

How Far Should Social Security Go? Few people oppose the use of direct governmental transfer payments under benefit systems such as OASDHI that provide moderate or socially adequate benefits related to previous earnings. But how much above the poverty level are socially adequate benefits? The 1972 amendments to Social Security were so substantial that they pose new basic public policy questions to Congress and the people. Is Social Security now just about right? Or are the benefits and their related taxes still too low, or already too high? Grudgingly insufficient, or out of control? How much income should be transferred from generation to generation, and among people in differing circumstances within a generation? How much choice should individuals have? These questions are closely related to the role that should be played by various mechanisms for income maintenance. Continued attention must be given to relative optimum roles of needs-tests benefits, OASDHI, private pensions, and private savings.

The benefit increases and the escalators incorporated in the 1972 amendments turned on the yellow caution light for many strong supporters of Social Security, and a red light for others. It now appears that fair treatment of all generations requires that each increase in benefits from now on, apart from the normal operation of the CPI escalator, should be looked at from the standpoint of the current workers who are financing the benefits, as well as from the standpoint of the recipients.

From Young to Old and Back Again. The public policy question of the extent of goods and services to be transferred from one generation to another has very human and very practical sides to it. In 1970, before the last three increases in benefits, Dr. Juanita M. Kreps, professor of economics at Duke University and a member of the Task Force on the Economics of the Aging, Special Senate Committee on Aging, in a few short paragraphs analyzed with insight the generational sweep of the Social Security program:

> For it is today's worker who produces the goods and services allocated to yesterday's worker, just as tomorrow's worker will in turn assume the responsibility for producing the goods and services that support the worker of today. Since we cannot store up goods that are produced now, though we know we will need such goods during fifteen to twenty years of retirement, we accumulate instead deferred claims against goods that will be produced in the future.
>
> Thus, the current worker whose payroll is taxed to finance purchases made by current retirees is the provider in this stage of his life and the recipient in the next, and he is surely plagued with some obvious misgivings: How much of his own present earnings rightfully belong to today's retired worker? How will the amount he pays in OASDHI taxes compare with what he gets back when he retires? Will tomorrow's worker support him adequately? If not, what recourse will he have against the society, once he has ceased to be a productive worker? None of these questions is eased by the constant pressure on the worker's financial resources, which must cover ever-rising living costs, lengthened educational periods for his children, and frequently direct assistance to his own aged parents. . . .
>
> There are no simple solutions to the dilemma of today's worker. He could easily consume all his earnings, leaving no claims (either public or private) for future retirement needs. Social policy cannot hope to satisfy all his present and future needs, for they far outstrip his lifetime earnings. All social policy can do is provide a mechanism that allocates aggregate output in some democratically agreed-to optimal fashion, the optimum allocation in this case having a lifetime as well as a temporary dimension. And just as there are differences of view as to how evenly income should be distributed at any point in time, so, too, men vary in the rates at which they discount the future—that is, in how highly they prize present over future consumption. . . . . The particular mechanism we use for allocating income to the aged, i.e., the payroll tax paid into a social security "fund," directs attention to the tax burden borne by the worker on behalf of the retiree, and points up an apparent source of economic conflict between the two generations.[36]

Below a certain level of benefits, sound social policy dictates extensive redistribution of income to the elderly. But the nation must also be fair to its younger, working members. Above a certain level of benefit payments, sound policy dictates a parallel concern for younger families and their financial problems.

Although the United States was late among industrialized nations in introducing social insurance, OASDI is now the primary element under our tripartite philosophy of old-age income support. During the years of Social Security's growth and development, public policy regarding old-age income was focused mainly on that program in a formative stage. With the 1972 amendments, however, the changed nature of the program has forced public policy attention onto the huge financial commitment the system entails, and on how to balance social objectives with financial realities. Just two years later another piece of federal legislation, the 1974 Pension Reform Act, marked a turning point in federal attention to another type of benefit plan—the private pension and its potential in our society. Private pensions have thus moved up in our set of national priorities. The next chapters turn to the issues surrounding private pensions.

— 4 —

Private Pension Plans

An annuity is a very serious business.
Jane Austen

Coverage under private pension plans has grown rapidly over the last two decades. The number of employees covered has about tripled, going from 9.8 million wage and salary earners in 1950 to a roughly estimated 30 million in 1970, or approximately half of the workers employed in the private sector. Table 4.1 shows growth since 1950 in coverage, in employer and employee contributions, and in beneficiaries and pension benefits. Most of the current analysis of aggregate pension coverage by official government sources is based on 1970 figures, which later sample surveys sustain as still valid because of lower rates of change in the mid-1970s.

Private pension plans with 26 or more members numbered about 18,000 in 1970.[1] The life insurance industry alone reported 401,840 pension plans in 1972, but 90 percent of these had an average of fewer than eight participants per plan.[2] A majority of covered workers participate in a few very large plans—more than half the covered workers in 1970 were in plans covering 10,000 workers or more. The Bureau of Labor Statistics estimated that about 20 percent of all active workers covered under private pension plans participated in the 17 largest plans. On the other hand, the more than 14,000 plans with between 26 and 1,000 participants accounted for about 14 percent of private pension plan participants.[3] Chart 4.1 shows that most plans are small, but most workers are covered by a few large plans.

CHART 4.1

Private Pension Plans and Covered Workers, 1969

Percent

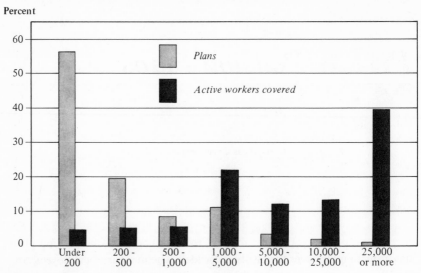

Number of active workers covered by plan

Source: Harry E. Davis and Arnold Strasser, "Private Pension Plans, 1960 to 1969 – An Overview," *Monthly Labor Review 93* (July 1970):47.

Table 4.1 Private Retirement Plans: Growth in Coverage, Contributions, Beneficiaries, and Benefit Payments, 1950–1970

Year	Coverage End of Year	Employer Contributions (millions)	Employee Contributions (millions)	Number of Beneficiaries End of Year	Amount of Benefit Payments (millions)
1950	9,800,000	$ 1,750	$ 330	450,000	$ 370
1955	15,400,000	3,280	560	980,000	850
1960	21,200,000	4,710	780	1,780,000	1,720
1965	25,300,000	7,370	990	2,750,000	3,520
1970	29,700,000	12,580	1,420	4,720,000	7,360

Source: Walter W. Kolodrubetz, "Two Decades of Employee-Benefit Plans, 1950–70: A Review," *Social Security Bulletin* 35 (April 1972):20.

About three of every ten workers covered under private pension plans are in multiemployer plans, plans covering more than one firm. Multiemployer plans are usually union negotiated and are especially important in the mining, construction, wholesale trade, printing, food, motor transportation, and service industries. Within these industries, multiemployer plans cover substantially more than half of all active workers participating in a pension plan. In manufacturing, on the other hand, multiemployer plans account for only about one of eight active participants; here, multiemployer plans are most important in the nondurable goods industries—principally in apparel manufacturing—where they cover about one of three workers who are under private pension plans in the industry.

Multiemployer plans have been the most rapidly growing plans over the last decade, particularly in the service, contract construction, and transportation industries. There were lesser pension gains in the industry areas in which single-employer pension plan growth had been achieved in earlier years, including retail trade, finance, insurance, real estate, communications, manufacturing, and utilities.

Most private pension plans are *noncontributory,* i.e., financed solely by the employer. The 1970 Bureau of Labor Statistics estimate is that 79 percent of private plans are noncontributory; 21 percent incorporate a contribution by the employee. Much of the recent increase in the proportion of noncontributory coverage is due to the previously mentioned growth in coverage under multiemployer plans, which are predominantly noncontributory, and to changes in large single-employer plans.[4]

The industrial patterns of plan financing reflect patterns of bargaining. Industries in which employees are highly organized usually have noncontributory plans, e.g., metalworking, contract construction, apparel, and transportation. Conversely, employee contributions are most frequently reported in the nonbargained plans, such as those covering workers in finance and textiles.[5]

Despite recent growth in private pension coverage, only about half of the people employed in the private sector work for employers providing a private plan. Most likely to be covered under a pension plan are unionized employees, higher-paid employees, and employees in larger firms; least likely are low-paid workers in small nonunion plants. In 1968, only a fifth of the workers in firms with average wages lower than $2.50 per hour were covered, compared with four fifths in those paying more than $5.00. Nine out of ten firms with more than 500 employees had private pension plan expenditures in 1970, compared with fewer than three in ten of those with less than 100 employees.[6]

Office workers are more likely to be covered by pension plans than nonoffice employees. The proportion of workers in office groups covered by retirement plans in 1968 exceeded that of workers in nonoffice groups, regardless of the size of the establishment's work force. The difference was largest (10 percentage points) among middle-sized firms, those with 100 to 499 employees, and smaller in firms with fewer than 50 workers (2 percentage

Table 4.2 Employees in the Private Sector Employed by Firms Reporting Pension Plans

	Total Private	Manufac- turing	Nonmanufac- turing
Type of Employee			
All employees	55%	73%	47%
Nonoffice	50	70	40
Office	67	83	62
Average Hourly Compensation			
Less than $2.50	20	28	18
$2.50 to $3.49	51	59	47
$3.50 to $4.99	74	86	66
$5.00 and over	81	93	72
Average Annual Earnings			
Under $5,000	30	36	29
$5,000 to $10,000	74	84	66
$10,000 and over	78	90	67
Employee Organization			
Union	82	84	79
Nonunion	44	62	37
Number of Employees in Establishments			
Under 100	27	32	26
100 to 499	62	64	60
500 and over	93	93	93

Source: Emerson Beier, "Incidence of Private Retirement Plans," *Monthly Labor Review* 94 (July 1971):38.

points) and in those with 500 workers or more (3 percentage points).[7] Table 4.2 gives an idea of the probability of coverage under a retirement plan for all industries together and for manufacturing and nonmanufacturing by showing the percent of employees in establishments reporting expenditures for retirement plans.

There is no real certainty as to exactly how many people are covered under private pension plans. Figures differ according to source, and the differences are considerable. The Institute of Life Insurance gave an estimated total for 1971 of 30,769,000 active workers under private retirement plans.[8] A 1972 Bureau of the Census survey analyzed by the Social Security Administration estimated that 23 million full-time workers in private wage and salary jobs were covered by a private pension or deferred profit-sharing plan.[9] The census survey characterized the 23 million as "almost half of those employed at the time of the survey." Another set of figures offered by the Social Security Administration, based on Institute of Life Insurance and Securities and Exchange Commission data, estimated a 1970 coverage under private pension and profit-sharing plans of 29.7 million employees.[10] A 1974 Social Security publication noted the differences in the various estimates of private pension coverage and suggested that there is "a need for a downward revision in the historical series" of estimates.[11]

Besides the approximately 50 percent (more or less) of nonagricultural wage and salary employees in the private sector who were not covered under a private pension plan in the early 1970s, members of various other groups are not covered: unemployed workers, agricultural workers, self-employed farm operators, unpaid family workers, and self-employed nonagricultural workers. These may amount to as many as 10 million persons.[12]

Table 4.3 summarizes the growth since 1950 of the proportion of wage and salary workers in private industry covered under pension plans. Rapid growth is shown during the 1950s and early '60s and then a much slower growth from the mid-1960s on. Most of the recent and more modest gains in coverage are attributed to expanded employment under existing plans rather than to the introduction of new plans.[13] Existing plans continue to report increases in benefits, lower retirement ages, and other changes.

Coverage under private pensions seems to be stalled at or just under the 50-percent level. The efforts of unions and the responses of employers have generally succeeded in getting some kind of pension coverage for workers in the larger, more prosperous industries and in the strongly unionized sectors of the economy. Generally left out are the large numbers of Americans employed in less well organized sectors, in smaller enterprises, in marginal firms or industries, and in self-employment and agriculture.

The limited coverage of private pension plans raises a dual question of public policy: the place of private pensions in our society and the role of Social Security. Can Social Security be expected to operate uniformly for all citizens and at the same time operate effectively for two very differently situated groups—those for whom Social Security provides a minimum level of benefits to which is added the protection of private or governmental pensions, and those for whom Social Security must provide the whole of retirement income beyond the individual's own savings and resources? Does lack of opportunity for private pension coverage for half of the private work force represent a failure to attend to a significant and visible gap? A crucial challenge now is to extend private pension coverage to "the other half."

Eligibility. Who joins an employer's private pension plan, and when, is determined by the participation or eligibility requirements. A length-of-service requirement is typically established as a means of keeping administrative costs low by eliminating the "ins and outs" of short-term employees. In addition, some plans have not permitted participation of persons in their early twenties, when wages generally are low, family responsibilities often high, and job turnover is frequent.[14]

A 1969 Labor Department survey found that about four fifths of all covered workers were in plans in which their coverage became effective immediately upon employment. The remaining workers were in plans which specified waiting-periods, which are more likely to be found in plans requiring

Table 4.3 Covered Employees as Percent of Wage and Salary Workers in Private Industry

1950	22.5%
1955	32.2
1960	42.4
1965	46.2
1970	48.3

Source: Walter W. Kolodrubetz, "Two Decades of Employee-Benefit Plans, 1950–1970: A Review," *Social Security Bulletin* 35 (April 1972):17.

an employee contribution than in the noncontributory plans. About 70 percent of contributory plans, covering 58 percent of workers under such plans, had some type of participation requirement. Only 36 percent of the noncontributory plans, covering 12 percent of the workers under these plans, had a participation requirement.

The 1975 Bankers Trust study of single-employer private pension plans (covering about 25 percent of all workers under such plans) found that 16 percent of pattern plans (those plans adopted by international unions and widely negotiated with individual companies and usually basing benefits on a flat rate) and 56 percent of conventional plans (plans with formula-based benefits incorporating years of service and rates of compensation) set eligibility requirements for membership. Such requirements were normally stated in terms of service requirements only or service plus age requirements.[15]

If plan participation is delayed until long after an employee joins the employer, and vesting of benefits depends on the completion of years of covered service, the combined delay makes difficult the attainment of assured retirement protection. Particularly where participation is delayed, early vesting once participation occurs is desirable so that an employee can begin accumulating credits toward retirement income. The Employee Retirement Income Security Act of 1974 now prohibits a retirement plan from excluding otherwise eligible employees who have reached age 25 and have completed one year of service. If plan benefits vest immediately, later plan entry is permitted, i.e., participation may be delayed until an employee has reached age 25 and has had three years of service.[16]

Retirement Age. Retirement plans state a "normal" retirement age, an age when full pension benefits can be received, assuming any applicable service requirements are met. Early retirement provisions may also be stated, usually including a service requirement and benefits reduced from those payable if retirement were delayed until the later normal age. Three out of four workers are covered by plans calling for age 65 retirement. Although the usual retirement age continues to be 65, as it has been for a couple of generations, important changes are occurring. They are discussed in Chapter 9.

The 1969 Labor Department survey found that just under 70 percent of all workers covered by private pension plans were in plans that had a normal retirement age of 65. One fourth were in plans permitting normal retirement at age 64 or earlier; 6 percent were in plans with no age requirement. The 1975 Bankers Trust study reported age 65 as the normal retirement age in 71 percent of conventional plans, age 60 to 64 in 5 percent, and the remainder either not stated (19 percent) or above age 65 (5 percent).[17] Table 4.4 shows Labor Department figures on normal retirement ages.

The Bankers Trust survey indicates that pattern plans are more likely to report service requirements for normal retirement (93 percent), and to report longer service requirements, than conventional plans (68 percent). Under the pattern plans, 77 percent required 10 or more years of service, while only 29 percent of the conventional plans required that length of service.[18]

Studies by the Bureau of Labor Statistics show that during the past decade the number of workers for whom early retirement at reduced benefits was available continued to grow, increasing to 87 percent of covered workers in 1969 from 75 percent in 1962. Most of the growth of early retirement provisions was under multiemployer plans, in which the percentage of affected workers rose from 29 percent to 74 percent.[19] The early retirement inquiries of the 1975 Bankers Trust survey revealed formal early retirement provisions (i.e., at the election of the employee without company consent) in 90 percent of the pattern plans studied and in 88 percent of conventional plans. Three out of every four of the latter plans specified age 55 with some period of credited service. The survey noted a trend toward the use of combined age and service requirements for early retirement and away from age as the only criterion.

In terms of the benefits paid to employees electing early retirement, the Bankers Trust survey found a trend toward higher early retirement benefits.

Table 4.4 Earliest Age for Normal Retirement Under Private Pension Plans, 1969

Normal Retirement Age	Percent Distribution of Covered Workers
65	69%
62–64	14
60–61	8
55–59	3
No age stated	6

Source: Harry E. Davis and Arnold Strasser, "Private Pension Plans, 1960 to 1969—An Overview," *Monthly Labor Review* 93 (July 1970):49.

A majority of the plans paid early retirement benefits greater than the actuarial equivalent but less than the full "normal age" benefit. Only 10 percent of the plans provided the actuarial equivalent for early retirees meeting service and age requirements. A similar but less pronounced trend was also found in conventional plans. There, 15 percent of plans paid the actuarial equivalent on early retirement, while the great majority (83 percent) provided more than the actuarial equivalent.

Early retirement without any reduction of the benefit was found by the Bankers Trust survey in a substantial number of the pattern plans because a large proportion of those plans maintain a 30-year service requirement for full pension. This is the type of plan initially achieved by the United Automobile Workers in a settlement with Chrysler in late 1973; it provided for full benefits for retirement at any age after 30 years of service. The Bankers Trust survey found that very few conventional plans, in contrast with the pattern plans, pay the full accrued pension upon earliest optional retirement date.[20] One of the reasons for this is the cost implications of younger retirement ages. With full benefits, retirement below age 65 raises the cost for a given benefit by 10 percent or more for each year the retiree is under 65. Cost aspects of early retirement are discussed in Chapter 9.

Benefits. The benefits paid by a private retirement plan depend of course on the plan's stated benefit level and, as a rule, on years of service under the plan credited to the retiring employee. The 1975 Bankers Trust study reported on the benefits currently being paid under pattern type plans and under conventional plans. Under the typical pattern plans—those normally paying a flat-dollar benefit for each year of service regardless of salary—the median benefit was $108 per year of service. The range was from $66 to $193. None of these plans was integrated with Social Security. Analysis of flat-dollar benefits by the Bureau of Labor Statistics estimates benefits ranging from a low of 6 percent of final pay for short-term employees meeting minimum vesting requirements to over 20 percent for pensioners having had 30 years of plan participation. The study notes that the addition of Social Security brings total benefits for long-term employees to 40 percent or more of the final earned-income level.[21]

Under the United Automobile Workers contracts with Chrysler and Ford negotiated for 1974, the minimum pension benefit payable for hourly workers on early retirement at any age after 30 years of service was $550 per month, payable until age 62, the starting date of Social Security early retirement benefits. The minimum benefit payable from age 62 was set at $395. Scheduled increases in the minimum are established to 1978. On reaching age 65, the early retiree receives the accrued normal retirement benefits plus an additional supplemental allowance. The normal retirement benefits, depending on the employee's wage category, became $8.75, $9.00 and $9.25 a month per year of service.[22]

For the conventional plans (plans relating benefits to salary and service), the 1975 Bankers Trust study found a continuing trend toward basing the benefit formula on "final-average" pay. Over a period of fifteen years the proportion of plans using a final pay formula for all or part of the benefits rose from 55 percent to 78 percent. In 1975 just 22 percent of the plans used the "career-average" approach. Over 90 percent of the plans used a final-averaging period of the five consecutive years of highest pay or the five years immediately preceding retirement.[23]

Conventional plans are normally integrated with Social Security, either through an offset formula, a step-rate formula, or an excess approach; under any of these, benefits are provided only on earnings above a present or former Social Security earnings base or specific dollar figure. The 1975 Bankers Trust survey indicated that career-average plans were most likely to use the offset approach (just over half), whereas final-pay plans overwhelmingly used the step-rate approach (81 percent). Only 13 percent of conventional plans were nonintegrated.[24] The trend in the breaking point used in step-rate plans has been away from a specified dollar point to one that ad-

Table 4.5 Median Pension Benefits for 30 Years of Service Under Conventional Pension Plans, 1975 (percent of final year's compensation)

Final Year's Compensation	Final Pay Plans	Career Average Plans	Total Plans	Social Security Benefit
$ 9,000	30%	28%	29%	39%
15,000	33	31	32	25
25,000	36	35	35	15
50,000	38	37	38	8

Source: Bankers Trust Company, *1975 Study of Corporate Pension Plans*, p. 29.

Note: 5% annual salary increase used in computations.

justs automatically with the changes in the Social Security earnings base, which are also automatic now.[25]

Pension benefits themselves vary considerably, of course, according to the employee's salary and service history. For illustration, the Bankers Trust study has calculated the median benefit payable under the plans surveyed based on the current service formulas, 30 years of service, and 5-percent annual salary increases. Over the last five years, the median benefits as a percent of career-average or final-average salary show no significant changes, but benefit ratios including Social Security show a substantial increase due to the dramatic increases in Social Security benefits. Table 4.5 shows the approximate pension benefits as a percentage of final year's compensation under conventional plans according to the above assumptions for final-year compensation ranging from $9,000 to $50,000. For example, an employee retiring on January 1, 1975, after 30 years of service, who earned $9,000 in 1974, received from the median plan a benefit equal to 29 percent of his final year's compensation. The Social Security primary benefit added an additional 39 percent, for a total retirement income of $6,120, or 68 percent.

Because the 1970–1974 period encompasses the sharpest inflation of any five-year period since World War II, a substantial number of private pension plans have increased benefits for persons already retired. The Bankers Trust report indicates an average benefit increase for employees who retired in 1970 of 11 percent under pattern plans and 9 percent under conventional formula plans.[26]

Provisions for disability retirement are frequently provided under private retirement plans. Certain age and service requirements are usually established, and the disability must meet a stated definition of total and permanent disability. The 1975 Bankers Trust study reported that 75 percent of the conventional, defined-benefit formula plans offered disability retirement provisions and that 97 percent of the pattern plans offered such a benefit.[27]

Postretirement survivor benefits are provided by the vast majority of pension plans. The 1975 Bankers Trust study found that the most frequent methods, which do not involve added cost, are either through the operation of a joint-and-survivor option elected by the retiree or through the refund of employee contributions. Under the first method the employee chooses an actuarially reduced pension payable for his lifetime upon retirement, with some or all of the reduced pension continuing after his death to his beneficiary. Under the second method, used by some contributory plans, the retiree's contributions in excess of pension payments already received at time of death are refunded with interest to the beneficiary. A growing number of plans were found to provide post-retirement death benefits that require an additional cost on the company's part.[28] From 1976 on the Employee Retirement Income Security Act requires employers to make available automatically (unless the employee chooses to cancel it) an actuarial equivalent 50-percent joint-and-survivor option.

Contribution Rates. The periodic Bankers Trust pension studies reveal a continued trend among corporate pension plans toward noncontributory plans—those requiring no employee contribution. Pattern plans are virtually all noncontributory. Only 50 percent of the conventional plans were noncontributory in the period 1960–65 and 56 percent in 1965–70, but 67 percent are noncontributory in the current 1970–75 period studied. The survey calculated the range of employee contribution rates reported. The highest rates ranged from 4 to 5 percent of salary, the lowest from 0.2 to 0.9 percent, and the median ranged from 1.2 to 2.8 percent, including both mandatory contributions and voluntary contributions leading to a defined benefit.[29]

This chapter has summarized most of the characteristics of pension plans in the private sector today, except for the important provisions for the vesting of benefits and for plan funding. These questions are given separate treatment in separate chapters (7 and 8) because of their close relationship to larger questions of public policy.

—5—

Public Employee Retirement Plans

A person who can't pay, gets another person who
can't pay, to guarantee that he can pay.

Charles Dickens

Over 18 percent of all employees in
nonagricultural establishments are employees of government.[1] And substantially all full-time government employees—federal, state, and local—are covered under a retirement plan provided by their employer. Thus, a worker who enters government employment is virtually certain to become a member of a public employee retirement system. Approximately two out of three government employees will also be under Social Security. By way of contrast, a worker entering private employment has only about a 50 percent chance of joining an employer offering a private retirement plan, but he will automatically be covered by Social Security.

There are over 2,000 separate public employee retirement systems. The 1972 Census of Governments (Bureau of the Census) counted 2,304 systems administered by state and local governments, as follows: *

---

* Statistics based on U.S. Bureau of the Census, *Finances of Employee-Retirement Systems of State and Local Governments in 1972–73,* GF 73, No. 2 (March 1974):1.

State administered	176
Locally administered	2,128
Counties	165
Municipalities	1,818
Townships	119
School districts	16
Special districts	10

State and local government employment has been one of the fastest growing lines of work. In 1973 there were 8,838,000 full-time state and local government employees and 2,515,000 part-time, a total of 11,353,000—more than double the 5,570,000 employees counted in 1960.[2]

The huge Federal Civil Service Retirement System covers most civilian employees of the federal government. Covered employees numbered 2,665,600 in 1974 (an increase of 17.5 percent since 1960).[3] A few categories of federal employees are not included in the Civil Service retirement plan. These include the President of the United States, certain U.S. judges, and employees of federal government units with their own plans: the military forces, members of the Foreign Service Retirement System, the Tennessee Valley Authority, the Federal Reserve Board, and the Federal Reserve System. Members of the Armed Forces are covered under the Uniformed Services Retirement and Survivor Benefit System. As of mid-1971, career and noncareer military personnel employed by the Department of Defense numbered 2,202,000 persons.[4]

STATE AND LOCAL RETIREMENT SYSTEMS

As noted in Chapter 2, the first public retirement plans were established on the local levels of government, first for policemen and firefighters, somewhat later for teachers, and finally for other categories of public employees, both local and state. By the early 1940s about half of all state and local employees had some type of coverage under a public retirement system. Further growth of coverage took place throughout the rest of the 1940s and the 1950s, when retirement plan coverage was extended to many employee groups not previously eligible.[5]

Administering Governments. Locally administered retirement systems are numerous, but they account for less than one fifth (17.4 percent) of the total membership of state and local plans. The 176 retirement systems administered by state governments accounted in 1972 for about four fifths of total membership, two thirds of the assets, and two thirds of all the recurrent benefit payments reported for state and locally administered systems.[6]

The distinction between state and local designation pertains to responsibility for plan administration. Many of the state-administered plans cover employees of local governments as well as personnel of state governments. Over the decade between 1962 and 1972 there was a considerable increase in the number of members of general coverage systems taking in both state and local government employees.[7]

Employee Groups Covered. A state may operate more than one statewide plan. Practices differ among the states as to the number of separate state plans and the distribution of employee groups among the plans. Some states operate one large retirement system for public school teachers and another for all the other employees of the state. Other states have a single retirement plan whose membership includes both public school teachers and other employees of the state. In many states, college and university teachers in public institutions of higher education are covered under the TIAA-CREF retirement system (Teachers Insurance and Annuity Association and College Retirement Equities Fund) rather than under the state teacher or public employee plan. Separate smaller systems may coexist with the principal state system or systems, covering judges, the state police or highway patrol, the forest service, or other distinctive branches of the state government. In some states employees of political subdivisions participate automatically in a state-administered statewide retirement plan; in others such participation may be optional, and in yet others local governments may operate their own retirement systems.

Membership Eligibility. Full-time public employees are normally eligible for retirement plan participation as soon as they are hired. Only about 10 percent of the public retirement systems impose an age or service requirement for plan eligibility; when such a requirement is stated, the waiting period is usually 6 or 12 months. Entry age requirements are rare, although in some plans employees hired at a high age, over 60 for example, are excluded from membership.

Public employees are normally required to participate in the retirement plan as soon as they become eligible to do so.[8] Part-time and temporary public employees are usually not eligible for plan participation, although some states make permanent part-time employees eligible for plan membership.

Relation to Social Security. Before 1951 public employees were not eligible to participate in the federal Social Security program. Since then, amendments to the Social Security Act have made Social Security available to state and local employees if certain procedures are followed by the employing governmental unit. The law makes it possible for Social Security coverage to apply to all members of a state or local retirement system or to only a portion of its membership. Of all members of state and local plans in 1972, 23 percent were in plans in which membership applied to some groups within the plan, but not to others.[9] Taking all state and local plan members together, data from the Bureau of the Census indicate that 65 percent have coverage under Social Security along with plan membership, and 35 percent are not covered under Social Security in their regular public employment.[10]

Benefit Determinations. About 90 percent of the members of state and local systems are covered under systems that express retirement benefits as a formula. This is the same conventional three-element formula as that employed under most private retirement plans: a stated percentage times years of service times final average salary. The remaining 10 percent are covered under plans of the defined contribution type under which the benefit is the amount of monthly income purchased by individually allocated accumulated contributions and interest earnings.[11]

The Percentage Factor. The typical public employee retirement plan applies a single percentage factor to total final average salary. The factor varies from 1 percent to 2 percent, depending on the system, with the most frequently found factors in the neighborhood of 1.5 percent. Thus, 30 years of service would result in a benefit of 30 times 1.5 percent, or 45 percent, of final average salary. A few public systems are integrated with Social Security and apply two percentage factors to portions of final average salary in order to balance the benefits above and below the Social Security earnings base. Under a nonintegrated plan, total benefits are much higher as a percentage of final average salary within the Social Security earnings base than above it.

The Salary Factor. The benefit formulas of most of the state and local retirement plans state the salary factor in terms of "the highest three years of average salary" or "the highest five years." The idea of consecutive years may also be included. These final-average approaches enable the plans to relate benefits to the best levels of wage or salaries the employee has earned. The number of career-average plans is negligible.

The Service Factor. The employee's length of service while a member of the retirement plan may determine eligibility for early or normal retirement, nearly always determines eligibility for disability retirement, and in every case is a factor in the defined benefit formula. Normally there is no limitation on the number of an individual's years of covered service that may be incorporated in the formula, but a few plans do state a maximum, such as 35 or 40 years, or state a maximum percentage of final average salary that may result from the formula; for example, 80 percent of final average salary is the limit in Ohio and Rhode Island. In Ohio the maximum rises to 85 percent for employees delaying retirement to age 70. The few systems which have this type of maximum are usually those with formula percentage factors in the neighborhood of 2 percent per year of service.

The Formula Result. The formula calculations result in a single life annuity benefit. All of the state and local retirement systems allow the retiring employee to elect a reduced income with provision for life income to a spouse. Some states provide means for increasing benefits after retirement in order to cushion the adverse effects of inflation on retirees' incomes.

State and local retirement systems traditionally have been more liberal than private plans in providing pensions for survivors of employees who die before retirement. Compared with private plans they also provide richer benefit levels for comparable periods of service, and they cost more.

Contributions. State and local government retirement systems typically require employee contributions. The only noncontributory public employee retirement systems are in the city and state of New York. The most frequently reported employee contribution rate under state and local retirement systems is 5 percent of total salary. The range among plans is considerable, however, and there are variations, including limits on the part of salary on which contributions are made, higher percentages on one part of salary than another (step-rate), and percentage contributions related to age of entry into the plan.

A 1966 Social Security Administration study of state and local plans whose members were not covered under Social Security reported that 93 percent of covered employees contributed on total salary, and that the contribution rates ranged from 3 percent to 8.6 percent of salary, with a concentration at the level of 5 or 6 percent.[12]

A 1965 Social Security Administration study of public plans whose members were covered under Social Security found that about 10 percent of total membership contributed on a step-rate basis. In most systems the contribution was a uniform percentage of total salary; a few of these systems placed a ceiling on the amount of salary on which contributions were based. Although employee contribution percentages were reported as ranging among plans from 2 to 12 percent, most members were covered by systems requiring employee contributions of from 3.5 percent to 5 percent of salary, a somewhat lower level than that required in plans where employees are not covered by Social Security.[13]

As noted, most of the retirement plans of state and local governments state their benefits in terms of a defined benefit formula. The portion of the cost of the benefit promise that is not covered by the accumulation of funds attributed to the employee's contribution is the employer cost. In a few of the state and local plans the retirement benefit is stated in two parts, on a defined contribution basis for the employee's accumulated contributions and as a formula for the employer-provided portion. (See Chapter 8 for a discussion of the defined benefit and the defined contribution approaches.)

Interest may be credited on the employee's contributions at a stated rate or at the current portfolio earnings rate of the retirement fund. In plans in which the rate is stated as a nominal figure (which may be well below the portfolio earnings rate), the employee in effect takes over part of the public employer's contribution to the cost of the retirement benefits. One of the questions public plan administrators face is the equitability of the treatment of the earnings derived from employee contributions compared with earnings credited to employer contributions.

Normal Retirement. State and local retirement systems often provide for "normal" retirement before age 65. Normal retirement age is defined as the earliest age an employee who has qualified for benefits may retire at his own volition and receive benefits according to a stated formula without actuarial reduction. With exceptions in the auto, aluminum, steel, and certain other industries, age 65 is the predominant normal retirement age in private pension plans.

The surveys of state and local retirement systems conducted in the mid-1960s by the Social Security Administration found that approximately 60 percent of covered employees participated in systems that permit normal retirement full-formula benefits before age 65.[14] Most systems stating a very low normal retirement age (55) accompany the provision with a service requirement of 20, 25, or 30 years, depending on the system. Plans which state an age 60 normal retirement age also favor an accompanying service requirement, generally varying among systems from 10 to 30 years. Generally, where the normal retirement age is low, the service requirement tends to be high. Data on public plans permitting normal retirement under age 62 indicate that in 1965 one out of five men retiring from the public systems in that year did so at an age under 62.[15]

Members of state and local retirement systems are generally not required to retire when they first become eligible to do so, that is, when becoming eligible for normal retirement. Information provided by the systems suggest that many employees do in fact continue to work after completing age and service requirements that would enable them to receive full-formula benefits. In this event, ultimate retirement benefits are increased by any increments in the service and salary formula factors. For employees who cannot qualify for a service-related normal retirement, the typical practice is to provide for normal retirement without service requirements at age 65 or, sometimes, as early as age 62.

Involuntary retirement is provided for by about 79 percent of state and local plans, according to Social Security Administration surveys. Age 70 seems to be the most frequently stated age of compulsory retirement. In some states and localities age 65 is stated as an age of compulsory retirement unless the employer specifically allows a continuation of service. A later age may then be stated beyond which the employer is not permitted to authorize continued service.[16]

Early Retirement. Normal retirement for age or age plus service results in no actuarial reduction of benefits; early retirement usually does. Most of the state and local retirement systems permit their members to retire with permanently reduced benefits at a younger age or with less service than that stipulated for normal retirement. Where early retirement at reduced (defined) benefits is provided for, age, service, or age-service requirements are stated—a frequently stated requirement is age 55 with a minimum service of 20 years.[17] Early retirement with benefits beginning at once should be distinguished from employment termination with vested deferred benefits that are scheduled to be started at a later age, usually the stated normal retirement age.

Another form of retirement under state and local retirement systems is retirement for disability. Nearly all the systems have some such provisions, although the benefits are in some cases quite low, especially for younger employees when the formula disability income benefit is related to length of service or is actuarially reduced for age. Most of the disability income provisions of state and local retirement systems were introduced before the general availability of group insurance plans for long-term total disability, plans which normally provide significant amounts of monthly income and at the same time defer the need to begin the retirement benefit until the normal retirement age has been reached.

Vesting. Among state and local government retirement plans, immediate vesting of benefits is about as rare as it is among private retirement plans. The Social Security Administration's study in the mid-1960s of state and local plans indicated that a fraction over 1 percent of public employees belonged to plans in which benefits vested immediately on employment or on attainment of membership status. Another 1 percent belonged to plans vesting benefits after one year of membership. About 75 percent of the surveyed plans contained a service requirement for vesting, and an additional 10 percent held a combined age and service requirement. About 4 percent had some kind of arrangement for gradual vesting starting after a stated period of service, and the remainder used a variety of qualification criteria.[18]

The concentration points of service requirements for vesting were at 5, 10, 15, and 20 years. Thirty-one percent of the members of plans stating a service requirement were in plans vesting after 5 years, 18 percent were in plans vesting after 10 years, 23 percent in plans vesting after 15 years, and 19 percent in plans stating a 20-year requirement. Vesting provisions of public retirement systems are discussed in greater detail in Chapter 7.

FEDERAL CIVIL SERVICE RETIREMENT SYSTEM

In addition to the 2,665,600 active employees of the federal government belonging to the Federal Civil Service Retirement System in 1974, 942,529 retired federal employees and 368,078 survivors of active or retired employees were receiving benefits.[19]

Membership. Membership in the Federal Civil Service Retirement System is automatic for all eligible employees except in the case of members of Congress and certain employees of the legislative branch, who have the option of becoming members. Employees of the federal government do not participate as federal employees in the Social Security program.

Contributions. The Civil Service Retirement System requires contributions from both members and employing agencies. Employees other than members of Congress and Congressional employees pay 7 percent of salary.

Members of Congress pay 8 percent of salary and Congressional employees 7.5 percent. Each employing agency contributes amounts equal to the deductions of its employees.

As part of a program designed to provide for the reduction of unfunded liabilities resulting from new or liberalized benefits put into effect after October 20, 1969, the government is required by law to make direct appropriations from general revenue in amounts that, paid in equal annual installments over a 30-year period beginning in 1969, will liquidate post-1969 liabilities. In addition, the government is required to transfer to the retirement fund each year an amount equal to the interest on all outstanding unfunded liabilities for that year, including liabilities incurred prior to October 20, 1969.[20] The huge and growing unfunded liability of this system is discussed in Chapter 8.

Vesting. Deferred retirement benefits vest after five years of service. A terminating employee who leaves his money in the fund is entitled to an annuity at age 62 if he has had five or more years of service. A member separated with 10 years of service may receive an annuity when he reaches age 60; with 20 years of service a member may receive a reduced benefit when he reaches age 50.

Benefit Calculation. The Civil Service Retirement System uses the defined benefit approach. "Final average salary" is defined as the highest average basic salary earned during any three consecutive years of service. There is no maximum on the number of years of service that may be included in the calculation. The annuity benefit may not exceed 80 percent of the employee's final average salary. The percentage factor is applied in three successive steps according to years of service:

1.5% × final average salary × first 5 years' service

plus

1.75% × final average salary × second 5 years' service

plus

2% × final average salary × service over 10 years.

The aim and effect is to provide a benefit weighted in favor of long-service employees. Employees who have rendered 20 years of service in "the investigation, apprehension, or detention of persons suspected or convicted of offenses against the criminal laws of the United States" are eligible to retire after age 50 and receive an annuity of 2 percent of final average salary multiplied by the total number of years of service.[21]

Normal Retirement. A number of combinations of age and service are provided for under the Civil Service Retirement System for normal or "service" retirement without actuarial reduction of benefits. Retirement is compulsory at age 70 after 15 years of service. Normal retirement is permissible at the option of the employee at age 55 after 30 years of service or at age 60 with 20 years of service or at age 62 and 5 years of service. A member of Congress may retire at age 60 after 10 years of member service, or at age 62 after 5 years of service. The full-formula benefit is provided under the various conditions just outlined.

For involuntary separations after 25 years of service, or after age 50 and 20 years of service, a deferred benefit may be started at the full-formula rate at age 55, or an immediate annuity is payable equal to the formula annuity reduced by one sixth of 1 percent for each full month the employee is under age 55 at the date of separation.

At retirement the employee may choose a reduced annuity with an income option that continues an annuity to his spouse or other beneficiary in the event of the retired employee's death. A retiree who was unmarried at the time of retirement and who later marries may elect a changed annuity income option and accept a reduction in his current annuity and the addition of an annuity payable to the spouse upon his death.

After an employee or survivor annuity begins, annuities are increased whenever the Consumer Price Index has risen 3 percent. An upward adjustment is effective on the first day of the third month after a rise in the CPI equals at least 3 percent for three consecutive months over the prior base. The percentage increase is equal to the percentage increase in the CPI plus 1 percent. This provision and its costly compounding effects are described in greater detail in Chapter 8.

Disability Retirement. A disability retirement benefit is available for employees who become disabled (total and permanent disability) after five years of service. The benefit is determined by application of the full-formula benefit to the years of service up to the time of disability. The minimum annuity benefit for disability is 40 percent of the employee's final average salary. The disability annuity cannot be greater than the annuity the employee would be entitled to were his service to include the period elapsing between the date of disability and the date he attains age 60.

Survivor Benefits. In the event a federal employee dies before retiring, the Civil Service Retirement System provides for annuities for surviving dependents, defined as the spouse and children. The dependent survivor annuities are paid upon the death of an employee in active service at any time following the completion of 18 months of active employment. The widow or widower's benefit is an annuity (beginning after the death of the employee) equal to 55 percent of the regular annuity payable. In determining the regular annuity of the employee who dies under age 60, the minimum annuity is 40 percent of the employee's average salary but never greater than the annuity he or she would be entitled to were service to include the period elapsing between the date of death and the date the employee would have attained age 60.

The annuity to the surviving spouse of an employee who dies before retiring terminates upon death or upon remarriage prior to attainment of age 60. If there are surviving children, annuities are also payable to them until age 18 or to age 22 if they are students. The minimum such annuity is $900 per year.

UNIFORMED SERVICES RETIREMENT AND SURVIVOR BENEFIT SYSTEM

The uniformed services of the United States include the Army, Navy, Air Force, Marine Corps, Coast Guard, and the commissioned corps of the Public Health Service and of the National Oceanic and Atmospheric Administration. All are under the same retirement system, the Uniformed Services Retirement and Survivor Benefit System. The system is administered by the Office of the Assistant Secretary of Defense for Manpower and Reserve Affairs.

The Uniformed Services System is composed of three retirement systems plus a survivor benefit system that provides annuities, life insurance, lump-sum payments, and funeral and burial benefits.

The retirement systems provide, respectively, for nondisability retirement, disability retirement, and reserve retirement.

At the end of the 1972 fiscal year, total retired military personnel and survivors receiving benefits numbered approximately 867,000. The number of persons on the retired rolls has been increasing rapidly in recent years. This is illustrated in Table 5.1. In the 10-year period between 1953 and 1963 the number receiving benefits increased by 144 percent, going from 147,216 to 358,830. In the next 10-year period, 1963 to 1973, the number increased 160 percent, from 358,830 to 946,080. The increases are directly attributable to the fact that a large number of personnel who entered the armed forces during World War II have attained eligibility for retirement. The Department of Defense projects further large increases and a total of 1,241,000 retired military personnel and survivors for the year 1978. Also predicted is a rise in annual costs from the $4.4-billion level in 1973 to $5.9 billion in 1978.

Financing. The Uniformed Services System is supported on a "pay-as-you-go" basis. Each year each branch of the service determines its obligation for retirement pay under the various categories of retirement (nondisability, temporary disability, permanent disability, and survivors' benefits) and submits the figure to the Department of Defense, which aggregates the amounts and submits to Congress the required budget for the year in question. There are no employee contributions. As indicated in Table 5.1, the payment budget for 1973 was approximately $4.4 billion, with estimated budgets for the future increasing to accommodate increased retirements and higher pay scales. Total liabilities accrued to the end of the 1972 fiscal year were estimated to be approximately $121.4 billion. No funds have been set aside to meet these obligations. The financing of this plan is discussed further in Chapter 8.[22]

Nondisability Retirement System. The nondisability system is the largest of the three component systems for members of the uniformed services. Originally, nondisability retirement occurred only at the advanced ages generally associated with superannuation and withdrawal from the work force. With a very modest military force and older retirement ages, only a small number of military men retired each year. However, the system has changed

Table 5.1 Annual Cost of the Uniformed Service Retirement and Survivor Benefit System

Fiscal Year	Number of Recipients	Annual Cost
1953	147,216	$ 356,385,000
1958	208,570	560,962,000
1963	358,830	1,014,775,000
1968	624,496	2,093,477,000
1973	946,080	4,442,249,000
1978 (projected)	1,241,000	5,866,000,000

Source: Office of the Assistant Secretary of Defense, Manpower, and Reserve Affairs, Actuarial Consultant, 1973.

gradually into its present state in which nondisability retirements can occur as early as age 37. The evolution is the result of the creation of a large American military machine and a policy of staffing the armed forces with young men and separating them at an early age. With approximately 725,000 nondisability retirees as of June 30, 1972, it is expected that for the next five years new retirees will be added at the rate of over 50,000 each year.

For regular nondisability retirement, a member who has completed 20 or more years of active military service may be retired at full service-related benefits regardless of age. In the case of a commissioned officer, at least 10 years of the 20 years of active service must have been as a commissioned officer. (See Chapter 8 for illustrations of the cost of such retirement provisions.)

Regular nondisability retirement benefits are computed by multiplying the basic pay to which the individual was entitled when retired by 2.5 percent times the number of years of service. The benefit may not exceed 75 percent of final basic pay.[23] For retirement with the minimum service requirement of 20 years, the benefit is 50 percent of final pay.

Disability Retirement System. The disability retirement system is the oldest of the three military retirement systems, tracing its origin to the Revolutionary War. In "normal peacetime years," according to the Department of Defense, the number of disability retirements for all services averages about 9,000 per year. Approximately 156,000 members, or about 20 percent of the total retired personnel of the uniformed services, were classified as disabled as of June 30, 1972.[24]

For disability retirement the disability must be determined to be permanent. Further conditions are that either the individual has at least 20 years of service or the disability is 30 percent or more under Veterans' Administration standards, and that either the individual has completed 8 years of active service and the disability is the proximate result of performing active duty, or the individual incurred the disability in line of duty during war or national emergency.

The disability retirement benefit is computed as basic pay multiplied by the percentage of disability as established under the Veterans' Administration rating scale, or by 2.5 percent times years of service, whichever is the greater. Retired disability pay cannot exceed 75 percent of the basic pay of the individual's retired grade.

Reserve Retirement System. The reserve retirement system is the smallest of the three component systems. It provides deferred annuities for reserve retirees. Since payments under this system do not commence until the member reaches age 60, the impact of the large reserve forces maintained since World War II is not yet reflected in the number of reservists receiving retired pay. Currently, they number about 48,500. By 1986 the number of reserve annuitants is expected to increase to about 132,000.[25]

Survivor Benefits. A survivor benefit plan provides for income benefits under stated conditions for survivors of members of the Uniformed Services System who die before retiring, and for the survivors of retirees. The survivor benefit plan is modeled after the postretirement survivor protection program for career civil service personnel.[26]

Social Security. Since January 1, 1957, armed forces personnel on active duty have been included in the Social Security program on a contributory basis and have paid Social Security taxes on the same basis as other covered employees.

Vesting. There is no vesting of benefits under the Uniformed Services System on termination of service prior to eligibility for retirement. Retirement benefits based on service of less than 20 years are provided for disability retirement only. The absence of vesting is regarded by system officials as a weakness of the plan. Current legislative proposals have been submitted to the Congress recommending vesting for a deferred benefit to commence at age 60, after 5 years of service if separation is involuntary, and after 10 years of service for voluntary terminations.[27]

This chapter and the preceding one have attempted to show the extent of coverage and the types of provisions in the retirement plans of both the public and private sectors.

Our next step is to examine private and public employee pension plans in terms of their long-range capacity to do the job intended. Basically, this involves financial strength—funding—and the capacity to assure people of benefit payments under the widest possible variety of circumstances—vesting.

—6—

Investments of Pension Funds

Cannot people realize how large an income is thrift?
Marcus Tullius Cicero

The invested assets of pension plans play several roles. They are the immediate source of most of the funds paid out as benefits and assure that funds will be available for these payments. They are a source of income that can either reduce the cost of the pension fund to the employer or increase the payments provided to plan beneficiaries, and they are now a major source of capital to drive the economy.

This chapter will examine how pension plans have invested in the past, how they invest at the present time, and how they may invest in the future. It will also examine how the countless investment decisions made by pension funds affect the economy and, in particular, financial markets.

MANAGEMENT OF PENSION FUNDS

For the purpose of analyzing their investments, pension plans can be divided into four classes:

1. Federal social programs and programs for federal government employees
2. Programs for state and local government employees
3. Private noninsured pension plans
4. Private insured plans

These four types have followed different investment patterns. Each is subject to different legal constraints.

The funds of the Social Security program and the Federal Civil Service Retirement System are invested in interest-bearing federal government obligations, in obligations guaranteed as to both principal and interest by the United States, or in certain federally sponsored agency obligations. These obligations may be acquired on original issue at the issue price or by purchase of outstanding obligations at their market price. In view of the limited scope of permitted investments this chapter gives little attention to the investments of these federal plans.

State and local employee pension funds are operated as distinct entities with separate reserves. The states' own plans are self-administered. Sometimes localities become part of the state system and their employees participate in and receive benefits from the state plan much as if they were state employees. In other cases, localities administer their own plans, including investing the assets held in reserve for pension obligations.

Private plans are either insured or noninsured. An insured plan is defined as one that is managed by an insurance company; all other plans are noninsured. About a third of all private plan assets are managed by insurance companies.

Banks manage about four fifths of the total noninsured pension assets. The percentage of all plan assets held by banks has been declining in recent years, but banks continue to manage the large plans, and the big banks manage most of the plan assets. In 1970, 3 banks managed over one third of all plan assets in the custody of banks, and 22 banks administered 75 percent of all bank-managed plan assets. There is some evidence in recent years that pension funds have been changing bank managers more frequently in a search for "performance," and that more large funds are now managing their own investments. More funds are also splitting their investments among a number of managers.[1]

PRIVATE PENSION PLAN INVESTMENTS BEFORE 1945

Prior to 1916 there were few private pension plans and nearly all of them were managed by the sponsoring companies. If the plans were funded at all, the employer would typically devote a fixed amount to the plan, with the thought of replenishing the fund from time to time as the original capital was depleted by benefit payments. There was no direct relationship between the capital provided to a plan and the value of the pension benefits that might ultimately be paid to its beneficiaries. Only 14 of the 20 pre-1916 plans surveyed by the National Industrial Conference Board were funded in even this rudimentary way.[2] As a result, total assets of pension plans prior to 1916 were negligible.

In the years following 1916, insured plans came into use. In the period from 1916 to 1929, some 40 insured pension plans were started, covering 55,000 individuals.[3] But the insured plans were too few in number to have much effect on the total of invested assets held by private pension plans. Accordingly, in the period 1916 to 1929 the only private pension reserves of significance were those of noninsured funds.

In 1922, the private noninsured pension funds had total assets of $90 million, of which $9 million was invested in U.S. government securities, $55 million in the sponsoring corporations' own bonds, $18 million in stocks, and $8 million in cash and other assets. By 1929, the total assets of pension funds excluding insured plans had reached $500 million. Of this, $50 million was invested in U.S. government obligations, $300 million in the sponsoring corporations' bonds, $100 million in stocks, and $50 million in cash and other assets. During these early days, about 10 percent of noninsured pension fund assets were in U.S. government obligations; this proportion did not change significantly until the period of World War II.[4]

Beginning in 1939, private pension plans began to invest more heavily in securities other than those issued by the sponsoring corporation. A small portion of these investments was placed in other corporations' common and preferred stock. A major part of the growth of noninsured private pension fund assets in this period was in securities of the federal government. In 1939, only 15 percent of the funds' assets were invested in federal securities. By 1945, this proportion had risen to 45 percent. The emphasis on federal securities was due to a desire to assist in the financing of the government's mobilization and war costs, and to a dearth of alternative investments available during wartime. Total noninsured private pension fund growth continued through the war years, so that by the end of 1945 total assets equalled $2.9 billion, an increase of over $1.85 billion in the six war years.[5]

PRIVATE PLAN INVESTMENTS SINCE 1945

Both insured and noninsured plans grew substantially throughout the post-World War II period. Table 6.1 compares the funds managed by insurance companies with those managed independently for selected years since 1950, the first year for which such data are available.

Insured pension plans grew tenfold between 1950 and 1974, but noninsured plans grew twice as fast, so that by the end of the period they represented more than two thirds of the total assets. Because insurance companies have been more heavily regulated than self-managed and trusteed pension plans, the two types of plans have tended to follow different directions in investing.

From 1945 to 1952, the total assets of noninsured private pension funds more than doubled, growing at the highest rate that these funds have experienced to date. During this period the noninsured private funds began a long-term move away from U.S. government securities. At the end of 1952, approximately 24 percent of noninsured private pension plan assets were invested in government securities, compared with 45 percent in 1945.[6] After 1952 the funds began to move out of government bonds at an even faster pace, so that by the end of 1971 these bonds constituted only 2.2 percent of the funds' assets.

Additionally, private noninsured funds began to increase the percent of assets held in common stocks. As illustrated by Table 6.2, the twin movements out of U.S. government bonds and into common stocks continued until 1972 to be the dominating tendencies of noninsured pension fund in-

Table 6.1 Assets of Private Pension Funds—Book Value ($ billions)

	1950	1955	1961	1966	1971	1973	1974
Insured pension reserves (including separate accounts)	$ 5.6	$11.2	$20.2	$29.4	$ 46.4	$ 56.0	$ 59.5
Noninsured pension funds	6.1	15.3	37.5	66.2	106.4	126.5	133.7
Total	11.7	26.5	57.7	95.6	152.8	182.5	193.2

Sources: 1966–1974: Securities and Exchange Commission, *Statistical Bulletin* 34 (April 1975):335; *Statistical Bulletin* 33 (April 1974):459. *1950–1961: Statistical Bulletin* 29 (May 1970):24.

Table 6.2 Assets of Private Noninsured Pension Funds ($ millions)

Asset Classes	1951		1961		1971		1974	
Cash and deposits	$ 330	4.2%	$ 700	1.5%	$ 1,600	1.3%	$ 4,300	3.8%
U.S. government securities	2,440	30.7	2,700	6.0	2,800	2.2	5,600	5.0
Corporate bonds	3,480	43.8	15,900	35.1	26,100	20.6	30,800	27.6
Preferred stock	370	4.7	700	1.5	2,000	1.6	700	0.6
Common stock	980	12.3	22,100	48.8	86,600	68.3	62,600	56.0
Own company	N/A [a]	N/A	3,000	6.6	7,700	6.1	N/A	N/A
Other companies	N/A	N/A	19,100	42.2	78,900	62.2	N/A	N/A
Mortgages	120	1.5	1,600	3.5	3,200	2.5	2,100	1.8
Other assets	230	2.9	1,600	3.5	4,500	3.6	5,700	5.1
Total assets	7,960	100.0	45,300	100.0	126,900	100.0	111,700	100.0

Sources: 1974: Securities and Exchange Commission, *Statistical Bulletin* 34 (April 1975):333–334. *1971: Statistical Bulletin* 31 (July 1972):28. *1951 and 1961: Statistical Bulletin* 20 (January 1961):13.

Notes: Assets include deferred profit sharing plans.

Data are rounded to nearest $10 million for 1951, nearest $100 million for 1961 to 1974. 1951 is computed at book value, 1961 to 1974 at market value. Figures may not add to totals because of rounding.

[a] N/A—Not available.

vestments. In 1973 and 1974, holding of government securities showed a substantial increase for the first time since World War II.

Between 1961 and 1974, the assets of private noninsured pension funds grew by $66 billion, thus more than doubling in size. Forty billion dollars of the total growth was in common stocks. Table 6.3 presents the net purchases for major institutional holders of stock. Since 1955 the value of stocks accumulated by private noninsured pension funds has exceeded the total accumulated by the three other major institutional groups of investors that acquire stocks for their own accounts: mutual funds, life insurance companies, and property and liability insurance companies.

Table 6.4 shows the stockholdings of institutional and individual investors. In 1961, the value of stocks held by pension funds was less than the value of stocks held by investment companies. Stocks were purchased at a rapid rate by private plans between 1961 and 1973 so that by 1974 the private plans held more than twice the value of stock held by any other institutional investors. The only class of investors owning more stock than private noninsured pension funds was that of individuals, either directly or through trust funds.

In spite of their large stock holdings, private pension funds have not dominated the stock markets. Compared with other institutional investors, pension funds have traded their stocks relatively infrequently. This is shown by data on "activity rates," which are defined as the average of purchases and sales divided by average market value of stockholdings, expressed as an annual rate (Table 6.5). Of all major institutional investors, noninsured pen-

Table 6.3 Net Purchases of Common Stock of Major Financial Institutions ($ millions)

	1955	1960	1966	1971	1974
Private noninsured pension funds	$865	$1,940	$3,445	$8,885	$2,412
Open-end investment companies	365	785	1,045	380	−287
Life insurance companies	60	185	280	3,455	1,255
Property and liability insurance companies	N/A [a]	240	80	2,225	−823

Sources: *1955–1971:* Securities and Exchange Commission, *Statistical Bulletin* 32 (March 1973):248. *1974: Statistical Bulletin* 34 (April 1975):329.

[a] N/A—Not available.

sion funds have had since 1968 the lowest activity rate, indicating relatively infrequent turnover of portfolio.

INVESTMENTS OF INSURED PENSION PLANS

Insured pension assets are usually commingled with other insurance assets and thus have been subject to the same constraints as are the other assets. Each insurance company is regulated by the state in which it is domiciled and also by those states in which it does business.

The long-term liabilities of life insurance companies traditionally are expressed as fixed-dollar amounts. These liabilities represent such obligations as the promise to pay a specified number of dollars of benefits upon death, or to provide continuing incomes of a certain dollar amount to annuitants. As a result, until recently, while a major investment vehicle for the private noninsured pension plans has been common stock, the prime investments for insurance companies, including assets held on behalf of pension plans, have been mortgages and bonds, the latter including direct placement obligations.

Table 6.4 Stockholdings of Institutional and Individual Investors ($ billions)

	1956	1961	1966	1971	1974
Private noninsured pension funds	$ 7.1	$ 22.9	$ 39.5	$ 88.7	$ 63.3
State and local retirement funds	0.1	0.6	2.1	15.4	16.8
Investment companies (shares not owned by institutions or personal trusts)	13.7	28.1	35.3	53.5	29.0
Life insurance companies	3.5	6.3	8.8	20.6	22.2
Property and liability insurance companies	5.6	9.3	11.0	16.6	12.6
Common trust funds	1.2	2.2	3.3	5.8	5.3
Mutual savings banks	0.7	1.0	1.5	4.1	3.3
Foundations	12.1	15.2	18.7	25.0	18.4
Educational endowments	3.4	5.0	6.2	9.0	6.2
Foreign investors	10.2	16.2	18.1	32.7	26.3
Personal trust funds	31.8	54.2	66.7	94.1	70.9
Domestic individuals	232.8	360.4	436.6	630.5	363.9
Total stock outstanding	322.1	521.4	647.8	996.0	638.2

Sources: 1956–1966: Securities and Exchange Commission, *Statistical Bulletin* 33 (August 1974):805–806. *1971–1974: Statistical Bulletin* 34 (May 1975):439.

Beginning in the early 1960s, insurance companies began to adopt variable annuities, with liabilities expressed as units rather than dollars. They also began to put the assets supporting pension obligations into separate accounts. Assets in separate accounts may be invested without being constrained by the restrictions that are placed on other insurance company assets. In 1974, over 66 percent of all separate account assets were in common stock. As shown in Table 6.6, some assets are held in preferred stock, mortgages, real estate, and cash. There is no legal or investment reason why, in the future, the holdings of these other investment vehicles for separate accounts could not increase relative to the holdings of stock.

In the seven-year period from 1967 to 1974, the assets of separate accounts grew nearly eightfold. While the total common stock holdings of these funds ($6.2 billion) is still negligible compared with the holdings of the private noninsured pension funds ($63.3 billion), the rate of growth suggests that within a very few years these separate accounts may become another important force in the stock market.

When benefit promises are expressed in fixed dollars, it is appropriate that the investments supporting these promises be fixed-dollar assets. Although differing in detail, the insurance laws of the 50 states reflect this judgment by requiring that about 90 percent of the investments of life insurance companies be fixed-dollar assets, such as bonds and mortgages, and by limiting the amount that can be invested in assets of widely varying value, such as preferred stocks, common stocks, and real estate. Indeed, from 1906 until 1950, life insurance companies licensed in New York could not invest in common stocks. This prohibition was partially a reflection of earlier insurance company excesses, but also reflected concern as to the risks of common

Table 6.5 Common Stock Activity Rates of Major Institutional Investors

	1966	1971	1973	1974
Private noninsured pension funds	12.6%	22.1%	17.3%	14.1%
Open-end investment companies	34.0	48.2	39.0	30.5
Life insurance companies	16.0	31.0	25.0	18.6
Property and liability insurance companies	8.6	23.2	20.3	19.8

Sources: Securities and Exchange Commission, *Statistical Bulletin* 33 (April 1974):404. *Statistical Bulletin* 34 (April 1975):329.

stock investments. For a great many companies, this historical set of circumstances resulted in investment portfolios that even today are composed largely of publicly issued government and industrial bonds, low-risk, low-return portfolios. These low-risk investments have in the past seemed to be acceptable to the public, which was seeking maximum security of cash benefits.

The low investment returns may have been suitable for assuring shorter-term cash life insurance benefits, but they were not very competitive with noninsured plans when used to fund retirement benefits. Very little effort was made to invest on a "total return" basis, which emphasizes optimum yield and capital gains over longer periods of time. Insufficient effort was made to obtain better returns by analyzing risk-reward relationships. It has been suggested that, until recently, many life insurance companies did not have investment staffs that would permit them to follow the total return concept. In a study of insurance company investment policies, Lawrence D. Jones of Harvard University observed: "For most [insurance] companies, the labor, capital, and material resources employed in making investment decisions represent a negligible portion of total resources utilized by the companies. Although not unknown, it is quite rare for the chief executive officer of a life insurance company to have had experience in the investment side of the business." [7]

To a considerable extent, developments in investment strategies for state

Table 6.6 Distribution of Assets Held in Separate Accounts—U.S. Life Insurance Companies ($ millions)

Year	Bonds	Stocks Common	Preferred	Mortgages	Real Estate	Cash	Other	Total
1967	$ 114	$1,055	$ 9	$ 14	— [a]	$13	$ 2	$ 1,207
1969	638	2,745	48	36	$ 1	52	99	3,619
1971	763	6,416	83	87	24	88	62	7,523
1973	1,581	7,900	53	171	186	64	75	10,030
1974	2,326	6,158	34	202	372	57	127	9,276

Source: Institute of Life Insurance, *Life Insurance Fact Book, 1975* (New York: Institute of Life Insurance, 1975), p. 81.

[a] Less than $500,000.

and local employee pension funds have paralleled those of private plans, but with a considerable delay. In the 1930s the private plans began making investments in securities other than those issued by the sponsoring corporations. It was not until the early 1940s that the state and local plans began to invest in other than state and local obligations.[8]

In the early 1950s, noninsured private plans began to invest in common stocks. The development of separate accounts in the early 1960s provided the vehicle through which the insured private plans could make major equity investments. The state and local funds began making major investments in common stocks in the late 1960s, although, with stocks constituting 23 percent of their assets in 1973, they have yet to have as high a percentage of their assets in stocks as do the private plans. Table 6.7 shows that bonds still account for the major holdings of the state and local plans.

CURRENT INVESTMENT TRENDS

Are some types of investments neglected by pension funds? Table 6.8 shows that, except for insurance companies, managers of pension funds have not chosen to enter to any great extent in the mortgage or individual loan markets. About 10 percent of total private pension plan assets have been invested in home or other mortgages, less than 2 percent in direct loans to individuals, and 4 percent in government securities. On the other hand, one

Table 6.7 Assets of State and Local Employee Retirement Plans ($ billions)

Asset Classes	1956	1961	1966	1971	1973
Demand deposits and currency	$ .2	$ .3	$ .4	$ .7	$ 1.0
Corporate shares	.2	.6	2.1	11.2	18.6
U.S. government securities	5.0	6.1	7.8	5.1	4.6
State and local obligations	3.1	4.3	2.5	2.1	1.4
Corporate bonds	3.0	8.5	20.2	38.1	49.4
Mortgages	.4	1.9	4.5	7.1	6.7
Other	.2	.4	.7	2.0	N/A
Total [a]	12.1	22.0	37.4	64.4	81.6

Sources: 1956: Federal Reserve Bulletin 55 (November 1969):71.19. 1961: Federal Reserve Bulletin 58 (June 1972):73.20. 1966–1973: Federal Reserve Bulletin 60 (October 1974):59.26.

[a] Totals do not equal 100% because of rounding.

third of the assets are in corporate and foreign bonds (principally corporate), and 45 percent in common stock.

Although direct data are not available, it does not appear that private pension funds and state and local retirement funds have entered to any great extent the private placement market. Most of the corporate stocks and bonds held by pension funds are the widely distributed and easily marketable offerings of major corporations. This neglect of private placements could mean that the investment patterns of pension funds are helping to distort the financial markets. By concentrating on the offerings of major corporations, the funds may thereby be underutilizing the substantial opportunities for long

Table 6.8 Distribution of Pension Assets, December 31, 1973 ($ billions)

	Life Insurance Companies		Private Non-insured Pension Funds		State and Local Retirement Funds		Total	
Corporate shares	$ 4.8	9.5%	$ 89.2	67.4%	$18.6	17.3%	$112.6	45.4%
Corporate and foreign bonds	18.6	37.0	29.8	22.6	49.4	55.9	97.8	33.4
Home mortgages	5.8	11.5	2.7	2.9	—	—	8.5	3.4
Mortgages other than on homes	12.0	23.9	—	—	6.7	11.0	18.7	6.8
U.S. government securities	.9	1.8	4.3	2.1	4.6	9.3	9.8	4.0
Loans, not elsewhere classified	4.7	9.3	—	—	—	—	4.7	1.5
State and local government securities	.8	1.6	—	—	1.4	2.9	2.2	1.1
Cash	.4	0.8	2.3	1.2	1.0	.8	3.7	1.0
Miscellaneous	2.3	4.6	4.9	3.7	—	3.1	7.2	3.6
Total	50.4	100.0	133.3	100.0	81.6	100.0	265.3	100.0

Sources: Federal Reserve Bulletin 60 (October 1974): A59-15; Institute of Life Insurance, *Life Insurance Fact Book 1974* (New York: Institute of Life Insurance, 1974), pp. 67–69.

Note: Pension assets of life insurance companies are estimated, based upon the Federal Reserve statements of assets by type, distributed in accordance with total life insurance liabilities (including reserves) and surplus.

range, productive investments in smaller companies and for new and emerging enterprises, as well as helping to cause a shortage of capital funds for these concerns.

Not only do pension funds invest heavily in common stocks, they concentrate on relatively few issues. Over 90 percent of the common stocks held by pension funds are listed on the New York Stock Exchange. Very few pension funds own stock not listed on the New York Stock Exchange except for stocks of major banks and insurance companies, some of which are now listed on the Big Board. Thus, rather than participating in all equity markets including stocks issued by many thousands of companies, pension funds largely limit themselves to a single market, the New York Stock Exchange, which in 1974 listed the common stock of only 1,567 companies.[9]

Furthermore, pension funds sharply limit their purchases among the shares of the NYSE-listed companies. The Securities and Exchange Commission's *Institutional Investor Study* determined that all institutional investors, including pension funds, tend to concentrate on the small number of stocks that have large total market values.[10]

The study found that [in 1969] significant portions of all institutional portfolios were invested in a relatively small number of stocks of the same large well-known companies. . . . The study found that institutions generally preferred the securities of larger companies to those of small firms.[11]

The current prices of stocks listed on the NYSE are widely reported. The SEC requires the disclosure of detailed financial information, and the NYSE and SEC limit and regulate the activities of insiders and specialists. There are numerous investment analysis services that regularly follow Big Board-listed issues; as a result, selections can be made among NYSE-listed stocks on the basis of readily available information, and this makes Big Board stocks excellent investment vehicles for less sophisticated investors, including many pension funds. Nevertheless, the concentration of investment funds in a relatively narrow class of stocks, those listed on the NYSE, does raise questions as to how the venture capital for smaller, emerging business is to be supplied.

Recently pension funds have been one of the largest net purchasers of common stock. The SEC's tabulations of the stock transactions of selected financial institutions show that, of the institutions studied (private noninsured pension funds, open-end investment companies, life insurance companies, and property and liability insurance companies), in the first half of 1974 private pension funds purchased $1.3 billion out of total net purchases of $1.355 billion.[12]

IMPACT OF PENSIONS UPON SAVINGS

The beneficial impact of pensions upon individual economic security would be reduced if families participating in pension plans save less than those who do not participate in pension plans. Whether, in fact, pensions tend to stimulate or retard other forms of savings depends upon how individuals view their pensions. If pensions are viewed as comparable to, say, savings accounts, then families may save less. They may reason that they have achieved part of their savings goals through their pension plans and thus can spend a greater proportion of their current income.

On the other hand, pensions may be viewed as being a different form of savings, for a different purpose. Then families will attempt to maintain other forms of savings at the same levels as they would have in absence of pension plans. Since pensions are in a fact a type of savings, the effect will be to increase total savings.

Finally, families may view private pensions as a partial step toward a goal that otherwise would be unachievable: the attaining of a truly adequate retirement income. Furthermore, the pension may serve as a constant reminder that provision must be made for the retirement years. Under these circumstances, pensions may induce families to increase their savings goals so that, at retirement, personal savings will be available to complement income from Social Security and private pensions. This effect, of course, would tend to die out once people felt their pensions plus Social Security were entirely adequate by themselves.[13]

Two surveys have attempted to measure whether families participating in pension plans saved more or less than those that did not participate. In the mid 1960s, Phillip Cagan surveyed a sample of subscribers to *Consumer Reports*. He concluded that "when households come under a pension plan, offsetting reductions in other savings do not occur." [14] About the same time, George Katona, using a more random sample that was designed to represent all households in the continental United States, also found that participation in pension plans tended to increase total individual savings.[15] These findings were reinforced by Vincent Apilado, who applied the techniques of multiple regression to such data as personal savings, the Consumer Price Index, disposable personal income, and the money stock.[16]

These findings conflict with evidence provided in both earlier and later studies. In particular, one recent study, based upon Canadian tax returns, concludes that the rich increase total savings in the presence of pensions, but that pensions may reduce the total saving of poor and middle-income classes.[17] While the best evidence seems to indicate that pensions do increase savings, the issue is still in doubt. Phillip Cagan and Roger Murray of Columbia University are only two of the experts who have pointed to the need for further information and urged that further research on this subject be conducted.

THE FUTURE GROWTH OF PENSION FUND INVESTMENTS

The recent growth in the size of pension fund invested assets has been impressive. As shown in Table 6.1, pension funds have grown faster in the last 10 years than any of the other major financial institutions. Will this continue over the next 20 years? The most recent systematic projection of pension assets was done in 1966 by Daniel Holland. His projections for private pension funds were made in terms of ranges. Based on recent data, it seems reasonable to conclude that the highest of his projections will be the most accurate. His high projection of private noninsured pension assets for 1981 is $214.2 billion, compared to $128.4 billion in total assets in 1971.[18] While projected magnitude in the growth of assets in the period from 1971 to 1982 is substantial, the estimate implies a decrease in the rate of growth over that experienced for much of the first half of the 20th century.

Holland's projections for the assets of state and local governments were not advanced with much confidence, and his 1971 projections proved to be substantially too low. The underestimate was due in part to an assumption that funding standards for such plans would continue to be poor, when in fact they have been improving. The growth of state and local government employment was also underestimated, as was the percentage increase in contributions per state and local government employee.[19]

We project that 1982 assets of state and local funds will be $180 billion. This figure was derived from Holland's estimates by adjusting for his underestimate of the 1971 total, incorporating the upgrading of state and local retirement plan vesting standards, and by assuming continued increases in the number of state and local employees. The estimate is based on guesses at future vesting and funding standards in state and local employment; accordingly, the estimated assets for 1982, nearly one-half trillion dollars, should only be viewed as suggesting future trends.

Table 6.9 summarizes actual 1961 and 1971 pension fund assets and estimated 1981 total assets for the various types of pension plans.

FUTURE PENSION FUND INVESTMENTS

One recent trend in pension investing is almost certain to continue: the differences in investment approach among the various nonfederal types of pension funds may be expected to decrease. We have already shown that, from about 1952 to 1972, the prime investment vehicle for private noninsured pension funds has been common stocks. Insurance companies have invested nearly all of their assets, including those reserved for pension funds, in publicly offered bonds, direct placements, and mortgages. State and local retirement funds have traditionally invested in fixed-income securities. However, the most recent data have indicated that the state and local funds are moving into common stocks, as have the insurance companies through the use of separate accounts. In short, state and local retirement funds and insurance companies are beginning to invest in the same types of securities as do the private noninsured funds.

But what the data do not show is the increasing interest of state and local

Table 6.9 Summary of Pension Plan Assets ($ billions)

Type	1961	1971	1981 [a]
Private plans	$63.5	$172.9	$306.0
Noninsured	41.9	128.4	214.2
Insured	21.6	44.5	91.8
State and local retirement plans	24.2	64.8	180.0
Total	$87.7	$237.7	$486.0

Source: Daniel M. Holland, *Private Pension Funds: Projected Growth* (New York: National Bureau of Economic Research, 1966), p. 8.

[a] Estimated assets.

and private noninsured funds in real estate, direct placements, and mortgages, all of which have heretofore been primarily associated with the insured funds.[20] Mortgages, for example, have certain advantages that make them natural investment vehicles for pension funds. As long-term investments for pension funds, mortgages and real estate provide stability and, at the same time, a constant cash flow of investment income.[21]

Why then, have mortgage investments not increased more substantially in the investment portfolios of private noninsured funds? A major reason is the different type of analysis necessary for mortgages and the impossibility of having the same type of data and information flow available that is present for common stocks. Information on common stocks, particularly the small group of NYSE stocks favored by private pensions funds, is readily available. Furthermore, at any given moment, there are a number of analysts more than ready to offer their comments on widely held stocks. Finally, most managers of private pension funds have been trained in investing in common stocks and feel comfortable in that investment vehicle.

Mortgages are a different matter. There is no governmental body trying to make sure that information on mortgages is complete and accurate, as the Securities and Exchange Commission does with common stocks. An institution making a mortgage loan needs to know a good deal about the borrowers, developers, and lessees of the property, and should be familiar with the neighborhood in which property is located. Each mortgage and each location is separate and distinct, while one share of a corporation's common stock is just like another of the same corporation. In addition, there is a good deal of technical law of the various states that must be taken into account whenever a mortgage is accepted.

Direct real estate investments would also seem to be good investments for pension funds. As Roger Murray has pointed out:

> The ideal pension fund asset . . . is one which possesses stability, and one with which is associated a predictable and constantly increasing growth rate. It is possible that no type of investment fits so neatly into the pension fund mold as does real estate.

However, there are particular problems with real estate as an investment for private pension funds.

> The ownership of real estate equities would appear to be a natural avenue of investment. . . . The tax-exempt status of a private pension plan, however, can be impaired by engaging in an unrelated business. The operation of income-producing

property, especially if the purchase is financed with borrowed funds and only an equity position is retained, is susceptible to being considered such an unrelated business.[22]

The problems related to taxation of unrelated business income can be resolved, although a level of expertise not normally present in a small fund is required. Another problem with real estate investments is that the tax benefits associated with such properties are of no use to pension funds. To a real estate operator, the tax benefits from accelerated depreciation, and his ability to introduce substantial financial leverage, usually justify his paying a higher price for property than a pension fund is prepared to pay without these possibilities.

Many of the problems that make it difficult for smaller pension funds to invest in real estate are potentially avoidable if they invest in long-term, well-run real estate investment trusts (REIT), which permit organizations and individuals to share in the benefits of real estate investments without themselves having to make the investments. As long as the trust distributes at least 90 percent of its net income to those that participate in the trust, it does not have to pay federal income taxes on the distributed income. The trust itself is responsible for avoiding the unrelated-business income tax problems. Thus, it is a potentially useful investment vehicle for those pension funds unwilling or unable to make direct investments in real estate but desirous of benefiting from such investments.[23]

In spite of the difficulties of real estate and mortgages as investment vehicles for pension funds, many funds are now beginning to make such investments, and others, both private and to a far lesser extent governmental, are giving serious consideration to such investments.

There also seems to be some interest on the part of noninsured pension funds in seeking out direct placement loans. They are not as liquid as publicly traded bonds, and the issuing companies are often neither large nor long-established. Direct placement loans are considered to be somewhat riskier investments and can command higher yields than do public investments. Thus they offer good investment returns to the pension fund able to invest in them and concurrently fill an important capital need for smaller businesses.

We have already seen that insured pension funds, which have traditionally been heavily invested in direct placement loans, real estate, and mortgages, are now through the use of separate accounts beginning to invest more heavily in common stocks. The private noninsured funds, currently heavy investors in common stocks, are contemplating or beginning to invest in real estate, mortgages and, to a lesser extent, in direct placements. State and local funds are investing more heavily in common stocks and are contemplating investments in mortgages and real estate. For nonstock investment vehicles, the larger funds will make direct investments; the smaller ones may well use conservatively managed REITs and comparable investment intermediaries.

As the managers of funds become more experienced with differing types of investments, the various categories of funds can be expected to become more similar in their investments. It is possible that 20 years from now the aggregate distribution of investments of state and local employee retirement funds will be indistinguishable from those of the separate accounts of insurance companies and of the private noninsured funds. If this pattern develops, it has potential for being useful, but it could create major problems.

The recent concentration by pension funds in relatively few stocks may have created distortions in stock prices by raising the value of these stocks relative to other stocks not so favored. If by 1981 the total assets of private and state and local pension funds will more than double their present size, distortions could be much more damaging if all pension funds are following similar investment philosophies. And such distortions might not be limited to the stock market. Real estate, or certain types of real estate, might become too popular with pension fund managers, as happened in the early 1970s with real estate investment trusts, with disastrous results.

On the other hand, if funds with sophisticated managements make direct, diversified investments, the number of acceptable investment opportunities increases enormously. There are, for example, tens of thousands of potential real estate investments that could be of interest to pension funds, compared with fewer than one or two thousand issues of common stock that currently seem acceptable. The presence of a larger number of potential investments would tend to disperse investments and reduce problems of concentration.

The resulting spread of pension fund assets over many types of investments would be beneficial to the economy, for the funds would be better serving their economic obligation to respond to the most pressing investment needs. Small businesses might have as great an access to this important source of capital as do today's large businesses.

—7—

Public Policy—The Vesting of Pension Benefits

He had forty-two boxes, all carefully packed,
With his name clearly printed on each:
But since he omitted to mention the fact,
They were all left behind on the beach.

Lewis Carroll

The Employee Retirement Income Security Act (also called the Pension Reform Act) was signed into law by President Ford on September 2, 1974, establishing preretirement vesting standards at the federal level for the first time. This legislation constituted a great forward step in federal interest in private pensions and greatly enhanced the pension expectations of individual workers.

But the 1974 Pension Reform Act is only a first step. Although it will bring about substantial improvement in many private plans, mainly those that have generally been behind in their vesting and funding provisions, it does not cover state and local retirement systems at all. Its vesting standards are modest. It mildly encourages individuals' retirement planning, but there is no incentive for employers to set up new plans to protect workers in private industry who are not yet covered. It is to be hoped that the act will not discourage the establishment of new plans or curtail improvements in vesting beyond the newly prescribed minimums.

Major federal interest in private pensions will certainly continue. Every future session of Congress will probably see bills introduced to improve or clarify various provisions of the 1974 act. At present it is important to examine carefully the subject of vested pension benefits and to discern how far we have come and how far there still is to go, all in the light of the interests of the individual, the employer, and society. The federal law quite properly chose vesting rather than "portability," "reciprocity," central repositories, or listing provisions as the mechanism for better pension protection for American workers when changing jobs. Should this choice continue for the future in contrast to the other possible methods of preserving pension benefits? This chapter discusses vesting principles and practices, costs, portability, reciprocity, and other aspects of mobility of pension rights. The following chapter discusses funding approaches and their effect on the security of pension rights.

THE GREAT VESTING DEBATE

Prior to the Pension Reform Act, Congressional debates, television programs, the news media, and many articles and books spotlighted certain defects of private pension plans, emphasizing in particular the plight of individuals without pension benefits after years of plan membership. Some of the horrible examples included workers who just missed their pension by not having enough service with their employer, some who worked for an employer whose business failed or was taken over by another concern, some who lost their job before benefits vested. But the message was the same—insecurity for the individual in old age.

At the turn of the century, when the early pension plans were being established, employers felt little pension obligation to any employee who did not stay alive, stay well, and stay put until retirement. Pensions were hardship payments, charity for nearby and visible former workers. If an employee died before retirement, his family usually did not receive anything. If he became disabled after long service, he might be taken care of. If he quit or was discharged, he probably received nothing.

Not many employers would admit that they now subscribe to the charitable and benevolent concept of retirement plans. Benefits are no longer discretionary and are usually related in some specific way to salary and service. Statements by employers about pensions today frequently express the thought that an employee earns the benefits credited to him by the employer during the time he works for that employer, and that benefits are definitely a part of compensation even though quite properly dedicated to specific benefit purposes. Now the job is to carry those statements through to actual pension provisions. Much remains to be done.

Before the 1974 pension legislation, the large majority of pension plans in business, industry, and public employment usually required 10 or 15 more years of service and, in many plans, the attainment of age 40 or 50 for an employee to receive ownership of the benefits he had earned working for the employer. Even after vesting occurred, many terminating employees under contributory retirement plans accepted a bird-in-the-hand option of return of their own contributions, thereby releasing their rights to employer-purchased benefits. On changing jobs, then, the individual who did not meet the employer's lengthy vesting requirements or who took the cash payment for his own contributions, had no souvenir of the retirement planning done on his own behalf. His pension benefits earned for those years were gone. No future employer could be expected to pick up the tab.

Most of the castigation of private pension plans in the last few years has centered on the vesting provisions, not levels of benefits, age of normal retirement, or survivors' benefits. It was largely the absence or delay of vesting that led Ralph Nader to claim that "pensions are no more certain than horseraces." [1] And Professor Merton Bernstein, commenting on delayed vesting of retirement benefits, stated that "unless Congress can do better than the Williams-Javits bills on vesting, the reform bill will constitute as big a fraud as the plans it purports to improve." [2] Of the minimum vesting choices contained in the pension bill finally passed, Professor Bernstein commented, "If that's private pension reform, make mine Social Security." [3]

The strong language from the critics is clear evidence that among all the successes and problems of private pensions, the question of vesting and portability had risen to top priority by the time the Pension Reform Act was passed. The act has substantially improved the pension prospects of workers in the mobile American labor force, but the newly established minimum requirements have by no means provided for a full solution to the problem of benefit forfeitures.

MOBILITY OF THE AMERICAN LABOR FORCE

Mobility of the American labor force is an essential factor in the efficient allocation of human and physical resources. It has permitted shifts from buggy-making to bicycles to railways to autos to airplanes and back to bicycles; from war production to peace endeavors; from production of goods to production of services; from old, dying industries to dynamic new endeavors. Companies and jobs disappear; other companies and jobs take their place.

Some workers stay with one employer from graduation from high school or college until retirement, but most change jobs several times during their careers. This mobility is an essential part of a dynamic society. It helps each individual develop his own career to the fullest and it adds strength and flexibility to the economy.

Pension forfeitures resulting from an employee's changing jobs where vesting has been delayed have been described as a form of industrial feudalism. Delayed vesting has also been called a kind of indenturing system, a golden chain that fastens a person to his employer. Long delays in vesting of pensions tend to result in misallocation of human resources. Attracting experienced personnel for a new or growing company or industry becomes more difficult, for it requires the breaking loose of workers' golden pension chains.

Vesting delays are especially harmful to middle-aged employees. The golden chain becomes stronger and stronger; an individual cannot afford to change jobs and at the same time give up his or her accrued pension rights. A potential new employer may not be willing to take on the triple expense of a salary high enough to counteract the job change risk, costs of current service pensions, and possible compensation to the new employee for forfeiting an unvested pension with the previous employer. Delay in the vesting of pensions is often a real factor in age discrimination.

A pension plan that vests benefits early allows the individual to stay with his present employer, attracted by good pension arrangements, job satisfaction, opportunity, even climate or location. Or it allows him to seek without loss a new employer where his individual capacities, skills, or preferences may be better met. Of course, the freedom to move is also the freedom to stay put.

The importance of job mobility without loss of pension benefits applies with equal force to blue-collar and white-collar employment. A production economy, we are now increasingly adding new economic dimensions as a service-oriented economy. Mobility of all types of workers, blue collar, white collar, and professional, may be expected to keep on increasing. The knowledge, skills, and experience of the carpenter, the electrician, the policeman, the machine tool operator, the computer programmer, the accountant, the chemist, the engineer, the salesman, the corporate lawyer, and the investment expert are best utilized when and where they are readily available.

Recent job tenure figures prepared by the Department of Labor suggest the present degree of mobility of the American labor force. The figures indicate that in 1973 only about a quarter of the 81 million American workers had been continuously employed at the same job for 10 years or more. Another quarter—labor force entrants, re-entrants, and job changers—had been at the same job for a year or less. Over the whole of the previous decade, the average length of time workers were employed on the same job (job tenure) declined, from 4.6 years in 1963 to 3.9 years in 1973. In the same decade the proportion of workers of all ages with 11 or more years of job tenure declined, for men from 36 percent in 1963 to 30 percent in 1973, and for women from 21 percent to 18 percent. Job tenure is more a function of age than other economic and personal characteristics. At age 40, median job tenure (1973) was 8 years; at age 50 it was 12 years, rising to 15 years at age 60, and then declining to 14 years at age 65.[4]

PERSONNEL RELATIONSHIPS

Among the most persistent arguments made against early vesting of private pension benefits are the personnel arguments regarding retention of good employees. Since these arguments will be used again whenever any improvements in vesting are proposed, a brief look at them seems indicated.

Vesting and Employee Retention. What about the view that in the area of executive and professional employment, plans incorporating delayed vesting help an employer keep his top-flight personnel? There are no statistics correlating the performance of professional, technical, and administrative workers with turnover. However, it would seem that forfeiture plans probably do reduce turnover among some professional and administrative employees, but perhaps primarily among those the employer least desires to retain. Lower performance staff members may be less likely to receive or to seek attractive offers elsewhere. A delayed vesting plan may encourage these individuals to try to stay put, at least until they become vested; in the prevested period another employment offer may not be enough of an improvement over the present job to make up for the pension loss. If, however, such staff members can take full deferred annuity provisions with them, they might better afford to move out of an unpromising situation and take the risks of seeking an offer elsewhere. Once such a move has been accomplished, each of the employers concerned may benefit, and so may the individual.

What about high-performance employees? Will a delayed vesting plan help to hold them as it may hold the others? Here again the effect may be the opposite of the expected. Although a large number of employees in the professional categories stay with a particular employer for many years, few in these categories at any one time expect to stay permanently or wish to be committed to do so. Good outside offers can often make up for loss of unvested benefits. For the best personnel, not even a golden chain can always bind them to a present employer.

Choosing the First Job. Young people in the early years of family life and home-buying are often unconcerned about a retirement plan. Yet younger employees may have more important reasons than anyone else to look closely at the vesting provisions of a retirement plan. Under immediate or early vesting, a young person does not have to choose his first employer under the assumption that he will have to stay put for as long as 10 or 15 years in order to achieve 100 percent vested pension rights. Nor need an employee be under pressure to leave the first employer early—"to get out while the getting is good"—lest too much be lost later on. Instead, he can remain longer at the employment of his first choice, building experience until the right spot opens up, either with that employer or another.

MECHANISMS FOR VESTING AND PORTABILITY

Over the years a good many ideas for handling the benefits of employees who change jobs before retirement have been suggested. Many years may elapse between a termination of employment with vested pension rights and the age at which benefits begin. Should such benefits be kept in cold storage? Should an individual's benefit rights from several employers be combined? What kind of records should be kept so an individual does not lose track of benefits to which he is entitled? Once society has determined that each segment of an individual's working life ideally should result in private or public employee pension benefits, what mechanisms should be used to assure the results? A number of mechanisms are in use or have been suggested.

Payments from the Regular Plan. Payment of future benefits from an employer's regular retirement plan provides a direct and simple method of handling vested benefits. Vested pensioners who leave the plan before retirement receive benefit checks later on (smaller, of course, than if they had stayed), directly from the same trust fund or insurance company that pays benefits to those who stay until retirement. Direct payment from the original plan, the normal method currently in use, avoids most of the serious problems of asset valuation and administrative costs involved in asset transfer mechanisms. Pensioners who have held several jobs and have vested under several plans cash several checks a month. This is sometimes cited as a problem, but it seems minor. The real complaint is that the employee who changes jobs before becoming vested does not have any retirement checks to cash except Social Security.

Payments from Multiemployer Systems. Another way of handling vesting is for each employer in an industry group to establish a retirement plan as part of a broader system. When an employee transfers from one employer to another in the system, he carries with him his benefit rights or credits from the first employer and immediately starts to increase these rights with the new employer, all within the same system. However, if the employee leaves the system entirely, he has to meet vesting requirements if his benefit rights are to be maintained on his behalf under the central pension system. Multiemployer-negotiated plans are of this type. The TIAA-CREF plans in the colleges and the National Health and Welfare Retirement plans for private charitable organizations provide multi-employer transferability together with full and immediate vesting.

Inter-System Portability. Although the term *portability* has been used to describe everything from vesting to reciprocity, it is most accurately used to mean direct transfer of funds from one employer's retirement plan to another to support specific benefits.

The idea of transferability to successive employers of both the benefit promise and the underlying assets seems to commend itself as a direct and sensible way to avoid the administrative expenses of maintaining many small benefit portions representing units of employment of terminated employees. Successive asset transfers could indeed transform one or more small benefits into a larger final single pension to be paid by the last employer. Asset transfers, however, run into serious problems of valuation, both of the assets and of the benefit obligation being transferred. These problems present difficulties even under defined contribution plans, and under defined benefit plans the valuation problem is so severe that portability is not likely to work.

A portability proposal has been advanced by Ralph Nader, who has advocated the establishment of a series of private independent (nonprofit) pension funds outside the control of employers and unions. Each employee would choose the fund to which his employer would make contributions for his retirement benefit credits; he could shift among funds or transfer when changing jobs.[5]

Reciprocity Agreements. As early as the 1930s some state teacher retirement systems, recognizing the need to facilitate transfers of public school teachers across state lines, proposed reciprocity agreements. These never amounted to much. A somewhat more fruitful endeavor grew out of the effort to provide some transferability among separate collectively bargained welfare plans in the early 1950s. A precursor plan was to waive the probationary period for members' entitlement to benefits such as hospitalization and short-term disability income. Later, separate pension plans mutually agreed to recognize service on a reciprocal basis in order to cover a larger part of an employee's working years under pension plans. This requires an approximate balance between persons transferring to and those transferring from a given member plan in order to avoid financial disadvantage to one plan or another.

A nationwide link-up of all multiemployer plans through mutually reciprocal arrangements is theoretically possible.[6] But reciprocity extended beyond a particular union or closely comparable employer groups could produce conflicts and a variety of technical complications, so that nationwide progress on this front seems unlikely.

The potential advantage of pension transferability of public employees among units of government—local, state, and federal—has been given considerable attention. Within a state there is usually provision for pension-credit reciprocity among separate retirement plans, but there is almost none between one state and another or between state and federal employment. Teachers, school superintendents, police chiefs, and city manager groups whose employment opportunities frequently cross state lines are among those that sought to develop multistate reciprocity or transfer arrangements. Except for city managers, their efforts have been largely unsuccessful. The solution seems to be improved vesting provisions within each separate retirement plan.

The permanent Advisory Commission on Intergovernmental Relations, a federal agency charged with the study of problems affecting the relationships of states with each other and the federal government, has given special attention to the barriers to public employee mobility caused by lengthy delays in the vesting of pension benefits. The 1963 commission report concluded that "provision should be made for an employee to change jobs without suffering any major loss of retirement credits. . . . In the long run, public employers and employees at all levels of government—federal, state, and local—will benefit from a better program for the preservation of retirement credits of employees who transfer from one governmental unit to another." [7]

Significantly, the commission placed its hopes for improvements in a recommendation that "the employee's benefits be vested when he has completed a period of service of not more than five years in the system. . . ." [8] Rejecting the idea that reciprocal agreements or complicated asset or benefit-right transfer schemes were practicable, the commission concluded that early vesting in each plan would be most effective in relaxing the grip of interstate immobility on public employees.

Information Clearinghouse. An idea for the central recording of information about already-vested benefits of terminated employees, initially proposed at the 1960 White House Conference on the Aging, was incorporated in the pension legislation passed by Congress in 1974. The Social Security Administration is to receive information reported to the Internal Revenue Service by each retirement plan regarding the vested deferred benefits of employees whose service was terminated before retirement age. This information will be provided to participants and beneficiaries upon their request and also upon application for Social Security benefits. [9]

It is not so important whether a retired worker receives three or four checks from three or four former employers, or one from a central clearing agency, or from one plan for a lifetime of participation. Nor is it so important whether an employee gains portability, or reciprocity, or pension repository claims. The key question is whether he receives full benefits covering his full working career. Continued emphasis on vesting as the central issue will bring large rewards in security for workers.

CASH VALUE OPTIONS IN CONTRIBUTORY PLANS

Now that the 1974 legislation has established minimum standards of vesting for workers in private pension plans, what happens when an employee leaves a contributory plan after becoming vested but before retirement? The law provides that no pension plan may include forfeiture of benefits based on *employer* contributions solely because of the withdrawal by a terminating participant of *his own* contributions if his benefits have become vested to the extent of 50 percent or more.

Generally, it would seem inadvisable for a terminating vested employee to take a return of his own contributions. From a public policy standpoint, it seems as reasonable to seek the preservation of deferred benefits based on employee contributions as it does to preserve vested benefits attributable to employer contributions. There should be no "cash value" termination provisions for employee contributions except in the circumstances outlined below:

(1) Prior to any vesting of employer contributions, it is of course reasonable to provide that a terminating employee be returned any contributions he or she has made to the plan.

(2) Where the total amount of a vested annuity involved is small, an option or even requirement to cash out could be acceptable. The 1974 act provides that where a terminating employee's deferred benefit is so small as to require a very small present value, employer-bought benefits may be forfeited and employee contributions returned.[10] However, it would be better to shift small amounts to a central clearinghouse or to an individual annuity with a life insurance company, where facilities for handling small amounts are available.

(3) A small cash payment—a retirement readjustment allowance—can provide a real help at time of retirement. It could be a doubling of the annuity amount for the first year or an amount equal to, say, 10 percent of the accumulated funds, to help cover moving expenses, purchase of a house, or even a long-awaited trip.

THE EFFECT OF PARTICIPATION ON VESTING

A retirement system need not include the young ages nor the first year or two of service in order to provide adequate benefits. However, it is not appropriate to combine extensive requirements for participation with long periods of delayed vesting. The 1974 federal pension law takes account of this by providing that an employer cannot exclude an employee from a pension plan that defers vesting after the attainment of age 25 or the completion of one year of service, whichever is later. For a retirement plan that provides immediate full vesting upon the commencement of participation, the act provides that a plan may not exclude participants after the later of attainment of age 25 or the completion of three years of service. This permits a longer waiting period for plans that have excellent vesting provisions.

LEVELS OF VESTING

Vesting of pension benefits means that at a stated point in time the employee gains an unforfeitable right to benefits under the plan, that the benefits based on service already rendered are to be his at retirement regardless of whether he leaves his job, is fired or laid off, or leaves the union.

Vesting may be immediate or deferred. It may be full or partial with increases on a graduated scale. Immediate full vesting provides the worker with assurance that each year of participation in a retirement plan will be represented by a full unforfeitable increment in the retirement benefit. Deferred full vesting means that if a worker leaves for any reason during the period of deferred vesting he has no entitlement to benefits, but if he stays beyond the vesting date he has full entitlement to benefits retroactively to his first participation in the pension plan.

Under graded vesting, during the grading period some portion of plan benefits, say 10 percent, becomes vested during each year of continued service. Deferred and graded vesting are sometimes combined.

The objective of vesting of retirement benefits is security in retirement for people who have completed employment periods of reasonable length, but who may not stay with a given employer until they reach the retirement age. Early and full vesting (and full funding) best assure the attainment of this objective. The minimum vesting standards set by the 1974 Pension Reform Act represent a step forward, but by no means a giant step.

MINIMUM FEDERAL STANDARDS

Under the 1974 federal pension law, private pension plans must provide full and immediate vesting in benefits derived from *employee* contributions.

With respect to *employer* contributions, the legislation requires minimum vesting standards under one of three available alternatives: (1) a 10-year/100 percent standard; (2) a 5- to 15-year graded standard; (3) a "rule of 45." [11]

Under the 10-year/100 percent standard, each employee must be 100 percent vested after 10 years of service.

Under the 5- to 15-year graded standard the employee must be at least 25 percent vested in his accrued benefit after 5 years of covered service, with 5 percent additional vesting for each of the next 5 years, and 10 percent additional vesting for each year thereafter, so that the employee becomes 100 percent vested after 15 years of service.

Under the "rule of 45," an employee with 5 or more years of covered service must be at least 50 percent vested when the sum of his age and years of covered service total 45, and there must be provision for at least 10 percent additional vesting for each year of covered service thereafter. In addition, each employee with 10 years of covered service regardless of his age must be at least 50 percent vested and there must be provision for 10 percent additional vesting for each year of service thereafter.

Regardless of the above minimums, the 1974 law requires that an employee must be 100 percent vested in his accrued benefit when he attains the normal or stated retirement age (or actually retires).

Generally, once an employee becomes eligible to participate in a pension plan, all his years of service with an employer (including preparticipation service and service performed before the date of the act) are to be taken into account for the purpose of determining his place on the vesting scale.

EXTENT OF VESTING

No genuinely comprehensive study has ever been made of the vesting provisions in all private and governmental retirement plans, but separate studies of segments of the employment market have provided some basic information on vesting. This information suggests, at least, the level of improvement to be expected from the new federal legislation.

One study by the Department of Labor, Bureau of Labor Statistics, found that in 1969, 77 percent of workers covered by private retirement plans were under plans with "some kind" of a vesting provision earlier than qualification for early or normal retirement.[12] A preretirement vesting provision was more likely to be found in single-employer plans than in multiemployer plans. The 1969 Labor Department study reported that 87 percent of workers covered under single-employer plans were under plans with provisions for vesting of benefits, while 51 percent of workers under multiemployer plans belonged to plans providing some kind of preretirement vesting. Multiemployer plans, of course, provide for intrasystem mobility of employees without loss of benefits regardless of the vesting provisions on employment termination.

But pension vesting has rarely been immediate. The combination of service and age requirements for the vesting of private pension benefits have been so numerous that it is difficult to summarize them. The Labor Department's 1969 study broke down its data in groupings that sometimes obscured the most prominent provisions: "service" categories, for example, were "5 to 10 years" and "11 to 15 years." A reader might assume a fairly even distribution of provisions within periods, but in fact virtually all of the stated periods within the 5-to-10-year groupings are exactly 10 years; almost no plans stated a lesser number. Thus, for "5 to 10 years" one must read "10 years," and for "11 to 15 years," "15 years."

Service requirements have been normal components of delayed vesting provisions. Age requirements, on the other hand, have been found recently in about half the plans as an additional requirement accompanying the service requirement.[13] The 1969 Labor Department study indicated that service requirements concentrated at 10 years and above. Forty-five percent of active workers were covered by plans providing for delayed full or graded vesting on completion of 10 years of service. Some of these plans meet the minimum standards of the 1974 federal pension act. Thirty-nine percent were covered under plans vesting after 15 years of service, 12 percent under plans vesting after 20 years, and 3 percent after more than 20 years. Only 1 percent were reported as covered under plans vesting in 5 years or less.[14]

Age requirements appeared to concentrate at 40 (or "40 or less" in the language of the Labor Department), 50, and 55, with about half at 40 and half above 40. Table 7.1 gives the Labor Department data from the 1969 compilation.

It has been easier to collect information about the requirements for vesting of benefits under pension plans than to determine the proportion of pension plan members who are vested. Documents filed with the Department of Labor have not been analyzed in terms of the proportion of plan participants who are at any one time vested in a plan. Some sample surveys have been made, however. In mid-1972 the Bureau of the Census conducted a survey under contract from the Departments of the Treasury, Labor, and Health, Education, and Welfare. It found that among 23 million full-time workers covered by a private pension or a deferred profit-sharing plan, about a third had achieved a nonforfeitable right to a pension from their current plan.[15] A comparable figure was reported in a 1971 sample survey of 865 private plans conducted by an actuarial consulting firm, which concluded that 30 percent of persons covered had vested benefits, and that another 36 percent "expected" to vest in plans which then covered them.[16]

Treasury Department figures released in 1972 provided data broken down by age for the 30.6 percent of total pension plan participants who had become vested in the benefits of the plan in which they were currently covered. By age groups, the proportion of vested employees ranged from less than 2 percent for employees under 30 years of age to 80 percent for employees 60 and over. Table 7.2 gives the age breakdowns.

Short-service and young employees can be expected to report vested benefits less frequently than long-service and older employees, given the nearly universal pattern of provisions for vesting delay. The Census Bureau survey confirmed this. About 60 percent of the workers with less than 10 years of employment did not yet have vested rights under their retirement plan. The

Table 7.1 Age and Service Requirements for Earliest Full Vesting Under Private Pension Plans, 1969

	Distribution	No Age Requirement	Age Requirement
All plans with vesting	100% [a]	51% [b]	49% [b]
Minimum Service Requirement			
Less than 5 years	1	82	18
5 to 10 years	45	74	26
11 to 15 years	39	26	74
16 to 20 years	12	43	57
More than 20 years	3	66	34

Source: Harry E. Davis and Arnold Strasser, "Private Pension Plans, 1960 to 1969—An Overview," *Monthly Labor Review,* (July 1970), p. 54.

Note: Statistics include both full vesting and graded vesting plans.

[a] Percent of plans.   [b] Percent of active workers.

rate of vesting rose as job tenure increased—from 20 percent of those having worked less than 5 years to 47 percent for those who had worked 15 to 19 years. The rate of vesting leveled off at about 50 percent for those who had worked 15 years or more.[17]

It is not surprising that the average time on the present job for all non-vested workers was found to be 7 years, contrasted with 14.4 years for vested workers. Yet one fourth of those who did *not* have vested rights had worked 15 or more years under a single employer.[18]

Of course, older workers were more likely to have achieved vested status; about 45 percent of the workers aged 55 or older were vested. Length of employment had much more to do with vesting than age. The census survey reported: "The proportion of vested workers rose only slightly as age increased for those with the same amount of service, but the proportion rose sharply as length of employment increased for those in a given age group." Illustrating this point, the survey found that the vesting rates for workers employed less than 10 years, for example, ranged from 19 percent for workers aged 30 to 39 to 28 percent of those aged 50 or over. For workers aged 40 to 49, on the other hand, vesting rates ranged from 23 percent for those who had worked less than 10 years to about 50 percent for those who had worked 15 years or more. Despite the positive effect on the chances of vesting of a combination of higher age and long service, only half of the men aged 50 or older who were employed 10 or more years had vested status.[19]

Table 7.2 Private Pension Plan Participants with Vested Benefits, by Age, 1971

Age	Total Participants	Participants Vested
Under 30	6,300,000	1.6%
30 to 40	5,300,000	13.2
40 to 45	3,000,000	36.7
45 to 50	2,900,000	44.8
50 to 55	2,500,000	56.0
55 to 60	2,000,000	70.0
60 and over	1,500,000	80.0
Total	23,500,000	30.6

Source: Treasury Department, December 1971.

The 1970 Bankers Trust Company study of conventional private pension plans concluded that in only 48 percent of the plans would an employee age 40 with 15 years of credited service be fully vested.[20] By 1975, similar age and service credits would have entitled the employee to fully vested benefits in 73 percent of the plans. Nine percent of the conventional plans studied in 1975 either imposed vesting requirements of 25 or more years of service or age 55 or older (regardless of a service requirement), compared with 23 percent in 1970.[21]

As interest in pension reform intensified in the late 1960s, it quickly appeared that very little research had actually been done to determine the extent of vesting among private pension plan participants. The studies mentioned above were among those that helped replace speculation with facts. These studies, though perhaps late in coming, aided in the formulation of vesting provisions in successive proposals before the Congress, improved the estimates of expected increases in cost resulting from earlier vesting, and

Table 7.3 State and Local Pension Plan Requirements for Vesting of Benefits, Effective January 1965 and 1966 (systems with 1,000 or more members)

	Number of Systems	Number of Employees (thousands)	Percent of Systems	Percent of Employees
Provision for Vesting of Benefits	138	3,591.8	64%	82%
Immediate vesting	5	47.0	2	1
Employee contribution of at least $500	3	160.1	1	4
Service requirement only	112	2,768.0	52	63
1 to 5 years	29	868.4	3	20
6 to 15 years	55	1,180.3	26	27
20 to 27 years	28	719.3	13	16
Age and service requirement [a]	12	352.3	6	8
Gradual vesting	4	141.4	2	3
Other	2	123.0	1	3
No Provision for Vesting	76	793.9	36	18
All Systems	214	4,385.7	100	100

Source: Tax Foundation, Inc., *State and Local Employee Pension Systems* (1969), p. 24.

[a] Minimum age ranging between 40 and 50 years; service requirement varying between 7 and 15 years.

ultimately contributed to the acceptability of the standards embodied in the Pension Reform Act of 1974.

VESTING AND PUBLIC RETIREMENT SYSTEMS

Vesting provisions among the public employee and state teacher retirement systems, state and local, are comparable to vesting provisions among private plans. Immediate vesting is rare. Most commonly, qualification for vested benefits depends on some specified period of service. More than half the systems set up a service requirement only; others add an age requirement. In 1966, more than one out of three of the systems (36 percent), covering one out of five participants (18 percent), provided for no vesting at all unless the employee met an early or normal retirement requirement.[22]

The Federal Civil Service Retirement System vests benefits after 5 years of plan participation. Participation in the plan occurs immediately on employment. The Uniformed Services Plan vests (nondisability) retirement benefits after 20 years.

Table 7.3 shows the vesting provisions in effect in state and local retirement systems with 1,000 or more members in 1965 and 1966, the latest years for which vesting data are available.

THE COST OF VESTING

Whenever the subject of improved vesting is raised—in Congressional hearings, plan negotiations, or general writing on private pension plans—the cost of vesting is advanced as a substantial deterrent. How great is the cost of improved vesting? Upon whom does it fall? What are the cost differences among various vesting formulas?

Cost/Benefit Ratio. Of course it costs money to pay benefits. A pension plan costs more if it pays more benefits. If there are lengthy vesting delays and high prevesting employee turnover, the pension plan costs less. But if an individual doesn't receive benefits in retirement, it is costly to him or her in both human and economic terms. And, beyond this, larger social and economic issues are involved because of the aggregate effect of many individual situations.

The question, then, is not whether to accept the cost of vesting benefits in private pension plans earlier than a prescribed minimum, but rather who is to accept it. If vesting costs are not to be borne by the employer's retirement system, the consequence is that no benefits from that system will be paid to persons who leave the employer before meeting minimum standards. If no pension benefits are paid to these employees, it is they who bear the cost of nonvesting. And the taxpayers may also have to pay the costs through welfare and related programs if Social Security benefits are not sufficient. In any event, the cost of vesting is ever-present, either as a cost to the employer for the benefits vested, a cost to the employee for benefits lost, or a cost to society for welfare benefits.

Business leaders are not unaware of these considerations. Many pension plans have improved their vesting provisions in recent years, reflecting the belief that the increased cost to the company is really rather light in terms of total product, sales, or payroll, or even in relationship to total cost for the pension plan. The new federal vesting standards will force improvement among the laggards. And many companies already are ahead of the new standards. It is to be hoped that progress will continue moving well beyond the new ERISA minimums.

Installation of a New Plan. Ideally, if a new business is being opened or a new company organized, it makes sense to start out with a good retirement system. Many employees probably will be of a relatively young age; the problem of retirement income itself will not become major for a number of years. There is no past-service obligation overhanging the plan, and early vesting should not be a financial problem. Full credit can be given to the workers from the outset in the form of good retirement benefits along with early vesting.

In establishing a new plan for an existing employer, one of the major problems is the fact that obligations for current service must be paid for out of current production, along with the payment from current production for past-service benefits granted by the new plan. The funding of past-service liabilities can be a real burden on an employer, especially heavy in low-profit or highly competitive industries. It can be a potential discouragement to the initiation of a plan. If an employer has no pension plan, and early vesting is considered too costly, it is better to establish a plan that delays vesting to the allowable maximum rather than have no plan at all. Since so many American workers in private employment are not covered by any private retirement plan, it would be careless for federal or state legislation to mandate a level of vesting for new plans that seriously retarded their installation.

Employer Costs of Improved Vesting. For any one pension plan, a fairly accurate estimate may be made of the cost of improving existing vesting provisions. Cost increases depend on the current provisions for vesting, the proposed new provisions, the age and wage distribution of the group, the eligibility and benefit provisions, and the actuarial factors that figure into the calculations, including employee turnover rates. In anticipation of pension reform legislation it was estimated that the addition of moderate vesting arrangements for plans having none could be expected to increase plan costs from 10 to 25 percent, or from 0.5 to 1.5 percent of payroll.

It is difficult to arrive at national estimates of the added cost for various types of improvements in vesting for all pension plans. When thousands of plans are involved, the differences in their provisions make it likely that broad cost estimates will incorporate large margins of error. Prior to the enactment of the 1974 Pension Reform Act, several studies were commissioned by federal agencies to assess the costs of the principal proposals for improvements in vesting that had been introduced in various House and Senate bills. A study by Professor Howard Winklevoss of the Wharton School of the University of Pennsylvania concluded that changing a 20-year vesting requirement to 10 years would increase plan costs under final-average formula plans by from 2 to 9 percent. The study found no appreciable differences in cost between a change from 20-year vesting to either 10 years, a graded 5- to 15-year schedule, or to a "rule of 50." The ranges in cost that were determined were due mainly, according to the study, to differences in the actuarial cost methods used by the plans.[23]

The Department of Labor estimated that a requirement of full vesting after 10 years of service, excluding years prior to age 25, which would immediately cover some 10 million workers, would cost one third of the private pension plans nothing or at most an additional 3 percent. About one fourth of the plans would be faced with plan cost increases of between 3 and 6 percent. Less than half the plans were expected to incur costs greater than 6 percent.[24]

A study of 491 large companies made in 1972 by McGraw-Hill Publications Company for Standard & Poor's InterCapital, Inc., indicated that on the average a mandated 10-year vesting rule would result in an increase in company pension contributions of 2 percent, with the average increases ranging among the 21 industries surveyed from 0.2 percent for the transportation equipment industry to 9.9 percent for the textile and apparel industry.[25] These are the orders of cost-increase that will be experienced by plans as they bring their vesting provisions up to meet the new federal standards.

By 1976, all private pension plans will have brought their vesting provisions up to the minimum federal levels, and at no excessive current service price if the foregoing studies prove accurate. Later, new studies of the cost of yet further improvements in vesting standards will be appropriate. Then, instead of the 10-year/100 percent minimum, it is to be hoped that we will be considering a 5-year/100 percent minimum; instead of a graded 5- to 15-year schedule, a 1- to 10-year grading, and instead of a "rule of 45," a "rule of 35."

Labor's Interest. Dr. Joseph J. Melone, when he was director of the McCahan Foundation for Basic Research in Security, Risk, and Insurance, suggested that organized labor is in a position to play a strong role in encouraging early vesting:

> It seems that a rapid expansion and liberalization of vested benefits will result only if employers receive more direct economic offsets to the additional cost of vested benefits. The most obvious offset would be for employees to recognize the adequacy of the wage package as a whole. The possibilities of this occurring depend in large part on the degree of importance attributed to this benefit by labor unions and employees.
>
> It would seem that labor unions are in an ideal position to encourage the adoption of effective vesting provisions. First of all, vesting is consistent with the objective and rationale of private pensions from the viewpoint of labor. And, second, unions are in a position, through adjustments of other wage demands, to offer the employer an economic justification for providing vested benefits. Vesting, therefore, fits in neatly with organized labor's goal of increasing the economic security of their members. However, if the union official looks upon the plan as being for the benefit of the union members and for the purpose of encouraging loyalty to the union, he may have little interest in negotiating a vested benefit.[26]

RECOMMENDATIONS

The following section makes recommendations with respect to vesting. It might be mentioned that those who now want stricter vesting requirements should recognize that the 1974 pension legislation sets up minimum, not maximum, standards. Any company or industry can set up plans with better vesting than the minimum. Many retirement plans already exceed the minimum proposed requirements, and the trend is strongly in that direction.

It is sound public policy to call on the private sector to accomplish everything it possibly can before recourse is had to public action or public requirements and mandates. It is noteworthy that the entire development of private pensions in this country has occurred with hardly any government regulation or legislation specifying minimum requirements, with the exception of the relatively few provisions of the Internal Revenue Service in return for appropriate tax treatment.

However, a great deal still needs to be done, despite pension reform legislation, especially in connection with assuring the mobile American work force that it is reasonably protected in old age through private pensions. The two major future developments that should be encouraged are the inclusion of a far larger number of workers under private pension plans, and maximum assurance for those who are so included that they will receive benefits upon retirement. While the following recommendations concern themselves with vesting, they are made with attention to the fact that installation of new plans must be encouraged, not delayed or made impracticable. Failure to provide any pension plan is worse than failure to improve vesting in plans already established.

What does early vesting seek to accomplish? Fairness for members of the labor force through real security in retirement; neutrality in hiring and therefore nondiscrimination by age and previous employment; coverage of a broad enough span of years regardless of employment changes in order to provide reasonable private supplements to Social Security retirement benefits. The ultimate objective should be full and immediate vesting of private pensions for American workers, with no forfeitures of earned benefits.

Recommendation #1. Continue to concentrate on earlier minimum vesting provisions; consider the 1974 Employee Retirement Income Security Act as merely the first step. This is the simplest and most direct method of assuring each worker that upon retirement he will have some pension benefits reflecting each of the major segments of his working life. Many ingenious devices have been suggested for handling the problem of the mobile worker: a clearinghouse, a series of nonprofit central pension plans, transfer of funds and benefit rights from plan to plan, and reciprocity. All of them share problems in complexity, difficulty of actuarial valuation of retirement benefits, and fairness of treatment both to those who change jobs and to those who do not. The most practical arrangement is to leave accumulated pension rights within each pension fund, coupled with a central listing of such rights with the Social Security Administration as provided under the Employee Retirement Income Security Act of 1974.

Recommendation #2. Provide a degree of flexibility in setting vesting requirements. The new federal legislation has inaugurated this approach with its three alternative minimum tests, a limited free choice for any pension plan. Future improvements should continue to offer alternative minimums.

Recommendation #3. Nothing short of full and immediate vesting for all plan participants is appropriate for the long run. We are in a transition period. The sensible way to go about improving requirements on vesting would be gradually to refine requirements, with the ultimate goal of full and immediate vesting for all pension plan participants. An interim goal of five-year vesting coupled with early participation requirements would be desirable.

Recommendation #4. Encourage new plans. In the future, when vesting standards have been raised, a new plan installed by an existing employer should not have to meet vesting requirements stricter than the current (1974 Act) prescribed minimums for a number of years. The main job is to fund past-service benefits and "get going" on current service. Therefore, a phase-in procedure permitting new plans to move gradually to stricter minimum legislative standards over a period of, say, 10 years, would be appropriate.

Recommendation #5. Eligibility requirements for participation in a retirement plan are appropriate. Thus, young employment ages need not be reflected in the final retirement benefit. But participation by the later of age 25 or completion of one year of service is desirable, and such a provision makes sense in connection with lifetime income patterns and achievement of ultimately appropriate retirement benefits. But legislation should require participation of workers in the employer's retirement plan, not merely prohibit their exclusion, by the later of age 25 or one year of service. If vesting is not delayed but is immediate, it is reasonable to provide for a somewhat later point in age or service after which an employee may not be excluded from a plan, a principle recognized in the 1974 act's provision for participation by the later of age 25 or three years of service under immediately vested plans.

Recommendation #6. Prohibit cash withdrawals of employee contributions to a pension plan. Retirement security will not be achieved if any dispersion of the benefit before retirement is allowed. Cash refunds—bait to cause an individual to give up vested benefits—should be restricted. The offer of return of the individual's own contributions if he will forfeit the otherwise vested benefits provided by the employer has been effectively eliminated by the 1974 act.

Recommendation #7. Establish a mechanism for central pooling of small benefit amounts. In our mobile society, the thrust of our private pension system should be toward early vesting in each retirement plan. However, there is a place for central pooling of smaller benefits earned through short service. Life insurance companies provide group and individual annuities that can readily be used for such purposes. Additional enterprising efforts could be inaugurated in the private sector to meet this need. The expenses would be paid by the users, that is, the employers who wish not to have to keep track of or fund benefits for a multitude of employees who have left some years before. However, legislatively mandated shifting of large amounts of funds to central repositories does not seem appropriate.

−8−

Public Policy—Financing Pension Benefits

All progress is based on a universal innate desire on the part of every organism to live beyond its income.
Samuel Butler

The ultimate purpose of a pension plan, of course, is to pay benefits to participants who become eligible to receive them. The inflow of funds, the establishment of reserves, and the pension checks are all organized around this central purpose. All retirement plans incorporate a systematic means for the determination of benefits for participants. Two main approaches to the making of pension commitments are used: "defined contribution" (or money purchase) and "defined benefit" (or formula) plans. An understanding of the differences between these two main categories will set the stage for later comparison and contrasts. Considerable attention is paid to defined contribution plans, since they are not usually covered adequately in pension literature, and because the new Pension Reform Act has resulted in increased interest in these types of plans.

DEFINED CONTRIBUTION PLANS

In defined contribution plans the pension commitment is specified in terms of *input* to the plan. The regular contribution to the pension plan is stated as a percentage of the current compensation of the plan participant. This amount is credited to an individual account on behalf of the participant.

As an example, a defined contribution pension plan might call for a contribution rate of 10 percent of each participant's salary, paid each month to an annuity contract. At retirement age the benefit is the fixed annuity that can be purchased by the total of employer and employee contributions and the compound interest earnings on the accumulating reserves. If the contributions are to a common-stock variable annuity, the annuity benefits will vary according to total units of fund participation purchased and the investment experience of the fund.

The percentage of earnings going into a defined contribution pension plan is usually the same for each participant, regardless of age or sex. Under a profit-sharing plan, the contribution may be defined as a percentage of annual net profits divided according to a predetermined distribution formula.

The defined contribution rate for the retirement plan is set at a level estimated to be sufficient to achieve a stated pension goal, assuming a career of service of 30 or 35 years. The pension goal might be stated as half of the average of salary over the last five years of service. A contribution rate is then selected that will enable the accumulation of funds sufficient to meet the stated goal.

Defined contribution plans are favored by small employers, partnerships, and the nonprofit sector. The largest of the defined contribution plans is the TIAA-CREF system for educational institutions. Some of the public employee and teacher retirement systems use the defined contribution approach for the determination of benefits from employee contributions. The Employee Retirement Income Security Act of 1974 may be expected to encourage the development of defined contribution plans because of the effectiveness with which they can provide earlier vesting, and their direct, uncomplicated funding methods.

Another type of defined contribution plan is a "cents per hour" or "cents per produced unit" plan. The contribution, rather than being expressed as a percentage of salary or wage, is a fixed amount per unit of time (hour, day, week, or month) or per unit of production (e.g., ton of coal). An employer contribution of 30 cents an hour, for example, might be made to a pension plan on behalf of each employee. This amount might be allocated to each employee individually for the purpose of an annuity (as under the variable annuity supplement for workers in the New York City construction industry), or it might be accumulated in a pooled fund out of which benefits are paid on a fixed-sum formula basis. Defined contributions of the cents-per-hour type are frequently used as the base for benefit financing among collectively bargained multiemployer plans of the fixed-sum formula type.

Financing Defined Contribution Plans. The financing process under a defined contribution plan is simple and direct. The salary of each participant is multiplied by the percentage contribution rate and the amount is credited directly to the individual's account in the pension fund. Each such credit earns its pro rata investment share. The participant can easily determine how much his employer has contributed on his behalf, how much he himself has contributed (if any), and the total fund to his credit including investment earnings.

Under defined contribution plans, the benefit itself is not precisely stated in advance, but is whatever pension can be purchased at retirement by the funds that have been accumulated on behalf of each plan participant. If contribution rates are increased or investment earnings are larger, the benefit is larger; the older the age of retirement, the larger the benefit; if a spouse is included, the periodic income is less because it must continue throughout two lives. All benefits are actuarially established in order to achieve equal lifetime equivalency among all participants.

DEFINED BENEFIT PLANS

Under most private pension plans the pension commitment is defined in terms of plan *output,* i.e., a definition of the benefit. The amount of the benefit is stated by formula and the formula is applied for each plan participant when he or she retires. The pension obligation created by the formula for all participants combined also becomes the base for the actuarial calculation of the plan liabilities and funding requirements.

Defined benefit formulas (also termed "fixed formula" or "fixed benefit") are of two types: "unit benefit" and "flat benefit." The unit benefit percentage formula is the type most frequently encountered in defined benefit plans. It is the usual approach in the single-employer plans that cover about 70 percent of workers under private pension plans. It is also the favored approach in government-sponsored plans for public employees and public school teachers.

A unit percentage plan might state its annual benefit as follows:

$$1\% \times \left[\begin{array}{c} \text{annual} \\ \text{compensation} \\ \text{throughout the} \\ \text{Social Security} \\ \text{wage base} \end{array} \right] + 1.5\% \times \left[\begin{array}{c} \text{annual} \\ \text{compensation} \\ \text{above the} \\ \text{Social Security} \\ \text{wage base} \end{array} \right] \times \text{ years of service}$$

In the above formula, the definition of annual compensation will specify whether it is to be the average annual earnings over the participant's entire working career (the "career average" approach), or the average annual earnings over a stated period of years near the retirement (or termination) age, such as the last five, the last three, or the final year's earnings (the "final average salary" approach). Sometimes an average of a stated number of years of highest earnings is used.

The flat benefit plan, in contrast, omits the wage-related feature of the unit percentage approach. The flat sum provides either the same benefit to all retirees, or, more frequently, varies the benefit solely on the basis of service. Thus, a flat-sum benefit formula might designate a benefit of $7 per month for each year of credited service. The flat-sum approach is extensively used in multiemployer plans and plans covering hourly employees only, as shown in Table 8.1.

Financing Defined Benefit Plans. Advance funding under the defined benefit approach requires the development of an actuarial cost method to in-

Table 8.1 Benefit Formulas in Defined Benefit Private Pension Plans

| | | Type of Benefit Formula | | |
Type of Plan	Percent Distribution	Flat Benefit	Salary-Related Unit Benefit	Total
Single-employer	71%	37%	63%	100%
Multiemployer	29	92	8	100
Contributory	21	22	78	100
Noncontributory	79	61	39	100
Salaried only	14	16	84	100
Salaried and hourly	39	25	75	100
Hourly only	47	86	14	100

Source: Harry E. Davis and Arnold Strasser, "Private Pension Plans, 1960 to 1969—an Overview," *Monthly Labor Review* (July 1970), p. 50.

form the employer of the rate at which the pension obligations that are accruing under the plan should be covered by the inflow of funds. The funding method chosen provides a plan for spreading the aggregate costs over the working lifetime of participants entering and attaining benefit eligibility under the plan. It also amortizes the liabilities represented by the credited prior service of employees who were at work before the plan was started.

Actuarial Cost Methods. Actuarial cost methods for funding differ from one defined benefit plan to another, since they can be selected to take into consideration a variety of factors. Among these factors are the age and sex composition of the covered group, the applicable mortality assumptions for active and retired employees, turnover rates in the various age categories, expected rates of future compensation, the type of retirement benefit, any disability and survivor benefits associated with the plan, expected investment earnings, and administrative costs.

Pension costs are basically classified as "normal costs" and "past-service costs." Normal cost is the cost that the chosen actuarial method assigns to years after the inception of the pension plan. Past-service costs are those the chosen method assigns to years before the plan came into existence.

A number of actuarial cost-funding methods are available for the orderly accumulation of reserves to provide the benefits of defined benefit pension plans. In practice, the terminology employed to describe these methods is not wholly uniform, although the Committee on Pension and Profit-Sharing Terminology of the American Risk and Insurance Association has established recommended classifications. Commonly employed terms, including the committee's terminology, are listed below: [1]

Committee-recommended terminology   *Other terminology in use*

Accrued benefit cost method   Unit credit method
Projected benefit cost methods:
   Individual level cost methods:
      Without supplemental liability   Individual level premium method
      With supplemental liability   Entry age normal method (individual basis)

   Aggregate level cost methods:
      Without supplemental liability   Aggregate method
      With supplemental liability   Attained age normal method; entry age normal method (aggregate basis)

Supplemental liability   Past service cost; prior service cost

Any of the above cost methods are regarded as acceptable under actuarial or accounting standards.

Under the accrued benefit (unit credit) method, the cost of each dollar of current service benefit related to current salary is met in the year in which it accrues. There is no attempt to anticipate or prefund benefits related to future wage or salary increases through the use of projections. In effect, a series of minimum benefit purchases is made for each participant year by year. The annual total of these purchases is the employer's annual cost. The accrued benefit method is nearly always used in connection with group deferred annuity contracts. It is almost never used with defined benefit final-average formula plans.

The other methods incorporate projected benefit costs based on assumptions regarding rates of change in compensation, with the objective of leveling out the premiums and funding more evenly over time. The methods may use assumed ages of entry into the plan or actual ages. A variety of approaches to the treatment of initial past-service liabilities and of liabilities resulting from plan liberalization are available under these standard cost methods.

The Effective Input Curve. Under defined benefit plans, the actual pattern of the input of contributions in the aggregate or per individual participant will depend on the actuarial cost method employed. In addition to the cost method, relevant factors in the employer's aggregate annual outlay will be the benefit structure and the age, sex, salary composition, and termination rate of the covered group. The aggregate employer cost each year may be expressed as a percentage of covered payroll, of total payroll, or in other ways. The overall percentage measures the total employer cost, but it does not indicate to a given participant the amount of money that is being set aside to fund his individual benefit, that is, the net addition to his annual compensation that could be said to be represented by employer payments to the pension plan on his behalf. Neither does it indicate to the employer how much it costs him to employ men or women of various ages and employment histories.

A revealing illustration of the cost of a defined benefit formula plan *per individual* is shown by the amount the employer must pay in each year to buy the year's promised benefit payable to the person at the normal retirement age. This is the accrued benefit (unit credit) actuarial cost method, which is used in the illustrations below.[2]

COMPARING THE TWO APPROACHES

Assumptions. Using an accrual (unit credit) approach for the defined benefit plans, let us compare employer costs and employee benefits under a defined benefit percentage formula plan and a defined contribution plan, each of which provides exactly the same retirement benefit for a man who enters at age 25 and retires at age 65. These are two alternative benefit packages any employer might wish to examine. (For both types of plan, contribution rates for women would be proportionately higher to provide the same monthly single life annuity because of the greater female longevity.) The comparisons are based on a formula of 1.5 percent of final five-year average salary per year of service for the defined benefit plan, and an employer contribution of 7.5 percent of each year's salary for the defined contribution plan. Both plans are paid for wholly by the employer (noncontributory). In addition, the following assumptions are made: immediate vesting of benefits, initial salary of $12,000 at age 25 increasing 3 percent per year to retirement at age 65, interest earnings assumed at 6 percent per year, administration expenses covered by 3.5 percent of each contribution, annuity mortality factors based on the A-1949 mortality table for males with the single life annuity option.

Table 8.2 shows the yearly input, the accumulating funds, and the benefits payable beginning at age 65 that have accrued at the end of each year of plan participation for a participant who has entered each type of plan— defined benefit and defined contribution—at age 25. Under the "Payment to Fund" columns is shown the actual amount of employer contribution that, taking into account interest, operational expense, and mortality assumptions, is required to fund the plan's benefit liability to date for the individual employee described by the benefit illustration. For the defined benefit plan, the accrual method is used in the illustration in order to indicate the actual funding situation of an individual employee at any one time for any year between age 25 and age 65. A level funding method—not unit accrual—would of course be used in actual practice in a final-average defined benefit percentage formula plan, with the method based on the plan's liabilities for the covered group as a whole. However, comparison of the two approaches as they affect an individual requires analysis of individual situations rather than aggregates. Ultimately, it is the individual who is the focus of the plan and the beneficiary of its benefits.

Comparisons of defined benefit and defined contribution approaches are rarely made. This is unfortunate, for it deprives individual plan participants of important information about the funding of their benefits. Often it is only the actuary of the defined benefit plan who knows for sure the actual effective allocation of funds per individual. Yet on termination of an individual employee's employment, no matter what the funding method a defined benefit plan has used, no more than the present dollar value of the individual's own formula-determined benefit is applied in his case. This is the kind of information the following pages aim to provide.

Career Participation. Comparing the two approaches on a career-long participation basis, the following characteristics may be observed:

¶ Under the defined benefit approach, the employer contribution is a low percentage of the entering employee's salary at younger ages, beginning at 1.52 percent of the salary of the 25-year-old participant compared with a uniform 7.5 percent of salary contribution under the defined contribution plan for participants of all ages. (Columns 4 and 7, Table 8.2)

¶ Not until the employee under a defined benefit plan reaches age 46 does the employer contribution on his behalf as a percentage of current salary equal the uniform 7.5 percent of salary rate under the defined contribution approach.

¶ The steady annual rise in employer contributions as a percentage of salary under the defined benefit plan brings the employer's annual cost up to a percentage of the employee's salary at the higher ages that far exceeds that of the defined contribution rate of 7.5 percent. By age 55, the employer's contribution has risen to 15 percent. It is 22 percent of the even higher salary at age 60 and amounts to nearly 30 percent of salary at age 64.

¶ The heavy weighting of employer contributions under a defined benefit plan at the higher ages is even more startling when expressed in dollar terms. This is a result of the much higher percentage contribution applied against a much higher salary. In the example, the employer cost for a person aged 30 under a defined benefit plan is $305, compared with $1,043 under a defined contribution plan. At age 64, the defined benefit plan cost is $11,271, compared with $2,850 under a defined contribution plan. The employer cost in dollars under a defined benefit plan in the illustration is 37 times as high at age 64 as at age 30, even though salary is only 3 times as high. These relationships are shown graphically in Chart 8.1. Under a defined contribution plan, both the salary and the employer cost rise at the same rate—both have tripled.

Table 8.2 Comparison of Benefit Accrual and Employer Costs Under Defined Benefit and Defined Contribution Plans

(1)	(2)	(3)	(4)	(5)	(6)	(7)	(8)	(9)	(10)	(11)
			Defined Benefit Approach			Defined Contribution Approach			Amount of Annuity Beginning at Age 65 Purchased to Age Shown in Column 2	
			Payment to Fund			Payment to Fund				
Years in Plan	Age	Current Salary	% of Current Salary	Amount in $	Accumulation of Principal + 6% Interest	% of Current Salary	Amount in $	Accumulation of Principal + 6% Interest	Defined Benefit Approach	Defined Contribution Approach
1	25	$12,000	1.52%	$ 182	$ 181	7.5%	$ 900	$ 898	$ 180	$ 891
2	26	12,360	1.61	199	390	7.5	927	1,877	365	1,757
3	27	12,731	1.70	216	629	7.5	955	2,942	556	2,599
4	28	13,113	1.81	237	903	7.5	983	4,100	753	3,417
5	29	13,505	1.92	259	1,215	7.5	1,013	5,357	955	4,212
6	30	13,911	2.19	305	1,592	7.5	1,043	6,720	1,181	4,985
7	31	14,329	2.38	341	2,028	7.5	1,075	8,196	1,419	5,735
8	32	14,758	2.59	382	2,530	7.5	1,107	9,792	1,670	6,464
9	33	15,201	2.81	427	3,108	7.5	1,140	11,518	1,936	7,173
10	34	15,657	3.05	478	3,771	7.5	1,175	13,381	2,215	7,862
11	35	16,127	3.31	534	4,528	7.5	1,210	15,391	2,510	8,531
12	36	16,611	3.59	596	5,394	7.5	1,246	17,557	2,820	9,181
13	37	17,109	3.89	666	6,380	7.5	1,283	19,891	3,147	9,813
14	38	17,622	4.21	743	7,501	7.5	1,325	22,404	3,491	10,427
15	39	18,151	4.56	828	8,775	7.5	1,361	25,107	3,852	11,023
16	40	18,696	4.93	922	10,219	7.5	1,403	28,013	4,233	11,603
17	41	19,256	5.33	1,027	11,855	7.5	1,445	31,135	4,632	12,166

Age	Age	Salary	Factor		Interest					
18	42	19,834	5.76	1,142	7.5	13,704	1,487	34,487	5,052	12,713
19	43	20,429	6.23	1,273	7.5	15,794	1,532	38,086	5,492	13,245
20	44	21,042	6.73	1,416	7.5	18,151	1,578	41,946	5,955	13,762
21	45	21,673	7.26	1,573	7.5	20,809	1,625	46,085	6,440	14,264
22	46	22,324	7.84	1,750	7.5	23,801	1,674	50,521	6,949	14,752
23	47	22,993	8.46	1,945	7.5	27,167	1,724	55,273	7,483	15,226
24	48	23,683	9.13	2,162	7.5	30,950	1,776	60,362	8,043	15,686
25	49	24,394	9.85	2,402	7.5	35,200	1,829	65,810	8,629	16,134
26	50	25,125	10.62	2,669	7.5	39,968	1,885	71,639	9,244	16,569
27	51	25,879	11.44	2,961	7.5	45,316	1,941	77,875	9,887	16,992
28	52	26,655	12.33	3,287	7.5	51,308	2,000	84,542	10,561	17,402
29	53	27,455	13.28	3,645	7.5	58,019	2,059	91,670	11,267	17,801
30	54	28,279	14.30	4,044	7.5	65,529	2,121	99,286	12,005	18,189
31	55	29,127	15.40	4,486	7.5	73,930	2,185	107,424	12,777	18,566
32	56	30,001	16.58	4,974	7.5	83,320	2,250	116,115	13,585	18,932
33	57	30,901	17.84	5,513	7.5	93,811	2,318	125,394	14,430	19,288
34	58	31,828	19.20	6,111	7.5	105,527	2,387	135,300	15,313	19,634
35	59	32,783	20.65	6,769	7.5	118,603	2,459	145,872	16,236	19,970
36	60	33,766	22.21	7,500	7.5	133,190	2,533	157,151	17,201	20,296
37	61	34,779	23.89	8,309	7.5	149,457	2,609	169,184	18,210	20,613
38	62	35,823	25.68	9,199	7.5	167,587	2,687	182,016	19,263	20,921
39	63	36,898	27.60	10,184	7.5	187,786	2,768	195,698	20,363	21,221
40	64	38,004	29.66	11,271	7.5	210,285	2,850	210,285	21,512	21,512
	Total			$112,927			$67,868			

Note: Benefit objective for both plans: 1.5% of final 5-year average salary times years of service for a 40-year career under one employer.

Assumptions used in preparation of table: 6% interest factor; A-1949 Mortality Table (Projected Scale B); 3.5% of contribution administrative expense factor.

CHART 8.1

Annual Employer Contributions—Noncontributory Defined Benefit and Defined Contribution Plans

(annual retirement income of $21,500 under both approaches)

Annual employer contribution

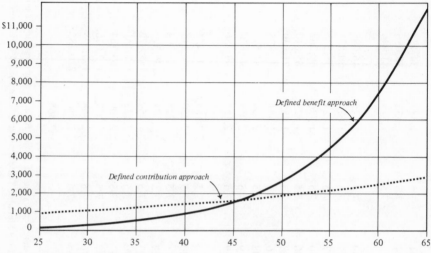

Age of participation (entry at 25; retirement at 65)

¶ The data in Table 8.2 indicate why contributions to a variable annuity plan should never be computed on an accrued benefit (unit credit) approach to funding. Two thirds of the defined benefit employer contributions ($74,316) for the 40-year period are heaped up in the last 10 years, compared with only 2.7 percent ($3,026) in the first 10 years. This places the participant at the mercy of relatively short-term swings in the stock market, and deprives him of the long-term dollar-cost-averaging experience for which variable annuities were designed.

¶ For the 40-year period of participation, the total amount contributed by the employer under the defined benefit approach is 66 percent higher than under the defined contribution approach: $112,900 under defined benefit versus $67,900 under defined contribution. The $45,000 higher cost under the defined benefit approach is the consequence of its lower interest earnings capacity.

¯¶ Table 8.2 also indicates the effect of compound interest growth on the funds contributed by the employer. The higher contributions in earlier years under a defined contribution plan result in higher interest earnings on the individually allocated basis illustrated. These interest earnings alone amount to 68 percent of the total $210,000 accumulation at age 65. Under defined benefit plans, total employer contributions for the entire 40-year period are higher, but are heaped up at the end of the employee's working career and yield only 46 percent of the total accumulation as interest.

¶ The combined effect of contributions and of compound interest earnings on the growing accumulations under the two types of plan is to produce by age 65 exactly the same annuity accumulation amount under both plans, but at all younger ages a greater accumulation under the defined contribution plan. The accumulation at any age is equal under both plans to the single-sum value of the deferred benefits purchased by that age. For example, at age 35 the employee under a defined benefit plan has accumulated a single-sum (present) benefit value of $4,528, while if he had been under a defined contribution plan, it would have been $15,391. Table 8.3 shows benefit values under the two plans at selected ages.

¶ At termination of employment prior to age 65, the deferred pension benefit under the defined contribution approach is substantially higher at every age than under the defined benefit approach. The same is generally true of survivor and disability benefits. This is primarily due to the combined effect of higher employer contributions at the younger ages under the defined contribution plan and the longer period of interest compounding on the larger input amounts in the earlier years.

Table 8.4 summarizes from Table 8.2 the retirement benefit an employee

Table 8.3 Present Value of Deferred Annuity at Selected Ages (accumulation of principal at 6% interest)

Age	Years in Plan	Accumulation	
		Defined Benefit Approach	Defined Contribution Approach
25	1	$ 181	$ 898
35	11	4,528	15,391
45	21	20,809	46,085
55	31	73,930	107,424
64	40	210,285	210,285

would receive at age 65 if he were to leave his employer at any one of the selected ages shown.

These data raise a question of how much the Pension Reform Act of 1974 accomplishes for employees covered by defined benefit plans. After 11 years in such a plan, from ages 25 through 35, assuming vested status, only $2,500 of the expected annual retirement benefit of $21,500 has been vested, against more than $8,500 of the benefit under a defined contribution plan.

Varied Entry Age. One should also look at the resulting annuity of employees who change jobs at different stages in their working career. If pension benefits are vested, an employee terminating service before the retirement age is entitled to a benefit payable later, when the individual has reached the plan's normal retirement age. In our example the full career benefit for an employee at age 65 who works for only one employer is a strictly comparable $21,500 per year under both defined benefit and defined contribution plans.

Under defined benefit plans, both the age at which an employee changes jobs and the number of times he changes jobs significantly influence the total accrued benefit payable at age 65. The age-65 benefit is the sum of benefits determined by multiplying 1.5 percent of the final average salary for each job times the number of years of service with that employer. A job change freezes the benefit at the average salary level on termination of employment. Table 8.5 compares the benefits payable at age 65 for an employee who makes no career job change with those for employees who move from one

Table 8.4 **Annual Retirement Annuity Earned as of Age Shown—Defined Benefit and Defined Contribution Approaches**

Age	Years in Plan	Defined Benefit Approach	Defined Contribution Approach
25	1	$ 180	$ 891
35	11	2,510	8,531
45	21	6,440	14,264
55	31	12,777	18,566
64	40	21,512	21,512

Note: Annuity payable beginning at age 65.

identical defined benefit plan to another, one at age 40, one at age 50, and one at ages 35 *and* 50. The lesser amounts of annual annuity payable at age 65 reflect the leverage of the final-average-salary factor in the calculation, since the salary of each of these employees was exactly the same in each year of employment.

By contrast, the age-65 accrued benefit for an employee under the defined contribution plan or plans is exactly the same, $21,500, whether he remains with the same employer for his entire working career or makes any number of changes to employers offering comparable defined contribution plans.

Although objective evidence is lacking, employers who have chosen a defined benefit plan may find costs so high for new employees in the upper age brackets that they may feel almost forced to discriminate against older job-seekers in their hiring practices. In order to eliminate this potential for discrimination, the Pension Reform Act of 1974 allows defined benefit plans to exclude people from any benefits under the plan if they are initially employed within five years of the normal retirement age. Thus the same Pension Reform Act that requires pension plan participation after one year for all younger people allows complete exclusion for the important five years just before retirement. Future amendments should require at least some benefits to accompany the last five years before normal retirement.

FUNDING BENEFITS

Of all financial institutions affecting individual lives, pension plans are, or should be, the most enduring—literally, "till death do us part." Since peo-

Table 8.5 Effect of Years of Service with Each Employer on Accrued Benefit at Age 65—Defined Benefit Approach

Years of Service	Annual Annuity	Benefit
No change (full 40 years with one employer)	$21,500	100%
Change after 15 years (age 40)	17,300	80
Change after 25 years (age 50)	16,700	77
Change after 10 years (age 35) and again after 15 more years (age 50)	15,475	72

ple usually outlast their jobs, and may outlast a company they work for, some permanent mechanism is needed to set aside enough money during working years to finance the retirement years. The manner and the amount of funding appropriate for pension funds needs to be given careful attention.

The determination of how much money should go into a pension plan, and when, requires financial projections for a very long time into the future. Sophisticated actuarial devices have been developed to analyze the level of benefits, the number and ages of participants, the projected schedule of retirements, life expectancies, and such additional benefits as disability benefits and benefits for survivors.

An additional set of financial considerations has to do with when the pension plan was established (Is it new and underfunded, or mature and well-funded?) and the kind of company or industry (growing or declining, profitable or marginal, stable or cyclical?). Each of these configurations influences the financing and funding of a retirement plan, and therefore the retirement security of the people it covers. Long-established, well-financed, and fully funded plans in a growing or stable industry or governmental unit offer participants maximum assurance of full promised benefits. New plans in an old company where there is a substantial overhang of nonfunded past-service benefit liability, inadequately funded plans in a declining industry or governmental unit, or plans where benefit promises have been allowed to run well ahead of funding do not give participants adequate assurance of full benefits.

A pension plan's financial health is measured in terms of the extent to which it is funded, i.e., the extent to which its pension promises already made could be fully discharged if termination were to occur at any time. It is fully funded if all benefit expectations reflecting service already rendered are covered by funds in hand. If a plan is not fully funded, then the security of participants with respect to benefits already earned may rest heavily on the future profitability of the firm or the future tax base of a governmental unit.

With respect to defined contribution plans, there is only one major cause of underfunding, namely, any past-service liability not yet funded, including liabilities created by the necessity of correcting for salary growth rate assumptions. Current service obligations are fully discharged for all employees each year.

There are three major sources of underfunding of defined benefit pension plans: (1) the past-service liability assumed by a new plan; (2) increases in the pension benefit formula or the addition of improved vesting, disability, survivor, or other benefits; (3) failure of the actuarial assumptions correctly to reflect plan experience.

Past-Service Liability. By the time a company gets around to starting a pension plan, it will have some "old, loyal," long-service employees, including, perhaps, the original entrepreneurs. This employee service already having been rendered, there is no available way to charge their pension costs against prior production. Since benefit credits are almost always granted to employees for past service, these credits will constitute the initial unfunded liability.

Interest. It is usually difficult, perhaps even impossible, for an employer to put up at once the full amount of an initial past-service liability. Under federal tax regulations, the minimum requirement until the passage of the Employee Retirement Income Security Act of 1974 was that the employer pay annually into the fund the interest on the newly created liability. It was desirable to do more than this, and many plans did. Ideally, there should always be a systematic program of liquidating the initial liability through an amortization process. But there was no federal encouragement to do this— quite the opposite, in fact. By federal law, the maximum proportion of a past-service liability that could be amortized each year was 10 percent, a limitation designed more for the collection of taxes than for the protection of pensioners.

The Employee Retirement Income Security Act of 1974 established new minimum funding requirements for past-service liabilities. Payments for initial past-service costs will henceforth have to be amortized over a period not to exceed 30 years. When benefit formula increases result in increased past-service liabilities, these too must be amortized with level annual payments over a 30-year period, beginning with the date of the increase.[3]

Normal Cost. The second portion of a defined benefit pension plan's liability is the so-called normal cost, the cost of benefits currently being earned by employees. Federal law for many years has required that normal costs be paid currently, but employers have had considerable flexibility in defining what normal costs will be. The new pension law continues the requirement that normal costs must be paid, and it establishes for defined benefit plans new criteria for determining whether or not the plan is meeting minimum funding standards. The minimum amount that an employer must contribute to a defined benefit plan now will have to include the normal costs of funding the plan under an accepted actuarial standard plus amortization of un-funded liabilities.[4]

Benefit Increases. A third portion of a defined benefit plan's liability accrues when a benefit formula is raised retroactively. Each time an im-provement in benefits is negotiated under a pension plan, for example, the benefit increase represents an increased liability under the plan. Liabilities arising from increases in benefit formulas are classified as past-service costs. They apply retroactively to the date each employee joined the plan, but not normally to credited service rendered before the plan's inauguration. In ei-ther case, the 1974 Pension Reform Act generally requires their amortization over a 30-year period.

Actuarial Assumptions. Liability determinations and funding programs based on actuarial cost estimates are subject to periodic review and revision. Good pension administration includes close monitoring of the estimates and assumptions. The standard list of actuarial assumptions includes mortality expectations for active employees and retired participants, sex and age dis-tribution turnover rates, disability expectations if disability benefits are in-corporated into the plan, present and expected levels of compensation, ad-ministrative costs, ages of retirement, and, finally, anticipated investment earnings. Changes in any or all of these will require new calculations, and these are made each year.

The numerous assumptions involved in determining pension liabilities offer flexibility to the employer and increase the complexity of the plans. Use by the employer of what from his point of view can be regarded as op-timistic assumptions can considerably reduce the stated normal costs of a plan. A more conservative approach might be more realistic but currently more costly. Thus, in the past an employer could arrange for a reduction of contributions into the plan by increasing one or more of the following: the investment earnings assumption, the turnover assumption, or the mortality expectations. The allowable flexibility permitted situations to develop in which plan costs were seriously underestimated, leading to increases in un-funded liabilities.

A partially unfunded pension plan is a serious matter if the employer goes out of business or if he is not in a position to meet normal plan costs plus in-terest costs on any unfunded portion of the liability. Since an important ob-jective of funding is truly to insulate pension plan participants from the ef-fects of adverse business experience of the employer, a pension fund should be fully funded for both prior and current service benefits.

Under the 1974 Pension Reform Act, new standards are to be applied to prevent the growth of normal cost deficiencies. Every year, defined benefit plans must file an actuarial report prepared by a qualified actuary.[5] The actuarial assumptions in use must meet a test of reasonableness and must be representative of the actuary's best estimates of the plan's anticipated experience. A new actuarial valuation must be prepared every three years. If actual plan experience turns out to be unfavorable, experience losses (due to variations from actuarial estimates) are to be amortized through increased contributions over a period no longer than 15 years from the time the deficiency is determined. Similarly, the minimum funding rules prescribe that actuarial gains are to be amortized over a 15-year period through decreased contributions.[6] These provisions are expected to result in timely corrections of plan weaknesses and in the general financial strengthening of defined benefit plans.

Plan Termination Insurance. The 1965 report of the President's Committee on Corporate Pension Funds recommended that serious study be given to "a system of *insurance* which, in the event of certain types of termination, would assure plan participants credit for accrued benefits." [7] Considerable doubt was expressed by actuaries and other pension professionals as to the technical feasibility of an arrangement for guaranteeing the obligations of private pension plans other than through the direct purchase of annuity or insurance contracts from life insurance companies. Studies by the Pension Research Council, under the direction of Dr. Dan M. McGill of the Wharton School of Finance and Commerce, helped with the analysis of the problem and the formulation of appropriate insurance solutions.[8] A number of legislative proposals were subsequently offered containing a variety of specific proposals for the structure and function of plan termination insurance systems.

The 1974 Pension Reform Act established a federal pension insurance system. A nonprofit body, the Pension Benefit Guaranty Corporation (PBGC), was set up within the Department of Labor, with the purpose of insuring private plan participants and beneficiaries against the loss of benefits arising from a plan termination. The PBGC guarantees the payment of vested benefit rights. The insured benefits are those promised under the plan, but they may not exceed the actuarial equivalent of the lesser of 100 percent of average wages during the individual's highest-paid five years of plan participation, or $750 a month. The limits are to be adjusted upward with changes in the Social Security wage base.[9]

Premiums charged to the covered retirement plans will finance the PBGC. It is expected that in the future premiums will be related to the size of a plan's unfunded liabilities. The PBGC will monitor adherence of plans to minimum funding requirements and benefit payments, sudden decreases in numbers of plan participants, and mergers and consolidations of plans or transfers of plan assets. The combined effect of the PBGC and the funding standard regulations established by other sections of the Pension Reform Act of 1974 can be expected to do much to improve the capacity of defined benefit pension plans to meet their benefit obligations and to assure participants that their pension plan can keep its promises, even in the event the employer goes out of business.

Until the 1974 act, as noted above, the financial obligation of a pension trust was limited to the actual assets of the plan; there was no recourse beyond that limit for those to whom benefits had been promised but for whom the liability had been insufficiently funded. Under the new pension law, the gap between the employer and the pension plan has been bridged. If the PBGC has had to pay benefits to vested participants upon plan termination, employers are liable for reimbursing the insurance corporation for insurance benefits paid. (This is in addition to any insurance premiums previously paid to the PBGC.) The liability is for 100 percent of the underfunding of the PBGC-insured benefits of the terminated plan, but in no event can it exceed 30 percent of the employer's net worth. If the employer fails to pay the required amounts, there is provision for a lien (having the same priority as that of a federal tax lien) to be placed on the employer's real or personal property. [10]

The new termination insurance provisions constitute a recognition in public policy that an employer who establishes a pension plan cannot thereafter isolate himself from the financial consequences of the promises made. The reform was long overdue.

PUBLIC RETIREMENT SYSTEMS

During the last few years, the intense spotlight of pension reform has focused on private plans. Pension plans for public employees have remained in the shadows. Yet, according to at least one pension expert, Dan M. McGill, chairman of the Pension Research Council, public plans are more in need of regulation than private plans. On the whole, public plans can be faulted on more than one count. Many have become overly generous, especially because of extravagant early retirement benefits or failure to integrate with Social Security benefits. Some are not meeting normal costs and more are seriously underfunded. Finally, their investment and accounting practices often leave much to be desired. There are exceptions, of course. In recent years, some states have grasped the problems of plan design and funding, and perhaps a larger number of states have changed laws that limited flexibility of investment policy.

In every respect, however, just how a state or local government handles its retirement plan is strictly up to it. Unlike private plans, public plans are not subject to the standards set by the Internal Revenue Service for qualification of plans or to the new Pension Reform Act of 1974. Literally no one—except a few taxpayers—is looking over the shoulders of public plans. And the interest of taxpayers is greatly attentuated by lack of information, the almost undecipherable complexity of the pension plans themselves, and the priorities usually assigned to other public issues and expenditures.

Another factor affecting public retirement plans often leads to departures from sound principles of funding. Unlike a private employer, who may be quickly affected by adverse changes in product markets, consumer preferences, competition, management inefficiency, or a host of other factors, and may have to close his doors, a state, city, or county is not affected by such factors in this manner. It is assumed that a unit of government will last forever and probably grow forever, always in a position to levy more taxes to cover unfunded benefit costs. In fact, the argument has been made that a state should follow a "pay-as-you-go" approach in financing its employee retirements, since it has the sovereign taxing power.

But as the size of state and local governments has grown, especially during the last 20 years, the increasing magnitude of unfunded or underfunded pension liabilities has changed the picture. Only now it is becoming more evident that the same rules that apply to the funding of private pensions must apply to pensions for public employees, and for the same reasons. Current operating costs of government should be borne by the current beneficiaries of that government; present taxpayers should pay the cost of current government services, including the current cost of making good in the future on retirement benefit expectations.

Recently a number of states have established pension commissions to take longer-range views of the question of pension benefits and financing. Illinois, Ohio, Minnesota, and New York are among the states which have attempted to get a better control over alarming increases in unfunded liabilities, "benefit leapfrogging" by various public employee groups, and successive introductions of generous benefits that were creating ever greater levels of financial liability, with benefits sometimes far exceeding those private employers could afford.[11]

When Social Security was made available optionally to public employees, instead of integrating the benefits to provide a uniform total benefit from employer contributions below and above the Social Security wage base from both Social Security and the public retirement plan benefits, some states simply added the benefits to existing coverage. In the state of New York, because of this and other liberal benefit provisions, some long-service employees can retire earlier than age 65 with total retirement benefits exceeding 100 percent of final salary.[12] Efforts are being made in a number of cities and states to begin the gigantic task of catching up on the funding of retirement plan liabilities.

Illinois. In the state of Illinois in the late 1960s, the legislature enacted a law requiring the various retirement funds covering public employees to begin the huge task of reducing unfunded liabilities; later, however, the legislature failed to provide the necessary appropriations. In 1974 teachers in Illinois won a court ruling that the legislature must make regular payments to reduce the $1.7-billion liability in the Illinois teachers' retirement system over a period of 50 years, as well as to provide for the funding of newly earned benefits. The ruling will increase the 1974 state expenditure for the plan to $245 million from $90 million in the previous year.[13] Altogether, the three retirement systems that cover teachers in Illinois—the Teachers Retirement System, the Pension and Retirement Fund of Chicago, and the State Universities Retirement System—are unfunded by $3 billion. Assets total $1.3 billion and liabilities $4.3 billion.[14]

Ohio. In the late 1960s in Ohio, some 454 local policemen's and firemen's pension plans were gathered together in a consolidated new fund, the Police and Firemen's Disability Pension Fund. (Statewide plans had been in effect for teachers since 1920 and for other state employees since 1935.) An actuarial study of the separate local police and firemen funds found that together they had only $75 million to bring to the new consolidated fund, but that $490 million of benefit promises had already been incurred to date.

Under the new plan, each city was charged with its own unfunded accrued liability. A report in *Pensions* magazine indicated that in 1972 normal costs for current service were 7 percent of salary contributed by police and firemen and 13 percent of payroll contributed by the cities. Funding accrued liabilities, which added a further expense, averaged 16 percent of payroll for the cities. This is a total exceeding one third of payroll.[15]

Los Angeles. Another example of serious underfunding and over-generous benefits is the City of Los Angeles Fire and Police Pension System. In 1971–1972, 32 percent of the city's property tax was consumed by the fire and police pension system. More than half of that is being paid toward a 70-year amortization of the unfunded vested liability of the system, a liability of approximately $1 billion. In 1959, the unfunded vested liability amounted to $310 million; since then, benefit liberalizations have tripled that amount. Assets are $200 million. Now, policemen and firemen who retire with 20 years of service get the minimum pension of $350 per month. The employee who remains on the job 10 years longer gets the maximum pension of 70 percent of salary on the date of retirement. In addition, the benefits rise when salaries of active members are increased. As reported by Barbara Patocka in *Pensions* magazine, the result is that some retirees are receiving a pension that is three times what their salary was when they were working. Members are also covered by Social Security. "The man with 30 years of service," Miss Patocka concludes, "may even see an improvement in his standard of living by retiring." [16]

New York. The state of New York in recent years has become increasingly alarmed about the situation in public pension plans. There have been several recent special commissions and inquiries, with reports that illustrate problems shared in common with many states.

The retirement plans of the city and state of New York are among the most generous in terms of benefits of any of the nation's state and local plans. The Federal Civil Service Retirement plan is in many ways the most generous among public employee plans, but unlike New York public employees, federal employees do not have Social Security on top of their plan.

The New York plans are underfunded, but proportionately greater unfunded liabilities are carried by many other public pension plans. It is a combination of features, each one in itself enough to burden a pension plan, that distinguishes the various New York plans.

The chairman of a commission designated by the New York State legislature in 1971 to look into the pensions of the state described some of the costly features involved:

1. Half pay after 20 years with no age requirement for policemen, firemen, and, in the city of New York, sanitation men.

2. Normal retirement at age 55 with half pay after 20 years of service, the general rule in New York City.

3. Full benefits at age 50 for New York City transit employees.

4. Pensions calculated by the state on a final average salary of the highest three consecutive years.

5. Pensions computed in the city of New York on either the final year's salary or the salary rate on the day of retirement. Abuses in scheduling of overtime in the last year of employment reached scandal proportions.

6. Pensions designed to assume no federal Social Security benefits, with Social Security then added on top.

7. Additional annuity payments by New York City to a union-managed fund from which additional retirement benefits are paid.

8. Exemption of state and city pension payments from state and local income tax. (There is no parallel tax exemption of retirement benefits for private pension plan members.) [17]

A 1970 study comparing the pension benefits paid by the state of New York with 50 of the largest private employers and unions in the state concluded that *none* of the private plans was as liberal as the state's plan.[18]

The appointment of a New York State Pension Commission in 1971 was a timely event. In 1971 the taxpayers of the state paid a total of $1.4 billion for pensions. The figure rose to $1.8 billion for that year with the addition of the Social Security contributions of public employers in the state.[19] By 1974 the annual total pension costs exceeded $2 billion.[20]

In New York City, the annual cost of retirement plans and Social Security rose from $260.8 million in 1961 to $753.9 million in 1972, an average rate of more than 10 percent per year. More than 315,000 city employees are members of the city-operated retirement systems; more than 75,000 retired employees or their beneficiaries receive benefits of nearly $400 million yearly. These New York City retirement systems have $6.6 billion in assets, more than twice that in liabilities ($14 billion), and an annual investment income of approximately $275 million.[21]

It was the refusal of the New York State legislature to enact a city-agreed pension settlement that led to a brief strike in June 1971 in which city employees raised and left open several drawbridges around Manhattan. The legislature refused to accept a 20-year half pay, 40-year full pay (with no age requirement) pension settlement for general city employees. Already generous, the current plan provides for 55 percent of final year's salary after 25 years. The striking employees wanted a plan that would provide the benefits accorded members of the city's uniformed services. It was at this point that the legislature appointed the New York State Pension Commission.[22]

The drawbridge strike in 1971 and near-default on New York City debts in 1975 gained national attention, revealing at least two elements of public pensions that had apparently not made themselves felt: the disorganized way in which various public pension benefit settlements had been made in the past, and the growing power of unions of public employees in their negotiations with local governments.

Political Forces. Failure to approach systematically the question of the cost of benefit liberalizations became a modus operandi in legislation long before the present era of large numbers of public employees, rich benefits, and powerful unionization of public employees. Now readjustments are difficult. The combined effects of benefit ratchets, leapfrogging by employee groups, and the ease of setting benefit increases without any formal requirements for funding them, has led state governments to continue to enact benefits that run far ahead of the provision for financing them. Some of the bills in the form of heavy increases in pension costs are already coming due, but the impact of cost for benefits already voted, however great it now is, will be even greater in the future.

Faced with escalating costs and demands, a number of states have appointed pension commissions for analysis, control, coordination, and long-term planning. If political considerations do not render them impotent, some long-term improvements may result. But the difficulties of coordination alone are enormous. In the New York State legislature, for example, some 216 bills pertaining to New York City pensions were enacted between 1960 and 1970. Yet, according to a 1972 report by the Economic Development Council of New York City, no running record of the changes was kept, "making it extremely difficult," the council concluded, "for public officials to weigh suggested new changes . . . and, with the turnover in elected officials over time, places them at a distinct disadvantage in determining whether the changes are reasonable or whether they will tend to 'feed the fires' for further liberalization elsewhere." [23]

A particularly difficult problem is the proper exercise of management responsibility by elected officials in their approach to pension benefits and financing. The 1972 New York Chamber of Commerce pension task force observed:

Public employee unions appear to be far more powerful than their private sector counterparts. There is a general failure to recognize the essential differences between public and private employer negotiations. The services provided by the City are not subject to the same law of supply and demand that a private employer faces. Consequently, public employee unions have less fear of diminished employment and are much less likely to be concerned with market forces. Similarly, the City does not approach the bargaining table with the resolve engendered in private employers by the absolute necessity to avoid pricing their products or services out of a competitive market. There is little or no competition for the City's services.[24]

UNDERFUNDING OF FEDERAL EMPLOYEE PLANS

The annual report for 1968 of the United States Civil Service Commission stated bluntly that "something has to be done about the civil service retirement system." Referring to an existing policy of "brinksmanship in retirement funding," the report pointed to an unfunded liability for fiscal 1968 "of more than $52 billion and a balance of $18 billion." [25] By 1974 the unfunded liability had grown to $77 billion.[26]

The huge unfunded liability has developed gradually, the product of years of inadequate financing. Employees have paid in their share for the contributory retirement plan, but the Civil Service Commission has frankly acknowledged that the government has "not made regular, systematic contributions in amounts sufficient to take care of liberalized benefits." [27] Consulting actuaries to the U.S. Civil Service pension system told the Congress in 1973 that "by all standards set by the government for nongovernmental pension funds, the retirement system is not adequately financed, with the result that considerable present expense is being passed on to future generations of taxpayers." [28]

Already, retirees from federal government service receive higher pension benefits than do their counterparts in private industry. At present, under the contributory federal plan employees pay in 7 percent of their salaries and the government matches this amount. Since the majority of private plans are noncontributory, it might seem that the federal employee contribution was making up the difference in benefit levels, but this is not the case. The huge cost of the federal plan is understated because of its continued and increasing underfunding. As was explained in Civil Service Commission testimony before a Senate Appropriations Subcommittee in 1968, "every time we increase salaries by $1, we are increasing the unfunded liability by $2.50." [29]

To magnify the problems already existing, Congress in 1970 added the most liberal cost-of-living increase to be found among all the pension plans in the nation, private or public. Failure in dealing with the problem of inflation as it affected the public generally did not deter either Congress or the Administration from insulating from the effects of inflation the more than one million beneficiaries of the system and, in the future, all retirees from the current federal work force of over two and a half million. [30] This is done through a provision of the law that provides a full cost-of-living pension increase whenever the cost of living has gone up by at least 3 percent since the date of any previous increase. The law adds to this an extra 1 percent every time the cost of living increases by 3 percent, a one-third extra premium on inflation. The stated objective of the extra 1 percent was to protect federal employees from the three-month lag; actually the 1-percent extra benefit is a permanent addition and is even included in the base for future benefit increases. Writing in *Business Week,* Arch Patton notes that "some wags have suggested that the one-third premium explains why Washington has done so little about curbing inflation: All the civil service employees make a profit on it." [31]

Between 1965 and 1974 the cost of living rose 69 percent; civil service pensions rose 85 percent. A man who retired with a pension of $500 a month was getting $925 a month. Increases between 1970 and 1974 alone have already added over $10 billion of unfunded increased future costs.

The effect of the automatic escalator in benefits for federal employees who will retire in the future is estimated by the Civil Service pension actuaries to require an increase in the current normal cost of the plan from the present 14 percent of payroll to 21.13 percent. Double-digit inflation could quickly bring the cost up to 30 percent or more of the federal payroll. And it must be remembered that this figure does not include amortization provision for the existing unfunded liability, the interest cost of which is now only partially included in the current costs and will not be fully included until 1980. As incurred liabilities rise because of the cost-of-living increases, this interest cost will rise too, perhaps then bringing the cost of the pension system in 1980 to 40 percent or more of payroll. If a 4-percent annual inflation rate is assumed, the 1974 unfunded liability would rise to $156 billion instead of $77 billion under a static assumption.[32]

Another reason for the high cost of the federal civil service plan is that it provides, as do many state plans, extremely expensive early retirement provisions. An employee may retire with a full pension at age 55 after 30 years of service. This provision roughly doubles the cost of providing a pension over what it would cost were age 65 to be the normal retirement age. It partially accounts for the high ratio of retired federal employees to the current work force.

Yearly actuarial reports of the Civil Service Retirement System point out to the Congress the growth and extent of unfunded plan liabilities. Adding, though gradually, the interest cost to current funding levels has represented a step toward more rational and responsible financing of the system. The cost-of-living feature, with its compounding 1 percent extra, adds enormously to the difficulty of the task.

The benefit structure and funding situation of the federal civil service plan raises many of the same policy questions regarding pension protection of employees that the public employee systems of the states do. Should not the same funding standards be applied to pension plans of public and private employers? Equitable treatment of all members of retirement plans—and of taxpayers—would seem to make sense if government employees are not to become a specially protected elite, benefiting from the capacity of governments to provide for taxation of citizens in the future who are unable to represent themselves in the legislative sessions of today. Or, on the other hand, retired public employees could become an endangered species if their unit of government ever entered a stage of contraction, or if taxpayers ever decided the tax burden for pensions was too great.

Another Federal Plan—The Military. Perhaps the most obscure of all public pension plans is the Armed Services Pension System. It provides the public with no annual report and its unfunded liabilities exceed even the gargantuan liabilities of its companion, the Federal Civil Service Retirement System. As figures shown in Chapter 5 indicate, the failure to establish a sound method of reserve financing for this system has created an annual burden of expenditure that is expected to rise to nearly $6 billion in 1978. The unfunded liability now exceeds $130 billion.

A PUBLIC POLICY FOR PUBLIC PLANS

Several points become immediately evident upon the examination of local, state, and federal employee retirement systems. Nearly all government employers provide a retirement plan for their employees, an excellent record, providing coverage far ahead of the private sector. On the average, the vesting provisions of these plans are at least on a par with those of private plans, and in some cases vesting is earlier, also a good record. Benefits of public plans are often provided for at ages or service periods enabling retirement with normal benefits as early as age 55, and for uniformed employees even earlier. This is extravagant. Such over-generous provisions can increase by as much as half the costs of these plans. Also extravagant is the frequent failure of the plans to integrate benefits with Social Security; over-generous early retirement benefits and failure to integrate with Social Security make some public employees a true pension elite, retirees who fare far better than their counterparts who have worked throughout their productive lives in the private sector. Perhaps most serious of all the defects is lack of prudent funding, representing a lack of willingness to face up to the actual costs of pension plans. While few of the state and local plans are operated wholly on a "pay-as-you-go" basis, many are dangerously close to it and most have accumulated liabilities substantially in excess of assets. This does not provide adequate security for public employee pensions, or fair treatment for future taxpayers. Coupled with this is the increase in the number of public employees during the last decade or two. As they begin to retire, a surge in the population of retired public employees will take place (augmented by the unusual opportunities for early retirement that are open to them). Promises made in earlier decades, but not fully funded, will have to be kept at tremendous cost.

Specific steps should now be taken to improve the soundness of public retirement systems—federal, state, and local.

1. Public employee plans should be required to meet the same standards for the amortization of past service benefits and the funding of normal costs that are applied by law to private pension plans.

2. If the above requirement is implemented, it will be necessary in most if not all states to rechannel tax revenues in order to begin the process of reducing unfunded liabilities and meeting normal costs. This should raise the consciousness of taxpayers regarding plan provisions.

3. For each legislative or collective bargaining proposal, independent current and future cost estimates should be required, and specific tax increases mandated to meet any increased costs.

4. In reexamining public plan provisions, careful attention should be given to the generous early retirement provisions so prevalent at present, and growing in use. Although it may be impossible to alter benefit promises and early retirement options available to persons presently participating in these plans, it would be desirable to consider bringing newly hired public employees into plans that provide for a normal retirement no earlier than age 65, with earlier retirement available only under standard actuarial reduction provisions. Splitting off new entrants into a separate plan or a plan with altered provisions for new entrants will not be easy. One of the main arguments mounted against it is that two employees in the same job and pay class would be treated differently in terms of the employer expenditure for the deferred pension benefit of each. Union leaders in particular have argued that a proposal for a split pension plan would do violence to the principle of equal pay for equal work or equal treatment of employees in similar situations. This argument could backfire were the public ever to decide that reform in early retirement provisions could only occur through depriving present employees of benefits promised them. A better method might be to provide a current salary differential for new entrants who would be accepting a return to age 65 as normal retirement age.

5. Are uniformed public employees—police, firefighters, and sanitation personnel—to remain as separate classes of pensioners when it comes to early retirement? This is perhaps one of the toughest problems of public administration. On the one hand it is reasonable to support the idea that the physically demanding and often dangerous situation of the uniformed services demands younger men and women. Early retirement seems appropriate in the light of the hazards faced and the demands made. Yet plan provisions frequently make early retirement attractive not for the purpose of binding up the wounds and exhaustion of an arduous life, but for the purpose of seeking another job at comparable pay with the additional advantage of receiving a

"retirement" income at the same time. A policy question that must be fairly and frankly acknowledged is whether public budgets can afford this result.

6. All public employees should participate in the Social Security system. Federal employees (except members of the Armed Forces Retirement System), and nearly all public employees in a half a dozen states, plus some in some pension systems in other states, do not now participate in Social Security. The burden and the benefits of an income transfer and redistribution system—Social Security—should be shared as broadly and as equitably as possible. All citizens benefit from the existence of such a system, whether they participate or not. Those who participate receive benefits directly. Employers and employees who do not contribute to Social Security, however, effectively increase the burden on those who do participate. The option for state and local employments to remain outside the Social Security program and the noncoverage of federal employment represent the last serious gap in this national scheme.

7. The contributions or the benefits of all public pension plans should provide their benefits so as to be integrated with Social Security.

8. The highest standards of actuarial evaluation, accounting, and disclosure of operations should be required of public pension systems. Perhaps model state laws should provide for this. Independent certified public accountants should examine each pension fund annually and the results of the audit should be published. The exact extent of unfunded liabilities should be determined by qualified actuaries according to a reasonable and clearly stated set of actuarial assumptions and established amortization schedules.

It would seem reasonable to establish as public policy that all types of employer-sponsored or jointly-administered pension plans be subject to the same rules of conduct, whether they involve public employers or private employers. The distinction between a public social insurance program and a public employee retirement system should be kept clear. By its nature a social insurance system, or Social Security, is a system for redistribution and intergenerational transfer, and it must depend on the willingness of each successive generation to support aged persons in return for the implicit promise that the supporting generation's turn will come. An employee retirement system, on the other hand, public or private, defers a part of wages until the retirement age, and is thus properly operated on the basis of reserve funding. Public policy should not permit heavily unfunded liabilities for public employee or private retirement plans to be created and thrust forward onto future generations, captive though they may be through precedent or sovereign power.

It is very much in the interest of present public employees and their governmental units to move toward sound retirement provisions and adequate financing and funding of public plans. A rapid shift of priorities from benefit leapfrogging to assurance of future payments of reasonable benefits would seem to be in the public interest. Public employees are just as deserving of legislative and regulatory protection of their benefits as are private employees. But to achieve adequate financing and funding, they will have to forego excesses in early retirement benefits, accept integration of benefits with Social Security, and be prepared for higher tax rates. All signs point toward intense public policy discussion of public employee retirement plans in coming years.

FIDUCIARY RESPONSIBILITY

Vesting protects the pension; funding protects the vesting. Sound investment policies and administrative procedures protect the funding. Standards for fiduciary responsibility and information disclosure are important elements of sound pension plans. Fiduciary misconduct is rare, but it is a possibility that must be guarded against.

Certain pension fiduciary requirements have been part of the Internal Revenue Code for many years, but lack of precise definition or of appropriate sanction has hampered effective application. In the past, the code has provided that a plan remains tax-exempt only so long as it is used exclusively for the benefit of the employees. Certain types of financial transactions were prohibited. But no authority was granted the IRS to recover misappropriated funds, and the penalties were levied against the plans as a whole rather than the individuals who had misused their trust.

More recently, the Welfare and Pension Plans Disclosure Act of 1958 was a disappointment to those who expected its disclosure provisions to result in information making possible the identification of instances of improper conduct. Finally, as indicated below, the 1974 pension legislation established fiduciary requirements at the federal level.

Some of the types of abuses against which legislative proscriptions are desirable are:

¶ Stealing money from the pension fund, or diverting money from the fund to support or make private investments.

¶ Gross mismanagement.

¶ Use of pension money to engineer corporate takeovers, as described by a Senate Labor Subcommittee counsel in the cases of Sharon Steel Corp., which used pension fund money for takeovers, and Genesco, which used pension fund money to buy and mortgage the stores of S. H. Kress, which it later acquired.[33]

¶ Heavy investment of pension funds in obligations or stock of the parent company.

¶ Loans from the pension fund to the parent company.

¶ Investment of an unduly large proportion of fund assets in a single issue.

¶ Purchases and sales of assets conflicting with the interests of participants. In one case, pension trustees who were also corporate officers purchased shares of company stock for the pension fund while simultaneously selling their own shares, creating a high market price that declined by two thirds when the fund ceased buying.

¶ Loans to corporations in which trustees of the pension fund were owners of the borrowing corporations.

One of the best-known cases of pension mismanagement was that of the jointly operated multiemployer Mine Workers Pension Fund. Large fund amounts from the United Mine Workers pension plan were held in noninterest-bearing accounts in the union-owned National Bank of Washington, making the UMW the bank's largest single customer. A U.S. District Court found that the bank accounts indicated a conspiracy between the union and the bank and that the pension fund trustees had full knowledge of the action. The coal companies' owner-designated trustee was simply ignored by the late John L. Lewis and trustee Josephine Roche in making the noninterest "investments." The court assessed the union and the bank damages amounting to $11.5 million, to be paid into the pension fund.[34]

Another type of questionable activity was reported by a study of the Penn Central Railroad prepared by the staff of the Interstate Commerce Commission. The study alleged financial impropriety on the part of the chairman of the pension fund's finance committee and another officer of the company involving the investment of funds from the company's two pension funds in stocks they had also purchased for themselves.[35]

A spectacular case in which a union-operated pension fund had to be placed in receivership came to light in 1971. A former president of the Barbers' Union testified in a federal court that he and others had received over

$300,000 in illegal fees and kickbacks in connection with the lending of more than $7 million of pension plan funds.[36]

While it is important to develop means of uncovering wrongdoing or conflict-of-interest situations, it is equally important to protect plan managers from undue interference in their exercise of judgment with respect to pension management and investment of funds. Investment managers must be able to carry out their responsibilities in a prudent and timely manner on the basis of information available to them without unduly limiting restrictions. Periodic independent audits and clear proscriptions of certain types of transactions should be formulated in order to protect employees and beneficiaries, and this can be done without inhibiting the proper management of pension funds.

"Prudent man" rules have been developed as one method of helping outside observers to determine whether a trust is properly managed. Presumably, the aim of the prudent man concept is to establish a standard of management behavior that remains within an acceptable spectrum of permitted decision-making and effectively discharges the trust position. Obviously, some pension plans will be better managed than others; there is a distinction between uprightness and competence. The problem of evaluating fiduciary behavior is one of setting "lower limits," the breach of which would make generally apparent a failure of the trust responsibility.

An early expression of the prudent man idea was voiced by Justice Putman in the case of *Harvard College v. Amory* in 1830: "All that can be required of a trustee to invest is that he shall conduct himself faithfully and exercise a sound discretion. He is to observe how men of prudence, discretion, and intelligence manage their own affairs, not in regard to speculation, but in regard to the permanent disposition of their funds, considering the probable income, as well as the probable safety of the capital to be invested." [37]

1974 Law. The fiduciary provisions of the Pension Reform Act of 1974 require that a fiduciary of a plan "act with the care, skill, prudence, and diligence under the circumstances then prevailing that a prudent man acting in a like capacity and familiar with such matters would use in conducting an enterprise of like character and with like aims." The law requires that each fiduciary of a plan act solely in the interests of the plan's participants and beneficiaries and exclusively to provide benefits to these participants and beneficiaries along with the payment of reasonable plan administrative costs.[38]

One feature of the new act is a requirement that fiduciaries diversify plan assets in order to minimize the risk of large financial losses. Thus, a fiduciary is not to invest the whole or an unduly large proportion of trust assets in one type of security or in securities dependent upon the success of one enterprise or upon conditions in one locality, one particular industry, or in mortgages in one particular class of property.

The 1974 act prohibits sales, exchanges, leases, loans, or extensions of credit between a plan and any "party-in-interest," including employers of plan participants, persons rendering services to the plan, unions (and their officers) whose members are plan participants, officers, fiduciaries and employees of a plan, and any relatives or agents of any of these.[39]

In the past, financial abuses have in some circumstances resulted from heavy investment of pension plan assets in the securities of the employer. The Pension Reform Act of 1974 generally limits the holding of employer securities or real property to a total of 10 percent of plan assets. An exception is made for assets of profit-sharing, stock bonus, employee stock ownership, or thrift or savings plans, since it is common for such plans to specifically provide for substantial investments in employer securities. The law generally allows a period of 10 years for disposal of assets that may be necessary in order to meet the 10 percent requirement.[40]

Reporting and disclosure requirements are established by the pension act to facilitate the flow of information required by the Department of Labor and the IRS to monitor fiduciary activity. Penalties are provided for failure of fiduciaries to meet the requirements of the law. A fiduciary who breaches trust requirements becomes personally liable for any losses to the plan resulting from the breach and to removal from office.[41] Violations relating to reporting and disclosure are also subject to penalty.[42]

Public Policy—Income Objectives and Retirement Ages

**There are few sorrows, however poignant,
in which a good income is to no avail.**

Logan Piersall Smith

Each retirement plan should establish a level of benefits suited to its situation. Both external and internal factors are involved, among them the characteristics of the business or industry in which the organization is engaged, current and probable future profitability of the firm, the effects of employee unionization, the degree of competition for personnel, and the type of jobs covered. Government policies and regulations are also involved. Willingness of employees to contribute is also a key element in the decision as to how large a plan's benefits will be. This chapter discusses the establishment of benefit objectives and the related question of the age at which benefits should begin.

BENEFIT OBJECTIVES

Retirement plans generally measure the employer's obligation and the employee's benefit in terms of the employee's service period and compensation rate. Even flat benefit plans, often found in multiemployer plans, relate benefits to broad wage categories.

The proportion of wages or salary that is to be continued as a retirement benefit is usually set by considering the benefit at normal retirement age in terms of a full career under the retirement plan, for example, 30 or 35 years of service. Shorter service produces smaller benefits.

Half-Salary Replacement Goal. A frequently assumed total retirement income goal including the primary Social Security benefit is half-salary after a career of 35 years, say from age 30 to age 65, under a single retirement plan. Or, the income replacement goal may be stated in graduated terms related to level of final pay. One such approach is a "60-50-40" guideline used by many employers, or a "70-60-50" guideline. That is, a goal of 60 to 70 percent of final average pay is set for employees whose earnings at retirement are in the neighborhood of the Social Security earnings base, 50 to 60 percent for those whose earnings range from the current OASDHI earnings base to $25,000 or $30,000, and 40 to 50 percent for those with higher final pay levels.[1] Thus, a plan might provide a benefit of 1 percent of final average salary within the Social Security earnings base and 1.5 percent of final average salary above the earnings base for each year of covered service. The integration with Social Security generally results in a total replacement benefit from Social Security plus the private retirement plan that is higher as a percentage of salary within the Social Security earnings base than for salary above the base.

It is common practice to ignore a spouse's Social Security benefit based on the employee's earnings in setting the benefit goal, since employee circumstances differ in this respect. In setting a general plan goal, however, the possibility of wife's benefits (50 percent of the primary insurance amount) might be taken into account in determining whether an employee would have a higher total take-home pay in retirement than while working.

A worker with long-term coverage whose earnings have typically been below the prevailing Social Security earnings base would find that the replacement portion of retirement income from the federal program alone might amount to 45 to 55 percent of final pay. If to this he can add a private pension benefit of 1 percent times 30 years of service, his total combined benefit can be in the area of 70 to 85 percent of final average pay. A worker whose salary has generally been equal to but no higher than the Social Security earnings base might expect a primary insurance amount at age 65 retirement of about 35 percent of final five-year average salary. Adding the private pension benefit could bring combined retirement income up to 65 percent of final average salary. The combined benefit of the employee whose salary has generally exceeded the Social Security base could be expected to be higher in dollar amount, but as a percentage of total salary it would be nearer the half-salary level. A higher total replacement income as a percentage of final pay for lower-paid workers is appropriate because retirement incomes must be sufficient to command at least basic minimum maintenance requirements.

A half-salary replacement goal assumes a definitely ideal situation in which a worker experiences no significant periods of unemployment, has been covered under private pension plans, and has not changed jobs or been laid off before attaining vested status under private pension coverage. It is to be hoped that increasing numbers of American workers will in the future qualify for full Social Security and private pension benefits. At present, those who so qualify are a minority.

Assuming full career Social Security and private pension coverage, the 1975 Bankers Trust Company study has summarized median combined benefits for 30 years of service under single-employer private plans covering about 25 percent of workers under such plans. As shown in Chapter 4, Table 4.5, a $9,000 final year's compensation provides a median private plan benefit of 29 percent of final year's compensation and a Social Security benefit of 39 percent, totaling 68 percent. A final salary of $25,000 produces a median private pension benefit of 35 percent of final salary and Social Security benefits of 15 percent, totaling 50 percent.

White House Conference Goal. Another expression of a retirement income goal is that of the 1971 White House Conference on Aging. That goal, which echoes the rather general language of the Older Americans Act of 1965, recommends "a total cash income in accordance with the 'American standard of living'." More specifically, the conference recommended as a minimum standard of income adequacy the intermediate budget for an elderly couple prepared by the Bureau of Labor Statistics (nationally averaging $6,041 in the fall of 1974), to be adjusted annually for changes in the cost of living and "rising" national standards of living. The Conference on Aging urged for single individuals a minimum annual total income "sufficient to maintain the same standard of living as for couples—not less than 75 percent of a couple's budget." For the elderly handicapped, who have higher living expenses, the conference recommended appropriate upward adjustments.[2]

Generally, it is appropriate to express minimum national retirement income goals in dollar amounts and pension plan replacement objectives in percentages of salary.

Upper Limits on Pensions? Should a pension plan ever provide benefits greater than 100 percent of salary? Although the question is not of practical importance to very many employees or retirees, from a public policy standpoint it involves the important matter of limits on how much may be put aside—tax deferred—to support pension income. The 1974 Pension Reform Act addresses the question, saying, in effect, that a pension benefit may exceed 100 percent of the average of the highest three years of salary only if the defined benefit amount is $10,000 per year or less; it may not exceed 100 percent if it is larger. For defined contribution and profit-sharing plans the limit is expressed in terms of input; no more than 25 percent of compensation may be paid into the plan each year.[3]

Disposable Income. A 50-percent combined Social Security and private pension income goal for a career of work compares *gross* (pre-tax) incomes before and after retirement. A more useful approach is to compare *disposable* (after-tax) incomes before and after retirement. Comparisons of disposable income before and after retirement provide much better guides for pension plan income objectives than do comparisons of gross incomes. They may also provide better insights regarding equitable tax policy and appropriate levels of social transfer payments from working to nonworking people through the Social Security system.

A gross retirement income equal to half of final salary provides a disposable income substantially greater than 50 percent of the person's take-home pay during his working years. Before retirement, salary is subject to deductions for Social Security taxes and perhaps retirement plan contributions, federal income tax, and perhaps state and local income taxes. Furthermore, there are certain types of expenditures a person may have to make in connection with work, but not after retirement. Work-related clothing and commuting can be expensive. Since 77 percent of retired married couples own their own homes, mostly mortgage-free, and 37 percent of single persons aged 65 or over do also, expenses in retirement may be reduced by the amounts of mortgage principal and interest no longer due; however, property taxes and upkeep frequently prove to be a burden to the elderly. The expenses of children for schooling and college, medical expenses for growing children, and other items are usually greater for the younger family than for the old. After a person retires there are no further deductions for Social Security taxes or pension plan contributions. A man or woman age 65 or over has a double income tax exemption. Social Security retirement benefits are not subject to federal income tax nor is that part of pension income that represents a return of contributions on which personal income tax was previously paid. Income above these exemptions and exclusions will be taxed first in lower brackets. For these reasons, a retirement income that is half of final salary produces a disposable income nearer two thirds of former take-home pay.

A 1972 Labor Department study describes the differing tax status and expenditures before and after retirement as "savings resulting from retirement." At low to moderate income levels the study found that a preretirement income equivalent would be effectively attained by a post-retirement income of from 70 to 78 percent of the preretirement total. Table 9.1 shows the calculations of tax savings.

Reasonable Standard. Most private retirement plans hope to provide a reasonable standard of living during retirement for typical long-service em-

Table 9.1 Disposable Income Before and After Retirement—Married Couples at Various Income Levels

Item	Total Preretirement Income				
	$4,000	$6,000	$8,000	$10,000	$15,000
Federal income tax	170	501	848	1,209	2,128
Federal OASDHI tax	208	312	416	468	468
Preretirement income after federal personal taxes	3,622	5,187	6,736	8,323	12,404
State income tax (12% of federal)	20	60	102	145	255
Preretirement income after federal and state personal taxes	3,602	5,127	6,634	8,178	12,149
Savings resulting from retirement	490	697	902	1,112	1,652
Retirement income needed to equal preretirement disposable income					
Amount	$3,112	$4,430	$5,732	$7,066	$10,497
Percent of total pre-retirement income	78%	74%	72%	71%	70%

Source: Department of Labor calculations in *Monthly Labor Review,* June 1972, p. 18.

ployees. Benefit levels are based on a presumed, though not necessarily explicitly stated, general level of income need. An important feature is that benefits are credited and paid according to the employee's service and salary history. A strength of private plans is that they provide flexibility for different answers to the question of how much to set aside from current earnings for retirement benefits.

Any large plan will of course cover single and married employees, members of large and small families, employees in good and poor health, long-service and short-service employees, and both highly compensated salaried employees and lower-paid unskilled workers. A retirement plan's need presumption cannot set a different goal for each of the individual personal and family situations represented by the plan participants. Nor can it test for other income sources and amounts. It can provide benefits in a systematic and evenhanded way by relating benefits for all to the objective criteria of employee service to the employer—salary and years of service. Consistency, uniformity, and equitable treatment of employees must characterize a private pension plan's benefit goals, despite the variety of individual circumstances that will exist. An individual who expects to need or want a larger income during retirement than that provided by the private pension plan plus Social Security must make the additional provisions on his own.

Retiring employees should of course be able to choose a form of retirement benefit that will include continuing benefits for a surviving spouse under an actuarially equivalent income option. The Pension Reform Act of 1974 requires that a pension plan must automatically provide for a joint and survivor annuity option, although an employee may specifically elect a single life annuity.[4]

HOW WELL WILL OBJECTIVES BE MET?

We are only now beginning to see the results of fairly broad worker participation in plans for security in retirement. Both private pensions and the Social Security system in this country are relatively new. Social Security began paying benefits only in 1940 and the private pension movement did not achieve real momentum until World War II and after. It would be incorrect to judge future performance of either program by levels of benefits provided in the past. The figures offered in Chapter 1 indicate that average incomes of persons who receive some private pension benefits in addition to

Social Security are significantly higher than those who must depend on
Social Security income alone. In view of the gradual increases in Social Security benefit levels, the Consumer Price Index escalator feature now built
into the system, the growth of private pension coverage during the last three
decades, and, most recently, the greater protection of private plan benefits
through the funding and vesting provisions of the Pension Reform Act of
1974, it appears that the income support structure for our retired population
is improving.

Social Security. The benefit objective of Social Security is related to career average monthly earnings, that is, a worker's average covered earnings
reported to the Social Security Administration since 1950 or from age 21,
whichever is later, up to the year the worker reaches retirement age. With
benefits weighted in favor of lower-earnings people, the percentage replacement of average *career* earnings ranges from over 90 percent at the lower
average wage levels for couples' benefits to about 60 percent at the top of
the Social Security wage base. Translated into a percentage of final earnings
just preceding retirement, the Social Security primary benefit generally can
range from 40 percent or more of final earnings for workers with wages
under the base to 8 or 10 percent for highly paid salaried employees.

By design, Social Security taxes and benefits are related only to the earnings base stated by the program. Since the philosophy of the program is to
provide a floor of benefits, however, supplements from separate employer-
sponsored pension plans are necessary in order to bring total retirement income up to a level more adequate than that provided by Social Security
alone. The supplementary function of private plans applies both within the
Social Security earnings base, where private plans provide a part of the total
benefit, and above the base, where private plans provide the whole benefit.
Integration of private plans with Social Security makes it possible to coordi-
nate two plans, social and private, in a way that can provide reasonably uniform benefits in an equitable manner over the whole range of earnings from
low to high.

Private Plan Benefits. An employee whose retirement has been preceded
by a career of private retirement plan participation without forfeitures may
expect a reasonable total retirement income combining Social Security and
private benefits.

Take, for example, an employee who retires at the end of 1975 under a
defined benefit plan providing 1 percent of final five-year average salary
under the Social Security wage base and 1.5 percent above for each year of

service. If the employee has participated in the retirement plan from age 30 to retirement at age 65, and his total salary has been $3,000 above the current Social Security wage base during each of the last five years, his benefit and its relation to previous earnings is as follows:

Preretirement:
    (1) Final year's salary $17,100
    (2) Final five-year average   13,980
    (3) Final five-year average within wage base   10,980

Postretirement:
    (1) Social Security primary insurance amount: $3,600
    (2) Private (defined benefit) pension:

$$(.01 \times 35 \text{ yrs.} \times \$10,980) \; \$3,850$$
$$(.015 \times 35 \text{ yrs.} \times \$3,000) \; \underline{1,575}$$
$$\$5,425 \qquad \qquad 5,425$$

Total retirement income: $9,025

In the example above, the Social Security benefit is 33 percent of the final five-year average salary within the Social Security wage base, and the portion of the private pension benefit calculated on the Social Security base brings the percentage up to 68. Overall, the total of the Social Security and the private pension benefit provides an income of 65 percent of the final five-year average salary just preceding retirement.

COMING CHANGE IN PRIVATE PENSIONS

Influence of Legislation. In the next few years, existing private pension plans will be considerably improved as they meet the requirements of the Employee Retirement Income Security Act of 1974. More people will be covered as a result of minimum entry age requirements. More people will get more benefits as vesting is improved and funding is strengthened. Participants will be protected from loss of benefits on plan termination. Reporting and disclosure requirements will bring plan provisions, financing, and transactions out into the light of day. Many plans, of course, have long met and even exceeded many or all of the new law's minimums. Now, however, all plans will be measured against stated public policy standards.

Employees Without Protection. More than half of the workers in the private sector have no private pension plan coverage because their employers do not have pension plans. Among such employers are those in industries with little or no effective union representation, small employers, businesses with low profit margins, marginal producers, and newly established businesses. Suggestions have been made that some minimum level of private plan coverage be mandated, comparable to mandated unemployment compensation insurance, minimum-wage laws, and Social Security coverage. However, the many problems associated with mandating private pension coverage have not been resolved.

Voluntary Individual Efforts–the IRA. The Pension Reform Act of 1974 contains provisions under which employees may be encouraged, within stated limits and through tax-deferment arrangements, to put aside pension funds on their own when their employer does not have a private pension plan. Such a provision has been available in Canada for many years. Under the new Individual Retirement Account (IRA), the law permits individuals not covered by a retirement plan to deduct from taxable income part of their compensation, provided the amount is set aside for retirement. The IRA may be established as a trust or custodial account, an annuity, or a retirement bond. The deduction is limited to the lesser of $1,500 a year or 15 percent of the individual's compensation.[5]

Prior to 1975, only self-employed persons were permitted to set aside for themselves and their employees tax-deferred funds to support pension benefits, as provided for under H.R. 10 (Keogh Act). The Pension Reform Act increased the Keogh Act limits to the lesser of $7,500 or 15 percent of earned income or compensation. In addition, the new law provides that a self-employed person may contribute and deduct $750 or less per year regardless of the 15-percent limitation.[6]

In principle, the new opportunity of putting aside funds for retirement through tax deferral on such amounts should result in increased retirement savings for workers not otherwise eligible for employer-sponsored retirement plan coverage. Whether aggregate long-term increases in pension protection will result from the provision, however, will depend on the extent to which the IRA is used by the lower-and middle-income employee groups whom it is intended to benefit.

OBJECTIVES CAN BE MET

The Social Security Act of 1972 and the Employee Retirement Income Security Act of 1974 should help raise the future retirement income security of many working Americans to levels that for the first time in history can be considered reasonably adequate. Top priority in public policy for pension planning should next turn toward provisions for workers in the private sector who presently are covered only by Social Security. Concurrently, attention must be given to the large sector of plans for federal, state, and local employees. This attention should include questions of Social Security coverage and public policy matters relating to soundness of funding, assurance of benefits, retirement age, and vesting in public plans.

Undoubtedly our society has the overall capacity to support the elderly in an acceptable manner. The retirement income objectives discussed earlier in this chapter can be met. But slackening growth in the economy and shifts in population age distribution will place severe restraints on our public policy decisions. These decisions must be made carefully lest we end up with either large gaps in our protection for the elderly or unacceptably large costs.

The task of providing adequate incomes for retired workers is not a small one. Under Social Security the current generation of workers pays through immediate income transfers the benefits being currently received by retired workers and beneficiaries. In 1974, the total Social Security taxes collected, excluding those for hospital insurance, amounted to $57.7 billion. Payments totaled $55.9 billion.

Under private plans, which essentially defer income and build up reserve funds to support future payments, the financial burden is also huge. Including public employee plans, annual benefits now approach $20 billion, and assets exceed $275 billion. The magnitude of the reserve-building job in private plans is illustrated by the fact that enough has to be saved during each two working years to support one retirement year. The average life expectancy for male annuitants at age 65 is approximately 17 years; for women, it is about 21 years. If vested retirement plan coverage starts at age 25 and retirement is at age 65, there will be 40 years of working life from which to finance about 20 or more years of retirement. The use of lifetime annuities assures that each individual will receive income as long as he or she lives whether that be to age 70, or to 90, or even 105. Obviously, if participation in a retirement plan does not begin until age 30 or 35, or nonvested benefits are lost by a job change, or retirement occurs earlier than age 65, the job of saving enough funds for retirement is made more difficult.

LEVERS AVAILABLE

There are five primary "levers" that affect the level of retirement benefits to be received by participants in private retirement plans. These levers are (1) entry age into a retirement plan; (2) the vesting provisions; (3) the benefit formula or contribution rate; (4) investment earnings; and (5) retirement age.

Participation. Year-by-year participation in one or more retirement plans throughout a working lifetime is essential if benefits at retirement are going to meet reasonable objectives. The amount of money that must be saved is just too large to permit any extended gaps in coverage or losses through forfeitures.

If membership in a pension plan covers only a few years of employment, it will not produce an adequate lifetime retirement income. The instances in which retirees report receiving small benefits from their private pension plan often reflect a short span of participation rather than the operation of a plan whose benefits are insufficient. It would be inequitable to pay the same pension benefit to a retiree with only 5 to 10 years of plan participation as to a retiree with 40 years of participation.

An early start is necessary if benefits are to be adequate. The Pension Reform Act of 1974 for the first time establishes participation requirements for private pension plans: employees may not be excluded from a pension plan after the later of age 25 or one year of service.[7] An employee who begins work before age 25 may have more than a one-year waiting period, although service between age 22 and 25 must be counted in determining where the employee stands on the vesting schedule.[8] For persons hired at age 25 or over participation must be made available after one year of service.

In the case of plans in which the employer pays the total cost (non-contributory plan), the law in effect requires coverage, since there is no reason for an employee to stay out of a plan paid for wholly by the employer. A plan to which employees contribute can be made either compulsory or voluntary.

The participation provisions of the Pension Reform Act recognize that it is reasonable from the standpoint of public policy to leave out of pension coverage people under 25. Earnings at the under-25 ages tend to be low, employment is sometimes intermittent and is sometimes mixed with attendance at educational institutions. But from about age 25 on it is important to have the most continuous pension plan participation possible. The one-year waiting period for new employees over age 25 cuts down recordkeeping for very short-term employment, but it also assures that when an employee has completed a year of service the employer may not exclude him from the important lifetime process of achieving vested status and of accumulating pension protection. This helps new employees get started quickly after each job change.

Special participation rules are provided under the Pension Reform Act for pension plans providing 100-percent immediate vesting. The act permits these plans to exclude an employee for up to three years before commencing participation. This takes account of the fact that under 100-percent immediate vesting, each year of participation provides an assured retirement benefit, whereas early participation in a plan with deferred vesting is without meaning if the employee leaves before benefits vest.

Vesting. In combination with plan participation, vesting is an essential lever for attaining adequate retirement benefits. We have described in Chapter 7 the alternative minimum vesting provisions of the 1974 Pension Reform Act. Many pension consultants have advised their clients that the 10-year vesting option—that is, no vesting during the first 10 years of plan participation and 100 percent vesting of all the previous 10-year credits once the tenth anniversary occurs—will be the easiest to administer, the best understood by employees, and perhaps cheaper than the "rule of 45" also available as a minimum vesting standard under the law.

Yet for many workers, especially younger ones, 10 years is longer than they will have a job with any particular employer. When this is the case, gaps in vesting are as harmful as gaps in participation. If, then, employment shifts are frequent, each time an individual forefeits benefits by leaving prior to the 10-year minimum (or other delayed vesting provision), the individual is rendered less secure in retirement. A large segment of a worker's working life will go unrepresented in his or her total retirement income. It can be seen that even under the standards of the new law, three or four job changes in a lifetime can leave a worker totally unprotected by the private plans belonged to. It is this irony of coverage without protection that still concerns observers who nevertheless recognize the substantial overall accomplishment of the new legislation in setting sound pension standards.

Contribution Levels. The benefits to be paid by a pension plan are, of course, related to the amount of money going into the pension plan. Under a defined benefit plan, the employer contributions to the plan are determined as those necessary to assure that the formula benefit promise can be kept. The dollar input is normally that determined by the actuarial processes described in Chapter 8. As noted there, the calculation factors used include the age and sex composition of the covered group, mortality experience, salary levels, labor turnover and disability rates, and the actual and anticipated investment earnings of the fund. The higher the formula benefit promise, the larger must be the contributions to the fund or its investment earnings. If the earnings rate increases, benefits could be liberalized, or employer input reduced. Studies indicate the input to private defined benefit pension plans currently amounts to about 6 percent of total payroll.[9]

Under defined contribution plans, as also noted in Chapter 8, the benefit is the retirement income resulting from input stated as a definite percentage of each participant's salary and the investment experience of the fund. Here also, the higher the input, the higher the benefit. If input is increased 10 percent, other things being equal, the benefit will be increased by 10 percent. If investment earnings increase, benefits also increase, since under the defined contribution approach increased fund earnings are allocated on a pro rata basis to the individual participants' accounts under the plan.

Typical defined contribution input varies among plans from 10 to 15 percent of salary, or it may be integrated with Social Security and stated as 10 percent of salary within the current Social Security earnings base and 12 percent or perhaps 15 percent of salary above the base. If the plan is contributory, the employee's share may be 5 percent, for example, of salary, with the employer making up the difference.

Table 9.2 Effect of Different Interest Earnings Rates on an Individual Retirement Account ($1,000 annual deposit)

Year	Total Paid in	Amount Accumulated at Interest Rate of 4%	6%	8%
1	$ 1,000	$ 1,000	$ 1,000	$ 1,000
5	5,000	5,420	5,640	5,870
10	10,000	12,010	13,180	14,490
15	15,000	20,020	23,280	27,150
20	20,000	29,780	36,790	45,760
25	25,000	41,650	54,860	73,110
30	30,000	56,080	79,060	113,280
35	35,000	73,650	111,430	172,320
40	40,000	95,030	154,760	259,060

Investment Earnings. Investment earnings in the form of dividends on equity investments and interest yields on security and mortgage investments can contribute substantially to the accumulation of funds required to finance retirement benefits. In addition, capital gains and losses on equity investment affect the growth of funds underlying the benefit promises of retirement plans.

Table 9.2 illustrates the dramatic effect of compound interest earnings on amounts regularly paid into a retirement plan. At a 4 percent earnings rate, for example, $1,000 paid into a plan each year for 30 years produces an accumulation of $56,080. An investment yield of just 2 percent more a year would produce $79,060 over the same period, or a 40 percent greater amount. At 8 percent, the accumulation would amount to $113,280, or 102 percent higher than at 4 percent.

CHOICE OF RETIREMENT AGE

The premise of a retirement plan is that at some stated age both the worker and the employer will be better off if they part company in an acceptable manner. The advance statement of a normal or mandatory retirement age helps prepare all workers, young and old, for that inevitable date, welcome to some, unwelcome to others. The plan benefits are designed to replace salary or wages. The retirement ages chosen have a powerful effect on the cost of benefits for the individual, for employers, and for society.

Although retirement plans are numerous and retirement ages conventional, there remains a paradox in the idea of retirement, an ambivalence that makes it difficult to bring together in one satisfactory policy so many conflicting objectives and views. On the one hand, retirement is regarded as a reward of leisure and comfort for a lifetime of productive work. Many workers do look forward to retirement and to a relaxation of demanding tasks and daily schedules. Yet it is widely recognized that work involvement provides important ego satisfaction in a work-oriented and work-ethic society and brings social status and recognition. Separation by mandatory retirement from the main stream of economic and social life and from close work associates can bring psychological trauma, feelings of isolation, loss of status.

Consequently, many people seek work after retirement for social and psychological as well as economic reasons. Perhaps some wanted to retire but then found that they had misapprehended the nature of the retirement experience. Studies of elderly people suggest that paid work has a powerful and positive impact on self-esteem, happiness, and relationships with other people.[10]

Why, then, must institutions of production and services set retirement ages and force at least some of our elderly workers into reluctant retirement? Certainly from the employer's point of view production does suffer if older workers cannot perform as well as their younger counterparts. Management and investors suffer if elderly employees at the executive level tend to meet old challenges rather than new ones, fail to respond to social and economic change, and block the progress of able younger managers. At the same time, it is recognized that mandatory retirement rules can also deprive an organization of workers and executives who represent a valuable resource.

Under these circumstances, it is difficult to set a retirement age policy that can please all the people all the time. Perhaps, as in other matters in human relations, there is no way to choose a retirement age that will deal equitably with all persons concerned. We can develop objective tests of eyesight, hearing, strength, and physical dexterity that are "age blind." Perhaps sometime we shall have developed yardsticks to measure other aspects of physiological age as nicely as we now measure chronological age, to measure the intangibles of mental elasticity and the variety of other capacities that make up good employees for many types of jobs. But as yet we have no such tests as criteria for retirement. The judgment of the worker or executive about his own abilities often differs from that of his associates or superiors. Although this tends to be true at any age, it seems to be an especially critical problem at the upper ages.

All of us can think of exceptional men and women in public life and among friends and associates who have retained striking intellectual or physical vigor well beyond the normal age for retirement. Perhaps, however, the conspicuousness of these exceptions merely supports the generally held conclusion that the ravages of time begin taking their toll of most people in their middle 60s or early 70s.

Selecting a retirement age is easy; selecting the "right" age is not. For most people, the word *old* has an intensely subjective meaning. The self is the pivot point; old is older than self, young is younger. This subjectiveness complicates the already difficult job of selecting a single, specific retirement age as the definitive separation between working years and retirement years.

In the normal course of events, the retirement age in a pension plan is chosen unilaterally by the employer or through a union negotiation process. The age selected will reflect the employer's view as to what is old for work in the particular industry or job, or the negotiated compromise of the views of union representatives and management, or, usually, just a "follow the crowd" decision. Hence, most private and governmental employments have fallen into the easy pattern of stating a fixed retirement age—62, 68, 70, but overwhelmingly age 65.

How did age 65 come to be so firmly fixed as the proper retirement age? Clearly it is arbitrary, as any other age would be, and it hits unevenly among individuals because they differ so much from each other in terms of physical and mental capacity. Jobs also vary greatly in the demands they place on physical and mental capacities. Perhaps the general use of age 65 was a matter of having to select some age, and somehow incorporates a recognition that age 70 may be too high and age 60 too low, considering the cost of providing retirement benefits and the nature of the aging process among large groups of individuals. It is interesting to note that Bismarck's early German social insurance scheme took age 65 as the age at which retirement disability benefits were first available. Later, in its free pension plan established in 1905 for college professors, the Carnegie Foundation for the Advancement of Teaching set age 65 as the earliest date on which non-disability related pensions were available. No pensions were payable until a professor withdrew from teaching; the pensions were increased in case of postponed retirement up to age 70 and were fixed from then on. Much the same system was used in the original 1935 Social Security Act. Benefits were first available at age 65 but were to be paid only when the worker substantially withdrew from the work force.

Age 65 continues to be the overwhelming choice of stated normal retirement age under private pension plans. The 1975 Bankers Trust study of single-employer plans reported normal retirement ages of less than 65 in only 5 percent of conventional plans. There was little significant change in the normal or compulsory retirement ages reported by the plans studied (covering about 8 million employees) during the 1965–1975 period.[11]

A number of writers and scholars in recent years have referred to "a trend toward early retirement." Cited as evidence are the "30 years and out" early retirement provisions of the United Automobile Workers' negotiated pension plan for hourly workers, similar plans negotiated by the steelworkers' union, certain special situation plans for baseball players or airline pilots, some of the early retirement provisions affecting policemen, firemen, other public employees and school teachers, and the increasing proportion of Social Security retirement beneficiaries who start their old-age benefits at ages under 65.

These developments, however, are the exception, not the rule. The only area where there has been rather widespread use of early normal retirement ages is in public service, where different classes of public employees have often leapfrogged each other in attaining preferential treatment. All told, there has been little movement from the normal retirement age of 65 throughout industry. A Social Security analysis done from July to December, 1969, of new beneficiaries with compulsory retirement provisions on their most recent job indicates that only 2 percent of such workers reported a compulsory retirement age under 65. Sixty-eight percent reported age 65 as the normal retirement age and 30 percent reported an age higher than 65.[12]

Normal retirement at ages earlier than 65, were it to become a national pattern, could result in significantly reduced gross national product, economic loss to workers due to increased demands on their income for transfer costs and income-support payments, and losses to elderly people themselves through deprivation of jobs, community involvements, and status. The enormous economic and social implications involved in any movement of our society toward earlier normal retirement ages deserve careful consideration.

LABOR-FORCE PARTICIPATION OF THE ELDERLY

Turning from stated normal retirement ages, we find that for many decades there has been a persistent and dramatic decline in the proportion of older people in the work force. In 1900 two out of three men age 65 and over were gainfully employed; this dropped to one in three in 1960, and only one in four in 1970. The labor-force participation for women aged 65 and over has stabilized over the past two decades at about 10 percent. Clearly, work-force participation for persons age 65 and over cannot for the foreseeable future contribute much to the security of the older population. Table 9.3 shows labor-force participation since 1950, with projections to 1985.

A work-experience survey based on Census Bureau data for 1971 showed that the lowest work-experience rates are among nonmarried women (including widows). Among elderly couples, at least one of whom was aged 65 or older, about 6 out of 10 reported some work during the year for those with one partner aged 65 to 72, and 3 out of 10 for those with one member aged 72 or older. Among nonworkers, those aged 60 to 64 were more likely than those aged 65 and older to cite ill health or unemployment as the major barrier to employment and were much less likely to view themselves as retired. Conversely, those aged 65 and older were more likely than those aged 60 to 64 to view themselves as retired and much less likely to report that ill health or lack of job opportunity hindered their employment.[13]

RETIREMENT—UNDER AND OVER 65

In 1970, 53 percent of the men claiming Social Security retirement benefits received reduced benefit awards. In other words, just over half "retired" at an age under 65. This information and other findings of the Social Security Administration's Survey of Newly Entitled Beneficiaries (SNEB) disclose a considerable amount of data about the age older persons leave the work force and the reasons for doing so as stated in questionnaire responses.[14]

Full Benefits at 65. There are substantial differences in the level and extent of earnings between men claiming currently payable Social Security retirement benefits as early as possible and those retiring at age 65 with benefits payable at the time of award. Those electing full benefits at age 65

Table 9.3 Labor-Force Participation of Persons 65 and Over

Year	Size of Labor Force [a] (millions)	Number of People 65 and Over in Population (millions)	Number of People 65 and Over in Labor Force (millions)	Percent of People 65 and Over in Labor Force
1950	63.9	12.4	3.0	24
1960	72.1	16.7	3.4	20
1970	85.9	20.1	3.2	16
1980 [b]	100.7	23.8	3.3	14
1985 [b]	107.2	25.5	3.4	13

Source: The Conference Board, *A Guide to Consumer Markets, 1972–1973* (New York: The Conference Board, Inc., 1972), pp. 15, 87.

[a] Includes Armed Forces.

[b] Based on estimates and projections of Department of Labor.

had higher earnings and more years of employment at those higher earnings. Their earnings in the years immediately before retirement were also likely to be higher. They were more likely to have had covered employment in the year just preceding the year of entitlement. Those persons retiring at age 65 were more likely to list a job-related reason for stopping work, such as compulsory retirement, as the most important factor in their decision to retire. Less than a quarter of the persons claiming benefits at age 65 said that health was the most important reason for stopping work.

Benefits Under Age 65. Men claiming reduced benefits payable at age 62 had on the average lower earnings and fewer years of employment than the men who drew full benefits, payable at award at age 65. Their primary insurance amounts were lower, a reflection of their lower earnings and gaps in their covered employment. Less than half the men who became entitled in 1970 to currently payable benefits at age 62 had covered employment in every year from 1951 to 1969, compared with about three fifths of those who waited until ages 63, 64, or 65. Thirty percent of those claiming benefits at 62 had been out of work for at least 12 months.

The factors entering into an individual's decision to start Social Security benefits early are relevant to issues of policy development for the financing and administration of retirement benefits. More than half (56 percent) of the men who claimed reduced benefits at ages 62 through 64 indicated that physical problems or an inability to keep up with the pace of work was the primary factor in their decision to take early benefits. Job-related reasons for early benefit claims were indicated by other responses; 55 percent of early claimants said they would have worked longer in their job if allowed. Over three fourths of those who said they worked in a place with a mandatory retirement age said they had not reached that age.

One of the questions was: "Did you want to leave your last job or would you have worked longer if you could?" Fifty-four percent of the newly entitled beneficiaries (of all ages) said they would have worked longer; 39 percent said they wanted to leave. Eligibility for a second pension apparently had a strong effect on the desire for early retirement; among those claiming reduced benefits at age 62, second-pension recipients were two and a half times more likely to have wanted to retire than those without another pension. Among men with second pensions claiming Social Security benefits at age 62, the willing retirees had a median combined income nearly $1,000 higher than those of unwilling retirees.

These data suggest that many of the people who start their Social Security benefits early do so because they are unemployed, often have been unemployed for some time, are less likely to be successful in getting a job because they have a background of lower wages and interruptions of covered employment, or because they are in ill health, are physically disabled to some degree, and can no longer cope with the requirements of the jobs they have typically held. They reflect for large numbers of persons a situation of unemployment and/or physical decline, rather than the desire to begin retirement early, and thus suggest that a system that would provide improved unemployment and disability benefits for older workers between the ages of 60 and 65 might function better than the present system that provides reduced old-age benefits from age 62 to 65.

Those employees who elect to begin benefits between ages 62 and 65 must accept permanently lowered benefits because of the actuarial reduction they suffer and the loss of income between ages 62 and 65 that could be applied to the final benefit calculation. In addition, early retirements increase the proportion of people receiving retirement benefits versus the working population, which in turn affects the flow of funds into the Social Security trust fund.

Recommendations. Three recommendations seem appropriate: First, disability benefits under Social Security should be made more easily and readily available from age 60 to 65; the definition of disability, strict at all ages now, should be eased above age 59. Second, unemployment compensation benefits should be made available for longer periods of time above age 60, that is, unemployment benefits could be made payable during continued availability for work but inability to find it for the entire unemployed period or periods prior to age 65 if the unemployment occurs after age 59. These two suggestions would meet the social needs for hardship benefits between ages 60 and 65. Then a third recommendation would be feasible: elimination of the reduced Social Security retirement benefits available from age 62 to 65 and payment of old-age Social Security benefits only to persons age 65 and over. Chapter 3 (Social Security) also discusses the public policy issues involved in setting an appropriate age for the commencement of social insurance old-age benefits.

GROWTH OF THE AGED POPULATION

A rapid increase has occurred since 1900 in the number of men and women age 65 and over. Chart 9.1 shows this growing age group, with projections to the year 2020. The number of women aged 65 and over in the United States may be expected to increase from 11,650,000 in 1970 to nearly 24,000,000 in 2020, and the number of men aged 65 and over from 8,416,000 in 1970 to about 17,000,000 in 2020. The larger number of women is of course the result of much greater female longevity.

Expected increases in the sheer numbers of aged persons by the year 2020 measure the magnitude of the task facing the country in the proper shaping of policies regarding income maintenance and social well-being of the 65-and-over population. In 1930 the total population of persons 65 and over

CHART 9.1

Growth of the 65-and-Over Population, 1900–2020

Millions of people

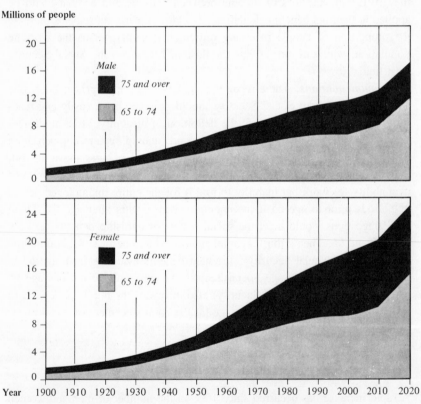

Source: U.S. Bureau of the Census, *Current Population Reports*, Series P-23, No. 43 (1973).

was 6,705,000. By 1950 it had reached 12,397,000, nearly doubling in 20 years. By 1970, it was 20,156,000. As Chart 9.1 suggests, projections indicate another doubling, to about 40,000,000 in the five decades between 1970 and 2020.[15]

The Census Bureau figures define as "elderly" people aged 65 and over. If our "elderly" population consisted of people 55 and over, the number in the "aged" population would double immediately. Table 9.4 shows the percentages of the total U.S. population represented by the age groups 55 and over and 65 and over. These figures help indicate the impact on society if an early retirement age of 55 were to become a normal retirement practice.

Our growing aged population is a consequence of a growing population and improvements in mortality. Whether the *proportion* of the aged in our society increases is determined by the birth rate. The "baby boom" following World War II provided an offset to the increasing ratio of older people, an effect destined to last until the members of the baby boom generation themselves enter the 65-and-over ranks. That surge group initially placed extra demands on the primary, secondary, and college-level educational institutions. Then, as the group moves through time it will compose the proportion of the population in the active work force. Finally, around the year 2010, the surge will swell the retired population. In the post-2010 era the working population under age 65 will be faced with staggering costs of previous economic commitments made on behalf of the post-2010 retired population.

FINANCIAL EFFECTS OF EARLY RETIREMENT

Provisions for early retirement under a pension plan—the starting of pension benefits at an age under 65—place a heavy financial burden on the pension fund if there is no actuarial reduction from normal-age benefit amounts. Just

Table 9.4 Percent of the Total U.S. Population at the Older Ages, 1900–2000

Age	1900	1930	1960	1970	1980	1990	2000
55 and over	9.4	12.3	17.9	18.9	19.7	19.1	19.0
65 and over	4.1	5.4	9.2	9.8	10.3	10.9	10.6

Source: U.S. Bureau of the Census, *Current Population Reports,* Series P-23, No. 43 (1973), p. 5 (Series E projections at 2.1 fertility rate).

how substantial this cost is does not seem to be widely understood. Public employee retirement systems in particular place a heavy burden on taxpayers when special employee groups, such as policemen and firemen, are provided pensions at full-formula level after 20 or 25 years of service regardless of age. Unfortunately, provisions for special hazard occupations appear to other public employee groups as fair for them too. The result has too often been the accelerated leapfrogging that brings similar privileges to other nonhazardous public employee groups, including full benefits at age 55 or 60 after a stated period of service.

In recent years federal, state, and local budgets have been getting closer scrutiny from heavily burdened and better informed citizens. One reason for the new taxpayer interest is that expensive early-age pension promises made in past times are now coming due, and for the first time the costs are becoming evident.

In industry as well, some of the settlements negotiated in recent years for "30 years and out regardless of age" threaten to saddle many private plans with dangerously higher pension costs. More and more plans could be affected as other groups demand the same thing. It was reported in early 1975 that the first two retirees in the United Auto Workers' plan under the "30 and out" provisions were aged 47 and 49, respectively.[16] It seems clear that pension plan provisions of this type can only encourage covered workers to start benefits early and turn immediately to another job. The result is that people are being paid once for not working while concurrently they are being paid a second time for working. The situation has already led to considerable discussion of federal "double dippers," military personnel retiring under the generous and costly "20 years and out" retirement provisions of the Uniformed Services Retirement System and immediately taking federal jobs under which they qualify quickly for Civil Service pensions.

Just how much is the cost of providing normal-age benefits at early-age retirement? Guesswork is not required. The extra cost under any particular retirement plan can be precisely figured. Several cost-swelling factors operate simultaneously. One is the increase in the average period over which retirement benefits must be expected to be paid if retirement occurs at an early age. Another is the decreased time available to the employer for the accumulation of funds to pay the retiree a benefit for life. Yet another is the lower total interest earnings on the funds involved due to the shortened period of fund accumulation; if the investment gains are lower, employers' contributions must take their place. The age of retirement with a full-formula benefit is, in fact, one of the most significant pension cost levers.

As an example of the increased cost of providing a given level of retirement benefit at age 55 or 60 rather than 65, we can take the defined benefit plan provisions used in several examples of plan costs in Chapter 8. This plan aimed at a retirement benefit at age 65 of 1.5 percent of final five-year average salary for each year of service. What would be the increased cost to provide for the same formula benefit under the plan, but beginning at age 55 without actuarial reduction instead of age 65? The answer is astonishing—an increase of well over 100 percent in cost. To be more precise, in order to provide the required funding for this change, to enable a 55-year-old employee to retire at once, the funds already accumulated on his behalf would have to be increased by 123 percent.

This explosion of employer cost should not be allowed to obscure the fact that even though the benefit is full-formula for the employee, it is applied to a final average salary covering the years of employment ending at age 55, not the higher average salary that could be expected later on at age 65. For this reason, the employee's full-formula age-55 early retirement income will be lower than if he had waited until 65 to retire, assuming a higher pay rate at the later retirement age.*

Suppose the proposal for early retirement were modified to provide for a normal-age full-formula retirement at age 60 instead of at age 65. Here again, the cost factor is still startlingly high—a 51 percent increase in the cost of financing immediate retirement for the 60-year-old employee. The percentage increase in the cost of providing a full-formula retirement benefit at ages earlier than normal retirement (age 65) would be as follows (assuming a normal retirement benefit of 1.5 percent of final five-year average salary with entry at age 25):

Age of Retirement	Required Percentage Increase in Accumulation
55	123%
60	51
62	29

* If the objective were to provide about the same dollar benefit at age 55 as at age 65, assuming a 3-percent annual salary increase from age 55 to 65 and thus relating the benefit to the higher expected salary at age 65, the cost of the early retirement benefit would be three times as high.

These figures give a powerful indication of the tremendous financial strain that is placed on a retirement plan by the apparently simple change of reducing the normal age of retirement. The figures for an individual above can be generalized; a five-year reduction in normal retirement age from 65 to 60 will increase an employer's retirement costs by about 50 percent. Providing for a normal-age retirement of 55 instead of 65 will increase an employer's retirement plan costs by well over 100 percent.

Another effect of retirement as early as age 55 is to reduce the ratio of the maximum number of supporting working years of pension plan participation to the average number of retired years, thus reducing the time available for the accumulation of funds to support retirement. Table 9.5 suggests the order of this ratio change.

In light of the order of increased costs for early retirement, we must seriously consider the immediate cost burden of early retirement proposals, which could become unsupportable. But there is an even more pressing issue. This is the public policy question of whether society should permit in its public or private retirement plans full benefit retirements at ages so young as to actually encourage workers to leave the work force as retirees only to reenter it at once as workers. Can the nation afford retirement systems in which some "retired" workers are drawing double pay at a time when half the private work force has no private pension coverage at all?

Social Security. Although Social Security is not a reserve-funded plan, its costs for a lowering of normal retirement ages would be affected in much the same way as costs of a private pension plan, or a public employee system. The Social Security Administration estimates that if full old-age benefits for workers were made available at age 62 instead of the present age 65,

Table 9.5 Ratio of Working Years to Average Retired Years

Normal Retirement Age	Maximum Retirement Plan Participation		Approximate Retired Life Expectancy [a]	Ratio of Supporting Years to Retired Years
	Age span	Years		
65	25–65	40	20 years	2:1
55	25–55	30	30	1:1

[a] Mixture of life expectancy for couples and single persons.

the extra cost would require a gradual increase in the Social Security tax from 5.85 to 7.40 percent on both employer and employee. If full benefits were to be payable at age 60, the payroll tax would have to be increased gradually from 5.85 percent to an estimated 8.18 percent on each. In terms of tax dollars, the maximum current annual tax for each would rise from $824.85 to $1,043.40 for full-benefit retirement at age 62, and to $1,153.38 for full-benefit retirement at age 60, or increases of 26 and 40 percent respectively. Thus a lowering of the full-benefit retirement age would bring the combined employer-employee wage tax at the full wage base to above $2,000 a year. The first year's cost of a change to age-60 retirement benefits at present age-65 benefit levels is estimated to be in the neighborhood of $6.6 billion.[17] The Consumer Price Index escalator would increase this figure for later years.

INFLATION

The greatest destroyer of old-age security is inflation. America has, during this generation, made extraordinary progress in reducing poverty and assuring reasonable incomes for many people through Social Security, private pension plans, personal savings, and various welfare arrangements. But inflation can seriously erode, and even destroy, all this work.

Since the start of this republic there has never been a period long enough to cover an individual's working and retired lifetime during which there has not been one or more difficult inflationary periods. During the first decade of the 20th century prices rose gradually and then jumped sharply during World War I. Following that painful inflation, there occurred a *decline* of one third in the cost of living from 1920 to 1933. But then World War II caused another serious inflation. Just as the cost of living started to decline in the post-war period, the Korean War set it off again. In the following decade, the Vietnam War again triggered inflation, an inflation that has persisted and to which other causes have also contributed.

This is not the place to analyze the various causes and cures for inflation. But it is important to emphasize that only central governments and their instrumentalities can effectively control inflation. If governments do not effectively control inflation, they indirectly make major policy decisions as to who is to bear the burdens of the cost of inflation. That choice nearly always results in hardship for the elderly.

The heaviest impact of inflation is on those with fixed incomes. The poor and the elderly are more likely to have incomes that are fixed than are the more affluent. Inflation is a tax that starts with the first dollar of earnings, and affects every dollar earned. Between 1970 and 1975 the cost of living increased by about 40 percent. Thus, the "real inflation tax rate" inflicted upon the person who retired on a fixed income just five years ago now amounts to 40 percent, and this "tax" is levied on full income, no matter how small or large, without exemptions, exclusions or deductions.

PENSIONS—MEETING PRICE LEVEL CHANGES

Security in retirement poses a difficult problem when it means providing not only a sufficient annuity income in dollars but also a reasonable income in current purchasing power. Traditional methods of saving for retirement have been effective in providing the dollar income; they have fallen short of the goal of providing a suitable purchasing power income throughout retirement. During the low prices prevailing in the 1930s, annuitants and others living on fixed incomes were receiving a larger "real," or purchasing-power, income than they might have expected; but during the entire post-World War II period their real income has been declining.

A variety of devices to soften the impact of inflation have been developed over the years. Also, some devices not specifically designed to cope with inflation have provided some protection.

Escalator Clauses. The most direct method is to provide cost-of-living escalators in pension plans. A Consumer Price Index escalator was added to Social Security in the 1972 amendments. This provision is discussed in Chapter 3.

The Civil Service Retirement System cost-of-living escalator was added in 1970. The states of Hawaii, Arkansas, Illinois, and Nevada have built escalator clauses into their retirement benefits for public employees in some or all classifications, as discussed in Chapter 5. A small number of industrial pension plans have automatic benefit-increase provisions.

These devices may become engines of inflation in themselves, or they may provide real economic security for retired people. In any event, the after-the-fact escalation of retirement benefits where service has already been rendered produces a difficult funding problem for public and private employers, and unknown future costs.

Final Average Salary Plans. In final average plans, contributions from the employer are related to current or projected salaries and wages year by year. The individual is assured a benefit equal to a certain percentage of his *final* average earnings or *highest* average earnings. Thus the individual may be assured a benefit equal to 1 or 1.5 percent times number of years of service times average earnings during the last, or perhaps the highest, five-year period.

These widely used plans represent one of the earlier devices that took partial cognizance of inflation, although inflation was not necessarily the reason for the adoption of the "final-five" formula. From the standpoint of individuals, these plans provide some protection against inflation that occurs far enough before their retirement so that their final salary used in the benefit calculation has adjusted to the new conditions. Unfortunately, persons within 10 or 15 years of retirement may find that their salaries have not kept up with inflation or with the more rapid increases in salaries at younger ages in an inflationary period. Final-five plans give no automatic protection for price changes occurring during retirement. Since people usually live 10 to 20 years after retirement, and sometimes much longer, this deficiency can be serious.

Final-five and similar plans also offer serious problems for employers. Persons now retiring are receiving benefits related to current salary levels. But much of their earnings, and therefore the funding of their retirement benefits, occurred during periods of lower wages prevailing in the 1960s, 1950s, 1940s, and even to some extent during the Great Depression. Actuarial cost methods calling for level annual contributions help meet the problem. However, the salary projection factors utilized have usually been too low, causing fund deficiencies. If the amount of underfunding is to be reduced, additional contributions must be made by the public authority in the case of state or local retirement systems, or from the general budgets of the companies, industries, hospitals, churches, and other organizations covered by final-five plans.

Ad Hoc Adjustments. In recent years some pension plans have added supplemental benefits for persons already retired under them, either through bargaining or at the employer's initiative. The 1975 Bankers Trust study reported that about 70 percent of the plans surveyed provided at least one increase since 1969, with an average increase over the whole period of $500 for a worker with 30 years' service.[18] Because of the financial ramifications, such benefit increases cannot be counted on as a widespread systematic solution to the problem of retirement benefit purchasing power.

Variable Annuities. Retirement programs that include variable annuities incorporate another approach to the inflation problem. Variable annuities differ from traditional pension systems in two fundamental ways. First, the risks and rewards of changes in the earnings and the value of plan assets inure to the beneficiaries of the plan, rather than, as is the case with most traditional pensions, to the sponsoring employers. Second, variable annuities invest largely in stocks in contrast to the portfolios of traditional plans. As a result, where retirement income under traditional plans remains stable in dollar terms, the income received by retired persons from variable annuities increases and decreases directly with the capital values and dividend yields of the investments of the fund.

Variable annuities take advantage of the fact that over intermediate and long periods of time stocks have been a good hedge against inflation. This has been demonstrated a number of times. One current study compared stock-price indexes against the wholesale price index for 24 countries. This study showed that in the vast majority of instances, stock prices over time increased at a rate faster than the rate of inflation.[19] Another recent study at Harvard examined the relationship between the business cycle and stock prices and concluded that stocks have been reasonably responsive to long-run inflation pressure.[20]

The original study in 1951 leading to the development of variable annuities initiated the interest in equity investments as a partial protection against inflation in old age. The study concluded that the optimum retirement program would include a variable annuity to help protect against inflation and a fixed annuity to help moderate the volatility of common stocks especially during an extended down market.[21] Data developed in the study demonstrated that, over periods long enough to encompass a normal working career and retirement years, individuals would have fared better in an annuity combining both fixed and variable elements than in a fixed-dollar annuity alone. The study also illustrated periods when retirement income from a combined fixed-variable annuity program would have declined while consumer prices were rising.

Chart 9.2, reproduced from the original study, suggests both the ability of a combined fixed-variable program to provide better protection against inflation over long periods and the divergences that occurred during shorter periods. It illustrates the experience of two hypothetical individuals who joined separate (theoretical) retirement plans in 1900, contributed $100 a year until they reached age 65 in 1930, and then retired in that year. One person contributed $50 a year to a fixed-dollar annuity and $50 to a variable annuity. The other contributed $100 a year to a fixed-dollar annuity. The chart also shows an "adjusted cost of living" income—the result of adjusting accumulating contributions and annuity income to the changing cost of living throughout the entire period.

The combined annuity and the adjusted cost of living lines show a reasonable degree of correlation over the period of annuity income payments. Thus, the study demonstrated the variable annuity's potential for compensating for increases in the price level over the long run. It should also be noted that the chart shows shorter periods, 1937 to 1942 for example, when the combined fixed and variable income declined significantly while consumer prices were rising.

Recent experience reinforces the findings of the 1951 study. Chart 9.3

CHART 9.2

Amounts of Accumulation and Annuity, 1900–1952—Fixed Annuity Compared with Combined Fixed and Variable Annuity

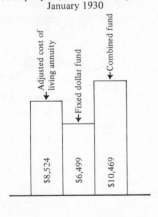

Accumulation 1900-1930
resulting from investment of
$100 per year; retirement at age 65,
January 1930

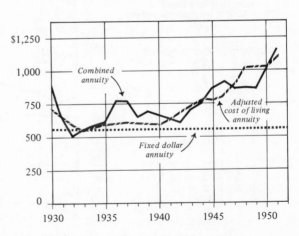

Source: William C. Greenough, *A New Approach to Retirement Income* (New York: TIAA, 1951), p.23.

was derived in much the same way as Chart 9.2, except that it is based on the performance of an actual variable annuity, CREF, combined with a fixed annuity, TIAA. The fixed-dollar annuity includes dividend increases made over the period. It was assumed that each of the persons began to participate on July 1, 1952, paying monthly premiums of $50 each to TIAA and to CREF, or, alternatively, $100 monthly to TIAA alone, and retired on July 1, 1962, at age 65. Throughout most of the period covered by the analysis, the fixed-variable annuity combination exceeded the increases in prices. However, in the period between 1972 and 1975 prices went up, while the annuity income dropped sharply.

Periods like 1937 to 1942 and 1972 to 1975 demonstrate that variable annuities are not a perfect hedge against inflation, especially over shorter periods, but when used with fixed-dollar annuities, to quote the 1951 study conclusions, they "offer promise of supplying retirement income that is at once reasonably free from violent fluctuations in amount and from serious depreciation through price-level changes." [22]

CHART 9.3

Amounts of Accumulation and Annuity, 1952–1975—Fixed Annuity Compared with Combined Fixed and Variable Annuity

Accumulation 1952-1962
resulting from investment of
$100 per month; retirement at age 65,
July 1962

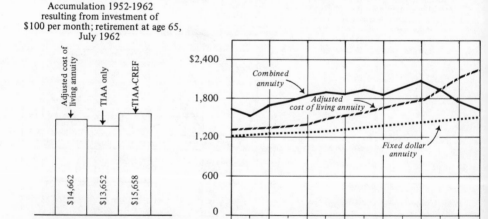

Source: Experience of Teachers Insurance and Annuity Association (TIAA) fixed annuity and combination of TIAA annuity and College Retirement Equities Fund (CREF) variable annuity, 1952 - 1975.

CONCLUSION

Rapid inflation should be recognized for what it is—a highly regressive tax that harms the economy and penalizes savers and pensioners. It is a tax that the elderly are especially defenseless against, a vicious social impost. The only fair and comprehensive way to meet this problem is through fiscal and monetary policies rigorously dedicated to keeping inflation at moderate rates. The pain of inflation for all segments of society is becoming more apparent. The continuing danger is that at the initial signs of recession, inflation controls are insufficiently applied for fear of deepening recession, so that desirable restraints are pushed farther down the list of national priorities. The result can mean serious distress for retired people, so that private pension plans must develop compensatory precautions, however unsatisfactory or costly they may be.

Under the Constitution, private property cannot be expropriated without due process and adequate compensation; when government confiscates private land for public use, recompense is made. This concept is not applied to the consequences of inflation, of course, but government policy can play a more decisive role in inflation control. Pending more determined application of appropriate measures, however, present pension plans may be expected to continue to try to improve their mechanisms for the provision of some protection against serious loss of purchasing power.

— 10 —

Foreign Systems of Social and Private Pensions

Nearly every country in the world, from Afghanistan to Zambia, has a social insurance plan of some kind. A 1973 report by the U.S. Department of Health, Education, and Welfare lists 105 different nations as having a social insurance plan for old age, disability, and survivors' benefits.[1]

Fewer nations have private pension systems. There is no count as to exactly how many. Private plans are most common in the industrialized Western nations. In a few countries private employers are required to provide pension coverage to complement a national social insurance scheme.

As we examine Social Security and private pensions in the United States, something can be gained by a brief look at the way some other nations have approached the same basic problems, at how other modern industrial nations have come to grips with the question of what should be the balance of responsibilities between social insurance programs on the one hand and employer-sponsored pension plans on the other. For this we have selected just seven countries, all of whose economic and social institutions and stage of industrial development are reasonably comparable to our own: Canada, Great Britain, France, West Germany, the Netherlands, Sweden, and Japan.

These nations offer a variety of approaches to the problem of providing income support in old age, a problem all of the nations share.

There is a general consensus that social insurance systems must provide for income replacement for aged and retired workers and their dependents, and for disability and survivor benefits, but there are considerable differences in the mechanisms employed to achieve these common goals. Also, different limits are set for the social programs in different countries. The same is true of private plans. In some countries private pension plans play a more important role in total retirement security protection than in others.

FOREIGN SOCIAL INSURANCE

Social Risks. The covered hazards in foreign social insurance systems, as in the United States, center on loss of earning power or loss of support—cessations of regular earned income over which the individual has little or no control. Thus a social insurance system will usually provide for old-age and survivor benefits, disability benefits, and will normally take into account the additional needs if there are dependents (wives, husbands under some plans, and children). Medical and hospital benefits, workmen's compensation, unemployment benefits, and special home care services for the sick and elderly are also often part of a social insurance scheme. The emphasis of this chapter is on old-age benefits.

Coverage. Employment is normally the basis of individual participation in social insurance systems. All employed persons are normally required to participate. In some countries, government employees do not participate because they are regarded as having equivalent protection under the retirement plans for civil servants, most of which antedate social insurance. In a few of the systems, nonworkers (housewives, for example) may also qualify and participate. In some, individual coverage credits or contributions from government continue during periods of unemployment. All of the social insurance systems described finance the benefits currently being paid out through the taxes and/or general revenue contributions currently being paid in.

Benefits. Benefits in the social insurance systems described are normally linked with the duration of an individual's participation in the system, with the level of an employee's wages or salary, and with wage-related contributions that he has made or that have been made on his behalf. There is usually an established minimum or weighted level of benefits that provides support to persons who have had relatively short employment histories or relatively low lifetime earnings. In some systems the minimum level is achieved through a flat benefit component of the total benefit. In others it is achieved through the use of a stated minimum benefit in a fully wage-related program. An upper limit is usually placed on the amount of an individual's earnings that are subject to social insurance contributions. Benefits are related to the "covered," or "pensionable," earnings.

Upward Adjustments. While old-age social insurance benefits are usually related to the earnings history of retiring employees, most systems attempt to incorporate means of recognizing the effects of inflation on wage rates or taxable wages over the long periods over which an employee will normally have made contributions. Thus, rather than relating the old-age benefit to the average of an individual's wages over 30 or 40 years, mechanisms are used to assign greater weight to wages received in the 10 or 5 years nearest the retirement age. So as to adjust benefits to changing living costs after old-age income begins, all of the systems incorporate automatic adjustments according to changes in a consumer price or wage index.

Starting Ages. The earliest age at which full social insurance old-age benefits may be started is age 60 in Japan, 65 in most of the countries reviewed (for women age 60 in two of these), and 67 in the Scandinavian countries. In some systems, an earlier-than-normal age for commencement of retirement benefits is permitted in cases of disability or ill health, or when an individual has been unable to find work for a stated period of time. Where old-age benefits may be begun earlier than 65 for other than these reasons, a penalty in reduced benefits becomes effective, and it may be substantial. Generally, public policy is framed so as to encourage employable persons to defer the beginning of social insurance benefits for old age until or even after the normal retirement age.

Financing. The financing of social insurance benefits is usually through a combination of employer and employee contributions, which in some countries is augmented by general revenue contributions. In one of the seven countries described, the old-age and survivor benefit system is financed by employee contributions alone (the Netherlands). In four countries both the employer and employee contributions are levied as taxes on an earnings base per employee (France, West Germany, Sweden, and Japan). In two countries the tax on employer and employee is levied on an earnings base and is accompanied by general revenue contributions (United Kingdom) or by an earmarked general sales tax (Canada). In one country the tax on employees is stated as a percentage of a range of taxable income (Sweden).

OCCUPATIONAL OR COMPLEMENTARY PLANS

Private "occupational" or "complementary" retirement plans are in operation in all of the countries covered in this chapter. In France, Sweden, and the Netherlands the supplementary plans are nearly universal through mandatory arrangements for the extension to all industry sectors of plans negotiated within one sector. In other countries, private plans are voluntary for employers and cover only the employees of the firms that have established plans, as in Canada, the Federal Republic of Germany, and Japan. In all of the countries, government-operated retirement plans cover government employees.

Private pension plans are subject to one degree or another of government regulation in all of the countries studied. In the countries in which private pension coverage is effectively mandated through legislation requiring extension to all of an industry of plans negotiated in one sector (France, Sweden, the Netherlands), immediate vesting is required. When private pension coverage is voluntary for employers there may or may not be a legislated vesting requirement. In Canada the federal vesting requirement for private pension plans is age 45 plus 10 years of service. In the United Kingdom legislation was passed in 1973 to mandate private pension coverage, but it has subsequently been repealed. In West Germany, 1975 legislation imposed a vesting requirement for the first time.

In countries in which the occupational schemes cover half or fewer of the working population, the general level of the old-age benefits of social insurance programs tends to be higher than in countries with extensive complementary plan coverage and with early vesting of the complementary benefits. In France and some of the Scandinavian countries, social security benefits providing reasonable wage replacement levels are complemented by a wide assurance of additional private plan benefits. West Germany's relatively high old-age benefit objective for its social security system is accompanied by a relatively weak private pension system.

In some of the countries in which the social security program provides a reasonably adequate benefit level of old-age income, private plan coverage is sometimes based on salary and wages above the taxable wage base or "pensionable income" of the social security system. The objective is to make total retirement income (from both sources) about the same percentage of previous earnings for everybody, regardless of income level preceding retirement.

Except in France, complementary private pension plans are based on reserve funding, as in the United States. In France private plans use a unique intergenerational transfer system with interindustry reinsurance, all under government regulation. In the other countries, where funding is more conventional, funding and fiduciary standards are normally established and enforced by the governments concerned, and funding schedules for unfunded liabilities are prescribed.

The remaining part of this chapter offers a closer look at the old-age income provisions in the countries selected for description.

CANADA

Although Canada is geographically close to the United States, has a federal political structure, and is economically similar, its social insurance and private pension institutions have developed somewhat differently. The Canadian national system of social security dates from the 1950s and '60s, more recent in origin than the U.S. system.

Canadian legislation, provincial and federal, affecting private pension plans dates from about 1965. Prior to 1965, legislation regarding private pensions dealt mainly with taxes; it now covers vesting, funding, fiduciary matters, and provides for reporting and plan supervision. Depending on the type of employment, regulation of private pensions is effected under provincial laws or under a Canada-wide law.

SOCIAL INSURANCE

The social insurance system of Canada consists of two parts: (1) a federal flat-rate old-age benefits program, started in 1952, and (2) the Canada Pension Plan, a national wage-related program of old-age, survivors', and disability benefits inaugurated in 1956. Before 1952, public old-age pensions were available only on a means-test basis.

The Flat-Rate Program. At its outset, the flat-rate Old Age Security Program provided a pension of $40 per month payable as a right without regard to need to every person age 70 and over who had resided in Canada for at least 20 years. During subsequent years, the amount of the pension was increased several times and the number of years of required residence in Canada was reduced until, in 1965, the flat pension was $75 per month and the basic residence requirement was 10 years.[2]

In 1966, when the wage-related Canada Pension Plan was introduced, further changes were made in the flat Old Age Security Program. The qualifying age for the flat benefit was reduced over a five-year period from 70 to 65. Provision was made for automatic increases in the amount of the flat pension up to 2 percent per year after 1967 according to a pension index developed for the Canada Pension Plan.

In 1967, an income-tested supplement was added, providing an additional benefit of up to 40 percent of the monthly amount of the basic flat pension to pensioners with no other income. The supplement was intended as a transition benefit for needy persons who, at the inception of the Canada Pension Plan, were too old to build up benefits under that plan.

The flat-benefit program is financed by earmarked general taxes. Currently, the taxes consist of a 4 percent tax on sales, a 3 percent tax on corporation income, and a 4 percent tax on taxable personal income up to $6,000.[3]

The Wage-Related Pension Plan. All employees and all self-employed persons between the ages of 18 and 70 are required to participate in the Canada Pension Plan. While it is a national program, provinces may "contract out" the employment within their borders if they establish a comparable social insurance program of their own. This is mainly for the benefit of Quebec, which has contracted out under a pension law almost identical to the national law. Benefits are fully portable between the national and Quebec plans.[4]

The national and Quebec wage-related Canada programs are financed by compulsory contributions from employees, employers, and self-employed individuals. The contribution rate on taxable earnings is 1.8 percent for employers, 1.8 percent for employees, and 3.6 percent of taxable earnings from self-employment.[5] Contributions are paid on annual earnings between specified lower and upper limits ($700 to $7,400 in 1974). The upper earnings limit is subject to an automatic readjustment in accordance with changes in an earnings index.

The old-age pensions of the Canada Pension Plan become payable at age

65. Under a work test, between ages 65 and 70 the amount of the pension is reduced if the recipient earns income from employment, with an allowable minimum pension specified.

The income goal of the plan is a pension of 25 percent of the "average of adjusted pensionable annual earnings" for a certain proportion of years between January 1, 1966 (or age 18 if attained later than 1966) and age 65. When benefits are to be calculated, recorded earnings are revalued so as to base benefits on wage levels nearer the retirement age than would a career average approach, which would average in obsolete wage levels prevailing many years before retirement. Benefits are adjusted quarterly based on changes in the cost of living.

Survivors' Pensions. A widow of age 65 or over is entitled to a widow's pension of 60 percent of the earnings-related pension of the spouse, and an additional amount if she is entitled to an age retirement pension in her own right.

A widow under age 65 is entitled to a widow's pension if she has unmarried dependent children, or is disabled, or has reached age 35 at the time of widowhood (with a substantially reduced benefit). A dependent child is one under age 18, or 18 through 25 if attending school, or a disabled child of any age.

PRIVATE PENSIONS IN CANADA

When the Dominion government was established in 1867 by the British North American Act, certain enumerated legislative powers were reserved for the provincial legislatures; the federal government was assigned jurisdiction over all matters not enumerated. Among the items reserved for provincial jurisdiction were "property and civil rights." In recent years, as the federal government has moved toward national regulation of pension plans, stumbling blocks arose out of contentions that pension plans, as contracts between employers and employees, involve property rights subject only to provincial jurisdiction. Some clarification has been achieved through amendments to the British North American Act that empower the federal government to make laws regarding pensions, with the proviso that no federal law shall affect the operation of provincial legislation relating to pensions. This made it possible for the Government of Canada to pass pension legislation applicable to employees under its own direct jurisdiction, but it did not allow the federal government to attempt to deal with the regulation of private pension plans on a nationwide basis.

Since it was judged impractical for any one province to enact regulatory legislation of pension plans which might conflict in an important way with laws on pension plans in other provinces, the federal government and the provinces in the 1960s resolved the issue by agreeing to the development of uniform pension legislation for province-by-province enactment, and to similar legislation affecting employee groups under the jurisdiction of the Government of Canada.

PROVINCIAL PENSION LAW

Uniform pension legislation in the provinces, generally designated as the Pension Benefits Act, has been enacted in the four provinces employing the bulk of Canadian industrial employees and incorporating about 80 percent of Canada's population: Ontario, Quebec, Alberta, and Saskatchewan. Other provinces are expected to follow suit. The uniform act was first passed in 1965 in the province of Ontario and is sometimes referred to as the Ontario Act.

The standards of the Pension Benefits Act, including funding, apply not only to the pension plans of private employers but to plans of governmental units of each province. The act does not make it compulsory for an employer to establish or maintain a pension plan. However, an employer who does establish a pension plan is required by the act to meet funding standards and certain rules on the vesting of pensions, investments, and other matters.[6]

Under the uniform act, a member of a plan must be fully vested at age 45 provided he has had 10 years of continuous service with the employer or has completed 10 years of membership in the plan, whichever occurs first. An employee who has worked for less than 10 years for his employer, but has worked for at least 10 years for several employers under a multiemployer plan, is entitled to a vested benefit. Earlier vesting, of course, may be provided for. The uniform law protects the vested benefit from forfeiture once it is acquired.[7]

Under the funding requirements of the act, current annual costs of a pension plan must be paid annually. Unfunded liabilities must be liquidated over a period of 25 years or less (beginning in each province on the day of enactment of the uniform law). Unfunded liabilities that arise after the effective date of the uniform law as a consequence of plan amendments or the establishment of new plans must be liquidated within 15 years. Liabilities arising from adverse experience must be funded within five years. The solvency requirements imposed by the act outlaw "pay-as-you-go" plans and "terminal funding" arrangements. On termination of a pension plan the employer is liable to pay to the insurer or trustee of the plan all amounts that would otherwise have been required to be paid to meet the tests for solvency prescribed by the regulations.[8]

Each province has established a Pension Commission to administer and enforce the provisions of its law through registration and supervision. Annual information returns are required.

FEDERAL PENSION LAW

The federal government's Pension Benefits Standard Act, covering pension plans subject to federal jurisdiction in Canada, incorporates essentially the same standards required of other plans through the uniform provincial legislation. The federal act became effective October 1, 1967.

The employments to which the federal act applies include the plans of the federal government of Canada and its departments and agencies, crown corporations, and to employment in railroad, water, and air transportation, communications and broadcasting, banking, and employments in the Yukon Territory and the Northwest Territories.[9]

Administration of the federal Pension Benefits Standard Act is under the direction of the Minister of Finance and is the immediate responsibility of the Superintendent of Insurance at Ottawa. The function of the Department of Insurance is to receive and review required reports and to make certain that each plan complies with the statutory requirements.

THE EXTENT OF PRIVATE PENSION PLANS IN CANADA

At the end of 1965 (latest available figures), Canada had more than 14,000 pension plans with nearly 2.3 million participants. Slightly over 57 percent of the labor force was employed by organizations with pension plans; about 38 percent of the labor force was participating in a plan. As in the United States, most members of pension plans in Canada are employed by large employers; 54 percent of all members of pension plans were with employers of more than 10,000 employees; 82 percent were with employers of more than 1,000 employees.

A large proportion of the private pension plans are contributory. In nearly 85 percent of the plans, covering about 78 percent of the total membership, the employees are required to make contributions. The most common employee contribution rate is 5 percent of earnings. Employer contributions to a registered pension plan are classified as a business expense for tax purposes. An employee is not taxed on payments made on his behalf by an employer to a registered pension fund. An employee may deduct from his taxable income any amount up to $1,500 in any one year that is withheld by his employer from his wages or salary and paid into a pension plan.

The earnings of a registered pension fund are not included in either the employer's or the employee's current income. Pension payments to retired employees are taxed as ordinary income.

The most common type of pension plan in Canada is the defined benefit plan; most of these plans base the benefit on an average of final or best earnings. Defined contribution plans cover approximately 7 percent of participants in all pension plans.[10]

UNITED KINGDOM

The principle of public responsibility for the relief of poverty in Britain goes back nearly five centuries to the Poor Law Act of 1601, preceding Shakespeare's death by 15 years. The law required the smallest unit of local government, the parish, to provide from local taxation for the needy, the homeless, and the sick.

The Poor Laws became increasingly inadequate and inappropriate to relieve the economic distress associated with the urban and industrial developments of the 18th and 19th centuries. The extent of distress and of local resources varied in different parts of the country. There were continuing disputes about which parish was responsible for particular individuals and to what extent. George Orwell's account in *Down and Out in Paris and London* of his own experiences with the remnants of the Poor Law system as a young man in the Great Depression of the '30s gives vivid expression to the effects of attempting to apply ancient laws to modern conditions.[11]

Unfortunately, the administration of the Poor Law system and its work houses created an enduring implication that poverty was the result of culpable idleness or antisocial attitude, an idea that persisted into the 19th and 20th centuries, when the role of economic forces outside any individual's control was becoming increasingly clear. The idea of individual guilt deterred many from seeking relief, hurt the self-respect of those who did, and weakened legislative attempts to introduce reform.

By 1900 a reaction had begun against the spirit of the Poor Law as it had evolved. New methods of public provision began to appear; the aged were of first concern. Under the Old Age Pension Act of 1908, the central government accepted responsibility for helping the aged poor with small cash pensions out of central government resources. The pensions were payable to people over 70 and were based on a needs test.

The first public system for the payment of benefits as a *right,* without an apparatus for the demonstration of need, came with the National Insurance Act of 1911, which introduced compulsory insurance against unemployment for workers in certain industries and against medical costs and loss of earnings through sickness for lower-paid workers. The principle of the payment of benefits as a right in return for contributions, instead of a test of need, was new to public provision, although it was already known through the mutual assistance plans of "friendly" or "fraternal" societies and labor unions, and in private insurance. The 1911 act was the first statutory social insurance plan in Britain.[12]

After the National Insurance Act of 1911, the scope and application of social insurance provisions outside the Poor Law rapidly increased. The Poor Law relief was renamed "public assistance" in 1929 and transferred to larger local government authorities. By 1939, social insurance and allied services in Britain included pensions based on need for the old and the blind, and pensions as a matter of right under an old-age, widows' and orphans' insurance scheme for manual and some other workers.[13]

As World War II began, public social programs in Britain were uncoordinated and there were numerous acknowledged gaps. Many different authorities administered the schemes.

THE BEVERIDGE REPORT

In 1941 the United Kingdom government, already looking ahead to the reconstruction of Britain at the end of the war, appointed a committee under Lord Beveridge to "undertake a survey of existing schemes of social insurance and allied service, including workmen's compensation, and to make recommendations.'' The committee recommendations appeared in the following year as the Beveridge Report, officially entitled *Social Insurance and Allied Services.*[14]

The Beveridge Report attracted a good deal of attention in other countries, including the United States, since it was addressed to the management of social and economic problems that were shared by many nations. Of special value, it appeared, was its thoughtful discussion of a philosophy of the role of the state, of employers, and of employees in the development of a unified system of social insurance and assistance.

Lord Beveridge's recommendations were designed in part to overcome the deficiencies he found in the hodgepodge of existing arrangements. Instead of a multiplicity of administrative authorities there should be one, a Ministry of Social Security. Instead of various levels of benefits for different contingencies occasioning a loss of earnings, some providing for dependents and others not, there should be consistent benefit amounts for all adults, with additions for dependents. The amounts should be sufficient to provide the minimum needed for subsistence in all normal cases.

The report enumerated the contingencies to be insured against under the comprehensive plan: sickness and other disability, unemployment, retirement from regular work, and widowhood where the widow was handicapped from earning for herself because of responsibility for dependent children, disability, or old age. Lord Beveridge argued that it was wasteful to pay pensions to elderly people still at work and to young fit widows without children. Cash grants were recommended for events causing special expenses: deaths, marriages, and births.

In addition to the social insurance scheme, Lord Beveridge envisaged a plan of national assistance for those who for one reason or another could not satisfy the contribution requirements for social insurance benefits.

Three Assumptions. Lord Beveridge's plan was based on three assumptions:

(1) that poverty resulting from size of family would be avoided by a separately established system of family allowances (done now through the Family Allowances Acts of 1945 and 1965);

(2) that mass unemployment would be avoided through appropriate government action (the government specifically accepted in 1944 a responsibility for maintaining full employment); and

(3) that comprehensive health and rehabilitation services would be available to all members of the community (done through the National Health Service Act of 1948).

Implementation. Most of the Beveridge recommendations were embodied in the National Insurance and Industrial Injuries Acts, effective in 1948. Between 1948 and 1973 the national insurance scheme was not greatly altered, although the levels of benefits and allowances were revised many times. The most substantial modification was the addition in 1961 of a layer of graduated contributions and benefits on top of the original flat benefit plan. The Beveridge Report had concluded that the benefits of the national insurance scheme would normally be sufficient without further resources to provide the minimum needed for subsistence.

In the years following the introduction of the social scheme, average earnings of employed persons increased considerably and the dispersal about the mean was widened. The report had espoused the principle that all employed persons would pay the same weekly contribution and receive the same pension amount on retirement at or after 65. An unforeseen result was to place a relatively heavier burden on lower earnings groups through the continued application of the uniform contribution. In response to this problem, the earnings-related layer was started in 1961, but even with this addition the benefits remained at a level just at or slightly below a subsistence level. Under these circumstances, it appeared that either more adequate supplementary coverage through employer-sponsored plans would be required, or else the social insurance plan would have to be enormously expanded.

STRENGTHENING AND COORDINATING
SOCIAL AND PRIVATE PLANS

In January 1969, the Labour Government published a white paper entitled *National Superannuation and Social Insurance: Proposals for Earnings-Related Social Security,* suggesting major changes in the social insurance plan.[15] The proposals were later embodied in a bill before the Parliament (1969); it had reached an advanced stage when Parliament was dissolved in May 1970 and the bill was "lost." The proposals and the bill were closely associated with the Secretary of State for Social Security, R. H. S. Crossman, and became known as the Crossman Scheme.

The successor Conservative government later issued another proposal,

Strategy for Pensions: The Future Development of State and Occupational Provisions.[16] The two proposals were not far apart, though the latter paper was more favorable to the mandating of earnings-related occupational (private) schemes, and expressed the view that the state should sponsor an equivalent earnings-related scheme for employees of employers who do not provide an occupational retirement plan.

Strategy for Pensions proposed a "partnership in which the State scheme provides basic pensions and occupational schemes provide pensions related to earnings." [17] The paper stated its view of the nature and purpose of a social program:

> The State scheme is the medium through which resources are transferred from people in work to those who have retired or are otherwise unable to work. It is a social scheme in which the range and level of benefits can and should depend upon social considerations and improvements in benefits can be shared with past contributors who are now the beneficiaries. The contributions needed to pay for, and establish a right to, these benefits are a social obligation that can be recognized more clearly and accepted more readily if it is not confused with the principles of insurance.[18]

The paper delineated the complementary role of occupational schemes:

> By contrast the essential role of the occupational scheme is to enable an employee to secure higher living standards for himself and his family in retirement by setting aside a part of his earnings. It is becoming increasingly recognized that wages are only one aspect of the total remuneration the employee gets for his services: pension rights should be as much a part of the terms of employment for the shop-floor worker as for the top executive. So a system where each form of pension is true to its own purpose holds out the best prospect of combining intelligibility with flexibility.[19]

and

> The security of a guaranteed basic pension through the State scheme is essential, but it is not enough. Every employee should have the opportunity to qualify for additional provision related to his earnings. . . . [F]or the great majority of people this can best be achieved through the expansion and improvement of occupational schemes.[20]

The Conservative government's proposals were generally followed in the resulting Social Security Act of July 1973, with provisions to become effective in April 1975.[21]

Following the election of February 28, 1974, which returned the Labour Party to power, the new government acted quickly to forestall implementation of certain elements of the Social Security Act of 1973 preparatory to issuing new proposals of its own in a subsequent white paper. In July 1974 an amendment was successfully carried in Parliament that endorsed the government's decision not to implement the State Reserve Pension Scheme and the "recognition" requirements for occupational pension plans. (The 1973 act required all employers after April 1975 to offer employees a private occupational pension plan or, as an alternative, to make provision for them through an especially established State Reserve Pension Scheme, a system based wholly on contributions paid in on a "value for money" basis, i.e., the defined contribution approach.) Labour's white paper issued in September 1974, *Better Pensions Fully Protected Against Inflation: Proposals for a New Pensions Scheme,* placed on the state greater responsibility for the provision of pensions through social security and resulted in the passing on August 7, 1975 of a new Social Security Act. Provisions are to become effective in April 1978.[22]

The proposals of both political parties have aimed at revising the system of income maintenance in old age to reduce the government's share of financing, to protect against inflation, and to provide more nearly adequate benefits. The controversy has been whether the primary means for accomplishing these goals should be the social security system or company benefit plans (occupation schemes). Labour has favored the former and the Conservatives the latter. The shifts in government have prevented the implementation of either approach. The portion of the 1973 act implemented in April 1975 is thus an interim measure, pending implementation in April 1978 of the Social Security Act of August 1975.

Provisions of the 1973 act that were implemented in April 1975 did not fundamentally alter the objective of the social insurance system—provision of a near-subsistence level social benefit. The most significant benefit change was suspension of the earnings-related benefit in the old-age insurance program and the interim strengthening of the flat-rate benefit, but with the important feature of a single earnings-related tax on all covered earnings up to a level that is approximately one and one-half times the average wage of employees in manufacturing. Previously, contributions were based on a two-tier flat-rate and earnings-related pattern. Employees with very low incomes benefit from the removal of the single flat-rate tax applied to persons at all income levels. Benefits were linked to living-cost changes. Graduated pensions already earned by April 1975 were preserved and paid with the basic flat pension on retirement. No new graduated pensions could be earned after the start of the new scheme.

The retirement age remains at 65 for men and 60 for women. The new earnings-related contributions are 5.5 percent of earnings for employees and 8.5 percent of payroll for employers, up to a maximum earnings of £69 a week for both. Employees earning less than £11 a week are automatically exempt from paying contributions but are still covered for flat-rate benefits.

Two other important measures were included in the legislation implemented in April 1975. One gives a new, more comprehensive definition of covered earnings. The other provides for vesting in private pension plans. Under the new provision workers who are at least age 26 and have 5 years of coverage in an approved private pension program must be fully vested as of 1980.

Labour government proposals for additional changes in social security provisions, outlined in the September 1974 white paper, were incorporated in the Social Security Act of August 1975, to be implemented in 1978. The flat-rate benefit is to be replaced by benefits based on a two-tiered system with a base-level amount guaranteed to everyone and earnings-related graduated benefits above the base level. The basic component is £1 for every £1 of earnings up to a lower earnings limit corresponding to the existing flat-rate pension in force when the new scheme begins. The additional component is to be 25 percent of earnings between the lower earnings limit and an upper limit that will be seven times the lower limit; the 25-percent benefit level will be achieved gradually at the rate of 1.25 percent of earnings between the lower and upper limits each year, until those workers contributing for 20 years qualify for the full 25 percent.

The new earnings-related employee contribution rate will be 6.5 percent of all earnings up to the upper limit. People earning less than the lower earnings limit will not be liable for contributions. The employer's contribution will be 10 percent of the same earnings range. Provision has been made for these rates to be reviewed before the new scheme is implemented.

The 1975 act permits employers to "contract out" of the second-tier or earnings-related component of the new system provided the benefits under an alternative occupational (private) scheme are at least as great as those available under the second-tier portion of social security. Contracting out through the implementation of occupational schemes would be voluntary. In general, the emphasis of the 1975 act is on helping lower-paid employees who will receive a higher proportion of their earnings as pension than will higher-paid employees.

FRANCE

Modern social security in France dates from legislation in 1945 that consolidated existing statutes, extended benefits to additional population categories, and gave nationwide application to what is known in France as the principle of *solidarité*, which expresses the idea that it is the duty of society to provide a minimum of security for all of its members.

Article 1 of the 1945 Social Security Code expresses the general objective of French social insurance: "The Social Security organization guarantees workers and their families against risks of all kinds which act to reduce or to eliminate earning capacity." [23]

An individual's old-age income protection through national social insurance is achieved in France through participation in one of three systems. The qualifying ages for retirement and the benefit amounts vary among the plans. About 60 percent of French wage and salary earners participate in the General Program. The remaining members of the work force participate in one of the Special Programs for wage and salaried employees, or in the Plans for Self-Employed Persons.

THE GENERAL SOCIAL SECURITY PROGRAM

The General Program for old-age pensions dates back to 1930, with subsequent improvements and extensions, and to the 1945 consolidation.

The General Program provides retired wage and salary earners a retirement benefit beginning at age 65 of 50 percent of average pensionable salary based on the 10 highest-paid years of work. Benefits may be begun at age 65 whether or not an individual continues employment. A worker who has reached age 65 is not required to pay further contributions for old-age insurance. The maximum benefit requires contributions for 37½ years. The pension is payable beginning as early as age 60, but at a much lower rate: 25 percent of the average best 10 years' pay, a level designed to discourage early retirements. However, a person who is forced to retire before 65 because of physical incapacity may begin benefits as early as age 60 at the normal 50-percent level. If an individual begins benefits as late as age 70, the benefit is increased to 75 percent of final average salary, and to 100 percent if benefits start at age 75.

The benefit amount is based on an individual's taxable wage base during working years, the "pensionable salary." The taxable wage base for 1973 was set at 24,480 francs (one franc then equaled 22.7 U.S. cents). The base is adjusted each year according to changes in national wage levels.

Additional old-age benefits are provided for a dependent spouse, care of children, and the assistance of *une tierce personne,* i.e., a person needed to perform household services for elderly persons. An old-age pension for a surviving spouse is provided for under the General Program, payable whether or not the insured person died before reaching the minimum pensionable age of 60. A surviving spouse is eligible for the pension beginning at age 55, recently lowered from age 65.

The General Program is financed by employer and employee contributions totaling 8.75 percent (1973) of the taxable wage base. The employee pays 3 percent of the taxable wage and employer 5.75 percent. An unemployed individual may pay into the General Program on a voluntary basis.[24]

THE SPECIAL PROGRAMS

Participants in the numerous special Social Security programs for old-age income in France are generally employed in public-service occupations that were already covered by government benefit programs when the General Program was established in 1945. Because of objections by the employed groups to changes in benefit arrangements, these programs were maintained and their participants were not brought under the General Program. Each special program is under the administration of the branch or organization of government that established it.

The main participating organizations are: the administration and services of the government, governments of departments and communes, the merchant marine, mining enterprises, railroad workers of the national railways and of secondary rail services, the Paris Métro, public utility companies, the Bank of France, notaries, the Opéra Nationale, Opéra-Comique, and Comédie Française.

The special programs are financed by contributions from employees and from the employing governmental units. In addition, the state contributes to the cost of the plans for miners, railroad workers, merchant marine, Opéra, Opéra-Comique, and Comédie Française.

The retirement age varies among plans, but generally it is 60 for governmental employees. For policemen, firemen, and other special hazard categories, the retirement age is 55.

Old-age benefits under the special plans vest after 15 years of service for deferred benefits payable at the normal retirement age stated by the plan. The benefits payable at the normal retirement age are set at 2 percent of the final year's basic wage or salary for each year of service.[25]

PROGRAMS FOR SELF-EMPLOYED PERSONS

The third part of the social security program in France is for self-employed persons, who are required to participate. Three separate institutions administer the coverage according to the segments served: (1) agricultural, (2) professional, and (3) industrial and commercial.

Benefits under the self-employed plans are based on contributions by participants and on government contributions. For self-employed people in the agricultural plan (1973), the benefits range from 1,500 to 6,000 francs per year depending on length of participation and age of retirement.

The coverage of the professional branch of the program includes accountants, physicians, architects, general insurance agents, consultants, artists, musicians, pharmacists, and veterinarians. The pensions payable range from 2,100 to 6,000 francs per year (9,000 francs for a family). Contributions are based on levels of professional compensation and of fund obligations. In 1972 contributions ranged from 550 francs per year for pharmacists to 1,300 francs for certified public accountants.

In recent years a decline in the number of self-employed persons in some covered categories led to fund deficits and to a law of reform in 1972 (effective 1973), which changed the contribution base for the industrial and commercial group to that of the General Program and substituted the General Program's benefits schedules. The result will be benefits that equal or exceed those payable under the former contribution rates.[26]

In addition to the old-age insurance program, the French social security system administers a system of family allowances, a workmen's compensation program, a disability pension system, and national health insurance.[27]

COMPLEMENTARY RETIREMENT PLANS

Extensive multiemployer retirement systems complement the social security system of France. Most of the plans have been developed under a system of nationwide collective bargaining between the principal labor organizations and the association of employers, the *Conseil Général du Patronat Français*. A French law of 1950 provides that multiemployer agreements between major employer associations and trade unions may be extended by government decree to all the employers and employees in the industry.[28] Employers who are not parties to an agreement are thus required to join the negotiated plans or establish comparable plans. This has resulted in extensive private pension coverage and in very large pension institutions, each covering thousands of employers and hundreds of thousands of employees.

Although privately administered, the multiemployer plans are subject to extensive government regulation with respect to composition of governing boards, investment of funds, financial reporting, and numerous substantive plan provisions. Private pensions are generally governed by the Social Security Ordinance of October 4, 1945, and subsequent regulations. Once a plan is established, employee participation is compulsory. Minimum employer and employee contributions are specified and vesting of benefits must be immediate. This combination of statutorily backed multiemployer pension negotiation, private administration, and strong government regulation has produced a layer of pension coverage above the basic social security level that resembles a social insurance program through its nearly universal and compulsory coverage, but also accommodates the diversity among private pension plans that results from their base in labor negotiation.

The French complementary pension plans are funded in a unique manner that markedly distinguishes them from the private plans in the United States. The financing of benefits is based on the principle of *répartition,* a redistribution technique through which the current workers in effect help finance the benefits of the current retirees in the plan. Full pension reserves in the traditional sense are not accumulated. The approach is nearer to what pension experts in the United States would call "pay-as-you-go" and is perhaps most comparable to the funding of social insurance systems. Necessarily, the French private system is surrounded with complex mechanisms designed to assure long-term payment stability.

Adverse experience with reserve funding explains the absence of the accumulating pension reserve funds on behalf of working employees to finance their benefits later on in retirement. Abandonment of traditional reserve funding methods came about because of the inflation that consumed the French franc between 1939 and the mid-1950s. These dozen and a half or so years of war and postwar inflation virtually wiped out the assets of private pension funds and insurance companies.

In 1938, just before the beginning of World War II, the cost-of-living index in France was readjusted to 100. By 1950, the index had risen to 2,100; by 1958, it had risen to 3,100. The effects were disastrous. For example, a person who had concluded a life insurance contract before World War II would have received as a benefit in 1952 only 4 percent of the purchasing power of the same benefit amount in 1938. If in 1938 it had been estimated that an insurance contract would provide the equivalent of one year's income 14 years later, the same amount would provide only two weeks of income in 1952 and about a week's income in 1958.[29]

The successor to reserve funding, redistribution, faces special problems of its own. One question is how to protect accrued benefit credits of employees and retirees if an employer goes out of business. The philosophy of reserve funding is that accrued benefits are assured by the accumulated reserves in the event of plan termination, with a plan's capacity to protect its participants judged by the extent to which resources (assets) match liabilities. Such protective assets are not established under redistribution.

Another problem under redistribution is how to assure benefits in the event of a decline in an industry, when lower levels of employment may be accompanied by an increasing proportion of retirees. If benefits are funded, retirees are protected, but if they must depend on the continuing fortunes of a particular industry, they are not as secure. A challenge to the redistribution method lies in the fact that active employee levels may decline as a proportion of retirees and that some industries and businesses may not only decline but may disappear altogether.

To meet these and other problems, the redistribution system has been furnished with extensive methods for coordination, stabilization, and mutual support among the various pension plans that use it. The aim is to assure pension funds in each of the industries that changes in the ratio of working to retired persons in specific areas will not result in fund or payment deficiencies, disproportionate requirements for contribution rates, or lower benefit levels compared with other industries. Pooling and reinsurance arrangements have been developed among the various plans in order to even out the consequences of changes in the fortunes of one or another industry or one or another group of employers. That all the plans are, in effect, multiemployer plans helps strengthen this pooling and mutual support approach. The basic philosophy brought into private pensions is, in fact, the solidarity concept—mutual support—which also underlies numerous aspects of social insurance.

The Cadres Plans. The first of the new-era pension plans was developed in 1947 through negotiations between associated employers and the French union for supervisory, professional, and executive personnel (for which there is no equivalent in the United States), the *Confederation Générale des Cadres* (CGC). The result was the *Cadres* plan for management and supervisory personnel throughout France. The negotiated plan provisions are uniform as to contributions and benefits over a large group of employers, but a number of separate pension institutions (*caisses*) administer the plan; an employer may choose for his management and supervisory group any particular *Cadre* pension institution he wishes.

The 70 or so pension institutions for the management and supervisory groups are coordinated and generally supervised by the *Association Générale des Institutions de Retraites des Cadres* (AGIRC). Through AGIRC, the affiliated institutions share their obligations, in effect pooling resources and liabilities. The participating *caisses* may be regional or national. They may serve the associated employees of a particular employer, a specific industry, or several industries. All of the *caisses* and AGIRC are under the jurisdiction of the Ministry of Labor. By the end of 1969 the *Cadres* plans covered more than 175,000 employers with more than 1,062,000 contributing employees and 201,000 pensioners.[30]

The statutory minimum contribution to the plans is 8 percent of the employee's salary in excess of the wage base for the General Program of social security up to a ceiling of four times the social security wage base. Currently, for the *Cadres* plans, the employee contributes 5 percent of applicable salary and the employer 9 percent.[31]

The *Cadre* benefit goal for the minimum contribution rate is an income beginning at age 65 of about 40 percent of the individual's preretirement salary excluding the salary base for social security benefits. The social security goal for benefits is currently about 50 percent of the average of the last 10 years' pensionable wage, for benefits beginning at age 65.

Other Employee Pension Plans. For nonmanagement employees, a similar pension arrangement was initiated by collective agreement in 1957. The agreement established a national supervisory and coordinating organization comparable to AGIRC, the *Union Nationale des Institutions de Retraites des Salariés* (UNIRS). Statutory action in 1962 made a pension plan compulsory for all employers whose employees were represented by national unions.

The plans under the supervision of UNIRS are comparable to those associated with the *Cadres,* with slight differences. Contributions and benefits are based on *all* of wages up to three times the social security wage base (rather than that part *above* the base). The contribution rate is lower, a total of 4 percent, shared by employer and employee on a three to two basis.

The benefit goal is a pension at age 65, in addition to social security old-age benefits, of up to 20 percent of the full range of earnings just preceding retirement. Combined, this would give a retirement benefit of about 70 percent of preretirement salary up to the wage base, and about 20 percent on the balance.

By 1961, negotiations among other employers and employees outside the UNIRS system had created other complementary pension plans for workers. In 1962 a new coordinating institution, *Association des Régimes de Retraites Complémentaires* (ARRCO) was established to cover both the new plans and the existing UNIRS plans. The ARRCO system now covers more than 8 million employees of more than 600,000 employers.[32] Some of the affiliated pension plans are very large and a number of them carry out extensive social services based on contributions agreed on in industry-wide negotiations.[33]

Among the several hundred *Cadre* and ARRCO pension institutions, with their coordinating and pooling institutions, accumulated pension benefits are immediately vested and are portable when job changes occur. Pension credits may be transferred from plan to plan. For the relatively few complementary retirement systems serving employees of a single employer, French pension law requires that pension benefits vest immediately.

Calculation of Pension Benefits. In establishing an employee's future pension entitlement under the redistribution plans, accumulation or formula "present value" calculations or projections are not made, as under private pension plans in the United States. Pension credits are expressed through a work point system. While the contributions on an employee's behalf are expressed as a percentage of his current wage or salary, as under defined contribution plans in the United States, they are immediately converted to pension points by dividing the contribution by an index number designated as the "reference salary." The result is a number of pension points credited to the employee's account. The point value changes each year to reflect changes in the reference salary index and changes in living costs and wage levels. During retirement the revaluation of points continues, so that retirement income responds to changes in living costs.

FEDERAL REPUBLIC OF GERMANY

The social security program of West Germany dates back to the compulsory insurance scheme for accidental injury introduced in Imperial Germany in 1883 and expanded in 1889 to cover permanent disability and old age.[34] This early system of social insurance became a model for every other country in Europe.

Prior to 1957, social insurance pensions in West Germany were based on covered earnings averaged over an individual's entire working lifetime, including periods of unemployment (no earnings credited) and, for almost every worker, spanning years of serious inflation. The resulting career average benefits did not accord very well with income needs at the time of retirement, nor was there a mechanism for maintaining the purchasing power of old-age benefits once they commenced.

MODERN SOCIAL INSURANCE

The 1957 and later changes have raised the goal of the old-age income program to a replacement rate of about 60 percent of last (covered) earnings, depending on the retirement age, for a working career, with benefits payable tied to a changing national wage index. In developing the 60-percent goal of replacement of pensionable earnings, the framers of the reform envisioned a total wage replacement rate of about 75 percent, with private pensions and individual savings making up the difference.[35]

Coverage. All wage earners are required to participate in the social security program, with the exception of police, military personnel, and civil servants (federal, state, and local), all of whom are covered under government employee plans. Voluntary social security coverage is available to civil servants and self-employed persons. All housewives, regardless of the coverage status of their husbands, may voluntarily participate.[36]

Contributions. Employer and employee each pay 9 percent (1973) of the employee's wage or salary up to a maximum wage of DM 27,600 per year (1973 ceiling; 1 DM then equaled 36.4 U.S. cents). The wage base for contributions coincides with the average West German wage, which is changed each year. The contribution for self-employed persons is 18 percent of income up to the wage base.

Benefits. The program provides old-age income, disability income, and income benefits to widows and surviving dependent children. The old-age benefit is calculated as 1.5 percent of the worker's assessed wages times years of insurance. "Assessed wages" represent a ratio of the worker's earnings to the national average over the period of coverage, multiplied by the current general computation base. The latter is changed each July 1 and corresponds to the average national wage level in the those calendar years preceding retirement. (The July 1972 computation base was DM 13,371.)[37]

The old-age benefit is based solely on the worker's wage history and is not increased on account of the presence of a spouse. It is increased if there are dependent children.

Widows' benefits are payable to a widow 45 years or older at the time of the husband's death, and to a widow with at least one child in her care. A widow's benefit is 60 percent of the benefit that was received by her husband. A child's benefit is 10 percent of the benefit of the insured if one parent survives and 20 percent if both are deceased. Children's benefits continue to age 18, or to 25 if the child is a student or is infirm.

Up to 1973, age 65 was the normal age for the start of old-age benefits for men, age 60 for women. In case of earlier withdrawal from the work force, an individual would be eligible for the old-age benefit only on reaching age 65 (men) or 60 (women). Effective in 1973, new legislation permitted flexible retirement. The fixed retirement age of 65 was replaced by a formula allowing workers the option of drawing the pension between the ages of 63 and 67. (As before, retirement at age 60 is allowed for men who have been unemployed for at least 52 weeks within the past 18 months and for women if they have spent at least 10 of the past 20 years in the labor force.) Retirement is at age 62 for severely disabled persons. Under the new flexible formula, normal retirement is at age 63 or 64, rather than 65, for any worker with 35 years of coverage. If a worker who is eligible for retirement before age 65 defers retiring beyond age 65, he will earn besides the 1.5-percent increase per year in his benefit an increment of 0.6 percent for each month worked between age 65 and 67. In addition, the periodic adjustments to wage increases will effectively increase the pension over that payable at age 63.[38]

PRIVATE PENSION PLANS IN WEST GERMANY

It has been estimated that private pension plans in West Germany cover about 60 percent of nonagricultural wage and salary earners, or about 11 million persons.[39] West Germany has elected a strong social insurance system for old-age benefits, leaving the private pension system as a largely voluntary effort. Prior to 1975, the private pension plans in Germany were not subject to very extensive statutory control. In this respect they resembled more closely private pension plans in the United States prior to the 1974 reform legislation than private plans among European neighbors. Private pension plans in Germany are concentrated among the larger employers. Estimates indicate that about two thirds of the firms with over 50 employees have pension plans, while about a quarter of smaller firms have them.[40]

As a result of passage of German labor law legislation effective January 1, 1975, employers were required to preserve a terminating employee's pension benefit, to protect an employee's rights against insolvency and to freeze the social security offset as of retirement. Additionally, employers are now required to review and adjust pension benefits at regular intervals of three years, with the first adjustment made before December 31, 1975.[41]

Vesting. Although exact figures are not available, it appears that, before the recent legislation, at any one time only a small percentage of private pension plan participants in West Germany had vested benefits. Under the new law the preservation of old-age, death, and disability benefits is compulsory. In case of termination of employment, the pension benefit becomes fully vested provided the employee has attained the age of 35 with at least 12 years of service and 3 years of membership in the plan or has been a member of the company pension plan for 10 years. Vested benefits can be replaced by a lump-sum refund if membership in the plan is less than 10 years. The law permits portability of an employee's benefits to the next employer, subject to the employee's agreement, but does not require the next employer to assume the new employee's pension claim.[42]

At this stage it appears that the new vesting requirements will have little impact, as Germany has a very low turnover of employment after the age of 35 or after 10 or 15 years of service, the age and service minimum required for vesting. It is possible, however, that the new law will provide the basis for broader vesting provisions in the future.

Types of Plans. Five basic types of funding arrangements are utilized in private pension plans in West Germany: (1) the balance sheet reserve system, (2) separate pension funds, (3) provident funds, (4) insured funds, and (5) voluntary participation for additional insurance through the social security system. Separate plans cover employees of the West German government and units of local government.

Balance Sheet Reserve System. The majority of private plans use this method (estimated to cover 70 percent of workers under retirement plans), also called "promise system," "retirement benefit pledge," or "book reserve" system (*Pensionsrückstellung*). No separately established segregated pension reserves are involved. The employer sets up an internal reserve to cover the expected benefit payments, but he continues to use the actual funds as working capital for company operations. If there are disability or death benefits under the pension plan, the risks are usually reinsured. Pension benefits are taxed as income to the employee when received.[43]

Separate Pension Funds. The *Pensionskassen* (independent pension funds) are similar to pension trust funds in the United States. They cover about 10 percent of workers under West German private pension plans. Regional multiemployer plans frequently use a pension trust, with its separate legal entity and protected reserves. Administration of the funds is usually through a joint employer-employee board. Investments are subject to the same regulation and supervision as insurance companies. These plans are often contributory. Employer contributions are deductible from taxable income as a business expense and are currently taxable to the employee above certain limits. Annuitants are not liable for income taxes on the benefits received.

Provident Funds. *Unterstützungskasse* (provident or support funds) cover another 10 percent of workers in private pension plans. The oldest form of private retirement funds in Germany, the provident funds are numerous and generally small in size; they may also provide medical care and other benefits. Employers may set up their own separate fund, or join a group fund. Government supervision is less than for *Pensionskassen;* tax treatment is the same. Money from the provident funds can be lent back to the employer at a "reasonable" rate of interest. There are no employee contributions, though employees have a right to participate in the management.

Insurance Plans. Individual or group contracts with insurance companies constitute this form of providing pension, disability, or death benefits. Less than 10 percent of workers under pension plans are covered by insured plans, usually the employees of small firms. The plans may be contributory.

Supplements through Social Security. Little-used but nevertheless available are arrangements through which additional voluntary contributions for old age, disability, and death benefits may be made to the social security system.[44]

THE NETHERLANDS

Old-age security in the Netherlands rests on a primary layer of income provided under the universal social insurance system and a secondary layer provided by private pensions or pensions for civil servants. Legislation requires the broad extension of private pension coverage in industries in which pensions have been negotiated. This has led to widespread private plan protection.

SOCIAL INSURANCE

As in most other Western European countries, modern social insurance legislation in the Netherlands developed out of early laws (1901) covering industrial accidents. Prior to World War II the social insurance legislation applied mainly to persons receiving salary or wages, but since the war the approach has been to cover as much of the entire population as possible, employed or not.[45]

The Netherlands social security program is divided into two parts: National Insurance, for old-age pensions and survivors' benefits (widows and orphans), and Employed Persons' Insurance, providing health insurance, disability insurance, and unemployment benefits. In addition, there are family allowance systems and a health insurance program.

The National Insurance Old-Age Pension Plan. The old-age pension plan is based on a 1957 act that provides for compulsory coverage of all Netherlands residents between the ages of 15 and 65. Participants pay a contribution of 10.4 percent of wages or other income up to 2,025 guilders per month (one guilder equaled about 37.5 U.S. cents in January 1976). The unique feature is that the same percentage contribution of income is required of persons not employed as well as those who are employed. The government makes the contributions for low-income persons and makes up any deficits. Collections are effected through income tax machinery. Wives who have little or no income and who do not pay contributions are, in old age, the beneficiaries of a special added pension for married couples. There are no employer contributions for the old-age pension program, but there are for the disability program.

To receive the full old-age pension, a person must have paid contributions from age 15 to age 65. A transition arrangement covers persons who reach age 65 without the maximum coverage due to their age at the time the plan was started. The pension may be claimed at age 65; retirement is unnecessary.

The full old-age pension is 492.50 guilders a month (1973). The supplement for a wife of any age is 205 guilders a month. The maximum benefits amount to approximately 45 percent of average current covered wages for single persons and about 60 percent for couples.

The pension payments are linked with the Netherlands wage index and are subject to adjustment twice a year by a percentage equal to the increase, if any, in the index.[46]

Survivors' Benefits. As under the old-age pension part of National Insurance, all Netherlands residents 15 years of age or older who have incomes are required to participate in the program for survivors' pensions. A contribution of 1.6 percent of the first 2,025 guilders of monthly earnings or income is paid by the individual. Employers do not contribute.

Widows' pensions are paid to age 65 if the widow was age 40 or over at the time of her husband's death. At age 65 the old-age pension takes over. A widow is also entitled to benefits if she is under age 40 and caring for a minor (unmarried) child at the time of her husband's death, or is pregnant or disabled. In addition, there are family allowances for children. The survivor benefits are linked to the wage index.

Employee contributions to the social insurance programs are taxed as current income. Employer contributions (made mainly to the Employed Persons and family allowance systems) are treated as deductible business expenses and are not taxed as income to the employee. Benefits are not taxed as income when received.[47]

PRIVATE PENSIONS IN THE NETHERLANDS

A large proportion of Dutch workers participate in private pension plans whose benefits supplement the basic benefits provided by social insurance. About 2.3 million employees (out of a total employed work force of 3.9

million) participate in the 85 industry-wide multiemployer pension funds or in the 1,600 single-employer self-administered or insured plans. The levels of benefits under different plans vary considerably.[48]

The first private pensions in the Netherlands were set up by the private railways in the early 20th century, following examples of pensions established for government employees. The private plans did not increase very rapidly in number until after World War II.

The first Netherlands public legislation covering private pension plans was the Industrial Pensions Fund Act following World War II. While leaving the establishment of pension plans entirely up to employers and employees in each branch of industry, the act authorized the Ministry for Social Affairs and Public Health, once a pension plan is established in an industry, to require all firms within the industry to participate in the plan if requested by the representative employee and employer associations in that industry. The effect of the statute has been to assure that pension gains in one part of an industry are generally shared by other segments of the same industry. The act also requires that pension fund boards be composed of equal numbers of representatives of employer and employee organizations.[49] Collective bargaining agreements normally establish the pension plans in each industry sector.

A 1954 law, the Pension Funds and Savings Act, spelled out further government requirements applicable to private pension coverage. Under this law, a firm whose employees are to be covered by pension benefits through negotiation or through extension to the firm by decree may join an industrial fund, establish a single-employer pension fund, or establish the plan through an insurance company.

The 1954 law also requires that benefits must vest after five years of plan participation. After age 25 for men and 30 for women, an employee terminating for any reason after five years of employment retains his accumulated pension credits and may not receive any surrender cash value. A government publication describes the vesting provision as helping "to prevent stagnation in the mobility of workers. . . ."[50]

The 1954 law also established certain pension funding requirements. Before 1954, some plans were operating on a "pay-as-you-go" basis, and others were not following strict actuarial principles. The 1954 act required full funding of pension promises and the filing of a plan description for approval with the Ministry of Social Affairs and Public Health. Each pension fund must submit an annual financial report to the Insurance Chamber (*Ver-*

zekeringskamer), the government office of life insurance regulation. Actuarial valuations are required every five years. The Insurance Chamber may authorize the gradual funding of past service benefits or benefit improvements over periods not exceeding 25 years.[51]

Benefits under private plans vary widely, ranging from modest amounts of less than 1,000 guilders per year for long service to as much as 70 percent of final pay. Benefits are usually related by formula to earnings and service. The social security wage base is often excluded for purposes of contributions and benefit calculations.[52] The plans usually incorporate disability benefits and widows' pensions.

A common contribution arrangement is a sharing of costs by the employer and the employee. Contributions for plans within the scope of the Pension and Savings Fund Act are deductible for income tax purposes by both employer and employee. Benefits are taxed as income.

The normal retirement age under private plans is almost invariably 65, corresponding with the social security retirement age.

Public employees in the Netherlands participate in the national social insurance system and in pension plans for public employees. In the latter, benefits vest after 10 years of service.

Recently the Dutch government asked the Labor Institute (*Stichting van de Arbeid*), an organization of employer and employee representatives, to study the future of private pensions in the Netherlands. Current reports on the study indicate that consideration is being given to a total retirement income goal for persons age 65, including social security and private pension benefits, of approximately 70 percent of final pay (up to a stated maximum). The study group is also seeking methods of avoiding steep last-minute increases in final pay for some workers in contrast to others, which result in inequitable benefit situations. To help cope with the effects of inflation on retirement benefits, this group has recommended the use of a supplemental index adjustment for private plans that would be financed on a pay-as-you-go basis, superimposed on the reserve funding of the basic private pension income.[53]

SWEDEN

The Swedish system of social insurance for old-age income is provided through the National Basic Pensions System and the National Supplementary Pensions System. Separate social insurance systems provide health insurance, industrial injuries insurance, and unemployment insurance. The Swedish system is very similar to that of Norway.

THE NATIONAL BASIC PENSIONS SYSTEM

The National Basic Pensions System normally applies only to Swedish citizens resident in Sweden. It provides old-age, disability, widows', and children's pensions. The pensions are flat amounts independent of contributions paid in and of the income or personal property of the pensioner and his spouse. Wife's supplements and income-tested municipal housing supplements may be paid at the option of each municipality in addition to the basic pensions.

Old-Age Pension. The basic flat pension is normally paid when the insured person attains the age of 67. On special application the pension may be granted earlier, but not before age 63. If drawn earlier than 67, the pension is reduced by 0.6 percent for each month by which the pension starting age falls short of 67. If the start of the pension is deferred until after age 67, the pension is increased by 0.6 percent for each month that payment is postponed, up to the age of 70.[54]

The annual amount of the old-age pension is calculated as a percentage of a base amount, calculated for January 1973 as 7,300 kronor. The base amount is changed when the consumer price index has changed by at least 3 percent. (One krona equaled about 23 U.S. cents in January 1976.)

The annual amount of the old-age pension (paid from age 67) is 90 percent of the base amount ($.90 \times 7,300 = 6,575$ kr in January 1973) for a single pensioner, and 140 percent of the base amount for a married couple.

Survivors' Benefits. The National Basic Pensions system provides a full widow's pension to widows caring for one or more children under the age of 16, and to widows who had reached the age of 50 at the time of the husband's death. If the widow is at least age 36 at the time of her husband's death and has no children under 16 in her care, she is entitled to a reduced widow's pension. The amount of a full widow's pension equals the amount of the basic old-age pension paid to a single person.[55]

Benefits for surviving children are paid at an annual rate of 35 percent of the base amount of the National Basic system for each child if both parents are dead, and 25 percent for each child if either of the parents is dead. The pension is paid until the child reaches the age of 16.[56]

The system also provides income benefits for partial and full disability. The amount of the full disability pension is the same as that of the basic old-age pension, paid from the age of 67. The disability pension is replaced by the basic old-age pension when the pensioner reaches the age of 67.[57]

Contributions. Persons insured under the National Basic system pay contributions between the ages of 16 and 65 at the rate of 5 percent of taxable income up to a maximum of 30,000 kronor (maximum tax of 1,500 kronor). Contributions are not deductible when taxable income is determined. Contributions provide about a third of the cost, the remaining two thirds of the cost of the basic program being financed from general revenue.

The National Basic Pensions are subject to personal income tax, but if the pensioner has no income or only a small income (up to a maximum of 1,500 kronor per year) in addition to his basic pension (including any municipal housing supplement), he is exempt from income tax.[58]

THE NATIONAL SUPPLEMENTARY PENSION SYSTEM

The National Supplementary Pension System (ATP) provides social insurance benefits that largely depend upon the income a person earned during the time he was actively working. The National Supplementary System applies to Swedish citizens and to foreigners resident in Sweden.

The supplementary pensions consist of (1) retirement pensions, (2) early retirement pensions or disability pensions, and (3) family pensions payable to widows and surviving children.

Contributions. For employed persons, contributions to the supplementary earnings-related pension system are paid by the employer. For self-employed persons, the contributions are paid by the insured individual.

The present contribution rate is 10.5 percent of pensionable earnings, defined as that part of income which exceeds the current "basic amount" under the Basic National Pension system, with a maximum of 7.5 times the current basic amount (7,300 to 54,750 kronor).[59]

Benefits. The income benefit from the earnings-related pension is 60 percent of the difference between average annual covered earnings (under the earnings-related plan) and the base amount, based on coverage from 1960, with the full pension provided if there are 20 years of coverage until 1980, or 30 years of coverage thereafter. For shorter coverage, the percentage is reduced accordingly. If retirement is delayed after age 67 there is an increment of 0.6 percent of pension per month of deferral until age 70. Provision is made for automatic adjustments of earnings and pensions in force resulting from price changes. As with the basic social security pension, there is a reduction in benefit of 0.6 percent per month for each month under age 67 at the start of benefits.[60]

Incapacity for work that entitles a person to disability pension benefits under the National Basic Pensions System also entitles a person to benefits under the National Supplementary Pension System. The full supplementary disability pension is equal to the amount of the old-age pension that would be payable from the age of 67.

Survivors' Pensions. Widow and child pensions are paid if at the time of death the insured was entitled to a National Supplementary old-age or disability pension. A widow's pension is 40 percent of the pension of the insured worker. If there are children under age 19, the widow's pension is 35 percent of the insured's pension plus 15 percent for the first child and 10 percent for each additional child.[61]

PRIVATE PENSIONS IN SWEDEN

Before 1960 the full National Basic Pension was so small that employers normally ignored it when setting the levels of benefits under private pension plans. The National Supplementary Pension System was introduced in 1960, and at the same time legislation provided for a 10-year program for the increase of benefits under the National Basic system. These developments influenced organizations of employers and employees to take up negotiations aimed at unifying the different private pension systems and adapting them to the two national pension systems.

The ITP Plan. ITP are the Swedish initials for "complementary pensions for salaried employees in industry and commerce." ITP pension agreements between the Swedish Employers' Confederation (SAF) and the salaried employees' unions established the private sector plan. Since October 1969, the collectively established plans must by law be extended to all member companies of the Swedish Employers' Confederation. The ITP plans have served as models for other pension agreements in the private sector.

Two alternative methods of providing benefits are used under the ITP plans. One is through the Swedish Staff Pension Society (SPP), a mutual insurance company founded in 1917 by the Federation of Swedish Industries and the Chambers of Commerce in cooperation with the unions of salaried employees. The main objective of SPP is to underwrite pensions under the ITP plan and occupational group life insurance. SPP is the only Swedish insurance company authorized to use a group basis when computing premiums for occupational pensions.

The alternative method is the FPG/PRI system. The FPG (Pension Guarantee Mutual Insurance Company) reinsures employers who elect to establish their pension reserves internally. The PRI (Pension Registration Institute) calculates funds required under employers' plans, records pension credits, collects funds from employers for pensions payable, and pays out pensions due.

Under the FPG/PRI system, the employer who is responsible for the pension commitments has to make transfers year by year to a special balance sheet account. The amounts transferred are in principle equivalent to the premiums that would be paid to the insured plan, the SPP. The pension commitments have to be secured by an insurance contract between FPG and the employer. In the event of an employer's insolvency, FPG buys pension insurance from SPP covering the employer's pension commitments for accrued pension rights.[62]

Contributions. For an insured ITP plan, premiums are uniformly set at between 8 and 9 percent of the total salary of the employees covered, and are paid by employers. The cost of disability and widows' pensions is about 0.6 percent of salary. FPG/PRI system costs are usually about the same, increased by the annual premium for guarantee insurance, 0.3 percent of the employer's unfunded pension liability. Per individual, the premiums under the SPP plan vary according to entry age, sex, and salary. Employer premiums to SPP and allocations within FPG/PRI are deductible as a business expense and not currently taxable as income to the employee. The pensions are taxable as income to the recipient.

Benefits. Under the ITP plans, salary up to a maximum of 15 times the base social security amount for January of each year is pensionable, that is, may be used for the purpose of the calculation of contributions and benefits. In addition to the ITP pension, benefits include disability pensions, widows' pensions, and family pensions.

Retirement age is 65 under ITP, two years earlier than under the basic and supplementary national pensions. Benefits are therefore stepped up for the two-year period. Before age 67 the pension is:

65 percent of final salary up to a maximum of 10 times the basic amount
($10 \times 7,300$ kronor in 1973),
and 32.5 percent of any additional salary up to a maximum of 15 times
the basic amount.

After age 67, the ITP pension is:

10 percent of the salary up to a maximum of 7.5 times the basic amount,
65 percent of salary between 7.5 and 10 times the basic amount,
and 32.5 percent of any additional salary up to a maximum of 15 times
the basic amount.

In 1962, measures were introduced to compensate ITP pensioners for
increases in the cost of living after the commencement of pension payments.
The increases, which apply under both the insured and the employer-
managed plans, consist of "bonus supplements" fixed once a year, limited
by the rise in the consumer price index, and determined uniformly for all
pensions commencing in the same calendar year.[63]

Vesting. The complementary pension plans in Sweden have incorporated
immediate vesting from the outset, and legislation now mandates it. In the
mid-1960s, a Royal Commission reviewed the old-age income protection of
Swedish citizens, and pension legislation was enacted as a result in 1968.
The legislation set standards for private pension plans, and generally covered plan funding, accounting standards, vesting, participation, insurance of
plan liabilities, and the reporting of financial operations. The Pension Registration Institute keeps records of the pension credits earned by employees
who move from employer to employer.

BLUE COLLAR WORKERS' PRIVATE PENSIONS

The ITP plan just described covers salaried workers in the private sector.
Until recently, there have been few collective agreements on pensions for
nonsalaried workers. In 1971, the Swedish Employers' Confederation (SAF)
and the Swedish Confederation of Trade Unions (IO) developed an agreement that included the introduction of a complementary pension insurance
plan, the STP (Complementary Pension for Workers), effective July 1,
1973. A special insurance company to provide the workers' complementary
pensions was established and it concluded an agreement with the Swedish

Staff Pension Society (SPP) to administer the plan. The new plan, financed by employers, is similar in most respects to the ITP plan.[64]

PUBLIC EMPLOYEE PENSIONS

Employees of governmental units in Sweden participate in the Swedish Government Pension System. The government plan is gradually being coordinated with the basic and supplementary national pension systems, so that government pension plans occupy approximately the same status as complementary pensions as do the ITP and STP plans. The statutory retirement age differs for posts in different categories, ranging from 63 to 66. The employer pays the full cost of the government pension system.[65]

JAPAN

Although Japan occupies a high place in the list of modern industrial nations, Japanese traditions and social institutions, contrasting in many respects to those of Western societies, have led to different approaches to support of the elderly. Despite the weight of tradition, however, the machinery for social insurance and pensions in Japan is changing, along with other institutions. It appears that developments in the future may tend to be along Western lines. In recent years the Japanese government has acknowledged that past concentration of national efforts in expanding industrial capabilities has blunted the pace of social reform.

SOCIAL INSURANCE

The program of social insurance in Japan is based on the Employees' Pension Insurance Law of 1944, as amended, and covers workers in enterprises in the private sector employing more than five persons. Public employees, teachers, seamen, and public utility employees participate in special systems. Persons not covered under the Employees' Pension Insurance Law are covered under the National Pension Program established in 1959 as part of the social insurance system.

EMPLOYEES' PENSION INSURANCE PLAN

Old-Age Benefits. The old-age pension benefits are made up of two parts: a flat annual benefit, consisting of 1,000 yen multiplied by months of covered participation up to a maximum of 360 (30 years), and a second tier of benefits based on earnings history. (One yen equaled 0.33 U.S. cents in January 1976.) The earnings-related portion is calculated as 1 percent of covered career average earnings multiplied by the years of participation. The calculation of the earnings-related portion includes an earnings revaluation procedure designed to compensate to a degree for increases in wage levels that have taken place over the earnings period. A minimum of 20 years' coverage is required.

The old-age social insurance benefit is commonly called "the 50,000-yen pension." A maximum social insurance pension of 600,000 yen per year (50,000 yen per month) is tax-free to the recipient. A recipient of old-age benefits who is supporting a spouse is entitled to a supplementary benefit of 2,400 yen per month.

The old-age benefits are payable at age 60 for men and at age 55 for women and miners. If the worker continues in employment after he becomes eligible for benefits, benefits are paid but are reduced by 20 percent during the period of continuing employment.

After benefits begin they are adjusted upward whenever the consumer price index increases by 5 percent or more.

Widows' Pensions. A widow is entitled to benefits if she is age 55 or over, disabled, or has children under 18 in her care. The widow of a person who dies while receiving an old-age pension is entitled to a benefit of 50 percent of the pension her husband received. Children's benefits are provided where such children are orphaned or under the care of a widow or widower.

The benefit for an eligible widow whose husband died before starting old-age benefits is 50 percent of the husband's old-age benefit calculated on the basis of a minimum of 20 years of covered employment.

Disability Benefits. Benefits are payable for covered employees who become totally and permanently disabled. The benefit is the same as if the employee had become entitled to old-age benefits with at least 20 years of covered employment. A "constant attendance" supplement of 25 percent of the amount of the pension is payable to disabled workers requiring such care. Additional benefits are paid according to the number of dependents the disabled worker is responsible for. Reduced pensions are payable for partial disability.

Contributions. The cost of the Employees' Pension Insurance Program is met by employee and employer contributions and from general revenues, which support about 20 percent of program costs. Employees pay 3.2 percent (men) or 2.4 percent (women) of covered earnings (up to 200,000 yen per month), and employers match the employees' contributions.

Japanese employees' wages are relatively low in the early years of working life under the traditional practice of "whole life employment." Wages become progressively higher with length of service and peak just before retirement. Thus, while the old-age social insurance pension may amount to 45 percent or 60 percent of average earnings, depending on whether the twice-a-year bonus is included in the calculation of earnings, it represents a much lower percentage of final earnings. The level of the 50,000-yen social pension is generally designed as a basic floor of protection, insufficient alone as an old-age income, but a basic amount upon which private employers may build supplementary protection.

THE NATIONAL PENSION PLAN

This part of the social insurance scheme covers self-employed persons and employees in very small enterprises. The plan provides benefits comparable to those of the Employees' Pension Insurance plan, including old-age pensions, disability benefits, and widows' and children's pensions.

Japanese residents aged 20 to 59 are compulsorily insured under the plan provided they are not covered under any other public plan or are spouses of such other persons.

Contributions. Each participant makes a monthly contribution of 550 yen. The balance of the cost of the scheme is provided from government contributions, currently equal to about half of the total amount contributed by participants. Disabled participants and widowed mothers are exempt from contributions.

Old-Age Benefits. A person is entitled to the old-age pension when he attains the age of 65 and has contributed for a period of 25 years. As a transition provision, the 25-year requirement is reduced to as little as 10 years for persons who had already reached the higher ages when the plan was commenced.

The amount of the National Pension annual benefit is calculated by formula: (number of contribution months) × 320 yen + (number of exempted months) × 320 yen × ⅓. A minimum annual benefit of 39,600 yen is paid after age 70. Although age 65 is set as the first age the benefit may be received, it may be delayed until age 70, with an actuarial increase in benefits.

The amount of a widow's pension is equal to half of the old-age pension her deceased husband received.[66]

PRIVATE PENSIONS IN JAPAN

Until recent years, the common practice among Japanese employers has been to pay retirement benefits in a lump sum. Until about 1950 there was virtually no other arrangement. The lump-sum payment in most companies was made at age 55, in others at an age normally between 55 and 60.

In the early 1950s some of the large companies in Japan began to adopt pension plans paying monthly income. There were several reasons: (1) because of the economic conditions following World War II, funds were lacking for the payment of the traditional lump-sum benefits; (2) the tax treatment of lump-sum benefits made annuities a more attractive method of receiving income; (3) it appeared that the tradition of family support of aged persons was beginning to change. Although the livelihood of the aged still largely depended on the care provided under the large family system, it was becoming more difficult to retain the custom that a child, usually the first son, should live with his parents and be responsible for supporting them in their old age.

Recent economic growth in Japan and increasing longevity, as well as an increasing proportion of older people in the population, has led to greater attention to income support methods for retired workers. The 1959 social security legislation encouraged this trend, and subsequent increases in social security benefit levels helped establish a floor upon which supplementary private coverage could be superimposed. About half of Japan's large companies have now established plans that provide for annuity benefits. Legislation in 1962 encouraged the introduction of tax-qualified pension plans and also removed drawbacks regarding the taxation of lump-sum benefits.

Private Plan Provisions. Under the tax-qualified pension plan provided by Japanese employers, benefits may be in the form of pensions or lump sums. Benefits are paid after a minimum of 20 to 25 years participation. The plans are usually noncontributory. Benefits may be based on an accumulation of funds or expressed as a percentage of final base pay. The benefits become vested only at retirement, a feature that corresponds to the Japanese tradition of a lifetime of work for a single employer.

Most of the private pension plans provide temporary annuities (annuities certain) rather than life annuities. Annual income is for 5 or 10 years. Consequently, pension plans in Japan are still inadequate to assure lifetime financial protection in old age. Since the age of compulsory retirement in Japanese industry is between 55 and 60, employers' contributions for pension plans would inevitably have to increase should they adopt life annuity pension provisions.

An optional "contracting out" provision of the social security system was adopted in 1966. Companies having more than 1,000 employees are eligible to install a contracted-out plan, which is permitted if the substitute plan assures a somewhat higher level of benefits proportionate to the employee's salary than does the social insurance plan. (The employer contracts out of the second tier of national social insurance, i.e., the earnings-related coverage.)

A contracted-out plan must provide a benefit with an actuarial value of at least 30 percent more than the social insurance benefit. In addition, certain other requirements must be met: the benefit of each employee must reflect the earnings of the employee during his entire service period, the benefits must be payable in the form of a life annuity, and contributions must be shared equally by employer and employee. Employers may pay additional benefits beyond the contracted-out portion.

Administration of contracted-out plans must be by an independent corporation, designated an Employees' Pension Fund. In 1970, there were 662 such plans, 111 of which were multiemployer plans. In 1970, approximately 3.4 million workers were covered under Employees' Pension Funds, out of a total of 20 million workers covered by private pension plans.[67]

NOTES

CHAPTER 1: INCOME OF THE AGED

1. U.S. Department of Health, Education, and Welfare, Public Health Service, *Life Tables* (1970).

2. U.S. Bureau of the Census, *Current Population Reports,* Series P-25, No. 470 (1971), pp. 40–42.

3. Ibid., No. 493 (1972), pp. 14–15.

4. Ibid.

5. World Health Organization, *World Health Statistics Report* 25 (1972):436.

6. Janet Murray, "Living Arrangements of People Aged 65 and Older," *Social Security Bulletin* 34 (September 1971):3.

7. U.S. Bureau of the Census, *Current Population Reports,* Series P-23, No. 43 (1973), p. 13.

8. Ibid.

9. The National Conference Board, *A Guide to Consumer Markets* (New York: The Conference Board, 1973–74), pp. 15, 87.

10. Patience Lauriat and William Rabin, "Men Who Claim Benefits before Age 65: Findings from the Survey of New Beneficiaries, 1968," *Social Security Bulletin* 33 (November 1970):3–4.

11. Virginia Reno, *Retirement Patterns of Men at OASDHI Entitlement, Preliminary Findings from the Survey of New Beneficiaries,* No. 2 (Washington, D.C.: Social Security Administration, 1971), p. 16.

12. Lauriat and Rabin, "Men Who Claim Benefits before Age 65," p. 22.

13. Ibid.

14. Virginia Reno, "Why Men Stop Working at or before Age 65: Findings from the Survey of New Beneficiaries," *Social Security Bulletin* 34 (June 1971):3.

15. Reno, *Retirement Patterns,* p. 15.

16. Ibid., p. 14.

17. Virginia Reno and Carol Zuckert, "Benefit Levels of Newly Retired Workers: Findings from the Survey of New Beneficiaries," *Social Security Bulletin* 34 (July 1971):4.

18. For a discussion of the practical and conceptual questions involving imputed incomes in data collection, see Lenore Bixby, "Income of People Aged 65 and Older: Overview from 1968 Survey of the Aged," *Social Security Bulletin* 34 (April 1970):5.

19. U.S. Bureau of the Census, *Current Population Reports,* Series P-60, No. 99 (1975), p. 9.

20. Ibid.

21. For a discussion of the research technique to measure adequacy of income, see U.S. Department of HEW, Administration on Aging, "Measuring Adequacy of Income," *Facts and Figures on Older Americans,* No. 1 (1971).

22. U.S. Bureau of the Census, *Current Population Reports,* Series P-60, No. 99 (1975), p. 16.

23. Ibid., pp. 13, 17.

24. U.S. Department of HEW, Administration on Aging, "Income and Poverty in 1972—Advance Report," *Facts and Figures on Older Americans,* No. 7 (1973), p. 3.

25. U.S. Bureau of the Census, *Current Population Reports,* Series P-60, No. 99 (1975), p. 9.

26. U.S. Department of HEW, "Measuring Adequacy of Income," pp. 4–5.

27. Bixby, "Income of People Aged 65," p. 19.

28. Ibid.; Susan Grad, "Relative Importance of Income Sources of the Aged," *Social Security Bulletin* 36 (August 1973):38.

29. Bixby, "Income of People Aged 65," p. 4.

30. Ibid.

31. Ibid., p. 23.

32. Ibid.

33. Ibid., p. 10.

34. Walter Kolodrubetz, "Private and Public Retirement Pensions: Findings from the 1968 Survey of the Aged," *Social Security Bulletin* 33 (September 1970):3.

35. Ibid., pp. 44–46.

36. Ibid., p. 45.

37. Lenore Bixby and Virginia Reno, "Second Pensions Among Newly Entitled Workers: Survey of New Beneficiaries," *Social Security Bulletin* 34 (November 1971):4.

38. Walter Kolodrubetz, "Private Retirement Benefits and Relationship to Earnings: Survey of New Beneficiaries," *Social Security Bulletin* 36 (May 1973):18.

39. Kolodrubetz, "Private and Public Retirement Pensions," pp. 7–8.

40. Janet Murray, "Homeownership and Financial Assets: Findings from the 1968 Survey of the Aged," *Social Security Bulletin* 35 (August 1972):4.

41. Ibid., p. 8.

42. Ibid.

43. Ibid., p. 12.

44. Ibid.

45. Ibid., p. 22.

46. Bixby, "Income of People Aged 65 and Older," pp. 10, 13.

47. U.S. Congress, Senate, Special Committee on Aging, *Developments in Aging: 1971 and January–March 1972*. S. Report 92–784, 92nd Congress, 2nd Session (1972), p. 258.

48. U.S. Department of HEW, Administration on Aging, *Invitation to Design a World, Second Reader,* AOA Publication No. 108 (1971), p. 3.

CHAPTER 2: THE BEGINNING OF AMERICAN
PENSION PLANS

1. Murray Webb Latimer, *Industrial Pension Systems in the United States and Canada,* 2 vols. (New York: Industrial Relations Counselors, 1932), 1:20–21.

2. Carnegie Foundation for the Advancement of Teaching, *Tenth Annual Report* (1915), pp. 74–75.

3. Latimer, *Industrial Pension Systems,* 1:22.

4. Ibid., pp. 22, 25, 27.

5. Ibid., p. 40.

6. Ibid., pp. 42, 47; U.S. Bureau of the Census, *Historical Statistics of the United States, 1789–1945,* Series D1-10 Labor Force (1949), p. 63.

7. See Abraham Epstein, *Insecurity: A Challenge to America* (New York: Smith and Haas, 1933), pp. 150–151.

8. Latimer, *Industrial Pension Systems,* 1:44–48.

9. Ibid., p. 44.

10. Ibid., p. 100.

11. Ibid., p. 99; Murray Webb Latimer, letter to the authors dated January 24, 1975.

12. National Industrial Conference Board, Inc., *Elements of Industrial Pension Plans* (New York: National Industrial Conference Board, 1931), p. 22.

13. Latimer, *Industrial Pension Systems,* 1:108.

14. Ibid., p. 106.

15. Ibid., p. 108.

16. Latimer, *Industrial Pension Systems,* 2:572.

17. National Industrial Conference Board, *Industrial Pension Plans in the United States* (New York: National Industrial Conference Board, 1925), p. 107.

18. Ibid., p. 101.

19. Conference Board, *Elements of Industrial Pension Plans,* pp. 34–35.

20. Latimer, *Industrial Pension Systems,* 2:707. On this point, Latimer noted the following in a letter to the authors (January 24, 1975): "Probably the majority of pension plans still provide for termination of the plan at the discretion of the employer, and even where there is a commitment to continue the plan, as often as not the commitment is contained in a document which is neither part of nor referred to in the pension plan. Further, the commitments to continue are mainly in the form of collective bargaining agreements with trade unions, the majority of which run for a period not to exceed three years. The average duration of commitments for continuation of pension plans or any part of them is probably less than two years.

"For my study, the only sources of the terms of pension plans were plans themselves. I did not examine trade union agreements to determine whether or not there were any employer commitments with respect to either the continuation of the plans or of specific provisions in pension plans. In view of what was then the hostile attitude of organized labor, I doubt if much was missed by any failure to examine trade union contracts; but the limitation in sources should be borne in mind. Thus, I found out after the study was complete that the St. Louis local of the International Brotherhood of Electrical Workers, in 1929 or thereabouts, secured a contractual commitment for employers to contribute to a pension plan. This agreement was apparently never put into effect, but there may have been others which will some day turn up."

21. Ibid., p. 708.

22. Luther Conant, *A Critical Analysis of Industrial Pension Systems* (New York: Macmillan, 1922), pp. 50–51.

23. Ibid., p. 51.

24. Ibid., p. 80.

25. McNevin v. Solvay Process Co., 32 Appl. Div. New York (1898), p. 610.

26. Latimer, *Industrial Pension Systems,* 2:683.

27. Dolge v. Dolge, 75 New York Suppl. (1902), p. 386.

28. Arthur D. Cloud, *Pensions in Modern Industry* (Chicago: Hawkins & Loomis, 1930), p. 128.

29. Paul Monroe, "An American System of Labor Pensions and Insurance," *American Journal of Sociology* 2 (January 1897):501–514.

30. Nicholas P. Gilman, *A Dividend to Labor* (Boston: Houghton Mifflin, 1899), p. 24.

31. Charles Dearing, *Industrial Pensions* (Washington, D.C.: Brookings Institution, 1954), pp. 23–26.

Murray W. Latimer has added the following footnote to the history of this period (letter to the authors, January 24, 1975): "General Charles D. Young, Vice President of Pennsylvania Railroad, who was in charge of the pension plan of the Pennsylvania Railroad, in the early 30s told me that the General Counsel of the railroad (John Dickinson, later the Solicitor General of the United States) was asked whether or not, under the Pennsylvania pension plan, the Company had the right to reduce pensions. Mr. Dickinson responded that the pension plan constituted a contract between the pensioners and the company, the conditions of which the pensioners had fulfilled. In Mr. Dickinson's opinion a reduction in pensions by the Pennsylvania would violate the contract, and thus make the railroad liable. When the 10 percent deduction from wages was agreed to by the railroads and the labor unions (which happened, as I recall, at the end of 1931) the employees demanded that the pensioners not be spared and refused to agree to the deduction unless the pensioners were included. Despite the opinion of General Counsel, Pennsylvania did reduce pensions to the larger of 90 percent of the original amount or $50 per month. I never heard of this except from General Young.

"The average employment on the railroads (Classes 1, 2 and 3) was 1,692,000 in 1928, 1,694,000 in 1929 and 991,000 in 1933. There was probably a total difference between peak and bottom of 800,000. But in the four-year period there was a reduction of probably more than 100,000 from normal attrition and a large group of the layoffs occurred among seasonal employees on tracks where a reduction of 150,000 from September to December was normal.

"The estimate of 250,000 people aged 61 or over in 1934 is a very substantial exaggeration. Dr. Julius H. Parmelee, Director of Railway Economics, testifying at the first hearing on railroad retirement legislation in January, 1933, presented a distribution of 1,216,000 employees by age and length of service. Of that number 4.25 percent were 65 or over, 8.44 percent were 61 or over and 11.19 percent (136,000) were 59 or over. Dr. Parmelee's tabulation included probably at least 200,000 employees who were no longer active. (Source: Hearings before Interstate Commerce on S. 3892 and S. 4446 on the subject of "Pensions and Retirement for Employees of Interstate Railways"—table inserted on page between 244 and 245—77th Congress, 2nd Session)

"Data collected by the Federal Coordinator of Transportation and the Railroad Retirement Board indicated that Dr. Parmelee's figures were reasonably accurate. The Federal Coordinator's study of 13 railroads found that, at the end of 1933, 9.2 percent of the employees were over 60. As of December 31, 1938, the Railroad Retirement Board data indicated the percentage of over-60 employees had increased to 9.9 percent after retirement of some 100,000. Many of the pensioners had not worked for several years and several thousand of them had retired before 65 because of disability. The railroads had a disproportionate share of older employees, but not as much as the Dearing statistic indicates. (See Annual Reports of the Railroad Retirement Board for 1940, page 210, and for 1950, pages 116 and 117)."

32. Murray W. Latimer has offered another view of the circumstances surrounding the establishment of the Railroad Retirement System (letter to the authors dated January 24, 1975):

"The financial condition of the railroad pension plans and company deficits had almost nothing to do with the demand for pension legislation. Nor do I think that there would have been further reductions in pension amounts. It is perhaps true that if the plans had been soundly financed that the railroads would have been able to make the adjustment which their employees demanded and have avoided the legislation. But the demand for the legislation was based primarily on the desire to secure the retirement of a substantial number of employees (but far short of 250,000) who were both blocking promotions and preventing recall of many people on layoff. The motives of the sponsors were very similar to those which characterized the Townsend movement, though there was little emphasis on the possible impact of larger railroad pensions on the total purchases of goods and services.

"The crucial provision in the legislation proposed by the Railway Employees National Pension Association was compulsory retirement at 60. The RENPA represented the vast majority of the railroad rank and file in 1931–1934. The brotherhoods and other 'standard' labor organizations were alarmed at the strength of the dissidents and drafted alternative legislation which failed to meet the demands of the rank and file. The first Railroad Retirement Act had a compulsory retirement provision, much watered down from the original, and this provision was condemned by the Supreme Court which, on this point, was unanimous. The 1935 and subsequent acts avoided compulsion.

"The 70-year retirement under the railroad voluntary plans—with some of the compulsory rules suspended—was producing only a small fraction of the retirements which the RENPA members thought essential. If the railroads had been willing to discuss adjustment of their plans to accelerate retirement and to meet the employees part way, it is quite possible that there would have been no legislative action.

"It was clear that all the labor organizations were willing to commit employees to substantial contributions. Arthur Young, head of Industrial Relations Counselors, was a friend of Frank V. Whiting, Chairman of the New York Central Pension Board and of the pension committee of the American Railroad Association. Mr. Young and I called on Mr. Whiting and urged him to work with the representatives of employees to develop a jointly contributory plan which would resemble some of the better industrial pension plans. Mr. Whiting was not interested and made it clear that he spoke for the industry. Given the temper of the times, legislation became unavoidable.

"When Joseph B. Eastman was appointed Federal Coordinator of Transportation in June, 1933, he established a section on labor relations headed by Otto S. Beyer, an engineer who had worked with the AFL railroad shop unions and the B&O and Canadian National Railways. Mr. Beyer realized the importance of pensions in any program aimed at bringing about an improvement in railroad operations and his views were reinforced by an advisory committee of experts which included Sumner Slichter, Douglas Brown, William Leiserson, and Isador Lubin.

"It was the opinion of this group that, while action should take legislative form and be as prompt as possible, essential facts had not been gathered and the analyses of the facts and the problems made by the interested labor groups were inadequate. In December, 1933, I was retained to plan and supervise the collection of data and make the analyses. The study proceeded with, I believe, unusual rapidity, but was not finished by June, 1934, when, with Congress about to adjourn the AFL groups, the brotherhoods and the RENPA compromised their differences, thus assuring immediate action. As Chairman of the newly created Railroad Retirement Board, I continued the studies begun for the Federal Coordinator of Transportation.

"As I have indicated, there was very little concern among railroad employees about the solvency of pension plans. Despite the reduction in many pensions, their purchasing power was as great, or perhaps greater, than in 1928 and there was no worry about the actual payment of pensions in 1933 and 1934. Most of the letters about pensions sent to the Federal Coordinator of Transportation came over my desk. There were few complaints about reduction in pensions and no concern at all about the security of payment of the reduced amounts.

"The Railroad Retirement Act was based on the assumption that it would involve only contributions from the railroads and their employees, with no subsidy from general revenues. I have no doubt that if there had been any expectation that any such subsidy would be needed the legislation would not have been enacted. The agreement in 1937 between the railroads and railroad labor organizations, which resulted in the termination of all litigation as to the constitutionality of the Railroad Retirement Act and in the amendments of 1937, was based on the assumption that the savings to Social Security resulting from the exclusion from Social Security of the disproportionate number of elderly railroad employees would be made available for railroad retirement. The mechanism was expected to take the form of a joint fund with the excess of railroad taxes above those levied for Social Security segregated and the railroad benefits in excess of those over Social Security accounted for separately. This arrangement was rejected by Congressman Crosser who was the sponsor of the legislation in the House and was not revived for almost 15 years.

"The main key to the 1937 agreement was the transfer of the railroad pensions to the railroad retirement account in the Treasury. Without this move the Pennsylvania, which was then the dominant force among American railroads, would not have become a party to the agreement and there would have been none. Most of the heads of railway labor organizations were opposed to the takeover of pensions and the largest of the labor organizations, the Brotherhood of Railroad Trainmen, withdrew from the Railway Executives Association in protest. They did not believe that the financial condition of the railroads was such as to warrant relief. If agreement to stop the litigation could have been reached without the takeover of pension payments, there would have been no advocates of that takeover among the labor people. The whole arrangement could hardly be called "bailing out of the railroads" since the immediate effect was the substantial increase in the aggregate costs for the industry. There were exceptions, as I pointed out in my testimony on the 1947 amendments to the Railroad Retirement Act. The taxes paid by some railways, notably the Pennsylvania, were less than their pensions would have been if the railroad pensions had not been paid from the Railroad Retirement account. But for most of the railroads the taxes were larger than the reduction in pension costs. (See Hearings on Railroad Retirement, H.R. 1362, 79th Congress, 1st Session, pp. 141–47)."

Through 1974, railroad employees who had a sufficient number of quarters of nonrailroad work qualified to receive Social Security payments in addition to their railroad retirement checks. In October, 1974, Congress overrode a veto by President Ford passing a $7 billion railroad retirement bill. The bill ended the dual payments system for future retirees. Those employees qualifying in the future under both retirement systems receive a Social Security payment and a supplemental railroad retirement payment that brings their benefit level up to the higher benefit payments of the Railroad Retirement System.

33. Sidney Webb and Beatrice Webb, *Industrial Democracy,* 2 vols. (London: Longmans, Green, 1894), 1:158.

34. James Lynch, "Trade-Union Sickness Insurance," *Trade Unionism and Labor Problems,* 2d series, John R. Commons, ed. (Boston: Ginn, 1921), p. 71.

35. Murray Webb Latimer, *Trade Union Pension Systems* (New York: National Industrial Conference Board, 1932), pp. 8–9.

36. Helen Sumner, "The Benefit System of the Cigarmakers Union," *Trade Unionism and Labor Problems,* John R. Commons, ed. (Boston: Ginn, 1905), pp. 527–545.

37. Latimer, *Trade Union Pension Systems,* p. 3.

38. Quoted in Abraham Epstein, *Industry, A Challenge to America* (New York: Smith and Haas, 1933), pp. 150–151.

39. Florence Peterson, *American Labor Unions* (New York: Harper and Brothers, 1945), pp. 128–146.

40. Lynch, "Trade-Union Sickness Insurance," pp. 79–80.

41. American Federation of Labor, "Retirement Plans in Collective Bargaining," *Research Report* (October 1949), pp. 3 ff.

42. Helen Sumner et al., *The Impact of Collective Bargaining on Management* (Washington, D.C.: Brookings Institution, 1960), p. 38.

43. U.S. Congress, Joint Economic Committee, "The Structure and Evolution of Union Interests in Pensions," by Jack Barbash, *Old Age Income Assurance, Part IV: Employment Aspects of Pension Plans,* 90th Congress, 1st Session (December 1967), p. 63.

44. U.S. Senate, Committee on Finance, *Recommendations for Social Security Legislation,*

Reports of the Advisory Council on Social Security, S. Doc. 208, 80th Congress, 2nd Session (1949), p. 2.

45. U.S. Congress, Joint Economic Committee, *Private Pension Plans,* Part II, 89th Congress, 2nd Session Testimony of Stanley S. Surrey and Sheldon S. Cohen (1966), pp. 412–437.

46. U.S. Department of Labor, Bureau of Labor Statistics, "Appraisal of Wage Stabilization Policies," by John T. Dunlop, *Problems and Policies of Dispute Settlements and Wage Stabilization During World War II,* Bulletin 1009 (1950), p. 166.

47. Joint Economic Committee, "Union Interests in Pensions," p. 66.

48. *New York Times,* May 14, 1946.

49. Joint Economic Committee, "Union Interests in Pensions," pp. 64–67.

50. Ben M. Selekman et al., *Problems in Labor Relations* (New York: McGraw-Hill, 1958), p. 480.

51. On the issue of costs and a contributory versus noncontributory plan at this time, Murray W. Latimer has added the following observations (letter to the authors, January 24, 1975):

"All of the steel companies, as far as I know, including Inland, took the position in 1949 that pensions were not to be the subject of bargaining in 1949. The basis of this contention was not that pensions were not wage rates, a matter that had been made moot by the Inland Steel decision, but rather that the specific agreement made by the Steelworkers had excluded pensions as a bargaining subject in 1949, along with some other matters which were subject unquestionably to bargaining. Inland, in the spring of 1949, did in fact enter into discussions with the Union, but without conceding there was any obligation on their part to do so under the Union contract. I was the spokesman for the Union in the discussions with Inland, as well as those with United States Steel, and there was no substantial difference in the character of the discussions with the two companies. And I have no doubt that if the Union had been willing to accept a contributory plan patterned after that of Inland there would have been a 1949 agreement without a strike.

"The controversy about the cost was largely a matter of form. In the cost calculations I used the methods and assumptions of the United States Steel actuary and the aggregate past service liability and annual normal cost resulting from my calculations for the Union were within 4 or 5 percent of the similar calculations made by the United States Steel actuary. I contended that for purposes of determining a "wage level equivalent," the normal cost plus interest on the past service liability, expressed in per employee terms, was appropriate. The companies refused to discuss "wage level equivalents" and contended that the proper annual cost was normal plus one-tenth of the past service liability which was then almost wholly unfunded. This difference, which is analogous to the proposition that the cost of a house depends on the periods of amortization of the mortgage, was unfortunately not understood by the Board. The actual contributions made to the new plans were calculated on bases far less conservative than I used for the Hearings."

52. Selekman, *Labor Relations,* p. 466.

53. Harry Becker, "Labor's Approach to the Retirement Problem," *IRRA Proceedings* (1949), pp. 120–121.

54. Selekman, *Labor Relations,* pp. 402–420.

55. U.S. Congress, Senate Committee on Finance, Hearings, *Federal Reinsurance of Private Pension Plans,* 89th Congress, 2nd Session (August 15, 1966), p. 48.

56. Clark Kerr, "Social and Economic Implications of Private Pension Plans," *The Commercial and Financial Chronicle,* December 1, 1949, in Reprint No. 16, University of California Institute of Industrial Relations, Berkeley (1949), pp. 4, 8.

57. Quoted by Kerr, "Private Pension Plans," p. 4.

58. Robert M. Ball, "Pension Plans under Collective Bargaining: An Evaluation of Their Social Utility," *IRRA Proceedings* (1949), p. 131.

59. Becker, "Labor's Approach," p. 118.

60. Ibid., p. 119.

61. Leonard Lesser, "Problems in Pension Contributions and Benefits," *IRRA Proceedings* (1952), p. 89.

62. U.S. Department of Labor, Bureau of Labor Statistics, "Multi-employer Pension Plans under Collective Bargaining," Spring 1960 *Bulletin,* No. 1326 (June 1962):1.

63. Adolph Held, "Health and Welfare Funds in the Needle Trades," *Industrial and Labor Relations Review* (January 1948), p. 3.

64. Ibid. The pooling idea was not so revolutionary as it was thought to be. The pooled multiemployer pension system for institutions of higher education, administered by the Teachers Insurance and Annuity Association, had been in operation since 1918 and in 1944 reported 250 participating institutions.

65. See James E. McNulty, *Decision and Influence Processes in Private Pension Plans* (Homewood, Ill.: Irwin, 1961), p. 55.

66. Western Conference of Teamsters Pension Trust Fund, *Annual Report* (1970).

67. Dorothy F. McCamman, *The Scope of Protection under State and Local Government Retirement Systems,* Report No. 12 (Washington: Social Security Board, Bureau of Research and Statistics, October 1944), p. 66.

68. See Rainard B. Robbins, "Pension Planning in the United States," mimeographed (New York: Teachers Insurance and Annuity Association, 1952), p. 13.

69. Paul Studenski, *Teachers' Pension Systems in the United States* (New York: D. Appleton, 1920), p. 16.

70. McCamman, *The Scope of Protection,* p. 66.

71. Studenski, *Teachers' Pension Systems,* p. 8.

72. Carnegie Foundation for the Advancement of Teaching, *Seventh Annual Report* (1912), p. 72.

73. Massachusetts House Document No. 1400, *Report of the Commission on Old Age Pensions, Annuities and Insurance* (1910).

74. Massachusetts House Document No. 1203, *Report of the Joint Special Committee on Pensions.*

75. Paul Studenski, "Financial Aspects of New York City's Pension Systems," mimeographed (New York: Citizens Budget Commission, 1933), p. 4.

76. Saul Waldman, *Retirement Systems for Employees of State and Local Government, 1966,* Report No. 23 (Washington: Social Security Administration, 1968), p. 1.

77. Robbins, *Pension Planning,* p. 62.

78. See Andrew Carnegie, *The Gospel of Wealth and Other Timely Essays* (Garden City: Doubleday, Doran, 1933).

79. Burton J. Hendrick, *The Life of Andrew Carnegie,* 2 vols. (Garden City: Doubleday, Doran, 1932), 1:38–39.

80. Carnegie Foundation for the Advancement of Teaching, *Second Annual Report* (1907), p. 79.

81. Carnegie Foundation for the Advancement of Teaching, *First Annual Report* (1906), p. 28.

82. Carnegie Foundation for the Advancement of Teaching, *Sixtieth Annual Report* (1964–65), p. 23.

83. Carnegie Foundation for the Advancement of Teaching, *Sixty-Seventh Annual Report* (1972), p. 33.

84. Church Pension Conference, Official Mailing List, 1973.

85. The Church Pension Fund, *The Church Pension Fund, 1917–1957* (New York: Church Pension Fund, 1958), p. 6.

86. Charles L. Burall, Sr., "Recent Developments in Church Pension Plans," *Pension and Welfare News* (March 1967), p. 40.

87. Ruth Reticker, "Benefits and the Beneficiaries of the Civil Service Retirement Act," *Social Security Bulletin* 4 (April 1941):29.

88. Ibid.

89. United States Civil Service Commission, Bureau of Retirement, Insurance and Occupational Health, *Annual Report of Financial and Statistical Data for Fiscal Year Ended June 30, 1972,* p. 6.

90. TVA Retirement System, *Annual Report* (June 30, 1972); Retirement Plan for Employees of the Federal Reserve System, *Thirty-Ninth Annual Report* 12 (December 31, 1972):20.

91. Charles L. Dearing, *Industrial Pensions* (Washington, D.C.: Brookings Institution, 1954) Appendix C, pp. 285–86.

92. U.S. Congress, Committee on Ways and Means, *Revenue Revisions of 1942,* 77th Congress, 2nd Session (March 3, 1942), p. 87.

93. Committee on Ways and Means, *Revenue Revisions of 1942,* Memorandum submitted by Randolph E. Paul (March 23, 1942), pp. 1004–5.

94. Ibid., pp. 2416, 2457.

95. Ibid., p. 2460.

96. Committee on Ways and Means, *Revenue Revisions of 1942* (April 10, 1942), pp. 2438–39, 2446.

97. Dearing, *Industrial Pensions,* p. 287.

98. U.S. Stat. 61 (1947) 136, Sec. 1 (b).

99. Ibid., Sec. 8 (5).

100. Inland Steel Co., 77 NLRB (April 1948), p. 1.

101. Inland Steel Co. v. NLRB, affirmed 170 F. 2nd 247 (C.C.A. 7, 1948), cert. den. as to the welfare fund issue, April 25, 1949, 336 U.S. 960, pp. 251, 253.

102. *New York Times,* September 11, 1949.

103. NLRB, *Legislative History of the Labor Management Relations Act, 1947,* 2 vols. (Washington, D.C.: U.S. GPO, 1948), 2:1305–6.

104. U.S. Congress, Senate, Committee on Labor and Public Welfare, *Welfare and Pension Plans Investigation, Hearings before a subcommittee of the Committee on Labor and Public Welfare,* 84th Congress, 1st Session (March 21, 1955), p. 1. For testimony regarding the operation of the United Mine Workers' Welfare Plans, see testimony of Louis S. Reed, John L. Lewis, Josephine Roche, Dr. Warren F. Draper, and Harry M. Moses, pp. 1015–58.

A comprehensive review of the colorful history of the United Mine Workers, from its founding in 1890 to a climax of conspiracy and murder in 1969–1970, is well-told in Joseph E. Finley, *The Corrupt Kingdom* (New York: Simon and Schuster, 1972).

105. U.S. Code 1964 Title 29, Sec. 301 *et seq.* August 28, 1958, PL 85-836. 72 Stat., 997.

106. U.S. Congress, Senate, S. 2688, 90th Congress, 1st Session (February 29, 1967).

107. U.S. Congress, House, H.R. 1045 and 1046, 91st Congress, 1st Session (December 10, 1969).

CHAPTER 3: SOCIAL SECURITY

1. Board of Trustees of the Federal Old-Age and Survivors Insurance and Disability Insurance Trust Funds, *Annual Report* (1975), p. 3.

2. Ibid.

3. *Social Security Bulletin* 37 (November 1974):43–48.

4. Lenore Bixby, "Income of People Aged 65 and Older: Overview from 1968 Survey of the Aged," *Social Security Bulletin* 33 (April 1970):24.

5. Abraham Epstein, *Insecurity, a Challenge to America* (New York: Smith and Haas, 1933), pp. 551–53.

6. *The Works of Theodore Roosevelt,* National Edition, 20 vols. (New York: Scribner's, 1926), 17:266.

7. U.S. Department of Commerce, Bureau of the Census, *Historical Studies of the United States, Colonial Times to 1957.*

8. U.S. Congress, *Supplement to the Report to the President of the Committee on Economic Security,* 73rd Congress (1935), p. 2, Table 3.

9. U.S. Congress, Senate, *Second Inaugural Address of Franklin D. Roosevelt,* January 20, 1937, 75th Congress, 1st Session (1937).

10. Theron F. Schlabach, *Edwin E. Witte, Cautious Reformer* (Madison: State Historical Society of Wisconsin, 1969), p. 109.

11. Franklin D. Roosevelt, *Review of Legislative Accomplishments of the Administration and Congress* (Message to Congress, June 8, 1934), U.S. House of Representatives Document No. 397 (73rd Congress, 2nd Session), p. 2.

12. Charles McKinley and Robert W. Frase, *Launching Social Security* (Madison: University of Wisconsin Press, 1970), pp. 9–10.

13. "The Social Security Plan," Detroit Free Press (January 19, 1935).

14. 49 Stat. 620 (1935).

15. Franklin D. Roosevelt, quoted in *The Princeton Symposium on the American System of Social Insurance,* ed. William G. Bullen et al. (New York: McGraw-Hill, 1968), p. 1.

16. Edwin E. Witte, "Twenty Years of Social Security," *Social Security Bulletin* 18 (October 1955):19.

17. U.S. Congress, Senate, *Future Directions in Social Security, Hearings before the Special Committee on Aging,* 93rd Congress, 1st Session, Part 1 (January 15, 1973), pp. 50–62.

18. James Bruce Cardwell, "The Future of Social Security," speech delivered before the Donaldson, Lufkin, Jenrette, Inc., and Alliance Capital Management Corporation, Tenth Annual Pension Conference, October 30, 1973.

19. U.S. Congress, *Future Directions in Social Security,* p. 2.

20. J. Douglas Brown, *An American Philosophy of Social Security* (Princeton: Princeton University Press, 1972), p. 3.

21. A notable exception to the general acceptance of Social Security is economist Milton Friedman, who has written that while present commitments make it impossible to eliminate Social Security overnight, "it should be unwound and terminated as soon as possible." Friedman's view is that Social Security combines a "highly regressive tax with largely indiscriminate benefits" and "probably redistributes income from lower to higher income persons." "Our goal," he writes, "should be to eliminate the payroll tax completely, to end the present complex structure of benefits and entitlements, to get the government out of the pseudo-pension business, and to combine the valid elements in the benefit structure with a single comprehensive program of assistance to the indigent." Wilbur J. Cohen and Milton Friedman, *Social Security:*

Universal or Selective? (Washington, D.C.: American Enterprise Institute for Public Policy Research, 1972), pp. 22–23, 40–41.

22. Schlabach, *Edwin E. Witte,* p. 151; Brown, *Philosophy of Social Security,* p. 65.

23. Herbert H. Tacker, "State and Local Government Employment Covered Under OASDHI," *Social Security Bulletin* 34 (April 1971):35.

24. Richard A. Musgrave, "The Role of Social Insurance in an Overall Program for Social Welfare," in *The Princeton Symposium,* p. 23.

25. Elizabeth K. Kirkpatrick, "The Retirement Test: An International Study," *Social Security Bulletin* 37 (July 1974):3–16.

26. Public Affairs Office, Social Security Regional Office, New York, by telephone September 24, 1974.

27. Elizabeth M. Heidbreder, "Federal Civil Service Annuitants and Social Security," *Social Security Bulletin* 32 (July 1969):20–33.

28. Integration rules for qualified retirement plans are set forth in the Internal Revenue Code and in IRS regulations.

29. Board of Trustees of the OASI and DI Trust Funds, *Annual Report* (1974), p. 57.

30. U.S. Congress, House, *Reports of the Quadrennial Advisory Council on Social Security,* H. Doc. No. 94-75, 94th Congress, 1st Session (March 10, 1975), p. 59.

31. Board of Trustees of the Federal OASI and DI Trust Funds, *Annual Report* (1975), p. 67, Table 23.

32. U.S. Congress, House, *Reports on Social Security,* p. 49.

33. Ibid., p. 61.

34. New York Stock Exchange, "The Capital Needs and Savings Potential of the U.S. Economy: Projections through 1985," New York, 1974.

35. Comparison based upon the 1973 flow of funds accounts and financial assets and liabilities, *Federal Reserve Bulletin* 60 (October 1974):A58–A59, 28.

36. U.S. Congress, *Economics of Aging,* "Toward a Full Share in Abundance," prepared statement by Dr. Juanita M. Kreps, p. 1924.

CHAPTER 4: PRIVATE PENSION PLANS

1. Harry E. Davis and Arnold Strasser, "Private Pension Plans, 1960 to 1969—An Overview," *Monthly Labor Review* 93 (July 1970):46.

2. "Private Pension Plans with Life Insurance Companies," *Tally of Life Insurance Statistics,* July 1975, p. 1.

3. Davis and Strasser, "Pension Plans," p. 47.

4. Ibid., pp. 47–49.

5. Donald M. Landay and Harry E. Davis, "Growth and Vesting Changes in Private Pension Plans," *Monthly Labor Review* 91 (May 1968):30.

6. Donald R. Bell, "Prevalence of Private Retirement Plans in Manufacturing," *Monthly Labor Review* 96 (September 1973):29; Emerson Beier, "Incidence of Private Retirement Plans," *Monthly Labor Review* 94 (July 1971):37.

7. Bell, "Retirement Plans," pp. 29–30.

8. "Number of Persons Covered by Major Pension and Retirement Programs in the United States," *Tally of Life Insurance Statistics,* February 1973, p. 1.

9. Walter W. Kolodrubetz and Donald M. Landay, "Coverage and Vesting of Full-Time Employees Under Private Retirement Plans," *Social Security Bulletin* 36 (November 1973):20.

10. Walter W. Kolodrubetz, "Two Decades of Employee-Benefit Plans, 1950–70, A Review," *Social Security Bulletin* 35 (April 1972):20.

11. Walter W. Kolodrubetz, "Employee-Benefit Plans, 1972," *Social Security Bulletin* 37 (May 1974):16.

12. Beier, "Retirement Plans," p. 37.

13. Walter W. Kolodrubetz, "Trends in Employee-Benefit Plans in the Sixties," *Social Security Bulletin* 34 (April 1971):27.

14. Davis and Strasser, "Pension Plans," p. 48.

15. Bankers Trust Company, *1975 Study of Corporate Pension Plans* (New York: Bankers Trust Co., 1975), pp. 6–7.

16. Employee Retirement Income Security Act of 1974, Sec. 202(a)(1).

17. Bankers Trust Company, *1975 Study of Corporate Pension Plans,* p. 24.

18. Ibid.

19. Davis and Strasser, "Pension Plans," p. 46.

20. Bankers Trust Company, *1975 Study of Corporate Retirement Plans,* pp. 10–14.

21. Arnold Strasser, "Pension Formula Summarization: An Emerging Research Technique," *Monthly Labor Review* 94 (April 1971):21.

22. *Employee Benefit Plan Review* 28 (October 1973):21; 28 (December 1973):14.

23. Bankers Trust Company, *1975 Study of Corporate Pension Plans,* p. 27.

24. Ibid., p. 28.

25. Ibid.

26. Ibid., p. 34.

27. Ibid., pp. 15–16.

28. Ibid., p. 22.

29. Ibid., p. 8.

CHAPTER 5: PUBLIC EMPLOYEE RETIREMENT PLANS

1. U.S. Bureau of the Census, "Labor Force, Employment, and Earning," Table No. 563, in *Statistical Abstract of the United States* (1974), p. 345.

2. U.S. Bureau of the Census, "State and Local Government Finances and Employment," Table No. 425, in *Statistical Abstract of the United States* (1974), p. 265.

3. U.S. Civil Service Commission, Bureau of Retirement, Insurance, and Occupational Health, *Annual Report of Financial and Statistical Data for Fiscal Year Ended June 30, 1974* (1974), p. 4.

4. U.S. Bureau of the Census, *Statistical Abstract of the United States* (1974), Table 505, p. 315.

5. U.S. Bureau of the Census, *Employee-Retirement Systems of State and Local Governments,* Census of Governments, 1967, vol. 6, no. 2 (1968):1.

6. Ibid., 1972, vol. 6, no. 1 (1973):9.

7. Ibid., p. 2.

8. U.S. Department of Health, Education, and Welfare, Social Security Administration, *State and Local Government Retirement Systems,* 1965 and 1966, Research Report Nos. 15 and 23 (1966 and 1968), pp. 8 and 12.

9. U.S. Bureau of the Census, *Retirement Systems,* 1967, p. 2.

10. U.S. Bureau of the Census, *Compendium of Public Employment,* Census of Governments, 1972, vol. 3, no. 2 (1973), Table 15.

11. Social Security Administration, *Government Retirement Systems,* Research Report No. 15, Table 2, p. 45, and Research Report No. 23, Table 4, p. 62.

12. Ibid., Research Report No. 23, Table 48, p. 86.

13. Ibid., Research Report No. 15, p. 41.

14. Ibid., Research Report No. 15, p. 8, and Research Report No. 23, p. 14.

15. Ibid., Research Report No. 23, p. 14.

16. Ibid., pp. 15–16.

17. Ibid., p. 21.

18. Ibid., Research Report No. 15, Table 10, p. 50, and Research Report No. 23, Table 10, p. 66.

19. U.S. Civil Service Commission, Bureau of Retirement, Insurance, and Occupational Health, *Annual Report of Financial and Statistical Data for Fiscal Year Ended June 30, 1974* (1974), p. 4.

20. U.S. Civil Service Commission, *Fiftieth Annual Report of the Board of Actuaries of the Civil Service Retirement System,* Fiscal Year 1970, 93rd Congress, 1st Session, House Document No. 93-37 (1973), pp. 8, 15.

21. Ibid., pp. 4–5.

22. Actuarial Consultant, Office of the Assistant Secretary of Defense, February 16, 1973.

23. U.S. Department of Defense, Office of the Assistant Secretary of Defense, "Overview of Uniformed Services Retirement and Survivor Benefits," 1973, and "Military Retirement," 1973 (mimeographed).

24. Ibid.

25. Ibid.

26. U.S. Department of Defense, Office of Information for the Armed Forces, *Survivor Benefit Plan for Retired Members of the Uniformed Services,* Department of Defense PA-11, 1973.

27. H.R. 12505, 93rd Congress, 2nd Session.

CHAPTER 6: INVESTMENTS OF PENSION FUNDS

1. Edna E. Ehrlich, "The Functions and Investment Policies of Personal Trust Departments," *Federal Reserve Bank of New York: Monthly Review* 54 (October 1972):265, 266.

2. National Industrial Conference Board, Inc., *Industrial Pensions in the United States* (New York: NICB, 1925), pp. 141–57.

3. Herman E. Kross and Martin R. Blyn, *A History of Financial Intermediaries* (New York: Random House, 1971), p. 166.

4. Raymond W. Goldsmith, *Financial Intermediaries in the American Economy Since 1900* (Princeton: Princeton University Press, 1958), p. 371.

5. Ibid.

6. Ibid.

7. Lawrence D. Jones, *Investment Policies of Life Insurance Companies* (Boston: Harvard University, 1968), p. 537.

8. Raymond W. Goldsmith, *A Study of Savings in the United States,* 2 vols. (Princeton: Princeton University Press, 1955), 1:1072.

9. The New York Stock Exchange, *1975 Fact Book* (New York: New York Stock Exchange, 1975), p. 32.

10. U.S. Congress, House of Representatives, *Institutional Investor Study Report of the Securities and Exchange Commission,* 5 vols. (1971), 3:1313–17.

11. Ibid., pp. 1332–33.

12. Securities and Exchange Commission, *Statistical Bulletin* 33 (October 1974):970.

13. See Roger Murray, *Economic Aspects of Pensions, A Summary Report,* General Series No. 85 (New York: National Bureau of Economic Research, 1968), pp. 54, 55.

14. Phillip Cagan, *The Effect of Pensions on Aggregate Saving: Evidence from a Sample Survey,* Occasional Paper 95 (New York: National Bureau of Economic Research, 1965), p. 82.

15. George Katona, *Private Pensions and Individual Savings* (Ann Arbor: Institute for Social Research, 1965), p. 88.

16. Vincent Apilado, "Pension Funds, Personal Savings and Economic Growth," *Journal of Risk and Insurance* 39 (September 1972):397–404.

17. Robert N. Schoeplein, "The Effect of Pension Plans on Other Retirement Saving," *The Journal of Finance* 25 (June 1970):635.

18. Daniel M. Holland, *Private Pension Funds: Projected Growth,* Occasional Paper 97 (New York: National Bureau of Economic Research, 1966), pp. 64–67.

19. Ibid., p. 135; Tax Foundation, Inc., *Facts and Figures on Government Finance, 1973* (New York: Tax Foundation, 1973), p. 24.

20. Robert Sutro, "Make Way for Mortgage and Real Estate Placements," *Pension and Welfare News* 8 (April 1972):41–49.

21. J. E. Henderson, "For Investment Return—Try Real Estate," *Pension and Welfare News* 9 (February 1973):63–64.

22. Murray, *Economic Aspects of Pensions,* p. 122.

23. The various types of trusts (equity, mortgage, and combination) are discussed in more detail in Sylvan M. Cohen, "REIT's Move to Sunny Spot on Real Estate Scene," *Pension and Welfare News* 8 (April 1972):30–36.

CHAPTER 7: PUBLIC POLICY—THE VESTING OF
PENSION BENEFITS

1. Ralph Nader and Kate Blackwell, *You and Your Pension—Why You Never Get a Penny* (New York: Grossman, 1973), p. 2.

2. U.S. Congress, Joint Economic Committee, "Private Pensions and Women," by Merton C. Bernstein, mimeographed (July 25, 1973), p. 9.

3. Merton C. Bernstein, letter to the *New York Times,* April 2, 1974.

4. Howard Hayghe, "Job Tenure of Workers, January 1973," *Monthly Labor Review* (December 1974), pp. 53–56.

5. Nader and Blackwell, *You and Your Pension,* pp. 158–68.

6. Dan McGill, *Preservation of Pension Benefit Rights* (Homewood, Ill.: Irwin, 1972), p. 206.

7. Advisory Commission on Intergovernmental Relations, "Transferability of Public Employee Retirement Credits Among Units of Government," Report A-16 (Washington, D.C.: U.S. Government Printing Office, 1963).

8. Ibid., p. 53.

9. Employee Retirement Income Security Act of 1974, Sec. 1031 (a) and Sec. 1032 adding Code Sec. 6057 (d).

10. Ibid., Sec. 204 (d) and Sec. 203 (a) (3) (D).

11. Ibid., Sec. 203 (a)–(c), Sec. 1012 (a) adding Code Sec. 411 (a) (2).

12. Henry E. Davis and Arnold Strasser, "Private Pension Plans, 1960 to 1969—An Overview," *Monthly Labor Review* (July 1970), p. 53.

13. Ibid., p. 54.

14. Ibid.

15. Walter W. Kolodrubetz and Donald M. Landay, "Coverage and Vesting of Full-Time Employees Under Private Retirement Plans," *Social Security Bulletin* 36 (November 1973):27.

16. Richard C. Keating, "Private Pension Plan Performance," *Financial Executive* (August 1971), p. 5.

17. Kolodrubetz and Landay, "Coverage and Vesting," p. 28.

18. Ibid., p. 28.

19. Ibid., pp. 29–31.

20. Bankers Trust Company, *1970 Study of Industrial Retirement Plans* (New York: Bankers Trust Co., 1970), p. 12.

21. Bankers Trust Company, *1975 Study of Corporate Pension Plans* (New York: Bankers Trust Co., 1975), p. 9.

22. U.S. Department of Health, Education, and Welfare, Social Security Administration, *State and Local Government Retirement Systems,* 1965 and 1966, Research Report Nos. 15 and 23 (1966 and 1968), pp. 50 and 66.

23. U.S. Department of Labor, Labor Management Services Administration, *Analysis of the Cost of Vesting in Pension Plans,* by Howard Winklevoss (Washington, D.C.: U.S. GPO, 1972).

24. U.S. Congress, Senate, *Economics of Aging: Toward a Full Share in Abundance, Hearings Before the Special Committee on Aging,* Part 10A—Pension Aspects, 91st Congress, 2nd Session (February 17, 1970), p. 1542.

25. Standard & Poor's/InterCapital, Inc., *Second Annual Pension Fund Management Survey* (October 1972), pp. 9, 10. Conducted by McGraw-Hill Publications, Department of Economics.

26. U.S. Congress, Joint Economic Committee, *Old Age Income Assurance: A Compendium of Papers on Problems and Policy Issues in the Public and Private Pension System,* Part VI, 90th Congress, 1st Session (December 1967), p. 135.

CHAPTER 8: PUBLIC POLICY—FINANCING PENSION BENEFITS

1. The pension terminology recommended by the Committee on Pension and Profit-Sharing Terminology of the American Risk and Insurance Association was initially presented in Joseph J. Melone, "Actuarial Cost Methods—New Pension Terminology," *The Journal of Insurance* (September 1963), pp. 456–64. Other commonly used terms are found in Ernest L. Hicks, *Accounting for the Cost of Pension Plans,* Accounting Research Study No. 8 (New York: American Institute of Certified Public Accountants, 1965), p. 26. Variations of the terminology are contained in H.R. 2, 93rd Congress, 2nd Session, "Employee Benefit Security Act of 1974," passed by the House on March 4, 1974.

2. Level cost projected methods aid the employer in achieving funding adequacy and stability, but a terminating vested participant is credited only with the benefit he has accrued to date, not with any additional funding based on projected future salary increments. The employee's departure effectively cancels the projected level contribution input pattern being followed on his behalf and fixes in its place his accrued benefit to termination with its lower associated accrued cost.

3. Employee Retirement Income Security Act of 1974, Sec. 302 and Sec. 1013 (a).

4. Ibid., Sec. 301 (a) and Sec. 302 (b).

5. Ibid., Sec. 103 (d) and Sec. 111 (b).

6. Ibid., Sec. 302 and Sec. 1013 (a).

7. President's Committee on Corporate Pension Funds, *Public Policy and Private Pension Programs* (1965), p. xii.

8. Dan McGill, *Guaranty Fund for Private Pension Obligations* (Homewood, Ill.: Irwin, 1970).

9. ERISA of 1974, Sec. 4002 (a) and Sec. 4022 (b) (3).

10. Ibid., Sec. 4062 (a) and (b) and Sec. 4068.

11. For a résumé of some of these developments, see Barbara P. Patocka, "Public Funds: The Herculean Task Is Under Way," *Pensions* 2 (May/June 1973):33–48.

12. Pension Task Force, Committee on Labor-Management Relations, *New York City's Pension Systems—A Report* (New York: N.Y. Chamber of Commerce, November 1972), p. 3.

13. James C. Hyatt, "Day of Reckoning," *Wall Street Journal* (June 26, 1974), p. 1.

14. Patocka, "Public Funds," p. 43.

15. Ibid., pp. 38–39.

16. Ibid., p. 42.

17. Otto Kinzel, "Costs of Public Pension Plans Threaten Private Plans," *Pension and Welfare News* (January 1973), p. 37.

18. Ibid.

19. Ibid., p. 36.

20. Joseph G. Metz, "Public Employee Pensions: Prospects for the Future," *Tax Review* 35 (July 1974):28.

21. Stuart N. Scott et al., *New York City Pensions* (New York: State Study Commission for New York City, 1973), pp. 1–4.

22. Kinzel, "Costs of Public Pension Plans," p. 35.

23. Economic Development Council of New York City, Inc., *Pension Changes in New York City, 1962–1972* (New York: Economic Development Council, 1972), p. 2.

24. Pension Task Force, *New York City's Pension Systems,* p. 27.

25. U.S. Civil Service Commission, *Annual Report* (1968), p. 29.

26. U.S. Civil Service Commission, *Annual Report* (1974), p. 4.

27. U.S. Civil Service Commission, *Annual Report* (1968), p. 30.

28. Arch Patton, "The Hidden Costs of Federal Pensions," *Business Week* (April 27, 1974), p. 26.

29. U.S. Civil Service Commission, *Annual Report* (1968), p. 30.

30. U.S. Congress, House, *Fiftieth Annual Report of the Board of Actuaries of the Civil Service Retirement System,* 93rd Congress, 1st Session, House Document No. 93-37 (1973), pp. 10, 38.

31. Patton, "Hidden Costs," p. 26.

32. U.S. Congress, House, *Fifty-Second Annual Report of the Board of Actuaries of the Civil Service Retirement System,* 94th Congress, 1st Session, House Document No. 94-203 (1975), p. 8.

33. "The Push for Pension Reform," *Business Week* (March 17, 1973), p. 49.

34. *Employee Benefit Plan Review* 26 (February 1972):26.

35. Ibid.

36. Ibid., p. 27.

37. Quoted in Bankers Trust Company, *The Private Pension Controversy* (New York: Bankers Trust Co., 1973), p. 59.

38. ERISA of 1974, Sec. 404 (a) (1).

39. Ibid., Sec. 406 (a).

40. Ibid., Sec. 407.

41. Ibid., Sec. 409.

42. Ibid., Sec. 501.

CHAPTER 9: PUBLIC POLICY—INCOME OBJECTIVES AND RETIREMENT AGES

1. See James G. Waters, "Solving for x in the Retirement Income Formula," *Pension and Welfare News* (March 1974), pp. 45–48, 51.

2. White House Conference on Aging, *Toward a National Policy on Aging,* 2 vols. (1971), 2:38; U.S. Bureau of Labor Statistics, *News* (August 1, 1975), p. 2.

3. Employee Retirement Income Security Act of 1974, Sec. 2004 (a) (2), adding Internal Revenue Code Sec. 415 (b) (1).

4. Ibid., Sec. 205.

5. Ibid., Sec. 2002.

6. Ibid., Sec. 2001 (a), (b), and (c) amending Internal Revenue Code Section 404 (e).

7. Ibid., Sec. 202 (a) (1) (A).

8. Ibid., Sec. 203 (b) (1).

9. Standard & Poor's/InterCapital, Inc., *Third Annual Pension Fund Management Survey* (November 1973), p. 3 (conducted by McGraw-Hill Publications, Department of Economics); U.S. Chamber of Commerce. *Employee Benefits 1973* (Washington, D.C.: U.S. Chamber of Commerce, 1974), p. 16.

10. Frances M. Carp, "Differences Among Older Workers, Volunteers and Persons Who are Neither," *Journal of Gerontology* 23 (1968):497–501.

11. Bankers Trust Company, *1975 Study of Corporate Pension Plans* (New York: Bankers Trust Co., 1975), pp. 23–24.

12. Virginia P. Reno, "Compulsory Retirement Among Newly Entitled Workers: Survey of New Beneficiaries," *Social Security Bulletin* 35 (March 1972):5.

13. Gayle B. Thompson, "Work Experience and Income of the Population Aged 60 and Older, 1971," *Social Security Bulletin* 37 (November 1974):3–20.

14. Julian Abbott, "Covered Employment and the Age Men Claim Retirement Benefits," *Social Security Bulletin* 37 (April 1974):3–16; Patience Lauriat and William Rabin, "Men Who Claim Benefits Before Age 65, Survey of Newly Entitled Beneficiaries (SNEB)" *Social Security Bulletin* 33 (November 1970):3–29; Virginia Reno, "Why Men Stop Working At or Before Age 65," *Social Security Bulletin* 34 (June 1971):3–17; Karen Schwab, "Early Labor-Force Withdrawal of Men: Participants and Nonparticipants Aged 58–63," *Social Security Bulletin* 37 (August 1974):24–38; Virginia Reno, "Retirement Patterns of Men at OASDHI Entitlement," Social Security Administration, *Report No. 2* (March 1971).

15. U.S. Bureau of the Census, *Current Population Reports,* Series P-23, No. 43 (1973), p. 2.

16. *Employee Benefit Plan Review* 29 (January 1975):48.

17. Social Security Administration, Actuarial Department, 1975.

18. Bankers Trust Company, *1975 Study of Corporate Pension Plans* (1975), pp. 34–35.

19. Phillip Cagan, *Common Stock Values and Inflation—The Historical Record of Many Centuries* (New York: National Bureau of Economic Research, 1974).

20. John Lintner, reported in the *Wall Street Journal* (December 17, 1973), p. 1.

21. William C. Greenough, *A New Approach to Retirement Income* (New York: TIAA, 1951), pp. 13–14.

22. Ibid., p. 14.

CHAPTER 10: FOREIGN SYSTEMS OF SOCIAL AND PRIVATE PENSIONS

1. U.S. Department of Health, Education, and Welfare, Social Security Administration, *Social Security Programs Throughout the World 1973,* Research Report No. 44 (1974), p. xi.

2. E. E. Clarke, "Canada Pension Plan," *Transactions of the 18th International Congress of Actuaries,* 3 vols. (June 1968), 1:622.

3. Ibid., p. 623.

4. U.S. Department of HEW, *Social Security Programs 1973*, p. 30.

5. Ibid.

6. Lawrence E. Coward, "Funding of Employee Pension Plans," *Transactions of the 18th International Congress of Actuaries*, 3 vols. (June 1968), 1:629.

7. U.S. Department of Labor, Labor Management Services Administration, *Canadian Regulation of Pension Plans*, by Frank M. Kleiler (1970), pp. 45–46.

8. Ibid., p. 48.

9. Ibid., pp. 71–72.

10. *Survey of Pension Plan Coverage 1965* (Ottawa: Dominion Bureau of Statistics, 1967).

11. George Orwell, *Down and Out in Paris and London* (London: Penguin Modern Classics, 1966).

12. *Social Security in Britain* (New York: British Information Services, 1975), pp. 3–4.

13. Ibid.

14. *Social Insurance and Allied Services* (Beveridge Report), (London: H.M.S.O., 1942), Cmd. 6404.

15. *National Superannuation and Social Insurance: Proposals for Earnings-Related Social Security* (London: H.M.S.O., 1969), Cmnd. 3883.

16. *Strategy for Pensions: The Future Development of State and Occupational Provisions* (London: H.M.S.O., 1971), Cmnd. 4755.

17. Ibid., p. 3.

18. Ibid., pp. 3–4.

19. Ibid., p. 4.

20. Ibid., p. 8.

21. *Social Security Act, 1973*, (London: H.M.S.O., 1973), chap. 38.

22. *Better Pensions Fully Protected Against Inflation: Proposals for a New Pensions Scheme*, (London: H.M.S.O., 1974), Cmnd. 5713; *Social Security in Great Britain*, pp. 33–35.

23. *La Protection Sanitaire et Sociale en France* (Paris: La Documentation Française, 1971), pp. 93–95.

24. Secrétariat Général du Comité Interministériel pour l'Information, Actualités-Service: Ce Qui est Fait pour les Personnes Agées, Note Numéro II, "Les Pensions de Retraite et Les Allocations de Vieilesse" (Février 1973), pp. 1–3.

25. Ibid., pp. 5–6.

26. Ibid., pp. 9–10.

27. *Social Security and National Health Insurance* (New York: Service de Presse et d'Information, 1971), pp. 12–15; *La Protection Sanitaire*, pp. 128–29.

28. Law No. 50-205, February 11, 1950.

29. Maurice Castelli, "Maintaining the Purchasing Value of Pensions," *International Insurance and Employee Benefit and Pension Management, Europe*, 2 vols. (New York: American Management Association, 1966), pp. 42–43.

30. U.S. Department of Labor, Labor-Management Services Administration, *European Regulation of Pension Plans*, by Frank M. Kleiler (1971), p. 77.

31. Ibid.

32. Ibid., p. 78. Figures for year-end, 1968.

33. One of the most interesting member plans of the ARRCO group is the CNRO (Caisse Nationale des Retraites des Ouvriers du Bâtiment et des Travaux Publiques), a large fund covering members of the building trades. This well-managed fund, under the direction of President Yves Pergeaux, has carried out extensive research in the field of aging, part of which has led to

the development of more than 40 residence communities for retired participants in various parts of France, and a program of vacations and vacation centers for retired and active union members.

34. *Encyclopaedia Britannica,* 1959 ed., s.v. "Social Security—The Growth of Social Insurance."

35. *Germany: Social Security Program* (New York: German Information Center, 1972), p. 1; U.S. Department of HEW, Social Security Administration, *Private Pension Plans in West Germany and France,* by Max Horlick and Alfred M. Skolnik, Research Report No. 36 (1971), pp. 4–6.

36. *Germany: Social Security Program,* p. 1.

37. U.S. Department of HEW, *Social Security Programs 1973,* pp. 80–81.

38. "Social Security Abroad: Flexible Retirement Feature of German Pension Reform," *Social Security Bulletin* 36 (July 1973):36–38.

39. U.S. Department of HEW, *Private Pension Plans in West Germany and France,* p. 7.

40. Ibid.

41. "Multinational Benefits Review," *Employee Benefit Plan Review* 29 (February 1975), supplement, pp. 2–4.

42. Ibid.

43. U.S. Department of HEW, *Private Pension Plans in West Germany and France,* pp. 8–9.

44. Ibid., pp. 12–13.

45. *Social Insurance,* The Kingdom of the Netherlands: Facts and Figures, No. 8 (The Hague: Government Printing Office, 1970–71), p. 1.

46. U.S. Department of HEW, *Social Security Program 1973,* pp. 160–61.

47. The Netherlands Consulate, Office of Information, March 12, 1975.

48. "Important Pension Legislation Being Developed in the Netherlands," *Employee Benefit Plan Review* 26 (July 1971):54–55.

49. *Social Insurance,* pp. 6–7.

50. Ibid., p. 7.

51. U.S. Department of Labor, *European Regulation of Pension Plans,* pp. 67–68.

52. Ibid., pp. 68–69.

53. "Important Pension Legislation," pp. 54–55; T. C. Braakman, M. A. Kwakman, and H. L. F. Verbraak, "Report . . . National Compulsory Pension Plan for Employees in the Netherlands," *Transactions of the 19th International Congress of Actuaries,* 5 vols. (June 1972), 3:361, 373.

54. Lennart Lagerstrom, *Social Insurance and Private Occupational Pensions in Sweden* (Stockholm: Swedish Staff Pension Society, 1971), p. 9.

55. Ibid., p. 10.

56. Ibid.

57. Ibid.

58. Ibid.

59. U.S. Department of HEW, *Social Security Programs 1973,* pp. 210–11.

60. Ibid.

61. Ibid.

62. Lagerstrom, *Social Insurance,* pp. 18–20.

63. Ibid., pp. 17, 20.

64. *AGS and STP,* Supplement to *Social Insurance . . . in Sweden* (Stockholm: Swedish Staff Pension Society, 1972), p. 2.

65. *The Swedish Government Pension Scheme* (Stockholm: Ministry of Salaries and Pensions, 1968).

66. *Outline of Social Insurance in Japan* (Japan International Social Security Association, 1972), pp. 50–70; "Two Types of Retirement Plans in Japan," *Employee Benefit Plan Review* 25 (June 1971):36–37; "Multinational Benefits Review," *Employee Benefit Plan Review* 27 (November 1973), supplement pp. 2–3.

67. "Retirement Plans in Japan," pp. 36–37; "Multinational Benefits Review," supplement pp. 2–3; T. Kato, "Development of Private Pension Plans in Japan," *Transactions of the 18th International Congress of Actuaries,* 3 vols. (June 1968), 3:513–17; Tadashi Araya, "The Sun Rises on Japanese Pension Funds," *Pension and Welfare News* 8 (December 1972):12–15, 46–48.

INDEX

Advisory Commission on Intergovernmental Relations, 161

Aged: definitions, 1–2, of "elderly," Census Bureau, 231; life expectancy, 1–2, 3–5, 29, 219; increase of in U.S. population, 2 (*chart*), 3, *1900–2020,* 229–31 (*chart, table*); increasing proportion of, 3 (*table*), 4–5; projection forecasts, *1970–2020,* 3, 5; sex composition, 5–6, 26; composition and characteristics of, 5–11; marital status and living arrangements, 6–7 (*table*); location of, 7–8; employment, 8, 19, 28, 226–29 (*table*); home ownership, 12, 22–23, 213; in nineteenth century, 28–29; *see also* Income of aged

Age of retirement, *see* Retirement age

American Express Company, 27–28, 30

American Risk and Insurance Association, Committee on Pension and Profit-Sharing Terminology, 180

Annuity plans, 34, 57, 177, 188–89 (*table*), 198, 219; variable, 56–57, 177, 238–40 (*table*); deferred, 187 (*table*)

Apilado, Vincent, 148

Apparel industry, 48, 111; International Ladies' Garment Workers' Union, 26, 48; New York Children's Dressmakers' Union, 26, 48

Armed services, *see* Military plan

Assessment plans, 41, 42, 49; *see also* Contributory plans

Austria, 69

Automobile industry, 46, 126, 225–26

Automobile Workers Union, United, 46, 47, 117, 232

Ball, Robert M., 47; quoted, 76–77

Baltimore and Ohio Railroad Company, 30, 38

Bankers Trust Company; study of single-employee private pension plans (1975), 115, 116–17, 118, 119–20, 212, 236–37

Barbash, Jack: quoted, 44

Barbers' Union: receivership of 207–8

Benefits, 32–33, 154–55, 176; "second pension" benefits to recipients of Social Security, 10–11, 20, 21 (*table*), 22, 26, 59, 67, 80, 84–85, 88, 98, 114, 211–12, 216; public pension plans, 196, 198, 203; fringe, 44; funding, 189–94; income objectives, 210–17; unemployment, 228–29; inflation and cost-of-living rises, effects on, 235–40 (*chart*); *see also under individual plans*

death, 40, 41, 49, 119, 130–31

dependents, 26, 131; under Social Security, 104

disability, 28, 31–32, 40, 41, 46, 47, 49, 119, 127–28, 130, 133, 229; under Social Security, 68, 72, 76; under OASDI, 73 (*table*), 81, 86, 103, 104; under SSI, 76

eligibility, age or service requirements and credits, 30, 31, 32, 46, 50, 52–53, 54, 55, 115, 116–19 (*table*), 124–25, 128, 129, 133, 155, 177, 181, 182–89 passim, 204, 212, 213, 216–17, 220–21; Solvay Process Company case, 35–36; defined benefit and defined contribution plans, 177, 181, 182–89 passim, 204

medical, 40, 41; under Social Security, 68, 81, 89, 103 (*see also* Medicare)

Social Security, *see under* Social Security

survivors, 49, 54, 56, 119–20, 130–33; under Social Security, 68, 71; under OASI, 73 (*table*), 81; under OASDI, 86, 104

widowers, 131; under Social Security, 75

widows, 41, 54, 55, 131; under Social Security, 75, 81

Bernstein, Merton C., 66; quoted, 155

Bethlehem Steel Company, 46

Blankenship v. Boyle, 65

Blind: under Social Security, 76

Cagan, Phillip, 148: quoted, 147

Canada, 218, 246–51; financing, 245, 247; disability benefits, 246, 248; funding, 246, 249, 250; flat-rate program, 246–47; Old Age Security Program, 246–47; legislation, 246, 248–49, 250; social insurance, 246–48; income supplement, 247; benefits, 247, 248; starting age, 247, 248;

Canada (*Continued*)
  coverage, 247, 250; contributions, 247,
  251; wage-related plan (Canada Pension
  Plan), 247–48; survivors' pensions, 248;
  provincial plans (Pension Benefits Act),
  249–50; federal employees (Pension
  Benefits Standard Act), 250
  private plans, 245, 246, 248–49; vesting,
  245, 246, 249; number and participation,
  250–251; defined benefit plans, 251
Carnegie, Andrew, 53–54
Carnegie Corporation, 55
Carnegie Foundation for the Advancement of
  Teaching, 51, 52, 54–56, 225
Carnegie Free Pension System, 53–56
Carnegie Steel Company, 30
Carriers' Taxing Act (1937), 21
Chrysler Motor Corporation, 46, 117
Church plans, 57
Cigarmakers' International Union of America,
  41
City employees, *see* Municipal employees
Civil Service Commission, federal, 200, 201
Clark, Sen. Champ, 79
Clothing industry, *see* Apparel industry
College and university faculties, 52–57, 123,
  290n64; Carnegie Free Pension System,
  53–54, 56; Carnegie Foundation for the
  Advancement of Teaching, 51, 52,
  54–56, 225; Commission on Insurance
  and Annuities, 56; Teachers Insurance and
  Annuity Association (TIAA), 56, 123,
  177, 240 (*table*); College Retirement
  Equities Fund (CREF), 56–57, 123, 177,
  240 (*table*); Illinois State Universities
  Retirement System, 196
Committee on Economic Security, 70–71
Community fund-raising organizations, 57–58
Conant, Luther: quoted, 35
Construction industry, 48, 111
Consumer Price Index (CPI), 74–75, 130, 216;
  and Social Security benefits, 74–75, 85,
  93, 94 (*table*), 100–3 (*tables*), 216, 235,
  236
Contributory plans, 32, 33, 51, 52, 56, 110–11
  (*table*), 115, 120, 289n51; vesting, 155,
  162, 163–64; defined contribution,
  176–78, 179 (*table*); financing, 178; *see*

also Employee contributions; Employer
  contributions

Death benefits, *see under* Benefits
Defined benefit plans, 178–82; employer costs
  and employee benefits, comparison with
  defined contribution plans, 182–89 (*chart,
  tables*); funding benefits, 189–94
Defined contribution plans, 176–78; employer
  costs and employee benefits, comparison
  with defined benefit plans, 182–89 (*chart,
  tables*); funding benefits, 189–94
Dent, Rep. John H., 66
Dependents' benefits, *see under* Benefits
Depression (1930s): effect of pension plans, 3,
  38, 39–41, 42–43, 69–70, 71, 237
Disability benefits, *see under* Benefits
Dolge v. Dolge, 36–37

Electrical Workers, International Brotherhood
  of, 42, 285n20
Eligibility requirements, *see under* Benefits
Employee contributions, 24, 25, 31, 49, 51,
  56, 57, 60, 61, 89, 111, 125–26, 128–29,
  177–89 passim (*tables*); vesting, 160,
  162, 163–64, 174–75
Employee Retirement Income Security Act of
  1974 (ERISA), 66–67, 91, 108, 115, 120,
  153–54, 161, 162, 163, 169, 171,
  172–73, 174, 176, 177, 188, 189, 191,
  192, 193–94, 195, 206, 208–9, 213, 215,
  217, 218–19, 220
Employee rights: protection of, 33–35; adjudi-
  cation of, 35–38; vesting, 61–62, 158,
  159, 161, 162, 173; labor, 63–65 (*see also*
  Taft-Hartley Act)
Employer contributions, 30, 31, 44, 46, 52, 56,
  59–60, 65, 111, 126, 128–29; exemption
  from federal taxes, 59–60; vesting, 162,
  164

Federal employees (Federal Civil Service Retirement System), 18, 20, 22, 58–59, 122,
  128–31, 135; exclusion from Social Security, 20, 68, 77, 79, 87–88, 128, 205;
  number covered, 58, 128; units not covered, 59, 122; membership and contributions, 128–29; vesting, 129, 153–55, 169;

benefits, 130–31; calculation, 129; investments, 136; underfunding of, 200–3; cost-of-living escalator in benefits, 201–2, 236
Federal Insurance Contributions Act (FICA), 80
Federal regulation, 59–67; Revenue Acts before *1942*, 59–60; exemptions of employer contributions, 59–61; tax laws, 59–63 (*see also* Internal Revenue Code); trust funds, 59–63, 208–9; labor, 63–65, 207; Welfare and Pension Plans Disclosure Act of *1958*, 65–66, 206; vesting standards, 163–64; Pension Benefit Guaranty Corporation, 193–94; mismanagement of pension funds, 207–9; *see also* Employee Retirement Income Security Act of 1974
Federal Reserve System, 59, 122
Financing, 33, 59, 132, 176–209; defined contribution plans, 176–78, 182–89 (*chart, tables*); defined benefit plans, 178–81, 182–89 (*chart, tables*); interest, 191, 222–23 (*table*); fiduciary responsibility, 206–9; *see also* Funding
Firemen, municipal, 49, 52, 122, 198, 205; Ohio Police and Firemen's Disability Pension Fund, 196–97; City of Los Angeles Fire and Police Pension System, 197
Firemen, New York State, 198
Ford Motor Company, 117
France, 258–65; contributions, 244, 258, 259–60, 261, 263, 264; industry plans, 245, 259, 260, 261–65, 300–1n33; reserve funding, 246, 261–62; disability benefits, 258; special programs, government employees, 258, 259–60; coverage, 258, 260, 261, 261–63, 264; starting age, 258, 260, 263, 264; 1945 Social Security Code, 258, 261; General Program, 258–59, 260; benefits, 258–59, 260, 261–62, 263, 264–65; survivors' pensions, 259; income supplement, 259, 262, 264–65; financing, 259–60, 261–62; self-employed, 260; multiemployer systems, 261–63; labor unions, 261–64; employee plans, 261–65; redistribution, 262–63, 264; cadres plans, 263, 264

private plans, 245, 246, 261–65; vesting, 245, 260, 261, 264; government regulation, 261, 263–64
Friedman, Milton: quoted, 292n21
Funding, 33–34, 47, 56, 57, 143, 180–81, 190, 206; actuarial cost methods, 56, 179–81, 183, 190, 192–93, 202, 205, 221–22, terminology, 180; accrued benefit funding method, 181, 182, 184–85 (*table*), 186, 189 (*table*), 192; benefits, 189–94, 204; fiduciary responsibility, 206–9; *see also* Financing

General Electric, 79
Genesco, 207
Germany, 69, 225, 265
Germany, Federal Republic of, 265–69; contributions, 244, 265–66, 268; coverage, 265, 266, 267; disability benefits, 265, 266, 267, 269; social insurance, 265–67, 268, 269; survivors' benefits, 266; starting age, 266–67; benefits, 266–67, 268, 269; legislation, 267; multiemployer plans, 268
private plans, 267–69; vesting, 245, 267–68; funding, 268–69; insurance plans, 268–69
Granite Cutters' International Association of America, 41
Greenough, William C.: cited, 239

Harvard College v. Amory (1830), 208
Health organizations, 57–58
Hoffa, James, 48
Holland, Daniel, 149–50

Illinois: State Universities Retirement System, 196; public employees plan, 196, 236
Income objectives, 210–17; half-salary replacement goal, 211–12; disposable (after-tax) income, 213–14 (*table*); reasonable standard, 214–17
Income of aged, 11–24; from work, 8, 19; from pensions, 10–11, 20–23, 26, 210–13; *1974*, 12–13; budgets of retired couples, 14–17 (*tables*), 212; number below Bureau of Labor Statistics budget levels, *1967–1974*, 15, 16 (*table*); from Social Security, 18, 19–20, 21 (*table*), 22

Income of aged (*Continued*)
(*table*), 26–27; sources, 18–24, since
1950, 18 (*table*), *1967,* 21 (*table*),
1968–1970, 22 (*table*); financial assets,
23–24, 24 (*table*); adequacy of, 24–26;
disposable (after-tax), 213–14 (*table*);
reasonable standard, 214–17
Income tax, federal, *see* Taxes, federal income
Individual Retirement Account (IRA), 218
Industry plans, 30–31, 34–35, 59, 111, 155;
employee rights in, 35–37; passbook use,
35–37; *see also specific industries*
Inflation: influence on pensions, 32, 33, 43–44,
119, 203, 235–36, 241; and Social Security, 70, 74–75, foreign plans, 244
*Inland Steel Company v. National Labor Rela-
tions Board,* 64–65
Insurance companies: management of pension
funds, 136; investment of pension funds,
138 (*table*), 140 (*table*), 142 (*table*); *see
also* Life insurance companies
Institute of Life Insurance, 113
Internal Revenue Act of *1942,* 43, 47
Internal Revenue Code (1942), 59, 60–63, 66,
80, 206; amendments, 63
Internal Revenue Service, 173, 195, 206, 209
Insterstate Commerce Commission, 207
Investment companies: purchases and holdings
of stocks, 140–42 (*tables*), 149
Investments, 57, 135–52; management,
135–36; state and local plans, 136, 144,
149 (*table*), 152; U.S. government securities, 137, 138, 139 (*table*), 140, 144
(*table*), 145 (*table*); bonds, 137, 138, 139
(*table*), 141, 143 (*table*), 144 (*table*),
145–46 (*table*); stocks, 137, 139 (*table*),
140–42 (*tables*), 144, 149, 150, 152;
common stocks, 137, 140–42 (*tables*),
145–47 (*table*); growth, 138 (*table*),
148–49; mortgages, 139 (*table*), 141, 143
(*table*), 144 (*table*), 145 (*table*), 150, 152;
private plans, noninsured, 140 (*table*),
144, insured, 141–44 (*tables*); real estate,
142, 143 (*table*), 150–51, 152; current
trends, 144–47 (*tables*); growth, 149–52;
direct placement loans, 151; mismanagement of, 207–9; *see also* Financing; Funding

Japan, 278–82; starting age, 241, 279, 280;
contributions, 279–80, 282; private plans,
245, 281–82; Employees' Pension Funds,
282; legislation, 278, 281; benefits,
278–79, 280–81, 282; disability benefits,
279, 280; survivors' benefits, 279, 280,
281; multiemployer plans, 282
social insurance, 278–81; Employees' Pension Insurance Plan, 278–80; National
Pension Plan (self-employed and employees of small enterprises), 280–81
Javits, Sen. Jacob K., 66
Jones, Lawrence D.: quoted, 143

Katona, George, 147
Keogh Act, 218
Kerr, Clark, 47
Kreps, Juanita M.: quoted, 107
Krug, J. A., 44, 65

Labor union plans, 26, 111; development of,
40–49; collective bargaining in, 47, 62,
64–65, 111, 285n20; trust funds, administration of, 65, 207; *see also names of
unions*
Latimer, Murray Webb: cited, 27–28, 31, 32;
quoted, 285n20, 285–86n31, 286–88n32,
289n51
Lewis, John L., 44–45, 65, 207
Life insurance companies, 109; private plans
management, 136, 138 (*table*); investment of pension funds, 140, 142–43
(*tables*); purchases and holdings of stock,
140–41 (*tables*), 142 (*table*), 149; pension
assets, distribution, *1973,* 145 (*table*)
Local plans, *see* Municipal plans; State and
local government employees
Locomotive Engineers, Brotherhood of, 41, 42
Locomotive Firemen and Enginemen, 41
Long, Huey, 70
Los Angeles Fire and Police Pension System,
197
Lynch, James: quoted, 40, 42

McGill, Dan M., 193, 194
Massachusetts retirement plan, 51–52
Medicaid, 25
Medical benefits, *see under* Benefits

Medicare, 10, 25, 72, 73 (*table*), 76
Melone, Joseph J.: quoted, 172
Military plan (Uniformed Services Retirement and Survivor Benefit System), 20, 58, 59, 122, 131–34, 272; veterans' pensions, 11, 133; inclusion under Social Security coverage, 59, 72, 88, 134, 205; number receiving, 122, 133, 134; financing, 132, 202–3; nondisability system, 132–34; disability system, 133; benefits, 133–34; reserve system, 134; vesting, 134, 169
Mine Workers of America, United, 44–45, 48; *Blankenship v. Boyle* case, 65; joint employer-union administration of fund, 65; pension mismanagement, 207
Minnesota, 196
Multiemployer plans, 26, 48–49, 111, 159, 160, 178, 179 (*table*), 210, 290n64; vesting, 159–61, 165
Municipal employees, 49–52, 122 (*table*), 123, 196–200; *see also* Firemen, municipal; Policemen, municipal; Teachers, municipal
Murray, Roger, 148: quoted, 150–51
Musgrave, Richard A.: quoted, 80

Nader, Ralph, 160; quoted, 155
National Health and Welfare Retirement Association, 57–58, 159
National Industrial Conference Board, 32, 33, 137
Negotiations of pension plans, 46–48, 225
Netherlands, 269–72; contributions, 244, 269–70, 272; industry plans, 245, 271, Industrial Pensions Fund Act, 271; disability benefits, 269; starting age, 269, 270, 272; coverage, 269, 271; legislation, 269, 271; benefits, 270, 271, 272; survivors' benefits, 270, 272; government employees, 271; multiemployer, 271; funding, 271–72; public employees, 272
  private plans, 245, 270–72; vesting, 245, 271, 272; Pension Funds and Savings Act (1954), 271–72; future, study, 272
  social insurance, 269–70; Employed Persons' Insurance, 269, 270; National Insurance, 269–70

New York Chamber of Commerce pension task force: quoted, 200
New York City, 198–200; policemen, 49, 198, 204; teachers, 49–50; pension plans study, 52; policemen, firemen, sanitation and transit employees, 198, 204
New York state, 197–98; Pension Commission, 198, 199
Noncontributory plans, 28, 31, 32, 33, 38–39, 46, 111, 115, 120, 289n51; *Solvay Process Company* case, 35–36; passbook use, 35–37

Ohio pension plan, 125
Ohio Police and Firemen's Disability Fund, 196–97
Old age: definition of, 1–2; decreasing employment, 10–11; *see also* Aged
Old Age, Survivors, and Disability Insurance (OASDI), 73 (*table*), 83, 85–86, 88–89
Old Age and Survivors Insurance (OASI), 73 (*table*)
Old Age Assistance Program, 43, 45, 76
Old Age, Survivors, Disability, and Health Insurance (OASDHI), 73 (*table*), 81, 211
Older Americans Act of *1965,* 212
Older workers, *see* Aged, *subhead* employment

Patocka, Barbara: quoted, 197
Pattern Makers' League of North America, 41
Patton, Arch: quoted, 201
Paul, Randolph: quoted, 61
Pay-as-you-go method, 44, 59, 132, 195, 203; Social Security, 91–96
Penn Central Railroad, 207
Pennsylvania Railroad, 31, 38, 285–86n31, 288n32
Pension Benefit Guaranty Corporation (PBGC), 193–94
Pension funds: management, 135–36; investment, 135–52 (*see* Investments); assets, *1961–1981,* 149 (*table*)
Pension plans: development of, 26–67, twentieth century, 30–67; mismanagement of, 66, 207–8

Pension Reform Act of 1974, *see* Employee Retirement Income Security Act of 1974 (ERISA)

Pension Research Council, 193, 194

Pepper, Sen. Claude: quoted, 65

Perfection Stove Company, 33

Plan termination insurance, 193–94

Policemen, municipal, 49, 52, 122, 204; Ohio Police and Firemen's Disability Fund, 196–97; Los Angeles Fire and Police Pension System, 197

Policemen, New York state, 198

Poverty level: definition, 13, 19; "near poor" threshold, 14–15, 16–17

President's Committee on Corporate Pension Funds and Other Private Retirement and Welfare Programs, 66, 193

Private plans, 109–20; as source of income of aged, 18 (*table*), 20–21 (*table*), 22 (*table*), 89; federal regulation, 59–67 (for analysis, *see* Federal regulation); investments, 98, 135, 136–44; number of and members, 109–11, 110 (*chart, table*); coverage, 110 (*table*), 111–13, 112 (*table*), 113–14; growth, 110 (*table*), 113–14 (*table*); contributions, employer and employee, 110 (*table*), 222; and Social Security, 114, 118–19 (*table*), 216–17; eligibility, 114–15, 116–19 (*table*), 212, 213, 216–17, 220–21; vesting, 115, 155, 162, 163–64, 166–68 (*tables*), 182, 219, 221; retirement age, 115–17 (*table*), 126, 219, 225; benefits, 117–20, 179–80, 216–17, payments, 110 (*table*); contribution rates, 120, 222; assets, *1950–1974,* 138 (*table*), *1961–1981,* 149 (*table*); total participation, by age, *1971,* 167 (*table*); defined benefits, 178, financing, 179–80 (*table*); future objectives, 217–19; foreign, 245–46, seven country systems, 246–82 passim (*see also names of countries*)

insured, 135, 136, 137; assets, *1950–1974,* 138 (*table*), *1961–1981,* 149 (*table*); investments, 141–44

investments: before *1945,* 136–37; after *1945,* 138–41

noninsured, 135, 136, 137, 138; assets, 138

(*table*), 139–40 (*tables*), distribution, *1973,* 145 (*table*), *1961–1981,* 149 (*table*); investments, 140 (*table*), 144

Profit-sharing plans, 113, 166, 177

Public assistance, 76, 89, 98, 106; as income of aged, 11, 24

Public employees, 10, 20, 49–52, 120–34, 226; benefits, 21–22 (*table*), 26, 49, 155, 178, 219; number of systems, *1972,* 120–21 (*table*); vesting, 127, 128, 129, 160, 161, 168, 203; funding, 194–200; exemption from federal standards, 195; steps to improve, 203–6; cost-of-living escalator, 236; *see also* Federal employees; Firemen; Municipal employees; State and local government employees; Teachers

Railroad employees, 20, 28, 31, 41, 42; decline of, 38–40, 286–87nn31,32; Railroad Retirement System, 39–40; Railroad Retirement Board, 286–87nn31,32; National Pension Association, 286–87n32; Social Security and, 287–88n32

Railroad Retirement Act (1935) and amendment, 39, 287–88n32

Railroad Trainmen, Brotherhood of, 41, 288n32

Religious denominations, *see* Church plans

Reserve funds, 33, 38, 59, 60, 62, 91, 176, 203; *see also under specific plans*

Retirement age, 10, 11, 31–32, 115–17; "pensionable," 3, 244; compulsory, 10–11, 29, 39, 50, 127, 130, 226; railroad employees, 28, 30, 31; steel industry, 30, 46; industry, 32; automobile industry, 46; college professors, 55–56, 225; delayed, 115; Social Security benefits, 75; private plans, 115–17 (*table*), 126, 219, 225; public employees, 126–27, 129–30, 203, 225, 226; state and local employees, 126–28; military, 133, 134; in defined benefit and defined contribution plans, 182, 186 (*table*), 189, 233; federal employees, 202, 211; choice, 223–29; ratio of working years to average retired years, 234 (*table*); foreign plans, 244

early, 116–17, 126–27, 133, 196, 202, 203,

204, 206, 228–29, 234 (*table*); financial effects, 231–35; effect on Social Security, 234–35; foreign plans, 244

Reuther, Walter, 46

Rhode Island pension plan, 125

Roche, Josephine, 207

Romania, 69

Roosevelt, Franklin D., 70–71; quoted, 71

Roosevelt, Theodore: quoted, 69

Scandinavian countries: early retirement age, 244; private plans, 245; social security, 245

Self-employed, 10, 13, 218; Social Security benefits, 80, age, 83; Keogh Act, 218

Sharon Steel Corporation, 207

Single-employer plans, 48, 52–57, 111, 167

Social insurance, foreign systems, 242–45; coverage, 243; benefits, 243–44; adjustments, 244; starting age, 244; financing, 244–45; federal regulation, 245–46; seven country systems, 246–82 passim (*see also names of countries*)

Social Security, 68–108, 216; age, of eligibility, 1, 10, 68, 72, 75, 76, 81, 103, 117–18, 216–17, at awards, *1968,* 9–11 (*table*); reasons of aged for taking, 10–11; supplementation by private pension ("second pension" benefits), 10–11, 20, 21 (*table*), 22 (*table*), 26, 59, 67, 80, 84–85, 88, 98, 114, by public pensions, 196, 198, 203; income from, 18, 19–20, 21 (*table*), 26–27; special age 72 benefit, 19, 75, 83; workers excluded, 20, 68, 77, 79, 87–88, 123–24, 128, 205; as partial income of public assistance recipients, 24, 76; coverage, 68, 72, 74, 79–80, *1974,* 68; background and history, 69–77, 215; contributions, 73 (*table*), 83–84, 216; basic principles, 77–96; as nationwide plan, 78; compulsory participation, 80; retirement, work, or earnings test, 81–82, 106; as replacement for earnings, 81–83, 89, 100–2 (*tables*), 211–12, 216; as right, 84, 88–89; future of, 96–103; decoupling the formula, 100–3, 100 (*table*), 103 (*table*); basic income transfer system, 104–8; and private plans,

114, 118–19 (*table*), 216–17; investments, 136; and public employee plans, 196; objections to, 292n21; *see also* Old Age Assistance Program; Old Age, Survivors, Disability, and Health Insurance (OASDHI)

benefits, 68, 71, 72, 74–77, 227–29; Survey of Newly Entitled Beneficiaries (SNEB), *1968,* 8–10, 227; special minimum, 74, 87–88; average, *1967–1975,* 74 (*table*), *1975,* 86, 89, *1940–1975,* 86, 87 (*chart*); Consumer Price Index and, 74–75, 85, 93, 94 (*table*), 100–3 (*tables*), 216, 235, 236; escalator clause (1972), 74–75, 93–94, 96, 106–7, 216, 236; delayed retirement, 75; wives, 75, 81, 103; widows' and widowers', 75, 104; Supplemental Security Income for Aged, Blind, and Disabled (SSI), 76; relation to social adequacy concepts, 84–88, 105–6; automatic increase (1975), 93–94; assumed changes, *1975–1979,* 94, 95 (*table*), 229; proposals, 103–4; early retirement, 234–35

financing, 83, 88–96; reserve fund, 72, 91, 99; taxable earning base, 72–73 (*table*), 75, 81, 82, 83, 88, 90–91, 96, changes, *1937–1975,* 91 (*table*), proposed increases, 97–98; trust funds, 80, 91–92, 94, 98–99, estimates, *1975–1979,* 94, 96 (*table*); contributions, *1973–1975,* 90 (*table*), changes in earnings base, *1937–1976,* 91 (*table*); pay-as-you-go (current), 91–96; employer contributions tax, maximum, *1937–1975,* 92 (*table*); trustees' assumptions for *1975–1980,* 94–96 (*tables*); approaching deficit crises, 95–96, 103–4; contributions, employee and employer, tax rates (OASDI), 96, 99, increases in, question of, 99; employer tax, increase in, question of, 99; tax collections, *1974,* 219

foreign, see Social insurance, foreign systems

Social Security Act of *1935,* 42, 43, 68, 71, 77, 79, 92, 225; amendments, 71, 72, 92, *1972,* 73–77, 100–1, 108, *1973,* 73

Social Security Administration, 74, 76, 161, 174, 234; studies, 125–27, 128

Social Security Advisory Council, 82, 86, 97, 98, 99, 101

Solvay Process Company, McNevin v., 35–36, 37

State and local government employees, 20, 21–22, 51–52, 122–28, 135; Social Security coverage, 72, 196; exclusions from Social Security, 79, 87–88; number of systems, *1972*, 120–21 (*table*); administering governments, 122–23; eligibility, 123; groups covered, 123; relation to Social Security, 123–24; benefits, determination, 124–25, 126, 127, 128; contributions, 125–26; retirement, normal and early, 126–28; investments, 136, 144; assets, *1956–1973*, 144 (*table*), distribution, *1973*, 145 (*table*), *1961–1981*, 149 (*table*); vesting, 128, 149, 160, 161, 168 (*table*), 169; exemption from federal standards, 195; funding, 195–200, 204; steps to improve, 203–6; cost-of-living escalator, 236; *see also* Municipal employees

Steel industry, 30, 45–46, 79, 126; Inland Steel case, 64–65

Strikes: relation to pension plans, 40, 41, 42, 44, 45, 46, 66

Studebaker Corporation, 66

Studenski, Paul, 50

Survivors' benefits, *see under* Benefits

Sweden, 272–78; contributions, 244, 245, 274, 276, 278; industry plans, 245, 275–77; vesting, 245, 277; coverage, 273, 274; disability benefits, 273, 274, 275, 276; benefits, 273, 274–75, 276–77; starting age, 273, 275, 276, 278; survivors' benefits, 273–74, 275, 276; legislation, 275, 277; Swedish Staff Pension Society, 275, 278; Pension Registration Unit, 277; public employees (Swedish Government Pension System), 278

private plans, 245, 275–77; blue-collar workers (Complementary Pension for Workers), 277–78

social insurance: National Basic Pensions System, 273–74, 275; National Supplementary Pension System, 274–75

Taft-Hartley Act, 45, 49, 63–65

Taxes, federal, 59–63; excess profits, 43; Internal Revenue Act of *1942*, 43; Internal Revenue Code, 59, 60, 173; nondeductibility of employee contributions, 60; self-employed, employer contribution, 80 exemptions, 59–60; beneficiaries, 59; contributions, employer, 59, 60, 63; profit-sharing plans, 59, 63; pension trusts, 59–60, 61, 63; Social Security benefits, 83–84, 96–97, 213–14

Taxes, federal income: preretirement, married couples, 214 (*table*); double, 213

Taxes, state, 214 (*table*); New York state, exemption of pension payments, 198; preretirement, married couples, 214 (*table*)

Teachers, college and university, *see* College and university faculties

Teachers Insurance and Annuity Association (TIAA), 56–57, 123, 177, 239–40 (*charts*); vesting, 56, 159

Teachers, municipal, 49–51, 52, 122, 123, 178; Illinois plans, 196

Teamsters' Union, 48, 49

Telephone and Telegraph, American, 79

Telephone Workers, National Federation of, 62

Tennessee Valley Authority (TVA), 59, 122

Termination of plan, 63, 181; insurance, 193–94

Townsend plan, 70

Trade unions, *see* Labor union plans

Trainmen, Brotherhood of Railroad, 41, 288*n*32

Transportation industry, 48, 111; *see also* Automobile industry; Railroad employees

Trust funds, 33, 65, 91; federal regulations of, 59–63, 208–9; trustees, 44, 46, 49, 207; *see also* Financing; Funding

Typographical Union, International, 40, 41, 42

United Kingdom, 69, 251–58; contributions, 245, 252, 254, 255, 256, 257; survivors' benefits, 252, 253; benefits, 252, 253, 254, 256–57; coverage, 252, 253–54, 257; starting age, 252, 254, 257; right to,

252, 255; occupational schemes, 252, 255, 256, 257; financing, 256

government proposals: Beveridge Report (Social Insurance and Allied Services), *1941*, 252–54; Crossman Scheme, 254; *Strategy for Pensions: Future Development of State and Occupational Provisions* (State Reserve Pension Scheme), *1971*, 254–55, 256; Labour and Conservative, *1969–1975*, 254–58

legislation, 245, 251–52, 253, 254; Poor Law Act of 1601 and successors (Old Age Pension Act of 1908, National Insurance Act of 1911) to World War II, 251–52; National Health Service Act of *1948*, 254; National Insurance and Industrial Injuries Act (1948), 254; Social Security Act of July *1973*, 255–56; Social Security Act of August *1975*, 256–58

private plans, 252, 255, 256, 257; vesting, 245, 257

U.S. Steel Corporation, 30, 79

Vesting, 26, 32, 47, 62–63, 79, 153–75, 206, 217; minimal federal requirements before 1974 Act, 61–62, 115; employee rights, 61–62, 158, 159, 161, 162, 173; impor-
tance, 154–57; factor of mobility of labor force in, 155–57; deferred, 156–57, 163, 165, 170; and employee retention, 157–58, 173; mechanisms for and portability, 158–62; payments from regular plan, 159; multiemployer plans, 159–61; employee contributions, 160, 162, 163–64, 174–75; reciprocity agreements, 160–61; information clearing house, 161, 162, 173; graded, 163; levels, 163; federal standards, 163–64, 172, 216; extent of, 164–69; service and age requirements, 165–68 (*tables*), 169, 174, 202, 216; cost, 169–72; recommendations, 172–75

Veterans' Administration, 133

Welfare, *see* Public assistance

Welfare and Pension Plans Disclosure Act of *1958*, 65–66, 206

West Germany, *see* Germany, Federal Republic of

White House Conferences on the Aging, 24–25, 212

Widows' benefits, *see under* Benefits

Winklevoss, Howard, 171

Witte, Edwin E., 70–71; quoted, 70, 71